Bl

in

Black and White in American Culture

An Anthology from *The Massachusetts Review*

Edited by
Jules Chametzky and Sidney Kaplan

NEW YORK / THE VIKING PRESS

TO MARTIN LUTHER KING, JR.

Foreword

A Decade of Discovery

The Massachusetts Review is a quarterly of literature, the arts, and public affairs, published independently with the cooperation and support of Amherst, Mount Holyoke, and Smith Colleges, and the University of Massachusetts. Its first number appeared in the fall of 1959, with F. C. Ellert as editor and Sidney Kaplan as managing editor. In 1961 Sidney Kaplan became co-editor. Since 1963, the Journal has been under the editorship of Jules Chametzky and John H. Hicks. Francis Murphy was a co-editor, 1965–1967.

This gathering of some forty pieces by writers black and white is drawn from the fiction, poetry, reportage, debate, document, essays (on literature, history, politics, society, music, and art) that have appeared in *The Massachusetts Review* between 1959 and 1969. All focus on the chiaroscuro of American life and thought, and reflect a decade very likely more decisive to our culture than any since the Civil War.

Because the book has its focus, unless it bore directly on the subject not everything published in *MR* by black artists and scholars was included. Nor does it include all book reviews, all matters bearing on black life in other countries, or every good special study (in these categories are fine essays by Henry Nash Smith on *Pudd'nhead Wilson,* Chadwick Hansen on Jim in *Huckleberry Finn,* Melvin Seiden on the Negro in *Absalom, Absalom!,* Mina Curtiss on Negroes in Russia). We regret all these and other omissions, but to have included everything would have resulted in a leviathan of a book.

When *MR* began, the sit-in by four black freshmen at a lunch counter in South Carolina that would open a new chapter in the Movement was still a few months away, and the demand for black studies that is today shaking the walls of Academe was scarcely to be foreseen. Like everyone else in this decade, we have been making discoveries about ourselves and our culture. Chief among these, for us, is that every aspect of the culture is touched by the "special enigma of the time"—the inhumanity of white to black. The truth of W. E. B. DuBois's assertion, that "the problem of the twentieth century is the problem of the color line," is inescapable.

This gathering of prose, verse, and picture is offered, then, not as a mere anniversary collection, but in the hope that, singly and cumulatively, it will contribute to the "moral growth of the intellect" that is indispensable to the achievement of our humanity.

JULES CHAMETZKY

SIDNEY KAPLAN

To the Public

... *The American people are fast opening their own destiny. ...*
One would say there is nothing colossal in the country but its
geography and its material activities; that the moral and intellectual
effects are not on the same scale with the trade and production.
There is no speech heard but that of auctioneers, newsboys,
and the caucus. ... Our books and fine arts are imitations; there is
a fatal incuriosity and disinclination in our educated men to
new studies and the interrogation of nature.

We have taste, critical talent, good professors, good commenta-
tors, but a lack of male energy. What more serious calamity
can befall a people than a constitutional dulness and limitation?
The moral influence of the intellect is wanting. ... We have a
bad war, many victories, each of which converts the country into
an immense chanticleer; and a very insincere political opposition.
The country needs to be extricated from its delirium at once.
Public affairs are chained in the same law with private; the
retributions of armed states are not less sure and signal than those
which come to private felons. The facility of majorities is no
protection from the natural sequence of their own acts. ... A
journal that would meet the real wants of this time must have a
courage and power sufficient to solve the problems which the
great groping society around us, stupid with perplexity, is dumbly
exploring. Let it not show its astuteness by dodging each difficult
question and arguing diffusely every point on which men are
long ago unanimous. Can it front this matter of Socialism, to which
the names of Owen and Fourier have attached...? Will it cope
with the allied questions of Government, Nonresistance, and all
that belongs under that category? Will it measure itself with
the chapter on Slavery, in some sort the special enigma of the
time...? There are literary and philosophical reputations to settle.
... We rely on the truth for and against ourselves.

RALPH WALDO EMERSON
in the first issue of the
Massachusetts Quarterly Review
December, 1847.

Contents

Part One

The Movement

Bright an' Mownin' Star

MIKE THELWELL

TRAVELING SOUTH FROM MEMPHIS on Highway 49, you cross over the last rolling hill and the Mississippi Delta stretches before you like the sea, an unbroken monotony of land so flat as to appear unnatural. So pervasive is this low-ceilinged, almost total flatness that one loses all other dimensions of space and vision. An endless succession of cotton and soybean fields surround the road.

A few weather-greyed shacks, stark, skeletal, and abrasively ugly, perch in a precarious oasis hacked out in the narrow, neutral strip between the road and the encroaching fields. Contemptuous of weather, time, and gravity, they stand apparently empty, long-abandoned and sheltering nothing but the wind. Then some appear, no different in point of squalor and decrepitude from the others, except that people stand before them.

At one point a single huge tree, off in a cotton field a distance, breaks the horizon. It is the first tree of any size that has appeared. This tree is an oak that bears small, gnarled acorns so bitter that there is no animal that will eat them. Its wood is very hard, but is knotty, faulted, and with a grain so treacherous and erratic that it cannot easily be worked. It is used for nothing more durable than a weapon. In this region they are called blackjacks, from the soot-like darkness of the bark, and find utility mainly in conversation as a metaphor of hardness, "tougher'n a blackjack oak."

This one is unusual beyond its mere presence and size, having both name and history. Its appearance, too, is unusual. The trunk and lower limbs are fire-charred to a dull black. These limbs are leafless and dead, but the topmost branches in the center of the tree continue to grow. In a strange inharmony the living oak flourishes out of the cinders of its own corpse. White folk call this tree the Nigger Jack, while Negroes speak of it hardly at all, save on those Sundays when the tree becomes the central symbol in some

[Reprinted from *MR*, Vol. VII, No. 4, Autumn 1966. Sources hereafter cited by volume, number, and date.]

hell-fire sermon, for it is widely known that the flames that burned the oak roasted the bodies of slaves judged dangerous beyond re-demption or control.

Once, it is said, some young black men from the county, re-turned from defeating the Kaiser, resolved to fell and burn the tree. On the night before this event was to take place, a huge and fiery cross was seen to shine at the base of the tree, burning through the night and into the next day.

For many years—the space of three generations—the land around this tree has lain fallow, producing annually only a tangled transient jungle of rabbit grass and myriad nameless weeds, for no Negro could be found who might be bribed, persuaded, or coerced into working there.

LOWE JUNIOR GRUNTED deep in his chest as the heavy, broad-blade chopping hoe hit into the dry black earth. He jerked it up, sighted on the next clump of wire-grass and weeds, and drove the hoe-blade into the furrow just beyond the weeds, and with the same smooth motion pulled the blade towards his body and slightly upwards, neatly grubbing out the intruder in a little cloud of dust without touching the flanking cotton plants.

"Sho' do seem like the grass growin' faster'n the cotton." He leaned on the hoe handle and inspected the grubbed-up weed. "Hit be greener an' fatter'n the cotton evrahtime. Heah hit is, middle o' June, an hit ain't sca'cely to mah knee yet." He ran his glance over the rows of stunted plants, already turning a dull brownish green, then squinted down the row he was chopping, estimating the work left. He saw much "grass" wrestling its way around and between the cotton. "Finish dishyer after dinner," he said, noting that the sun had already cleared the tip of the blackjack oak which stood some ten rows into the middle of the field. Drag-ging his hoe he started towards the tree's shade.

Lowe Junior was tall, a gaunt, slightly stooped figure as he shambled with the foot-dragging, slightly pigeon-toed, stiff-backed gait that a man develops straddling new-turned furrows while holding down the jerking, bucking handle of a bull-tongue plow. His boots and the dragging hoe raised a fine powder of dust around his knees. When he reached the tree he leaned his tool against the trunk and stretched himself. He moved his shoulders, feeling the pull of the overalls where the straps had worn into his flesh during the morning's work. Holding the small of his back, he arched his middle forward to ease the numb, cramping ache that hardly seemed to leave the muscles in his back. Then he straightened up and stood for a while looking out over his cotton.

Then Lowe Junior turned to the tree and took a pail which hung from one of the broken stubs. He touched the blackened trunk, running his hands over the rough cinders. "Thet fiah oney toughed yo' up, thass all . . . an there ain't nothin' wrong with thet." There was something familiar, almost affectionate, in his voice and action. When he first started working this section, he had carefully avoided the tree, sitting on the hot earth in the rows to eat and rest. But he had become accustomed to the tree now, was grateful for its shade, and he found himself accepting it as the only other living thing he encountered during the day. After all, he assured himself, "Hit cain't be no harm to no tree, fo' a certain fack."

He eased himself down ponderously, almost painfully, like a man too old or too fat, and began to eat. In the pail were butter-beans boiled with country peppers, wild onions, and slabs of salted fatback. This stew was tepid, almost perceptibly warm from the midday heat. The coating of pork grease that had floated to the top had not congealed. Lowe Junior briefly debated making a small fire but decided against taking the time. He ate quickly, stirring the stew and scooping it into his mouth with a thin square of cornbread, biting into the gravy-soaked bread, then chewing and swallowing rapidly. Finishing his meal he drank deeply from a kerosene tin filled with water and covered with burlap (wet in the morning but now bone dry), which stood among the roots of the tree.

He stretched himself again, yawned, belched, spat, and braced himself firmly against the tree. He lay there limply, his eyes closed as though to shut out the rows and rows of small, drying-out plants that represented the work of his hands, every day, from can see to can't, since early in the spring.

"Ef hit would jes' rain some . . . seems like the mo' a man strain, hits the harder times git. Li'l rain now, an' the cotton be right up, but soon'll be too late." Weariness spread in him and the effort even of thinking was too great. He just lay there inert, more passive even than the tree, which at least stood. Even if by some miracle this cotton in the section he was "halfing" for Mr. Riley Peterson survived the drought, rains coming in August or

September would turn the dust into mud and rot whatever cotton was ripening in the bolls—or else wash it into the mud.

A sudden panic came upon Lowe Junior, stretched beneath the tree. He could hardly feel his body, which was just a numbness. He felt that he could not rise, could not even begin, for his body would not obey him. For a brief moment he was terrified of making the effort lest he fail. Then he sat up suddenly, almost falling over forward from the violence of his effort. "Better study out whut t' do. No profit to layin' here scarin' m'se'f. Quarter section be a lot o' farmin' fo' a man. Sho' ain't be able to keep t' grass outen the cotton by myse'f."

This was a problem for him, had been ever since he had asked Mr. Peterson to give him this quarter section. He was young but a good worker; still Mr. Peterson might not have given it to him had it not been for the fact that no other tenant would take it. Lowe Junior did not want to ask for help with the chopping because, in "halfing," the cost of the seed, fertilizer, ginning, and any hired help came out of the tenant's half. Already most of his half belonged to Mr. J. D. Odum, the merchant in Sunflower who had "furnished" him. He knew that he would have to have help with the picking, and did not want to hire any help before then, when he would at least have an idea of the crop's potential. "Man can en' up with nothin' thet way," he muttered. "Hit'll happen anyways, tho. Figured to put in eight mebbe even nine bale fo' my share come the crop . . . now be the grace o' the good Gawd ef ah makes fo' . . . man doan feel much even t' keep on . . . Lawd, hit be better t' die, than t' live so hard." He found little comfort in those grim lines from the old blues to which his grandmother was so partial. She was always incanting that song as though it had a special meaning for her.

After his father died, and his mother went off to the North to find work, it was the old woman, pious and accepting, who had told him the old stories, raised him in the Church, and interpreted for him the ways of their world. He remembered her story of how God had put two boxes into the world, one big and the other small. The first Negro and the first white man had seen the boxes at the same time and run towards them, but the Negro arrived first and greedily appropriated for himself the larger box. Unfortunately this box contained a plough, a hoe, a cop-axe, and a mule, while the smaller box contained a pen, paper, and a ledger book. "An' thass why," the old woman would conclude, her face serious, "the Nigger been aworkin' evah since, an' the white man he reckon up the crop; he be sittin' theah at crop time, jes' afigurin' an' areckonin'; he say

> Noughts a nought,
> Figgers a figger,
> All fo' us folks,
> None fo' the Nigger."

He had been fifteen before he even began to doubt the authenticity of this explanation. Now the old lady was ailing and very old. But she had not lost her faith in the ultimate justice of the Lord or her stoic acceptance of whatever He sent. It was a joke among the neighbors that when the good sisters of the Church went in to see the old lady, now failing in sight and almost bedridden, her answer to the question, "How yo' keepin', Miz Culvah?" invariably was "Porely, thank d' Lawd." Lowe Junior chuckled, got up, dusted off his clothes, and went out into the sun.

THAT EVENING he stopped work early, just as the sun was setting, and started home, trudging slowly over the flat dusty road past fields, a few as parched and poor as his own, and large ones where elaborate machinery hurled silvery sprays over rows of tall lush plants. A wind swept the fine cool spray into the road. He felt the pleasant tickling points of coldness on his face and saw the grayish dust coating his overalls turn dark with the moisture. Minute grains of mud formed on his skin. He looked into the dazzling spray and saw a band of color where the setting sun made a rainbow.

> D' Lawd give Noah d' rainbow sign,
> No mo' watah, d'fiah nex' time.

"Thass whut the ol' woman would say, an tell evrahbody thet she seen d' Lawd's sign. Be jes' sun an' watah, tho." He did not look at the green fields. Looking straight ahead into the dust of the road, he increased his pace. He wanted only to get home.

Just where the dust road meets the highway, at the very edge of a huge field, was the shack. Tin-roofed with gray clapboard sides painted only with the stain of time and weather, it had two small rooms. As Lowe Junior came up the road, it seemed to be tossed and balanced on a sea of brown stalks, the remains of last year's bean crop which came up to the back door.

In the front, the small bare yard was shaded by a pecan tree already in blossom. Small lots, well-kept and tidy, grew okra, butter-bean, and collard green plants on both sides of the yard. Lowe Junior walked around the shack to a standpipe in back of the stoop. He washed the dust from his head and arms, filled his pail, and drank. The water was brown, tepid, and rusty-tasting. He sprinkled the okra and bean plants, then entered the shack. The fire was out, and the huge pot hanging over the fire, from which he had taken his dinner that morning, had not been touched.

"Mam, Mam," he called softly, "Yo' awright?" There was no answer, and he went into the old woman's room. The room was stifling-hot as the tin roof radiated the day's heat. The air was heavy with the smell of stale urine, old flesh, and night sweat. The old lady lay against the wall, partially covered by an old quilt. A ray of sunlight beamed through a small knothole and lighted up the lined and creasing skin pattern on one side of her face. A single fly buzzed noisily around her open mouth and lighted on the tuft of straggling white hairs on her chin. Her eyes stared at a framed picture of the bleeding heart of Jesus, violent red and surrounded by a wreath of murderous-looking thorns and a hopeful glow, which hung on the opposite wall above the motto, "The Blood of Jesus Saves."

Lowe Junior searched his pockets slowly, almost absently, for two coins to place over her eyes. His gaze never left her face and, as he looked, the ray of sunlight gradually diminished, seeming to withdraw reluctantly from the face, finally leaving it to shadow.

Failing to find any coins, he straightened the limbs, pulled the quilt over the face, and went to tell the neighbors.

When he returned, the thick purple Delta darkness had descended with a tropical suddenness. He added more beans, fatback and water to the stew, and started the fire. Then he lit a kerosene lantern and took it into the yard to a spot beneath the pecan tree. He hung the lantern on a branch and began to dig.

THE NEIGHBORS found him still digging when they began to arrive in the little yard. The first small group of women was led by Sister Beulah, a big, imposing, very black woman with a reputation for fierce holiness. She stood out from the worn and subdued group not only because of the crisp whiteness of her robe and bandanna but also in her purposeful, almost aggressive manner. She led the women to the side of the hole.

"Sho' sorry t' heah 'bout Sistah Culvah, but as you knows . . .," she began.

"She inside," Lowe Junior said without looking up, "an' ah thanks yo' all fo' comin'."

Interrupted in mid-benediction, Beulah stood with her mouth open. She had failed to officiate at buryings in the community only twice in the past twenty years, and then only because she had been holding revivals at the other end of the state. She had never quite forgiven the families of the deceased for not awaiting her return. She resented Lowe Junior's thanks, the first she had ever received for doing what she thought of as an indispensable service. May as well thank the grave.

"Thet boy sho' actin' funny," she murmured and swept into the shack to take charge of preparations.

More neighbors straggled into the yard. Another lantern was brought and hung in the tree, widening the chancy and uncertain perimeter of light in the otherwise enveloping blackness of the Delta night. Each man arriving offered to help Lowe Junior with the digging. Some had even brought tools, but Lowe Junior stonily refused all offers.

"Ah be finished time the box get heah," he answered without looking at the men. "Sho' do thank yo', tho'."

So the men sat and smoked, speaking only in murmurs and infrequently. The women passed out steaming plates of stew and tins of coffee bitter with chicory. Lowe Junior declined all food. The plates in the shack were emptied and rotated until all were fed. After a muttered consultation, one of the men approached Lowe Junior. He was old, his hair very white against his skin. He was very neat and careful of himself, moving with great dignity. His faded overalls were clean and shiny from the iron. He stood quietly at the side of the hole until Lowe Junior stopped work and looked up at him. Then he spoke, but so softly that the other men could not make out his words. The yard was very silent.

"Brothar Culvah. The peoples ain't easy in min'. They come to he'p yo' an heah yo' takin' no he'p." Lowe Junior said nothing.

"In time o' grief, praise Jesus, folks, they wants t', an' mo'n thet, they needs, t' he'p . . . they come t' pay respeck t' the daid

an' share the burden an' sarrow o' d' livin'. Thass how hits allus
bin . . . Son, when folks offer comfort an' he'p, a man mus'
accep' hit, 'caus hit's mebbe all they got."

Lowe Junior looked at the old man.

"Yo' unnerstan' what ah'm asayin', son?" he asked gently.
"The peoples doan feel like as if they got anythang t' do heah,
anythang thet they needs t' be adoin'."

Lowe Junior looked into the darkness. His voice was low and
without inflection. "Hit ain't no he'p to give, ain't no sarrow
t' share. Hits jes' thet the ol' woman was ol', an now she daid.
Ain't no sarrow in thet."

They became aware of a sound. It came from the shack and
at first did not seem to intrude or in any way challenge the dark
silence. It began as a deep sonorous hum, close in pitch to the
sound of silence. Then it grew, cadenced and inflected, gathering power and volume until it filled the yard and was present,
physical and real. The men picked up the moan and it became
a hymn.

> hhhmmmmmmmMMMay the Circle . . . be Unbroken
> Bye an bye, Lawd . . . Bye annnn Bye

"Peoples can sang," Lowe Junior said. "Praise Jesus, they can
allus do thet."

The old man walked away, silent. He sat on the stoop ignoring the questioning looks of the others. He hunched over, his
frail body gently rocking back and forth, as though moved against
his will by the throbbing cadences of the singing. He sat there in
isolation, his eyes looking into the darkness as at his own approaching end, his face etched with lines of a private and unnamable old
man's sorrow. Deep and low in his chest he began to hum the dirge.

Lowe Junior chopped viciously at the earth. The people intoned
the old and troubled music that they were born to—the music
which, along with a capacity to endure, was their only legacy from
the generations that had gone before, the music that gathered
around them, close, warm, and personal as the physical throbbing
of their natural life.

When the hole was to Lowe Junior's chin, the Haskell boys
came into the yard carrying the coffin. It was of green pitchpine,
the boards rough-planed so that all depressions on the surface of

the boards were sticky with sap. The men also brought two boxes so that the coffin would not rest on the ground. The Haskells stood by the hole, wiping their gummy hands on their overalls.

"Yo' reckon hit'll be awright?" Ben Haskell asked.

"Shol'y. Sho', hit'll be jes fine. Yo' done real good; hits a coffin, ain't hit?" Lowe Junior still had not looked at the coffin, which was surrounded by the neighbor men. The Haskells stood silent, looking at him.

" 'Sides, ol' woman . . . allus was right partial t' scent o' pine. Yassuh, hit'll be right fine," Lowe Junior said. Ben Haskell smiled, a diffident embarrassed stretching of his mouth. "Yo said cedar, but see, quick as yo' needed hit, pine wuz all we could git."

"Thass right," his brother assented.

Leastwise, Lowe Junior thought, Mist' Odum wouldn' give yo' all cedar fo' credit. He repeated softly, "Yo' done good, real good." The Haskells beamed, relieved, and expressed again their sympathy before moving away.

THE YARD WAS NOW FULL, some twenty persons stood, hunkered, or sat around. Set on the boxes in the center of the group, the raw white coffin dominated the scene like an altar, filling the air with the pungent odor of crude turpentine.

Lowe Junior walked around the coffin and approached the steps of the shack. The neighbors' eyes followed him. Sister Beulah met him at the door. He saw the faces of the other women peering down at him from behind her. All conversation ceased.

"Brothah Culvah, this yer ah'm agonna say ain't strictly mah business. Some would say hit rightly ain't *none* o' mah concern atall." She paused, looking at Lowe Junior and the men in the yard. Nothing was said, and she continued. "But lookin' at hit anothah way, hit what ah'm gonna say, *is* mah business. Hits bin troublin' mah min', and hits lotsa othah folks heah, what ah knows feel d' same way." When she paused again, there was a faint assenting Ahmen from the people.

"So ah'm agonna say hit . . . Now, yo' all knows me, bin apreachin' an aservin' the Lawd in these parts fo' thutty year, an live heah thutty year befo' thet." Murmurs of "Thass right" came from the group.

"Yas, thass the Lawd's truth, an ah knows Sistah Culvah, Miss

Alice we used t' call her, from the fust come off t' plantation an' nobody evah had a word o' bad to say 'bout her, praise Jesus. Yas, an' ah known yo' po' mothah, an yo' se'f, Brothah Culvah, from evah since." The murmurs from the neighbors were stronger now. Encouraged, Sister Beulah continued. She was now speaking louder than anyone had spoken in the yard all evening.

"She wuz a good woman, a go-o-d woman, she knowed Jesus an' she wuz saved. Hits true, towards the las' when she wuz porely an' gittin' up in age, she couldn' git to meetin' to praise her Gawd, but yo' all knows she *lo-oved* the Church." She took a deep breath. "Now, ah knows thet back then, in slavery times, when the ol' folks could' do no bettah, an' had to hol' buryin's an' Chris'nin' an' evrah-thang at night. But, thank Jesus, them days is gone. They's gone. Hit ain't fittin' an' hit ain't right an' propah t' hol' no buryin' at night, leas' hit ain't bin done herebouts. The body o' the good sistah, now called t' Glorah, ain't even bin churched. Yo' knows thet ain't right. Ah knows thet, effen she could have somepin t' say, she'd want hit done right at the las'! Ah *kno-o-ows* in mah heart she would."

"Yas, yas, ahah, praise Jesus." The neighbors agreed.

"An Brothah Culvah, yo' a young man, yo' a Gawd-fearin' man, an' ah knows yo' wants t' do right. Cause . . . yo' know hit says . . . the longes' road mus' ha' some endin', but a good name endureth fo'evah." On this dramatic and veiled note of warning the huge white-draped woman ended.

Everyone was quiet, but there was a faint expectant shuffling of feet as the people looked at Lowe Junior.

" 'Tain't no call t' fret yo'se'f," he said. "Ol' woman wuz ol' an now she gone. Ah be aburyin' her tonight." There was a quickly stifled murmur from the people. No one spoke, and Lowe Junior continued more softly.

" 'Tain't thet whut yo' say ain't got right to hit, Sta' Beulah, 'cause hit do. But hits no law say thet effen yo' buryin' t' do, hit cain't be done in the night."

"Yas, Brothah Culvah, effen yo' *got* t' do hit. Doan seem like t' me hits no hurry . . ." Beulah said.

"Yas'm, hit is a hurry. See, ah feel like ah should take care o' this thang personal. Ol' woman raise me from when ah wuz young, ah wants t' take care o' the buryin' personal."

"Whut's wrong with t'morrow? Yo' answer me thet."

"Be no tellin' jes' where ah'll be t'morrow," Lowe Junior said, lifting one end of the coffin and asking Ben Haskell to help with the other end. They took it into the shack to receive the body.

"Hey, Lowe, yo' sho' nuff fixin' t' leave?" Ben could not keep the excitement out of his voice.

"Thass right." Lowe Junior's first knowledge of his decision had come when he heard himself telling Beulah, a moment before.

"Yo' mean yo' ain't even gon' stay t' make yo' crop?"

"Any one o' yo' all wants t' work hit is welcome t' my share. Ah'll sign a paper so Mist' Peterson and Mist' Odum'll know." Temptation and fear struggled in Ben's eyes, and finally he said only, "Ah'll tell d' other'ns . . . but supposin' no one wants t' take hit?"

"Yo' mean 'bout Mist' Peterson . . . well, he got mo' cotton. Fack is, he got 'bout all theah is."

"Lawd's truth," Ben agreed, and went quickly to share the news with the men in the yard. There the women were grouped around Sister Beulah who was threatening to go home. After what she judged to be sufficient entreaty to mollify her hurt dignity, she agreed to remain and conduct the burial, but only because "hits mah bounden duty to see to hit thet the pore daid woman gits a propah Christian service." She led the women into the shack to put the old lady into the coffin.

After everyone had taken a last look at the corpse, Ben Haskell nailed the lid on and the coffin was brought out and placed on the boxes. During the singing of "Leaning on the Everlasting Arms," two of the women began to cry. Lowe Junior stood a short distance off under the shadow of the pecan tree and looked out over the darkness. He took no part in the singing until the lines of "Amazing Grace,"

> Ah wunst wuz lost but now ah'm Found,
> Wuz blind but now ah See.

In a loud but totally uninflected voice, he repeated "Wuz blind but now ah See."

This unexpected voice, coming as it were from behind her, distracted Sister Beulah who had begun to "line out" the succeeding lines for the benefit of any backsliders who might have forgotten them. She stopped, turned, and glared at Lowe Junior, then continued in the joyful and triumphant voice of one whose seat in the Kingdom is secure beyond all challenge.

" *'Twuz Grace thet taught mah heart t' feah,*" she exulted; "*An' Grace mah feah relieved.*" Her face was illuminated, radiant with the security of grace.

When the coffin was being lowered and was a quarter of the way down, the rope under the head slipped, and it thudded into the hole, almost upright. The people stood in momentary shocked silence. Sister Beulah at the head of the grave raised her massive white-sleeved arms to the sky as though appealing for divine vindication of this sacrilege, the result of Lowe Junior's stubbornness. Lowe Junior quickly lay flat on the edge of the grave, and shoved the high end of the coffin with all his strength. He grunted with the effort and the box slid into place with a heavy thump, followed by the rattle of dirt and pebbles from the sides.

At that moment the sky lightened. They all looked up and saw the risen moon peering from behind a wall of dark clouds that had not been there when the sun set.

"Glorah, Glorah!" a man shouted hoarsely, and the ritual resumed. Sister Beulah had thought to preach her famous "Dead Bones Arisin" sermon, capped with a few well-chosen words on the certain doom of impious children, but recent events had lessened her zeal. Almost perfunctorily, she recounted the joys and glories of Salvation and the rewards awaiting the departed sister. Then they piled dirt on the coffin, patted down the pile, and departed.

LOWE JUNIOR SAT ON the steps. Barely acknowledging the final murmured consolations, he watched the neighbors leave. He realized that he was not alone when the old man approached the stoop.

"Ah heah yo' is leavin', Brothah Culvah. Done any thankin' on wheah yo' goin' an' whut yo' gonna be doin'?"

Lowe Junior did not answer. He in no way acknowledged the old man's presence.

"Thass awright, yo' doan have t' answer 'cause ah knows— yo' ain't! Jes' like ah wuz when ah wuz 'bout yo' age. An ah lef' too, din' know wheah ah wuz agoin' nor whut ah wuz lookin' fo'. Effen yo' doan know whut yo' seekin', Brothah Culvah, yo' cain' know when yo' fin' hit."

Now Lowe Junior was looking at the man; he seemed interested in what he was saying. It was the first interest he had shown in anyone else that evening.

"See, Brothah Culvah, ah travelled aroun' some when ah wuz yowr age, and heah ah is now. Ah never foun' no bettah place nowheahs." He shook his head. "Fo' usses, theah wuzn't none, leastways not thet ah could fin'."

"But at leas' yo' looked," Lowe Junior said.

"Thass why ah'm asayin' t' yo' whut ah is. 'Cause ah did. Brothah Culvah, yo' a good worker, yo' knows farmin' an cotton, but whut else do yo' know? Ah disbelieves thet yo' even bin so far as Memphis."

"Well," Lowe Junior said, "t'morrow thet won't be true. But ah 'preciates yo' kin'ness."

The old man hobbled into the darkness, shrouded in his own knowledge.

Lowe Junior sat on the steps and watched him leave, until finally he was alone. He went to the tree, blew the lamp out, and sat in the darkness. . . . When the sun came up next morning he had not moved. The astringent pitchpine smell still hovered in the still air. Lowe Junior saw that the morning sky was covered by a heavy, metallic-grey cloud that had come swirling up from the Gulf in the dark. He entered the shack and looked about him for something to take. In the old woman's room he found nothing. He returned, picked up his hoe, turned around in the small room, saw nothing else that he wanted, and started to leave. On the steps he changed his mind and re-entered the house. In the old woman's room he took the picture of the Sacred Heart from the frame. Then from a small wooden box he took a Bible which he held by the covers and shook. Three crumpled bills fluttered to the floor. He gave the book a final shake, tossed it into the box, then picked up the bills and carefully wrapped them in the picture. He placed the package in the long deep side-pocket of his overalls. He picked up his hoe from the steps and started out. At the dirt road he turned, not towards the highway, but east towards his section. Soon he could see the top of the oak in the thin dawning light.

"Sho' nevah put no stock in all thet talk 'bout thet tree," he mused. "Burned like thet on the sides an so green t' the top, hit allus did put me in min' o' Moses an' the burnin' bush. But ah wager a daid houn', ain't no Nigger agoin' t' work thisyer lan' now."

He stood for awhile looking at the tree, at the lean runted plants. "Sho' do feels like ah knows yo' evrah one, evrah row and clump o' grass like hit wuz the face o' mah own han' or mah own name."

He strode up to the tree, set his feet, and swung the hoe against the trunk with all the strength of his back. The hickory handle snapped with a crack like a rifle in the early morning. The blade went whirring into the cotton rows. He felt the shock of the blow sting the palm of his hands, and shiver up into his shoulders. He stepped away from the tree and hurled the broken handle as far as he could into the field.

"Theah," he grunted, "yo' got the las' o' me thet yo' is gonna git—the natural las'."

He started back towards the highway at a dead run. There were tears in his eyes and his breath was gusty. He tired and slowed to a walk. He saw the first raindrops hitting heavily into the thick dust of the road, raising sudden explosions of dust and craters of dampness where they struck. Before he reached the cabin, torrents of water were lashing the face of the Delta. When he reached the highway, he turned once to look at the mean little house, gray and forlorn in the storm. He saw a pool already spreading around the roots of the pecan tree.

The dry earth gave off an acrid smell as the water dampened it. "Be nuff now fo' evrah one, white and black," Lowe Junior thought and laughed. "Sho' doan mattah now effen they takes ovah mah fiel'. Hit be all washed out, evrah natural one."

The rain swept down with increased violence. He was completely drenched, streamlets ran down his face, washing away the dust. "Ah nevah seed the like. Sho' now, be hongry folk heah this year. Even white folk be hongry in the Delta this winter." He walked steadily down the highway stretching into the distance.

Prologue

JAMES O. LONG

THEY HAD LEFT the grim-faced body that swung from the tree hanging there long enough for the newspaper to get a picture of Sheriff Turner and his two deputies and Constable Twigg standing there beside it with shotguns and pistols. And when it finally did come out in the Jackson paper, the Negro who had been hanged by the neck, had somehow twisted or been twisted by the mysterious forces that twist things, hung, so that not the Negro but only his anonymous behind was presented to the camera; the whole thing cropped just above the waist anyway, which was, after all, in good taste, and the armed men looking competent and dangerous and running about a step and a half behind events, and not much more useful or concerned than if they had been guarding a spoiled side of beef from the unlikely event that someone would want to steal it. And Twigg was grinning a toothy, frozen grin that his mother had taught him to grin whenever a camera was pointed at him.

Nobody had known how to tie a hangman's noose, so they just settled for a square knot and slipped it around his head and yanked him off the ground. This just went to prove that the reason they tie a man's hands and feet behind him when they hang him is not to keep him from getting loose, but to keep him from making a fool of himself.

And so they had seen him kick, those shadowy faces strewn on both sides of the road, and they had watched him make an undignified fool of himself, spitting, gagging: arms and legs going all together and his body whipping like a snake with its head mashed, not really trying to get loose, but actually trying to run, his feet up about shoulder-high off the ground, trying to run, and the nigger boy they brought down to teach a lesson, watching his daddy hang, just lying there on the ground laughing and rolling his eyes and people hitting him with long willow switches like it was him and not his daddy that the white girl said raped her.

[I, 3, Spring 1960]

And somebody with a long willow switch came running up in the light of the fire they had built up under him to see him better and let him have it across the shanks a time or two like flicking a mare with a buggy whip, and two or three voices shrieking and laughing and calling, one of them: "At's it, Will, make the black son-of-a-bitch go!"

And then when everybody was afraid he was really going to die; they had let loose of the rope and he fell down on the road and didn't have any better sense than to move, and so they got him up on his feet and whipped him with long willow switches some more until he fell down on his knees and didn't even make a sound, not even when the switches, lashing down like coachwhips, cut open the flesh about his neck. "Hell, he ain't got no feelins," one hollered. "Look here," and he cut down again with the willow limb. "Like a damn mule," one of them said. "Stand up!" they hollered. "Talk!" They got him on his feet but he didn't fall because too many pressed around him, and his eyes were rolled up at the sky. The sky was August; it was not black or blue, but aquamarine with a moon ambitionless as a whippoorwill singing its monotonous, senseless song.

Where they had piled sticks and cardboard they had a fire going and every now and then somebody would hit it with a stick and scatter it and there would be shouts and laughter and shrieks. And so when the second time they hoisted him up, and he didn't make quite as big a fool of himself as he did the first time, some boys drug some burning sticks out of the fire, flinging it a little of the way at a time and kicking it until it burned under him. "Hey," somebody hollered. "We don't want no cruelty here. Git that fire from under 'im." But somebody had found a great big pasteboard box and they threw it on there, and presently it blazed up. And there was some tar-paper and somebody threw some paint at the fire but it went all the way across and splattered some people on the other side. The paint was bright orange, and bathed in the firelight it glistened like blood on their clothes and hair. One of them hollered, "Blood!" and the others laughed. The tar-paper had smoked for a while, and then it caught up in a thick curl of red. His trouserleg blazed and he kicked one short undignified kick and his arms went straight out like he was trying to reach for the moon. There he hung, flaming like fury with his dark face streaming with all the waters of his life, with the pigment of his skin until slowly his eyes glowing white with the pain inside them, fixed straight ahead as those mysterious forces that turn things that hang from ropes turned him, and his gaze looked down upon them all.

When he had blazed, there had been shrieking and shouting, but now, the flames had died down into a flickering light, and the tumult subsided into calm. Again and again the specter twisted on pendulum, a gentle breeze rocking him to and fro, and around and around. One of those with the "blood" on him wiped at his hair.

Uneasily, almost imperceptibly, they had drawn back from the fire. And the specter had seemed to move. One of the boys hollered, trying to scare everybody, but his single, everlasting shout died in its own echoes; and there was a hiss that grew louder and louder and they murmured when the specter's chest grew bigger and bigger, and his lips had curled back exposing white teeth against the dark hollow of his jaws, a sound like a moan escaped out of him. Some ran home, then and there, not knowing that the heat had merely built up gases inside him that were now finding their escape.

And so, one by one they retreated into the August night. And one by one, the lights went out in the valley, and three moons hung over Turnbo that night: the pale-brass moon in the sky, and the two gleaming, prophetic moons reflected in the eyes of the man who swung to and fro, turned by the mysterious forces that turn things that hang by strings and ropes.

Alabama Tenants: 1937

WILLIAM CORRINGTON

And we stumbled from dark beds
under an unrisen sun
each of our frowsy heads
filled with poverty's classic abstraction.
To turn away an old year's stubble,
feeling hungry mules lost traction
in the still-frozen trouble
of furrows remembering snow.
Our hands on the thick plowshafts
seemed in that cold to grow
part of the tool. Above us, rafts
of lightless cloud like pelt
from something dead since the fall
began to leak a chill anonymous belt
of rain across numberless small
fields. We pulled our rags about
us and went on breaking land,
remembering flood and drought,
too numb to hope for a stand
of crop enough to break
the formal grasp of hunger and its pain
nesting in our bellies like a snake.
We stood like broken tools in the rain
pressing this hard earth, no mother,
startling haggard mules into a lope
across eternal furlongs where cotton
will rise to bring us something less than hope,
and hold us there, amidst the land, forgotten.

[VII, 4, Autumn 1966]

English Comp.

W. W. & ROSELLEN BROWN*

My home town
Is Canton, Mississippi.
It is located in Central Miss., and is said to be
one of her finest shopping centers.
I think you know about this so called friendly town.
When ever I'm coming home
and look at that sign that says "Welcome to FRIENDLY CANTON"
I know that sign was meant for someone
not me.

I was glad when you asked us to write about our home town,
because I want someone else to know of its evils.
This town is so evil
until you can see it in white men's eyes.
It is some men around here that know me
personally that are clansmen,
take for instance the Sheriff,
we been knowing each other every since I was four years old
going to his grocery store with a penny for bubble gum.
Would these men kill me if they got a chance?
I wish I knew the answer.

I will tell you about my people of the town:
My people make the white man treat us
like this.

If any decent white man would ride down North Hickory Street
            on a Saturday Night
one could see what I mean.
I will attempt to describe what goes on down this rat hole:

[VIII, 2, Spring 1967]
*The words are W. W.'s; Rosellen Brown, his teacher, set them as a poem.

This place is called the "Hollow"
because it is a narrow street. It (left side) contains a

sandwich shop	On the right side
cola stand	it is full of
honky tonk cafe	the same thing
barber shop	mainly
low down blues playing cafe	cafes.
funeral home	
and a fish shop.	

The foundation for every sort of disorder
from murder to rape.
People come here (some) for one purpose, that is
to get drunk.
Dressed in overalls, white shirts and red socks.
Some woman in after five dresses
loud colors with high heels.
I won't forget the old men either
sitting around on the streets eating sardines and crackers
and spitting tobacco juice
on the walking isle.

The thing I hate most is when I see
cops herding Negros into cars.
One night when I was passing through
going home,
two women had gotten to fighting over some man with knives.
One had gotten cut up in the face.

Though it is full of whiskey,
bootleggers,
cuthroats,
clansmen
and what not,
Canton is my home sweet home.
I love it from my heart,
I guess anyone would find faults with
his or her home town.
My mother was born here,
so was I.
There is a spot that I would like to be buried here.

The place has changed a lot,
there used to be trees all up and down the street that I live.
Now there is nothing
but dead roots.
The trees are like the people,
getting old and passing on
like the silent river.
I can remember when I was four years old,
the people I knew were in their prime,
now they are old and grey.
It makes me want to cry by just thinking of them.

Canton is a place full of flowers and flower trees,
if I may say so
it smells as sweet as it looks
in the spring.

In the Inner City

LUCILLE CLIFTON

in the inner city
or
like we call it
home
we think a lòt about uptown
and the silent nights
and the houses straight as
dead men
and the pastel lights
and we hang on to our no place
happy to be alive
and in the inner city
or
like we call it
home

[X, 1, Winter 1969. Copyright © 1969 by Lucille Clifton.]

The South that is
Man's Destiny

ROBERT COLES

I CAME TO THE SOUTH a New Englander by birth and over a quarter of a century of living and growing up. In the middle of a psychiatric residency I was called to Mississippi to serve my required two years in the military as a doctor, in this case as the chief of an Air Force neuropsychiatric hospital. Now it is six years later, yet I write this in Mississippi. The Air Force is a memory, but the South has become a real, a fresh part of my life. If at first it was a region that I cared little to know, in fact a dismaying one which had taken me from several assignments I would have preferred, it presently is one whose continuing pull upon my mind and heart makes it hard for me to stay away for very long.

It is so easy to categorize and give names to experiences once we are done with them, and often so very sad that we do, because the effort takes away much of their original and spontaneous character. I suppose we need to try—it helps others understand, and makes us feel less anxious because more organized and in control of our fate. As I look back at the past years in the South, I recall how easily I slipped into its very distinctive life and how pleasant I found that life to be. Only now do I stir anxiously at the thought of just how long, weeks turning to months, it took me to develop the dim awareness that became the vague uneasiness which marked a change in my thoughts and habits while living there.

One way of putting it is that I was a white, middle-class professional man, and so I fitted into that kind of Southern society, only to begin to notice slowly the injustice so much at hand and, as a consequence, eventually take up my particular effort against it. (There would be those various categorical "stages" in such a development, ranging from faint glimmers to horrified, full

[VI, 2, Winter-Spring 1965]

recognition.) In the South, of course, anyone who begins to discover "injustice" in the world is in fact noticing the existence of
a caste system wherein Negroes have an inherited position in a
social organization which both needs them and yet gives their
skin color priority over any individual attainments or accomplishments they may manage to amass.

It seems strange to me now that I could spend so many months
in Mississippi and Louisiana without any particular worry about
much except my work and my day-to-day life. At other times I
understand *that* fact more than anything else I know about individuals and their society. We live our lives, after all, moved by
our energies and interests as they involve themselves in the world
around us, or indeed as they are also shaped by the world. I am
sure that I can be charged with a period of extreme insensitivity,
but I think the major conclusion which I now draw from my
first stay in the South was less one of willful accommodation to
its social evils than of intense preoccupation with a brief but
demanding interlude in my life—a new kind of job in a new location. How many struggles can most of us take on during our
lives? The world cries out with its innumerable trials and horrors
—the betrayal of human life made cheap and stripped of its dignity,
in every nation. The very nature of the human mind forces us to
limit our interests and compassion, or else we drown in their dif-
fusion and our own extreme pain. If this kind of talk is rationalization, it is also, alas, a remark upon our common fate and limitations
as human beings.

In any event, toward the end of my second year South I was
interrupted one day on a biking trip by the sight and sound of a
vicious battle on the Gulf of Mexico. To this day I can remember
my mind working its way toward some comprehension of what was
happening, fighting its way through its old attitudes for a moment,
then slipping back to them in relief. I saw a scuffle, and at first I
wondered why people would want to behave that way. For a few
seconds, I suppose my lifetime—and I don't think only mine—
was recapitulated: its innocence, its indifference, its ignorance, its
sheltered quiet, its half-and-half mixture of thickly justified moral
inertia and well-intentioned effort. For a while I could only see
people fighting. I heard shouts and cries. Some nasty and vulgar
words fell upon my ears. I recall thinking for a moment that it was
a Sunday, a beautiful Sunday; and it was a shame that people

could be so mean-spirited and irreverent, on Sunday, on any day, on such a clear, warm morning in early spring. I pedaled faster; I almost had the scene out of sight; but I can remember today slowing down, hesitating, only able to stop by lifting my body from the seat of the bike, by using my dragging, scuffing feet. I let the bike lie on its side, and stood still.

Every time I think of that scene—and it is often—I think of the first discrimination I made: not only was there a fight, but among the people I could see several *women.* A woman screamed that a man had smashed her watch and stepped on her glasses. Before I saw that she was a slender, middle-aged *Negro* lady, that he was a young, athletic *white man,* I felt the sympathy and horror that the weak share with the weak against the powerful. With that feeling I also knew for a moment that I would not easily be able to go to the woman's aid. In another flash, however, I realized I could justify my reluctance: it was a *racial* incident; the truth of what was happening was that the people were not simply people, the men and women not simply that.

I can still feel myself standing there, benighted, frightened, seized with curiosity, suddenly quite restless. I was not morally outraged. I did not want to join in the Negroes' protest for equal access to that essentially useless, shallow bit of seashore. Eventually, I simply wanted to go away; and I did. Riding home I condemned *all* the antagonists—for fighting, for choosing to fight for such absurd stakes, for being the kind of people who *would* fight. I am not very proud of those minutes. Yet if I forgot them, I would be even more ashamed.

That night I worked in the Emergency Ward of the Base Hospital, a duty which fell on each doctor with unnerving regularity. I had come to know the local police quite well during those evenings; they were on call, too, and we shared the long stretches of dark silence in that small town. The incident I had inadvertently witnessed was directly in the minds of both policemen, and their insistent talk about it made it impossible for me to forget it. We had never before mentioned the subject of race, but not, so far as I know, out of self-conscious or fearful avoidance in any of us. I liked those two men. They were kind, polite, and quite intelligent —considerably more so than many I had met in similar situations in certain Northern hospitals.

Like the event itself, I recall the first words: "They'd be dead now if it weren't for the publicity they get these days," followed by an avowal from his companion that "they will be if they try it again. We're never going to have mixing in this state." They had been talking with me; suddenly I felt them talking to me—at me. Their voices tightened. They spoke as crisply as a Southern drawl will permit—the honey in it had crystallized. They seemed aloof, yet fiercely determined to make their feelings clear to me, to the others nearby—now I realize, to themselves. I found myself slipping into a psychiatric posture with them, noticing their defensive anger, their accusations—diffusely directed at history, at Northerners. I decided that *they* were afraid, but I really didn't know why. I said little in reply. I wondered how men so strong, so appealing, so sensible *still* could be so aroused by an event I had managed to put out of *my* mind. Then a patient came in, and I was strangely glad to see him. His minor infection kept me exceptionally busy. Even if he hadn't been there, I remember thinking, I would not have told my friends that I had seen the "swim-in." I remember, also, realizing for a brief second that I had no *reason,* except my own anxiety, not to tell them. I saw their mood, observed their tension, felt their resentment, sensed their irritability, and feared my own involvement in any of them. Psychiatrists, of course, learn to watch for the unreasonable, avoid entanglement with the irrational. I imagine it was handy for me to call upon such professional practices.

By morning we had talked of town news, the fishing and shrimping, the new shopping center going up, the meaning to the area of a projected increase in the base population. That dawn we left, the same friends to one another. During the next weeks I continued with my usual tasks of work and play; but something had happened, something easy enough to talk about and describe now. Then, however, it was really nothing but an indistinct glimpse into a problem, sometimes disappearing into no vision at all, sometimes becoming a sharp and painful image. I can recollect, for instance, picking up the Jackson and New Orleans papers, reading in them of the coming probability of school desegregation in nearby New Orleans. It was well before the fateful day of its start, but the New Orleans papers were bitter and the Jackson papers almost incredulous. (I am writing this in Jackson, in September of 1964, over five years later, just before school desegregation starts there; now *its* papers are bitter; the New Orleans papers worry themselves about crime and gambling.) Somehow that news didn't manage to slip by me the way much news does, out of the impossibility of keeping abreast and involved with all the information that pours upon us these days. It wasn't simply my reading, however, that was being affected. I started noticing where Negroes lived, where they didn't, where they were in evidence, where they were not, and how they behaved with white people, and white people with them.

This new consciousness took root over several months. I find it hard to do justice to whatever growth and consolidation of feeling may have occurred during those months, because to think about that time now often invites in myself a certain scornful disbelief—that I could have lived so long under such a clearly oppressive social, political, and economic system, only to have been so blithely, so very innocently unaware of its nature. Yet I was.

Today there may be other problems than blindness facing many people living in the South. Large numbers of people in the region have awakened to the racial problem, and many of them, like me, must be freshly sensitive to the limitations which all human beings find upon their involvements and sensitivities. As if that were not enough, many probably are also coming to know that strong commitments push and tug at one another with their various demands, so that new kinds of indifference—even arrogance and hate—can follow old blind spots or prejudices. For example, there is the fighter's need to shed himself of much of the ambiguity of life, to sacrifice perspective, kind-heartedness, and even, at times, good judgment to the interests of the hard battle. When I look back at my first days there I am glad that I came to know the South as I did; but I also feel torn and paralyzed when I think of those times too long. I enjoyed one kind of life then, and that kind is gone for me.

Of course the South has always had its moments of paralyzed nostalgia. Nostalgia can be for anyone a valuable way to avoid the terrible strain of the present by forsaking its reality for the more pleasant world of memory. There is a painful ambiguity to Southern life: the genuine beauty of the landscape, the very real tradition of generosity and neighborliness, the longstanding sense of persecution, moral as well as economic, at the hands of powerful and hypocritical countrymen from other areas, all that aside from the presence of the Negro, with reminders of his history and his lot everywhere in evidence if not accusation. Effective protest, even against many open and declared social evils, does not always come about easily; and segregation in the South has hardly been considered anything but a way of living for both whites and Negroes, each in their own way knowing for generations the futility or risks of trying to change so awesome and peculiar a social system.

The protest I witnessed at the seashore in Mississippi showed that whatever balance it took to keep a "way of life" from being seen as a social evil was beginning to be undone. Not only was the protest no accident, but the restraint of the town's police was necessary, too—whatever their solemn excuses for it. The South was feeling the swift encouragement (and consequent apprehension) of a chain of events from far and near, grounded in world history as well as our own as a nation. My life is no "average white Southerner's" (hopefully none of our lives submit to approximations like that), and I am not sure that sit-ins such as I saw that day affect the majority of the South's white population as they do many of us who live elsewhere. Yet I think most people of the South—Negroes and whites alike—have experienced some of that same surprise I did, a jolting flash when one kind of world begins to collapse, another begins to appear, and it all becomes *apparent*.

My work of the past five years has been to study what happens to people in the midst of such social changes, how they relinquish their old ways and take up new ones, how, that is, they manage the various stresses and exertions of doing so. I shall never know how those Negroes and whites I saw that day on the Gulf Coast of Mississippi felt, but I think I have some fair notion about how others like them have felt in equally tense if not so vicious encounters—the children in desegregated schools in Louisiana, or in Georgia, where I lived for two years; the sit-in students from all over the South, and the whites who have been confronted by them; some leading segregationists, whom I came to know over a good number of months; and most recently, some sharecroppers and migrant workers, the poor of both races, whose hands harvest our cotton and food for little enough indeed.

Doing such work has required constant travel throughout the region, to the point that I know much of it better than any part of the North where I have lived. Even before I started studying some of the problems in the South, however, I had become somewhat sensitive to it through the astonishing contrast there with all that New England taught me to expect from nature and people. The very names of the towns were surprising. Some were familiar enough, but there are special preferences, too, such as the Greek and Roman names given to town after town in state after state: Rome in Georgia, Mississippi, and Tennessee; or Sparta in Georgia, Tennessee, and North Carolina. The ancient city of Carthage on the Gulf of Tunis is no more, but of fourteen cities which carry on its name over the world, six of them are in the South. There are other names, less classical, but in their sum a story of the region: Laurel, Enterprise, Liberty, Eufala, Senatobia, Natchitoches, Yazoo, Magnolia, Opelouses, Amite, and the Fayettevilles and Waynesboros, telling of flowers, ideals, Indians, and the French or English who lived there or came to do so.

The difference from the rest of the nation depends upon more than villages named in honor of Indian tribes or patriots to be celebrated; the South is not only its history, of those towns, of slavery, of rebellion. The mind recalls the past, but the senses recognize the living present. The skin feels the bouts of winter warmth, and must live with the near daily heat in summer, dry in Atlanta, steamy in New Orleans; for it *is* the South, and the weather is indeed kinder in winter and tiring, slowing in the summer. Whole theories of human nature have centered themselves on climate, and most often they seem single-minded or excessive, except for a moment in February when a soft wind rises from the bay and comes into Mobile, and with it a warm sun which brings out azaleas and high spirits both; or a time in midsummer when the damp heat in Louisiana has gone on long enough to make nerves already worn thin become alive beyond control.

The earth, too, is special, much of it red with copper. The growth is different, the tropical plants and palm trees, the famous wisteria and symbolic magnolia. The water is particularly abundant and rich in its variety: wide rivers, their tributaries weaving through the entire region, and the still smaller bayous, and canals, and the swamps with the mist over them. Lakes are everywhere, and much of the oceanside shows a tropical green band where it touches the shore.

The people have their own ways, too—their words, their food and stories, their kind of churches and praying. It's been noted so often, but an outsider like me coming from Northern or Western cities is surprised at first by the very names that are not Anglo-Saxon; those names, of course, shared by Negroes, who are not simply confined to ghettoes as they are so predominantly in the North, but are everywhere. They take care of homes and often live near them; they work in stores, gas stations, office buildings, and on the farms which still dominate the area; they cultivate and harvest crops, sharing in some of the profits in exchange for land and house, or moving from state to state to wait for harvests and gather them.

White and Negro alike, the people are, I suspect, church going beyond all others in the nation. The land seems covered with churches, and their denominational variety is astonishing. Revivals are common, and strict tithing by no means rare. The Bible is read literally in many towns throughout the section, still rural, strong on family and unashamed patriotism. Many whites have not yet surrendered their intensely suspicious regional and national pride, and many Negroes have till now found no reason to let go of the apathy and dependency, the alternation of good-natured frolic and sulky aloofness which characterized for so long their lack of pride in both themselves and their condition. Both races share some of the social forms of the society—the expressions like "Y'all come back," said frequently out of meaning as well as ritual, or the food, like pecan pie, grits, and okra, which come upon any visitor fairly soon and which one "favors" or is "partial to."

All of these distinctions of weather and terrain, of folk and folkways are individually interesting in their appeal, or for that matter, lack of it; but cumulatively they indicate that the Southerner in his daily life is perhaps specially identified by the marks of his region. Yes, the federal roads are coming in, television with its widespread news and "culture" is everywhere, and national loyalties have always contended with local ones. The region, though, for good and bad has had a stubborn power, not only in its social and economic system, but its history, its earth, its language and literature. Changes afoot there may well be influenced by those forces as well as bring to bear their own influence upon them. Certainly what I have described about the South's particular nature is familiar to most of us, and has been repeatedly described before. I had read those descriptions, and "knew" their message before going to live there. Yet the experience of those differences of living and thinking made for a sharper kind of awareness in me of the very real effect of those differences on the outsider who comes to live there as well as the life-long inhabitant of the section. Too much can be made of these "local" variations; but then too little significance can be granted them in an age that recognizes perhaps rather exclusively the grossest kinds of political and economic power, or dwells with a certain preoccupation upon the unqualified power of early childhood experiences.

My work has been concerned with changes in Southern life as it moodily breaks with the past. For well over a generation a "new South" has been anticipated and hailed, and its arrival is now certain. Walking through Atlanta or Charlotte the people can be seen in all their hurry, dressed out of New York, their office buildings as new, ugly, and efficient as those in other "growing" sections. The airports are the same proud boxes of never-ending buoyant music, and the runways as hungry for jets as all others. Yet Southerners have resisted as well as yielded to and even welcomed our modern nearness to one another. In studying the adjustment of white and Negro children (and their parents and teachers) to school desegregation I have learned to expect just that unusual blend of affection and reserve, accommodation and resentment which characterizes not only racial relations as they change in form and substance these days, but the South itself—recasting itself, but in its own fashion.

No one interested in the individual as he encounters a society in swift transition will be bored by Mississippi or the Carolinas. The ironies in both human beings and their social and political life are constantly revealed. Some of its people hurt and exploit others, but the region itself has been ruthlessly exploited over the generations. Many of its people are poor, ignorant, and capable of an absurd kind of defensive chauvinism, but many are sturdy, hard-working, kind people, so that as a whole every bit of Faulkner's vision seems sound. For all the shrill and resentful ones about, there have been many who fought hard in the past as warriors in hopeless causes, or as people reduced to poverty and defeat; and now their descendants fight against hateful mobs and the mean conditions of life which generate them.

These past one hundred years have not been a pretty story, and distress has not fallen upon one race alone. The kind of political tyranny practiced by whites over Negroes has gained little for large numbers of whites, and the saddest part of studying whites hating Negroes by forming mobs, or being nasty to them in schools, or sharing their fate on the collapsing farms of the region, or in the flow of migrant farmers which travels through it each year, is how very treacherous that "psychological" satisfaction of racial superiority has really been to the lives of those who have lived on it, and sometimes almost on it alone.

A nation within a nation, emerging from years of exile and hardship, its people today are showing individual dignity and courage as well as fear and desperation. Today, when some of us wonder whether our social order is in fact becoming drab and lifeless through its ability to make many of us fearfully similar and compliant, the South still clings to its almost Biblical struggles between those willing to risk and dare and those anxious to flee and hide. Perhaps out of no special virtue except its own tragic history (very much with it even now) the people there are fighting one another, taking sides against one another, questioning one another with an intensity and consistency which is rare indeed in our country at this time.

The protagonists have been ordinary people, but all of them have found themselves in a place and a time which have given heroic and symbolic proportions to their struggles. I am thinking, in this connection, of a white woman in New Orleans whose four children, with only a very few exceptions, defied the mobs attempting a total boycott of an elementary school on one little Negro girl's account. Why did this woman, deeply of the South, not by any means committed to "integration," hazard her life, the lives of her husband and children? I was in the company of those who tried to find the answer; a reporter, a sociologist, a psychiatrist, each of us worked at our common curiosity about human nature and its motives. I think we were all baffled, and—I suspect largely because of the way we think these days—we were all eager for the categorical solution, afraid of the clumsy, undefined, paradoxical flow of life and its events which may, in fact, be the truth of it.

Again and again—I talked with this woman over a period of two years—she came back to her only reply: she hadn't *planned* to dispute the angry, threatening crowds; she didn't think she was actually in favor of desegregation when all the uproar started; perhaps she was now, though; but she had always believed in education for her children, and she also felt a deep loyalty to the South's tradition, as she put it, "of good manners."

Poke and shove this woman's mind, I think her exploration will be found to hold firm. One day she was at her most open, and

most persuasive: ". . . my heart is divided, and at the worst of it
I thought we'd die, not just from dynamite, but from nervous ex-
haustion. I wasn't brought up to have Nigras at school with me
or my children. I just wasn't. . . . If I had to do it over, I wouldn't
have made this system, but how many people ever have a say
about what kind of world they're going to live in? . . . I guess in a
sense I did have my way with those mobs. But I didn't plan to, and
we were near scared to death most of the time. . . . People blame
the South for the mobs, but that's just part of the South. If I did
right, that's part of the South, too. . . . They just don't know how
a lot of us down here suffer. We didn't make all this, we just were
born to it, and we don't have all the opportunity and money down
here that they do in the North. . . . I told my children the other day
that we're going to live to see the end of this trouble, and when we
do I'll bet both races get on better down here than anywhere else
in America. . . . Why? Because I think we're quieter down here, and
we respect one another, and if we could clear up the race thing,
we really would know one another better. . . . We've lived so *close*
for so long. . . ."

A full transcript of what this woman has said at various times
tells more than any comments from those who have heard her.
She is not alone in her courage. The South is filled with an underground of sly liberals in the midst of situations hardly likely to
support their efforts. It is filled with a tradition of solid, dignified
Negroes, and ashamed, confused whites, enough of both so that it
would take a bold man indeed to separate and weigh their respective suffering. It is also, however, filled with bitter, spiteful whites,
and fearful apathetic Negroes, some of them capable of exploiting
their own people or demeaning them.

Perhaps nowhere in America is there so much that is good and
bad about human beings so clearly in evidence. Few would want
to keep the region's special virtues at the price of its outrageous
faults. Yet, it is a beautiful land to see, and its people in their guilt
and distress may have a good deal to teach us all. This nation
as a whole has known little frustration and defeat for some time.
The South has lived intimately with both, and it may have some
wisdom to offer from that experience. This is surely a time in our
national life when we need any help we can get about how to live
properly and sensibly in the face of prolonged uncertainty, ambiguity, and even the frustrations which come from not winning every

battle in every war. The South has not only seen the gloomy and tormented side of man's destiny (the woeful spell seems about to end); it has seen it and known enough of it perhaps to realize also the redemptive promise and power in human suffering. Sorrow may be fated, but to survive it and grow is an achievement all its own.

Fish are Jumping an'
the Cotton is High

Notes from the Mississippi Delta

MIKE THELWELL

THERE IS AN IMMENSE MURAL in the Hinds County Courthouse in Jackson, Mississippi. On the wall behind the judge's bench is this mansion. White, gracefully colonnaded in a vaguely classical style, it overlooks vast fields, white with cotton which rows of darkies are busily (and no doubt, happily) picking. In the foreground to the left stands a family. The man is tall, well-proportioned, with a kind of benevolent nobility shining from his handsome Anglo-Saxon face. He is immaculate in white linen and a planter's stetson as he gallantly supports his wife, who is the spirit of demure grace and elegance in her lace-trimmed gown. To the right, somewhat in the background to be sure, stands a buxom, grinning, handkerchief-headed Aunt Jemima, everyone's good-humored black Mammy. In this mural, progress is represented by a work-gang of Negroes, building, under the direction of a white overseer, what appears to be an addition to the great house. Although this painting is not wired for sound—a concession, one imagines, to the dignity of the court—it requires little imagination to hear the soothing, homey sound of a spiritual wafting on the gentle wind from the cotton fields. The general tone is certainly one of orderly industry, stability, and a general contentment. "Take a good look at them," a Negro lawyer said to me, "because they are the last happy darkies you are likely to see here."

Actually, this mural is so inept in technique and execution, that at first flush one is inclined to mistake it for parody. But Mississippians, especially the politicians, have never demonstrated the sense of security or humor that would permit them consciously to parody themselves, although they seem incapable of escaping self-parody in their public utterances. That this mural, consciously or not, is a burlesque of a parody of a stereotype which has never had historical or social reality goes without saying, but the mere fact that the mural exists and is intended to be taken seriously, or at least with a straight face, is equally important. Because, despite the fact that the Deep South is an area of as vast geographic, economic, and even sociological differentiation as any region in the nation, it is this plantation image of the South that persists in the sentimental sub-conscious of the American popular imagination. It is this image, or some derivative of it, that people tend to see when the Deep South is mentioned.

In point of fact, the area in which the huge cotton plantations of *Gone With The Wind* popular fame existed, and to an extent still do, is limited to a relatively small, specific geographic region. This is a narrow band of very level, fertile black earth which runs erratically south, then west from the bottom of Virginia through parts of the Carolinas, central Alabama, picks up in south-west Georgia, and runs through north-western Mississippi and into Arkansas. This very generally describes the region known as the "Black Belt," where the institutional replacements of the huge ante-bellum plantations exist, and where the descendants of the slaves still greatly outnumber the descendants of their masters, and where the relationship between these two groups shows only a superficial formal change. In Mississippi, this area is called the Delta, a term which, in its precise geographic meaning, refers only to the wedge of land between the Mississippi and Yazoo Rivers, but which extends in popular usage to most of the north-western quarter of the state. The area of the Delta coincides almost exactly with the Second Congressional District of Mississippi, the home of Senator Eastland, the Citizens' Council, and of the densest popula-tion of Negroes in the state. It is here, were it to exist anywhere, that one would find the image of the mural translated into reality.

WHAT CAN BE SAID about this place that will express the impact of a land so surrealistic and monotonous in its flatness that it ap-pears unnatural, even menacing? Faulkner comes close to express-ing the physical impact of the region: "... *Crossing the last hill, at the foot of which the rich unbroken alluvial flatness began as the sea began, at the base of its cliffs, dissolving away in the unhurried rain as the sea itself would dissolve away.*"

This description suggests the dominant quality: a flatness like an ocean of land, but within that vast flatness, a sense of confinement, a negation of distance and space that the sea does not have. And there are the rivers—in the east the headwaters of the river called Big Black, and sluggish tributaries, the Skuna, Yalabusha, and Yacona, which flow into the Tallahatchie, which in turn meets the Sunflower to become the Yazoo which was called by the Indians "the river of the dead." The Yazoo flows south and west until it meets the Mississippi at the city of Vicksburg. These rivers are, in Faulkner's words, ". . . *thick, black, slow, unsunned streams almost without current, which once each year ceased to flow at all, then reversed, spreading, drowning the rich land and subsiding again leaving it even richer.*"

I once entered the Delta from the west, from Arkansas, over a long, narrow old bridge that seemed to go for miles over the wide and uncertain Mississippi. It was mid-summer and a heat that seemed independent of the sun rose from the land. The slightest indentation in the road's surface became a shimmering sheet of water that disappeared as you approached it. The numbing repetition of cotton-fields blurring in the distance wore on one's nerves and perceptions. This has been called the richest agricultural soil in the world. So it may have been, but it also is tough and demanding—no longer boundlessly fecund, it now yields its fruits only after exacting disproportionate prices in human sweat and effort. An old man told me, "for every man it enriches it kills fifty," and some folks joke that "the Delta will wear out a mule in five years, a white man in ten, and a nigger in fifteen."

For long stretches of highway where the fields are unbroken by any structure or sign of habitation, one might be in another century, except that a few things serve to place you in time. Even if tractors are not visible they are suggested by the certainty that there could not be, no, not in all the Southland, enough Negroes and mules to have planted all this. And there are the airplanes. On smooth strips next to the cotton these toylike little craft, fragile and buoyant as children's kites, are tethered to the ground. The gentlest wind causes them to rear and buck against their moorings like colts. At times they are seen at absurdly low levels, skimming the top of the crops they are "dusting" against the boll weevil. They are used increasingly on the large plantations. One pilot, unnecessarily reckless, you think, crosses the highway *underneath* the telegraph wires and directly over your car. You remember, in that moment, the outdoor rally in Indianola that was bombed from one of these planes one night.

The billboards along the highway are also indices, not only of time but of place. They exhort you to support your Citizens' Council, to save America by impeaching Earl Warren, and challenge you to deny that "In Your Heart, You Know He is Right." "KILLS 'EM FAST, KEEPS 'EM DYING," is the message of another, and it is only when you are nearly abreast of the sign that the small print reveals that an insecticide is being advertised, and nothing larger than a boll weevil is the proposed victim.

But the combination of plane and grisly advertisement reminds you of a report from Panola County, in the heart of the Delta. The SNCC worker who wrote the report is distressed by the fact that many small Negro children in that area are plagued by running, chancre-like sores on their faces or limbs. These lingering and persistent ulcers are attributed by the community to a side-effect of the "pizen" sprayed on the cotton. Children of all ages pick cotton in the Delta, and apparently this insecticide enters any exposed break in the skin and eats away at the flesh like an acid. "What can we do," the report asks, "isn't there some law. . . ?" Perhaps, you think, it may be this particular brand of pesticide that "keeps 'em dying."

THIS IS "THE HEART OF DIXIE"—as numerous signs proclaim— the very center of the myth and the image, but what is its reality? For you right now, its only reality is heat, and an almost unbearable cumulative discomfort, sweat burning your eyes, oven blasts of dusty air when you open the window, the metal edge of the window that keeps scorching your arm, and all around a punitive white glare that is painful to look into.

For the SNCC workers who are your companions the reality seems to be a certain tense caution. They work the Delta and know the road, but in curious terms. Their knowledge is of the condition of the jail, idiosyncrasies of the lawmen, and the make, model, and color of the cars they drive. They choose a route, not necessarily the most direct, but one that avoids certain towns and the jurisdictions of certain local officers. They watch the background intently for the car that may be the sheriff, the Highway Patrol, or one of the new radio-equipped prowl cars of the Klan. A car or pick-up truck filled with youngish white men, stripped of license tags, is always ominous, especially if they keep passing and inspecting your car. Often, because it is legal to carry openly displayed weapons here, the cars will be fitted with racks on which rifles and shotguns are conspicuous. This should not suggest that violence is an inevitable consequence of using the highways. But the tension is always present, for when a car follows you for a few miles, passes you a number of times, then streaks off down the highway, you have no way of knowing their intentions. "Man, watch for a '63 Chevvy, light grey, no plate on front an' a long aerial. See anything that look like it shout."

The tension in the car draws to a fine edge. All know the car, and the reputation of the patrolman who polices the next fifty or so miles of highway. Two of the young men in the car have been "busted"—arrested—by him and as one says, "Once is enough. That man would rather whup yore head than eat shrimp . . . an' he's a sea-food lover."

This trooper is regarded with a mixture of fear and contempt by the Negroes in the County. He is reputed to stop every Negro he encounters, driving or on foot, to check their licenses and to find out where they are going and why. He is particularly fond of "interrogating" adolescent girls. As your companions talk about him a sort of grim, parodic humor attaches to him. His first statement, they say, is invariably, "All right Nigger, pull to the side, take off your hat, spit out your gum, an' lemme see your license." It makes no difference if you are hatless and have never chewed gum. And because, for SNCC workers anyway, the response is either silent compliance or a denial that their name is Nigger, his next utterance is usually "Dammit Nigger, don't you know to say Sir?" But this day he does not appear.

On another occasion I saw him making an arrest. Like most things in the Delta, he verges on being a caricature, drawn with too heavy a hand. He is not tall, but blocky and heavy. His hair is thinning, his face is round, full-cheeked, cherubic save for small pale-blue eyes behind absolutely innocuous gold-rimmed glasses. In the heat his complexion could not be called merely florid, it was red, deeply and truly red. His khaki-colored military-style uniform was too tight and stained with damp circles at the armpits and the seat of his pants. His ponderous, hard-looking belly sags over the belt which slopes down almost to the junction of his thighs. Most striking are his hands: blunt, stubby, very wide—with the skin of the fingers stretched tight, like so many plump, freckled and hairy link sausages. Two images stay with me: one of a boneless, formless, shapeless face; another of the chunky figure, standing spraddle-legged and tugging at the cloth of his trousers where it bunched in tight wrinkles between his thighs. I often wonder about this man. From all accounts he is a sadist, and one with entirely too much opportunity to indulge his impulses, but there is also present a pathetic, somehow pitiable, banality about him. Besides, he represents the most easily solved of the problems in the Delta.

Driving along the highways in the Delta you occasionally pass people walking—a single man, two, or sometimes what appears to be an entire family. Usually the man is in front in overalls, or blue denim pants and jacket, and with a wide-brimmed straw hat against the sun. The children follow behind in single file, with the woman usually at the end. They often carry tools, but more often cardboard boxes and newspaper-wrapped bundles tied with string. These little caravans become visible while you are some distance down the highway. If they have shoes then they walk on the hot but smooth asphalt; if they are barefoot they take to the weeds. When they hear your car approaching they step off the highway and face the road, motionless, waiting with a quality of dogged, expressionless patience to resume their plodding journey. Sometimes, but rarely, a child will wave, a vague and tentative motion of the arm somewhere between greeting and dismissal, and that is the only sign. No smiles. Often you find such a group miles from any house, village, side road, or anything that might be called a town. One wonders where they sprang from, where they hope to go, and why. They are almost always—I cannot remember seeing any white families walking—Negroes.

INDIANOLA IS the capital of Sunflower County, a county distinguished because it contains the 4,800-acre plantation of U.S. Senator James O. Eastland, the state prison farm at Parchman, and is the home of Mrs. Fannie Lou Hamer, the ex-plantation worker who has become the symbol of the resistance.

Although this is your first time there, you recognize when you have come home. When the pavement runs out—the streetlights become fewer or nonexistent and the rows of weather-textured, grey-grained clapboard shacks begin—you experience feelings of relief, almost love. This chaotic, dilapidated shanty-town represents community, safety in numbers, friendship, and some degree of security after the exposed vulnerability of the highway.

Even if you wanted to, you could not escape the children of all sizes and shades who abandon their games in the dusty streets or weed-filled lots for the excitement of a new arrival. Noisy with impatient curiosity and quick vitality they surround you, shooting questions. "Is yo' a freedom fighter? Yo' come for the Meeting? Is yo' start up the school? Have any money?" Or proudly, "We does leafletting, yo' want us to give out any?" Big-eyed and solemn they await the answers, ignoring their elders' warnings, shouted from the porches, "Yo' all don't be botherin' that man now, heah?" They must have some bit of information so that they can go scampering importantly up the porches to inform the old people. The community grapevine.

And on the porches, the people are almost always old, at least no longer young. Frequently they are the grandparents of the children because the true parents, the generation in between, are at work, or have left the state in search of work. This gap between generations lies like a blight on every Negro community, and especially in the Delta. You see it in any kind of meeting, in the churches—any gathering of Negroes in Mississippi consists predominantly of teen-agers and older people..

So the old people on the porch rock and fan and listen politely, perhaps too politely, expressing a cautious, noncommittal agree-ment that is somehow too glib and practised. And their eyes flick over your shoulder to see who may be watching. It may be the Man. The quiescent, easy agreement is another aspect of the mask, and one has no right to judge the only practical response that they have fashioned, the only defense they had. For if they survived yessing the white man to death, why not you? "Thou seest this man's fall, but thou knowest not his wrasslin'."

The motion and energy, the openness and thirst to know of the children in the road forms a tragic counterpoint to the neutral caution of the porches. So short a journey and symbolically so final. The problem comes clear: to create within the community those new forms, new relationships, new alternatives that will preserve this new generation from the paralysis of fear and hopelessness.

IN ALL THE SHANTY-TOWNS that cluster at the edge of every Delta city and town, the population steadily increases as increasing numbers of Negroes are driven off the plantations and off the land. Everywhere you get the impression of hopelessness and waiting. Large numbers of human beings in a kind of limbo, physically present and *waiting*. And what they wait for is the cotton. At planting time, chopping time, and picking time, busses and trucks come into the shanty-towns before the sun is well up. The people—men, women, and children—file on in the numbers needed and are taken to the plantations where they work a twelve-hour day for $2.50, or 30 cents an hour. Each year fewer and fewer people are needed for less and less work. If the fall is unusually wet, then it is a little better. The dust becomes a black and adhesive mud miring down the ponderous cotton-picking machines. Then, for a few hectic weeks almost the entire community can find work getting the crop in before it rots. Still, denied education and the skills that would give them mobility, these waiting people are superfluous, the obsolete victims of a vicious system that depended on large numbers of human beings being kept available in case they were needed. One plantation owner in the county is quoted as saying, "Niggers went out like the mule."

One way to understand this primitive and haunting place and the gratuitous human misery that it breeds, is to figure out who is in charge. Two forces rule the Delta: racism and cotton. Though the whitefolks put up a great show of control and dominance they are at the mercy of both. It is Cotton—not even Anglo-Saxon, but an immigrant from Egypt—that determines how the society is organized. And as a ruler, it is as ruthless, capricious, and sickly as the final issue of some inbred and decadent European house. Delicate, it must be protected from more vigorous hybrid weeds, and from a small beetle from Mexico. Drought will burn it out, water will rot it. Extravagant and demanding, it has—in alliance with human cupidity—all but exhausted a land of once incredible fertility which must now be pampered and fertilized excessively before it will produce. This process is so expensive that the final, grudging yield must be bought by the United States Government which alone can afford it. The federal government has a surplus at present of some fourteen million bales. This spring the federal cotton allotment has been reduced by one-third in the Delta. Even fewer Negroes will have work of any kind. The millionaire planter Eastland and other landlords, however, will still profit handsomely from their federal subsidy. While awaiting a federal check that runs into hundreds of thousands of dollars, the Senator will, if he maintains his average, make three speeches deploring the immorality of government handouts and creeping socialism, by which he must mean the distribution of food surpluses to starving families in his county.

AT SUPPERTIME the "freedom house" is full of bustle, the local kids pass in and out, a couple of carloads of SNCC workers from other parts of the state have stopped by on their way through. The shouted laughter and greetings are loud, the exchange of news marked by a wry humor. A young man from the south-west corner around Natchez tells stories about a local judge, nicknamed by the lawyers "Necessity," because in Horace's observation "necessity knows no law." But this judge is a favorite, because his records invariably contain so much error that although he never fails to convict, the higher court hardly ever fails to reverse him. Frequently, they say, his mind wanders, and he interrupts the proceedings of his own court with, "Your Honor, I object."

Another worker just down from Sharkey County, which is very rural and contains no city of any size, complains loudly about conditions. "Even the mosquitoes threatening to leave the county. They organized and sent Johnson a telegram saying that if the Red Cross didn't come down and distribute blood, they weren't staying." He wouldn't be surprised, he adds, to find when he returned that they had gotten relief.

The meeting is called for eight, but will not really get started much before nine, as the women must feed their white folks their suppers before going home to feed their own families. But folks start gathering from seven. They use the time to "testify"; to talk about whatever troubles their minds—mostly the absence of food, money, work, and the oppressiveness of the police. They talk about loss of credit, eviction, and voting, three things which form an inseparable unity in the Delta. Some young men are there from Washington County. They say the people over there got together and told the owners that they wouldn't work anymore for thirty cents. After the evictions they started a tent city, have a "strike fund" collected in the community, and are planting a "freedom garden" for winter food. Everyone cheers. What they want is co-operation. "If they sen' buses from Washington County don't go. Be workin' gainst us if you do."

"Thass right. Nevah. Freedom."

In the clapping, shouting, stomping excitement there is brief release from tension and fear. But over it all hovers an unease, the desperation of the unanswered question, "Whut *is* we gon' do." Winter is coming. "*Whut is we gon' do?*"

A lady wants to know. She is from "out in the rural" she says and two nights ago was awakened by what sounded like people crying. A man, his wife, and seven children were coming down the road carrying bundles. The children were crying and tears were in the man's eyes. They had no shoes. He said that evening the owner had given him twenty dollars and told him to find someplace else. He had worked that plantation all his life, had less than three years of school, and had never been outside the county. "Ah tell yo' that man was *shock,* he wuz *confused.* I want to know, what is we gon' do."

A portly, middle-aged lady answers her. This lady is known for a tough nerviness, an insouciant streak of daring best characterized by the Yiddish word *chutzpah,* or by the sheriff in the term "smart nigger." She also has a heart condition of some fame and strategic value. (As she gets up, you recall the time she was in jail and convinced the jailor, after two minor attacks and a constant and indignant harangue, that she was quite likely to die, and that he was certain to be held responsible, if she were not allowed to have her "heart prescription." And she got it, too. You remember her, dramatically clutching her ailing heart, breathing laboriously, and accepting with a quick wink the druggist's bottle of sour mash bourbon.) There were two little boys walking down the road, she says. They were throwing stones at everything they met. They came upon a chicken which the larger boy sent off with a well-placed stone. He does the same for a pig, a cow, and a mule. Then, they come to a hornets' nest. When the bigger boy makes no effort to hit that target the other asks, "Ain't yo' gonna pop that nes'?" "Nope, sho' ain't." "Why ain't y' gonna hit thet nes'?" the smaller asks. "Well, Ah ain't gonna hit thet nes',"—she pauses, looks at the audience, winks, shakes her head—"I ain't gonna hit thet nes' *because dey's organized.*"

They like that story, even if it is only a partial answer, saying *what,* but not *how.* So they nod agreement and murmur that "we'uns gotta be *together,* an' we gotta keep on, keeping on, no matter how mean times git." There is in these Delta communities a great spirit of closeness and cooperation. When a family is evicted, the children may be absorbed into the community, two here, one there. Or an entire family that finds itself suddenly homeless (landlords aren't required by any law to give notice) may be taken in by another family whose home is already too small. Without these traditions the folks could not have endured.

In the meetings, everything—uncertainty, fear, even desperation—finds expression, and there is comfort and sustenance in "talkin' bout hit." A Preacher picks the theme up with a story of his own. "Wunst times wuz very bad fer the rabbits."

"Fo' the *Whut?*" comes a chorus. The old man smiles, "Fer the *rabbits.* Yes Sir, Ah tells yo' they wuz bein' hard *pressed.* Them ol' houn's wuz runnin' them *ragged.* Got so bad it seem like they couldn't git down to the fiel's to nibble a little grass. It looked like they wasn't gonna be able to make it."

"*Yeah, Yeah, Tellit,*" the people shake their heads in sympathy.

"They wuz *hard pressed* fo' a fack. So fin'lly, not knowin' what else to do, they calls a meetin'. Yessir, they call a *mass meetin'.*"

"*Ahuh, Freedom.*"

"So they talked an' talked, discussed it back an' fo'th, how the houn's wasn't givin' them space even to live."

"*Thass right, tell it.*"

"But they couldn't meet with no solution. It jes' didn't seem like hit wuz nothin' they could do." The speaker shakes his head. "No, it didn't seem like they could make it. So fin'ly thisyer ol' rabbit, he wuz ol' anyways an' fixin' to die anyhow, he sugges' that since they wuzn't making it *nohow,* they should all jes' join together an' run down to the *river an' drown theyself.*"

Everyone in the church is listening very closely. There is the beginning of a low murmur of rejection.

"But since nobody said any better, they put hit in the form of a motion, an' someone secon' hit an' they take a vote. It passed [pause] *unanimous.* So on the nex' moonlight night, they all git together jes' as the motion call fer, link they arms and start fer the river, fo' to drown theyself. Hit wuz *a-a-l* the rabbits in the county, an' thet wuz a long line, jes' hoppin' along in the moonlight to go drown theyse'f. It wuz somethin' to see, chillun, it sho' wuz. An, yo' know, they hadn't gon far befo' they come upon the houn's, out looking fo' rabbits to chase. Them ol' houn's be so surprise at seein' all them rabbits commin' towards them steady, *they thought they time had come.* They be so surprised they turn roun' and run so fas' they was outen the county, befo' sun come up. Rabbits had no mo' trouble."

"*Talk 'bout Freedom.*"

THERE IS LITTLE of subtlety or delicacy here, it is a region of extremes and nothing occurs in small measure. All is blatant, even the passing of time. Night in the Delta is sudden and intense, an almost tangible curtain of blue-purple darkness that comes abruptly, softening and muting the starkness of the day. The moon and stars seem close, shining with a bright yellow haziness like ripe fruit squashed against a black-board. The wind is warm, very physical and furry as it moves with suggestive intimacy over your face and body. Like the sea; the Delta is at its most haunting and mysterious in the dark. The air is heavy with the ripe smell of honeysuckle and night-blooming jasmine, at once cloying and aphrodisiac. A woman's voice, deep-timbered, husky, and *Negro* is singing an old plaintive song of constant sorrow with new words. The song becomes part of the rich-textured night, like the tracings of the fireflies. In the restless and erotic night you believe. For the first time you can believe the blues, tales of furtive and shameful passions, madness, incest, rape, and violence. Half-intoxicated by the night, by its sensuous, textured restlessness, it is possible to believe all the secret, shameful history that everyone seems to know and none will admit except in whispers. It is easy to believe that the land is finally and irrevocably cursed. The faceless voice singing to the darkness an old song with new words, "*They say that freedom . . . is a constant sorrow.*"

JUST OFF THE ROAD STANDS THE SHACK. There is a quality of wildness to the scrubby bush around it, and because it is set on short wood piles, it appears to have been suddenly set down on the very top of the carpet of weeds around it. The greyed wood siding has long since warped so that a fine line shows between each plank, giving the shack the appearance of a cage. Crossing the porch you step carefully, avoiding the rotted holes. The woman inside turns dull eyes towards where you stand in the doorway. She is sharing out a pot of greens onto tin plates. The cabin is windowless and dim but is criss-crossed by rays of light beaming through the cracks in the siding and from gaps in the roof where the shingles have rotted and blown away. This light creates patterns of light and shadow on everything in the room. As the woman watches you, at least inclines her head in your direction, her children sidle around her so that she is between them and the door. You see that there are only five —at first it seemed as though the cabin was full. None of them is dressed fully, and the two smallest are completely nude. As the mother gives you the directions back to the highway, she ladles out the greens and each child seizes a plate but stands looking at you. They are all eyes, and these eyes in thin tight faces blaze at you. The full, distended bellies of the children contrast with the emaciated limbs, big prominent joints, narrow chests in which each rib stands out, the black skin shiny, almost luminous. You cannot leave, so you stand gently talking with the mother, who answers your questions with an unnatural candor. She seems beyond pride. As you talk, she sits on a box and gives her breast to the smallest child even though he seems to be about five. This doesn't surprise you unduly for you have learned that in the Delta, Negro mothers frequently do not wean their children until the next one arrives. What will substitute when there is not enough food?

You find out that she is twenty-four, was married at fifteen, had seven children but two died, the father is in Louisiana chopping pulpwood, the nearest work he could find. He sends money when he works. She lives in this abandoned cabin because it was the only rent-free house she could find after they were put off the plantation. As you leave, you see them framed in the doorway, the mother in unlaced man's shoes, one brown, the other black, holding her smallest child with the unnaturally big head and eyes.

You wonder how they are to survive the winter in a cabin with walls that cannot even keep the dust out. But this is Tallahatchie County, where thirty-three per cent of all Negro babies die in the first year of life, where Negroes live, grow old, and die without ever being properly examined by a doctor, and children die of cold and hunger in the winter. One reason given for the high infant mortality rate—you meet women who admit to having birthed ten children of which three or four survived—is that in this completely agricultural county, families survive the winter, when there is no work for the men, on the ten or twelve dollars the mother makes working as a cook or maid. When her time of labor approaches she dares not stop working.

BUT ALL OF THIS was some time ago. All I know of the Delta now is what I hear. I am told that snow blanketed it in January and I am glad I was not there to see it. I am told that in December two hundred and fifty families were given notice to be off the plantations by January first. This means that some 2,200 human beings are without home or livelihood, and none of the programs of the federal government—social security, unemployment compensation, or job retraining—affects them. By spring, they say, some 12,000 people will be homeless. I am glad I was not there to see the ghostly silent caravans trudging through the snow at the side of the highway. A lady in Sunflower County told me on the phone that families were at the tent city asking to be taken in.

Throughout the Delta the plantations are automating, driven by the dual pressure of cutting costs and the potential effect of the 1965 Voting Rights Bill in a region with a Negro majority. The state of Mississippi wants its Negro population thinned out. They make no secret of it. Governor Johnson has said in praise of his predecessor that under Ross Barnett's regime "116,000 Negroes fled the state." And the state has still not been able to find any way to use the 1.6 million dollars appropriated by the Office of Economic Opportunity to be used to finance the distribution of surplus food in the Delta. Before this grant, it had been Mississippi's position that they simply could not afford the cost of *distributing* the free food. I am just cowardly enough to be glad I am not there to see.

Four Photographs from Mississippi
by Bob Fletcher, reproduced by permission of SNCC.
[VII, 2, Spring 1966]

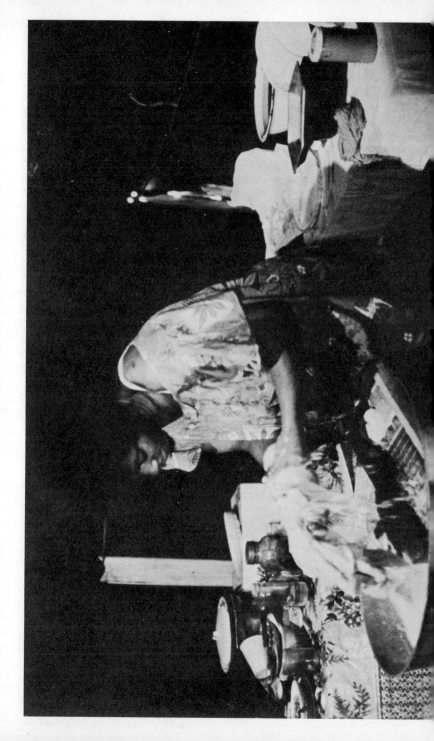

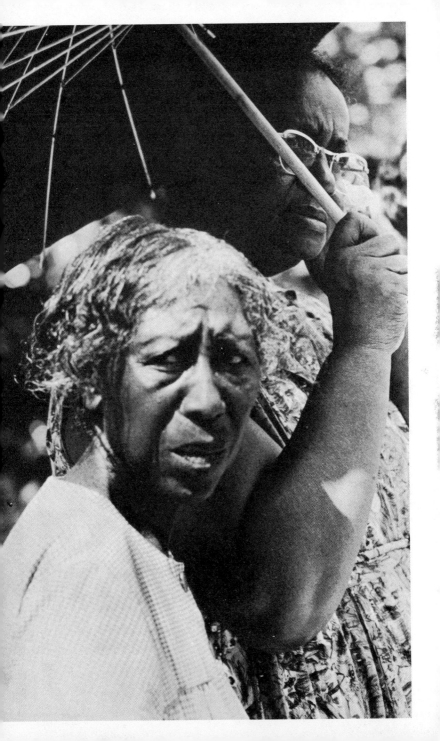

"Bye, Lena"

CHARLOTTE PAINTER

GEORGIA JUNEAU went out to the country to visit her grandma. It was something she always did. As a little girl, she played in the mud with the two colored girls from the tenant shack, crazy old Dinah's girls. They made mud-cakes, brownies, pies, and pones, until she was about eleven. Then, she started giving slumber parties at grandma's and later, when she was at college, houseparties that went on until dawn or after. And when she was a married woman, grandma's was the best place to meet secret dates, for the old lady wasn't too wide awake anymore, and there were no neighbors around to notice what cars came and went. There were only old Dinah's two colored girls.

Old Dinah herself had a moaning cry that would pierce the middle of the night: "Old Tom Turkey's gonna get me!" Nobody thought anything of it. It was just something she always did. And her two girls would quiet her down.

"I'm just crazy about those two gals," Georgia confided one day to her best friend Tooter Bemis when she was ten. "My mother's going to pack up a box of my old clothes and leave them at the door of Dinah's shack." Her mother did so, and thereafter, it was something *she* always did.

"They make me wish I was colored," said Tooter enthusiastically. "I just love the way they talk."

And so there was a natural reason for Georgia and her friend Tooter, when they were in high school, to get a kick out of a certain game. It was just one of those games that spring up from nowhere, like London Bridge or Knock-knock. All the girls were playing it. And it became something Georgia and Tooter always did.

They would come upon one another in the hallways or school yard and the following exchange would take place.

"Hello, Lena," the one would say.

"Hello, Tina," the other would say.

[VIII, 2, Spring 1967]

"What you doin?"

"Peelin taters. What *you* doin?"

"Peelin maters."

"How you like it?"

"Mmm. Ah like it. How *you* like it?"

"Mmm. Ah like it."

"Where you workin?"

"Down at Thompson's. Where *you* workin?"

"Down at Johnson's."

"How you like it?"

"Mmmm. Ah like it. How *you* like it?"

"Mmm. Ah like it."

"Who's yo feller?"

"Tommy Thompson. Who's *yo* feller?"

"Johnny Johnson."

"How you like him?"

"Mmm. Ah like him. How *you* like him?"

"Mmm. Ah like him."

"Bye, Lena."

"Bye, Tina."

You had to keep a straight face all the way through. You were supposed to drag out the Mmm's in the last part, the part about the boy friends, and to wave bye-bye at the end and go on your way without another word. And you had to be careful not to ask anything out of turn. One 'How you like it?' misplaced or forgotten, one giggle, and the score went against you. For a spell, Georgia, who was a lot smarter than almost anyone in her class, had twenty points against Tooter, and a total of about a hundred points against all the other girls who played with her. "There's nothing to it," she would say of the game. "That's what I like about it. It's just plain nothing." And she would tap her forehead.

Once she said, "I'd like to see crazy old Dinah's girls play this game."

It happened that she didn't have a chance to teach old Dinah's girls the game until many years later, after she and Tooter were married women. But one afternoon, Georgia found she had some time on her hands. She had waited an hour at grandma's for her date, who was two hours late himself. She decided to teach the two girls the game to pass the time. She and Tooter hardly ever played the game themselves anymore. Georgia didn't see as much of her old friend as she used to. And thinking of that, Georgia became depressed. "What happened to the things we always did?" she wondered. Then, the telephone rang, and her date told her he couldn't make it. At that, a strange sense of loss became strong enough to make her cry. Except that the colored girls were waiting outside where she had told them to meet her.

In the yard, she lined them up and taught them the words. It turned out Georgia had been right. The girls played the game like a couple of naturals.

There was only one problem, and that was keeping a straight face. That took a lot of drilling. They often had to stop to pass their brown hands over their mouths to wipe away their grins. Whenever that happened, Georgia made them start all over again.

"You're a kick!" cried Georgia at length. "Do it again." She got them to do it over and over. Then she made them switch roles, so that the one whose feller was Johnny Johnson had to remember to say Tommy Thompson, and that broke them up. She always made them start again from the beginning after they recovered from their giggles. They were a long, long time getting the smiles wiped completely off their faces. It would be hard to say exactly how long.

"Where you workin?" went the first of Dinah's girls toward the end.

"Down at Thompson's. Where *you* workin?" went the other.

"Down at Johnson's."

"How you like it?"

This time, Georgia looked at old Dinah's girls more closely. To her surprise, she saw that they were grown women now, too. What did they do with themselves? she wondered. Did they still live in that old shack out back with Dinah? Did Dinah still moan in the night about old Tom Turkey? The girls were dressed as neat as two peas, and in clothes she didn't recognize. They weren't dresses *she* had ever had, that was for sure. "Where *are* you working these days?" she said to one of the girls.

But the girl seemed not to hear, and the dialogue continued. "Who yo feller?"

"Tommy Thompson. Who *yo* feller?"

"Johnny Johnson . . ."

Georgia raised her voice. "I said, 'Where're you working these days?' "

But no answer came.

"How you like him?" asked the one girl.

"Ah doan like him," said the other.

Georgia laughed. "Listen. I know it takes a lot of concentration, this game. But stop a minute. I want to talk. You realize how long it's been since we talked? Since we used to make mudcakes, just about."

But the two colored girls seemed not to hear. They went on and on.

"How *you* like him?"

"Ah doan like him."

"Thass bad news, Lena."

"Ah knows it, Tina."

"How his dangle?"

"Long as Monday. How *his* dangle?"

"Short as Sunday. How you like it?"

Georgia gave a queasy laugh. "What's going on here, you two?" she asked. "You getting fresh?" But the dialogue continued.

"Doan much like it. How *you* like it?"

"Doan much like it."

"He a white man?"

"White as perch. *He* a white man?"

"White as birch."

"How you like it?"

"Doan much like it. How *you* like it?"

Georgia stood over them angrily. "Stop this. Stop it this minute. Who do you think you are?"

"Mah name's Lena," said the one.

"Mah name's Tina," said the other. "Who you-all?"

Georgia began to scream. "I'll tell you who I am. I'll get my daddy to come out here, and you'll see you can't get away with this kind of sass. He'll show you a thing or two!"

"How *his* dangle?" Lena asked her.

"Sad as Sad'dy," answered Tina.

"Get out! Get out!" screamed Georgia helplessly. "You're crazy just like old Dinah. Crazy, crazy!" But the two went on with their discussion.

"How yo baby?"

"He get hongry. How *yo* baby?"

"He get hongry."

"How you like it?"

"Doan much like it. How *you* like it?"

"Doan much like it. You try white folk?"

"He doan like 'em, little bugger."

"My boy eat 'em."

"How *he* like 'em?"

"Fair. Ah sprinkle on some sugar."

"My boy doan like 'em."

"Try Tabasco. Dat sometime help."

"Done tried it on the little whelp."

"Still doan like 'em?"

"No, just doan like 'em."

"Ah'd sooner pigs when Ah can get 'em."

"Doan squeal so loud-like when you hit 'em."

"Thass right, Tina."

"Take white folk feet—they just ain't sweet."

"And the heart's so hard, and the bacon's fat."

"And the gizzard's like a leather hat."

"It ain't so hot."

"And the gut's all rot."

"And the brains ain't fit for a hound to eat."

"You so right, Lena."

Georgia Juneau could bear no more. She fell to her knees, sobbing. "Oh please stop, please. Can't we be friends? Just like before? I wasn't poking fun at you. I liked the way you talk—that's the whole point of the game. Can't we go on the way we always did? Oh—who's come down here and stirred you up? No, wait, don't go, please. Don't desert me!" she cried.

But the two gave no sign of having heard. They linked arms and sauntered down the dusky road.

"Ah wouldn't monkey with 'em—'cept for gettin hongry."

"Thass right, Tina."

"But we got to make do with what the Lord provides."

"Thass right, Lena, with what the Lord provides."

Changing People

Negro Civil Rights and the Colleges

HOWARD ZINN

SINCE 1960, THE NEGRO COLLEGES in the United States have been a source of national excitement, a breeding place for the small band of youthful abolitionists sparking the Negro revolt, and a cause of worry. The worrying is being done by a number of the administrators of Negro colleges, who have had trouble keeping the new militancy from surging against the orthodox patterns of authority on Negro campuses. But there may be faint tremors, too, in the highest circles of American education. The reason for this is the momentum of the civil rights revolution, and its effect on increasing numbers of college students, Negro and white.

This is not yet a mass movement; the bulk of American students remain only slightly touched by the concerns which grip a few thousand of them, which have changed the lives of a few hundred. Too many American educators are still hemmed in by catalogues, transcripts, and machine-graded examinations. But there is a gleam of possibility widening slowly in the cloistered corridors of the American educational system.

I CAME TO BE AWARE OF THIS as I observed the student revolt from my own fascinating observation post—the campus of a Negro college in the Deep South. Through seven years, I watched slow awakening, volcanic eruption, and the growing signs of what might be either a passing disturbance, or the beginnings of fundamental change.

The student outburst could have come any time after 1954, the year of the Supreme Court decision, or after 1955, the year of the Montgomery bus boycott. It came in 1960, on the first of February, when a few students from a Negro college in Greensboro, North Carolina, staged the first lunch-counter sit-in and started a national commotion which has refused to die down. In the next eighteen months, sit-ins or other forms of demonstration took place in over one hundred cities of the deep and border South; about 3600 students and supporters were arrested; tens of thousands participated in one way or another.

That this was a double threat, to the status quo of both Negro and white leaders of segregated society, was soon evident. Punitive action was taken, particularly in state-supported colleges where Negro presidents, either following or anticipating the stated desires of white overseers, began to get rid of trouble-making students and faculty members. At the largest Negro college in the United States, Southern University in Baton Rouge, Louisiana, sit-in leaders were dismissed from the school, after which two hundred and thirty-six students withdrew in protest and several faculty members resigned. Most of the Negro faculty members remained silent as students and colleagues were removed from campus. Part of the blame for this, undoubtedly, should be laid to the economic pressure on Negro teachers, who face color discrimination even in the academic world.

In some Negro colleges, as at Fisk University, the administration supported the students from the beginning, without equivocation. Perhaps the most typical response was that shown at the six associated Negro colleges of the Atlanta University Center, where the presidents, troubled by the eagerness of their students for direct action, tried to slow them up and divert them to more respectable avenues of protest, but then, when the demonstrations became a fact, declared their support. An example of this public approval and private discomfort is one experience a faculty member had, trying to get one of the colleges in the Center to put up bond money for a student in jail on a traffic charge. Administrators at the college were prepared to do it, as a college will often take the responsibility for its wards, but when they found out their student had been returning from a demonstration, they suddenly withdrew their offer, leaving the young fellow in jail. This was a college whose president publicly was a supporter of the demonstrations.

On the Spelman College campus in Atlanta, where students gathered frequently in my home, I could watch the immediate effect of the Greensboro sit-ins. I could also witness the internal turmoil that followed, for the revolution against the old South carried implications of a revolution against the old Negro leadership. Presidents of the Negro colleges in Atlanta assembled the students, who were anxious to begin demonstrating, and suggested that before direct action, they publish a statement of grievances as a full-page ad in the *Atlanta Constitution*.

Negro students, like subordinate groups everywhere, have learned sometimes to slide around obstacles rather than attack them frontally. They agreed to the advertisement, but worded it in such a way as to make follow-up action inevitable. In their dramatic and eloquent full-page proclamation, called "An Appeal for Human Rights" (which startled the city's white population, never confronted with such bold demands by Negroes), they listed the indignities suffered daily by Atlanta Negroes, and concluded with a promise to "use every legal and non-violent means at our disposal" to end segregation.

Six days after that promise—it was March 15, 1960—several hundred Negro students, in a maneuver planned with near-military precision, went into town to sit-in at ten restaurants, resulting in the arrest of seventy-seven of them who refused to leave their seats. The morning of the sit-in, some Spelman girls came to my house to borrow my car "to go shopping" in town. In a sharp break with their college's tradition of conservatism and gentility, fourteen Spelman girls went to jail that day. Sit-ins and picketing continued for over a year before Atlanta merchants, including the Rich's Department Store, agreed to desegregate their lunch-counters.

In the process, a striking change came over the Negro student in the segregated college of the Deep South. Quiet girls from little Southern towns became heroines; studious young men became mature leaders of complex movements for social change. Lives were altered, directions reversed, overnight.

I saw it in my own students. Marian Wright, the girl who drove my car downtown that first dramatic day of the Atlanta sit-ins, was from a little town in South Carolina. She spent some time in jail, reading. Before she left Spelman she had become one of the leaders of the student movement in Atlanta. She went on to Yale Law School and graduated last year, spending summers meanwhile with "The Movement." She intends to be the first Negro woman civil rights lawyer in the state of Mississippi.

Another Spelman student, Ruby Doris Smith, silent and unobtrusive on campus, just another one of five hundred girls stepping cautiously into a new world, took part in a demonstration in Rock Hill, South Carolina, that first summer after the sit-ins and spent a month in jail. The following summer of 1961, when the Freedom Rides were organized, Ruby Doris rode on one of those buses into Jackson, Mississippi, and ended up spending two months in Hinds County Jail. Meals consisted of syrup and biscuits, red beans, and black-eyed peas. She and her twenty-four fellow prisoners waited for the lights to go out at night, and then sang freedom songs.

That the student upsurge of the spring of 1960 was not a passing mood, and that it presaged changes in more than Southern racial patterns, became clear when, a few months after those first sit-ins, protest leaders from all over the South met in Raleigh, North Carolina. There they formed the Student Nonviolent Coordinating Committee. A year later, sixteen students deserted their colleges and became full-time professionals in a new and dangerous educational venture. By early 1964, the number of ex-students who were manning outposts in Albany, Georgia; Greenwood, Mississippi; Selma, Alabama; Danville, Virginia, and a dozen other troublespots in the deep South, had grown to one hundred and fifty.

THE REVOLT OF THESE STUDENTS against the power of white segregationists in the South, and against the older, more conservative Negro leadership, has brought, as one of its least-noticed but most important consequences, a wild flowering of discontent with traditional education in America.

This discontent has two targets. One is orthodox *Negro* education—the special pattern of life, both academic and social, which has dominated the campuses of Negro colleges ever since their establishment shortly after the Civil War. The other target is traditional *American* education—those values and that philosophy which, despite brave Commencement Day addresses, represent the reality of higher education in America.

That perceptive and irrepressible sociologist, the late E. Franklin Frazier, spoke to an audience of Negro students, faculty, and administrators in Atlanta in 1957 and dropped a series of emotional grenades among them as he castigated "this vicious thing called Negro education." Frazier, one of the great Negro scholars of our time, attacked the values and educational aims of Negro colleges, which he said were directed at producing carbon copies of those false objectives fostered in white bourgeois society. "Most of our schools," he complained, "are finishing schools for the Negro middle class."

To the critique of Frazier might be added the fact that paternalism and authoritarianism have long plagued students and faculty at many of the Negro colleges. Students have found their activities controlled at every turn, their freedom to speak and write restricted, their liberties doled out in spoon-size portions. A study made in 1962 by an inter-racial team—Roberta Yancy and Mary King— who traveled throughout the South and visited dozens of Negro college campuses, revealed the severe limits on academic freedom for students. And faculty members of Negro colleges often find themselves as much victims of administrative tyranny as do the students.

I do not want to overemphasize the specialness of those shortcomings which have plagued Negro colleges. The same disabilities —pallid middle-class ambitions connected with money and prestige, a condescendingly paternal attitude towards students by administrators and faculty standing on their piles of degrees, the hierarchy of authority which puts huge power in the hands of college administrators, the consequent restrictions on the academic freedom of both faculty and students—mar so many American colleges. That these qualities exist in exaggerated form in Southern Negro colleges can be attributed to a factor which is easily forgotten in the present glow of liberal admiration for everything Negro: that these institutions suffer from a hundred years of segregation. And segregation breeds fear, defensiveness, insecurity, even among its proudest victims. A *New York Times* news story from Elmira said: "Students at Elmira College have petitioned the Board of Trustees to review actions of the president of the college. They say his actions have created an atmosphere of fear on the campus."

When the sit-in spirit swept through Spelman College, some of the dynamic overflow became focused inward, at the restrictions, the pretenses, the absence of a spirit of freedom, which had been part of campus life there for so long. Girls who were going to jail, challenging the taboos of the dominant white society around them, could hardly be expected to return to campus and submit once again to the old way of life. One girl wrote in the student newspaper:

We admit that Spelman is a good school and a beautiful campus. . . . But why shouldn't we be able to enjoy scenery other than that of Spelman College? . . . Why can't we venture outside of 'our world' into the 'big world'. . . . We sit and watch the birds and the squirrels as they seemingly enjoy life, while we, the most intellectual species, must sit confined behind the Spelman Wall!

In the spring of 1962, the "proper young ladies" of Spelman College, who had done battle—nonviolently, of course—with white merchants, state troopers, and the Governor himself, rebelled against the college administration. In a petition signed by over half the student body, they listed their grievances. Spelman College, they declared, "is not preparing today's woman to assume the responsibilities of today's rapidly changing world." They called for a series of reforms in the curriculum and in the social regulations. Berating the student leaders for their presumptuousness, Spelman's president prevented publication of the petition in the student newspaper and denied a scholarship to one of the leaders of the petition drive. But the battle continued.

Similar clashes—though perhaps less direct—took place at some other Negro colleges. That this situation differs only in degree from that in white colleges is shown by events at Elmira College in New York, at almost exactly the same time.

ALONG WITH THIS GROWING RESISTANCE to the Negro college tradition there is the beginning (only the beginning—I don't want to exaggerate its scope) of revolt against the whole value system of American education today. For a Negro student who has gone through the intense learning experience of a direct clash with an entrenched social structure to sit in class and regurgitate stale subject matter from ponderous textbooks—or even interesting subject matter from streamlined textbooks—seems pallid and unrewarding. In the civil rights movement, a student learns public speaking from appearances at church rallies, practices writing grammatical and pungent leaflets, learns about the law and the courts as they really operate, gets interested in the economic structure of his community. He discusses the philosophy of nonviolence, and other questions of ethics, in bull-sessions with fellow activists. Now, I am idealizing this, but students caught up in it are likely—even if subconsciously—to measure that ideal against the caricature of education they find so often in the academic world.

The result is either total withdrawal from college, or a painful mental tug-of-war where the student zig-zags from "the movement" to college, back and forth, unable to decide. Knowing that too often college is divorced from the reality of social struggle, and also that the struggle itself does not quite supply either the practical requirement of occupational training or a thoroughgoing theoretical foundation in the humanities and the social sciences, each student involves his problem in his own way.

Lenore Taitt studied history with me at Spelman—a voluble, charming girl, and soon a happy warrior in the movement, which she joined in her senior year. When she graduated, she went on to the Atlanta University School of Social Work, but all through the first semester she was restless. In December of 1961, the Southern Regional Council sent me down to Albany, Georgia, to do a study of the racial crisis there. It had been set off by the arrest of eight students, Negro and white, who rode down from Atlanta to Albany together in a train, and then were taken into custody at the terminal by the Albany police chief. Lenore Taitt was among them. I tried to visit her at the Dougherty County Jail in Albany and got as far as any visitor could get—the barbed wire fence around the stone jailhouse, from which we could shout to each other, Lenore invisible behind a thick mesh window. After her release she went back to the School of Social Work, but with frequent trips to the office of the Student Nonviolent Coordinating Committee until she finally graduated.

It was in Albany, too, late one evening outside a Negro church, with the sound of freedom songs drifting into the street, that I met a tall, dark-skinned, forceful young man named Stokely Carmichael. He was a field worker with SNCC, but also a major in philosophy at Howard University. A veteran of the sit-ins and freedom rides, jailed in Mississippi and in Maryland several times, he continued to go to school, but spent his Christmas vacations and summers in the deep South. In Greenwood, Mississippi, last summer, far from Howard University, I met him again, heard him talk to sharecroppers in a rundown little church out in the cotton country.

The field staff of SNCC, all over the deep South, consists mainly of youngsters who have left college completely to work for the movement. Some go back after a year in the field; others remain. The taste for academic education stays with them, but the memory of their college classes is usually a sour one. And among the great mass of Negro students, who have not left school, there is the constant pull, the glamor, attached to those few who once sat with them in the lecture halls and now appear in the newspapers as protagonists in the nation's great social crusade. The magnetism is strong, and every so often it pulls another student away, suddenly, into the maelstrom.

Among the five million white students in the nation, the effect of the civil rights drama has been complex: many react as they do to their classes, with a combination of boredom and annoyance, impatient to get out in the real world of credit cards, a comfortable income, and a shrewd marriage. For others, the movement has had the faint scent of forbidden fruit—enticing, but distant and unknowable. For a handful, the heavens suddenly lit up and all the stars changed their position; these few were catapulted, by the emotional force of the movement and the passion of their own response, out of the safe world of college education and into a new sphere of danger, commitment, and promise. With each month, more and more white students become involved, either partially, on their own campuses, or totally, hurling themselves into the most tense trouble areas of the Deep South.

With some, it started innocently enough. In 1960 and 1961, several of the Negro colleges in the South were involved in student exchange programs with Northern colleges: a few Negro students would spend a semester in the Northern institution, and a few white students would replace them in a Southern Negro college, immersing themselves completely in the social and academic life there. What happened was more than the administrative organizers of the exchange bargained for; many of the white exchange students underwent a personal revolution which sharply changed the direction of their lives.

Catherine Cade, an alert enthusiastic student from Carleton College, came to Spelman in the fall on exchange. During her first week in Atlanta she was already participating in a sit-in at the Georgia State Legislature. Soon, she was on picket lines regularly. When she went back to Carleton, it was with a feeling of being forcibly torn from where she belonged. The next summer, she returned to work full-time for the Student Nonviolent Coordinating Committee.

With another exchange student, the effect was even more sweeping. Anna Jo Weaver, a tall, studious, quiet girl from the Far West, came to Spelman, and when the exchange period was over, refused to go back. She had become a part of the movement in

Atlanta, and so stayed on as a regular Spelman student, spending most of her time in SNCC activity, sitting-in, picketing, being arrested again and again in the cause of desegregating one or another public facility in Atlanta.

Beyond the exchange programs, white students have been attaching themselves in ever greater numbers to what is essentially still a Negro student movement. A few pioneers were there at the very beginning of the movement. The day I stood and waited for Lenore Taitt to emerge from Dougherty County Jail, I met some of her fellow prisoners. One of them, tall, husky, with a week's growth of beard, but smiling through it all, was Bob Zellner, a white youth from Alabama. Zellner was still a student at Huntington College in Alabama when he began to be involved in civil rights activity. After graduation, he became a field secretary for the Student Nonviolent Coordinating Committee. He has been beaten, jailed, threatened with mutilation, arrested numerous times; most recently, in Danville, Virginia, policemen broke down the door of a church to take him into custody on charges of leading demonstrations there. After two years of front-line battle, he is beginning graduate work at Brandeis University, hoping to return South later as a civil rights lawyer.

Bill Hansen, another white student, from the Midwest, was arrested many times at demonstrations in Maryland, went to Albany, Georgia, at the height of the trouble there, was arrested again. In the Albany jail, he was beaten; his jaw was broken. He has no immediate plans to return to school. Right now, he is a SNCC field secretary in Pine Bluff, Arkansas.

Hansen and Zellner were among the first white professionals of the Negro revolt. But the numbers are growing. Last summer, the SNCC office in Atlanta was filled with white students devoting their summer to the cause. Once such students arrive, some of them find it impossible to turn back.

A year ago, at a civil rights conference at Sarah Lawrence College, I met a student from Trinity College named Ralph Allen, just one of many clean-cut, well-dressed delegates, politely listening to speeches about the Southern movement. Six months later, I saw him in a Negro drugstore in Albany, Georgia, needing a shave, wearing an old T-shirt, just returned from Terrell County, Georgia ("Terrible Terrell"—as it is known to Negroes there), where he was working on voter registration. In Terrell he was beaten and repeatedly threatened with death. Last year he spent four months in jail in Americus, Georgia, charged with "inciting to insurrection" (he had been arrested at the scene of a Negro demonstration) which in Georgia at the time was subject to the death penalty.

THE FEW HUNDRED STUDENTS—white and Negro—who have rebelled against the social neutrality in the American college system by deserting it, either temporarily or permanently, represent, I believe, only the visible part of an iceberg of discontent which chills the millions of other students who remain in school. These others don't express their dissatisfaction by joining the civil rights movement. Some of them simply join fraternities or sororities; others find excuses for leaving school; others go through the ritual and graduate, but they couldn't care less. Most of them don't even know why they are dissatisfied. But if I had to single out the most crucial cause, I would say it is the divorce of higher education from the life-or-death problems of this century; the fact that colleges *play* with social issues—fondle them, examine them at a distance, talk endlessly about them—but rarely *live* with them.

Negro faculty and administrators in the South have not—with a few exceptions—shared the sense of commitment shown by thousands of Negro students. Teachers grumbled that their students, out demonstrating, were cutting classes. To become a "first-class" institution means, to many Negro administrators, to adopt the sterile values, the studied non-commitment, of the white colleges: to build more buildings, raise more money, get more foundation grants (the prestige of receiving a grant is often more important than the substantive activity which it finances), add more Ph.D.'s to the faculty.

Traditionally, the ideal student—in both Negro and white colleges—is the student who keeps his nose for social concern to the academic grindstone; who attends classes, gets high grades, becomes a campus "leader" in the proper organizations, makes out well on his Graduate Record Examinations, and gets admitted to a first-rate graduate school, thus bringing honor to the institution. But the militant Negro student—being joined now by the thoughtful white—is beginning to cause some turbulence in the ordered atmosphere of the academic world, and to set many of us to thinking, not only about society, but about the proper role of education in it.

There is increasing talk, and the beginnings of foundation support, for educational projects which will combine civil rights activity in the deep South with intensive reading and seminars right there in the field, supplemented by brief periods of concentrated education in social science and humanities away from the field. If plans like these do not alter the nation's educational outlook in a fundamental way, they may at least serve as a yardstick against which our college system can measure its commitment to the idea that education means *changing people.*

The burgeoning of new plans, which try to connect academic education with involvement in social struggle, is an attempt to escape the bureaucratic requirements that beset academic life. It also suggests that a combination of expert knowledge, skill in communication, and personal commitment to a life of social action, rather than alone the number of degrees amassed, may become the criteria for a new type of teacher.

Is this a taste of the future? We don't know, but it is suggestive of what the most alive, the most socially curious students in the country are seeking. It is the educational counterpart of that revolution which is giving the nation a sense of mission it has not had in a long time. And in this revolution, as so often happens, the teachers are being taught by the students.

Corollary to a Poem by
A. E. Housman

ANDREW GOODMAN

How dismally the day
Screams out and blasts the night.
What disaster you will say,
To start another fight.

See how heaven shows dismay
As her stars are scared away;
As the sun ascends with might
With his hot and awful light

He shows us babies crying
We see the black boy dying
We close our eyes and choke our sighs
And look into the dreadful skies.

Then peacefully the night
Puts out the reddened day
And the jaws that used to bite
Are sterile where we lay.

Spring 1964

[VI, 1, Autumn-Winter 1964-65]
Before going to Mississippi, Andrew Goodman was a student in a course at Queens College, New York, with Professor Mary Doyle Curran; he wrote and handed in this poem after a class discussion of Housman's "To an Athlete Dying Young." It is printed here with the permission of his parents, Mr. and Mrs. Robert Goodman.

Civil Rights and
White Intellectuals

G. C. ODEN

L ET IT BE SAID straight out that the role of the white intellectual in the present movement by Negroes for their civil rights is one that is neither easy, enviable, nor small. As to how true this is, I would remind you of the penalty exacted of Andrew Goodman and Michael Schwerner within the first twenty-four hours of their arrival in Mississippi; full-face you with the memory of last summer when, stemming from historic rejection by the white community, Negroes took their anger and desperation to the streets; bid you to consider that in the white intellectual's support of Negro goals he must interpret his position to 170,000,-000 other white Americans. Nevertheless, his role is clear and definite, but to assess it we must examine the background against which it is to be seen to be understood.

To begin with, recognize that the civil rights movement is, at base, an attempt to insure individuality, to preserve from false restrictions freedom of choice. In this country, the hysterical point upon which the exercise of one's individuality rests is race, and to such extent, that it presents to the world the miserable spectacle of an overwhelming white majority standing on the neck of an infinitely smaller black minority. It goes then, almost without saying, that the Negro has had built into him the ambition to be more than the secondary architect of the removal of the oppressive boot. But it must also be seen that by the very nature of his indignity, and in the very essence of his cause, the Negro has come up with his only area of human intercourse where race is not a visible handicap to opportunity, and where he can achieve a more broadly based pinnacle of leadership than does exist for him, in the main, throughout the business and professional life of this country.

Civil rights is the supreme area wherein the Negro can engage in exploration of himself as a valuable human being blessed with initiative, drive, perseverance, creativity—attributes he is seldom allowed to develop in his regular fields of employment, where he is limited to strait-jacketed competition with his white counterpart. Civil rights is also the place where he can feel his is a real contribution to life, meaningful in the larger history of the world. Such a view is systematically denied him in his usual endeavors; particularly the Negro man against whose image the measure of his race is taken and against whom the vigor of segregation has worked its most unconscionable wrong.

Allied to the observation that the civil rights movement is an avenue for self-expression, must also be the understanding of why the Negro insists his self-expression be exactly that if the dialogue between himself and the power structure of the white community is to be true, honest, and, therefore, meaningful.

When the Negro was transplanted to these shores, his burden was to contend with a culture and civilization different in kind and substance from that from which he was kidnapped. His incorporation into society was not envisioned or planned for beyond his labor. Maintained in ignorance and servitude, his lot was to depend upon those white men and women of sensibility who chose to speak in behalf of the Negro. It is to their credit—and America is indebted to them for speaking so long and so well—that the Negro was set free.

However, "adrift" might reflect a more accurate description of his situation. Thrown upon his negligible resources in this hostile land, once again he found himself dependent upon the efforts of those humane whites who would not abandon him to a corrupted destiny. There were, of course, some Negroes who had achieved education and a status of which the white community took notice. Upon these, more often than not, it conferred leadership of the black community. Factually, these leaders were often as powerless among their own people as they were in terms of the white community. To make matters worse, the power structure within the white community would listen to the demands by these Negroes only when the demands fitted with what they were willing to give. It is in opposition to both these situations that the civil rights movement has taken its major turn and things are not likely to be as once they were.

As has been stated, it has been the Negro man who suffered most under slavery and continues to do so this narrow side of it.

The Negro woman, who presented less of a threat to white masculine ego and so gained for herself greater education, was allowed wider latitudes of behavior, and still, today, makes the most populous inroads into the business and professional worlds. However, in recent years, as more and more Negro men have achieved better education, wider opportunity and experience, he has increasingly taken over the summits of leadership heretofore roosted upon by the Negro woman.

The importance of all this is that the civil rights movement, with newer diversity and broader reflectiveness of the variegated aspects of the community, has produced its own spokesmen. Their disciplined following within the ghetto have earned for them their titles as leaders, and it is from these leaders the Negro demands the putting forth—unwatered-down—of his broad spectrum of expectation. It is the celebrated appearance of these men that places the white intellectual in the role he now must assume, the role in which he is likely to remain.

Today the Negro speaks for himself, and it is the place of the white intellectual to let him. From here on in, the white intellectual is no more than a joint venturer. His speech and his actions may be no more in behalf of the Negro but for himself as a decent moral person seeking to live in a just society. His obligation is to stand with the civil rights movement whether an action is personally to his liking or not. His demeanor must be one of humility, as opposed to omniscience; his attitude that of love.

Admittedly, his is a tough role. It means the white intellectual must rid himself of the paternalism inbred in him from years of stewardship of the black man's right to speak. From topside he must move alongside the Negro. It means he must, without rancor, devalue his color, granting to the Negro his choices—his right to design the social action by which he opts for freedom now. It further means that he must recognize that all of his relations with Negroes are highly specialized, and that knowing a Negro "on the job," having a Negro housekeeper or maid, or playing golf with a Negro business or professional man has not gifted him with all there is to know about the problems of being a Negro in these United States. Lastly, it means that into the thickets and thorns of his own community the white intellectual is bound to go beseeching the restoration of that morality towards the Negro which it has so sadly eschewed. Then and only then can come that grand alliance between the races to work towards meeting the joint needs of their impoverished in the later-than-we-think areas of housing, employment, and education.

There has been much talk about the Great Society. Such a society will be one where color, rightly, is an insignificance. The civil rights movement aims for such higher consciousness, and the white intellectual has his part to play in the ascent. Guilt accrues to the white intellectual by virtue of his historic role in the subjugation of the Negro. If now he will work with his guilt, taking the strength to be found in reflection and join with the Negro in his pursuit of simple equality, then may mankind yet qualify as a more fitting resemblance of the one in whose image he has supposed himself to be made.

Toward Black Liberation

STOKELY CARMICHAEL

O NE OF THE MOST pointed illustrations of the need for Black Power, as a positive and redemptive force in a society degenerating into a form of totalitarianism, is to be made by examining the history of distortion that the concept has received in national media of publicity. In this "debate," as in everything else that affects our lives, Negroes are dependent on, and at the discretion of, forces and institutions within the white society which have little interest in representing us honestly. Our experience with the national press has been that where they have managed to escape a meretricious special interest in "Git Whitey" sensationalism and race-war-mongering, individual reporters and commentators have been conditioned by the enveloping racism of the society to the point where they are incapable even of objective observation and reporting of racial *incidents,* much less the analysis of *ideas.* But this limitation of vision and perceptions is an inevitable consequence of the dictatorship of definition, interpretation, and consciousness, along with the censorship of history that the society has inflicted upon the Negro—and itself.

Our concern for black power addresses itself directly to this problem, the necessity to reclaim our history and our identity from the cultural terrorism and depredation of self-justifying white guilt.

To do this we shall have to struggle for the right to create our own terms through which to define ourselves and our relationship to the society, and to have these terms recognized. This is the first necessity of a free people, and the first right that any oppressor must suspend. The white fathers of American racism knew this— instinctively it seems—as is indicated by the continuous record of the distortion and omission in their dealings with the red and black men. In the same way that Southern apologists for the "Jim Crow" society have so obscured, muddied, and misrepresented the record of the reconstruction period, until it is almost impossible to tell what really happened, their contemporary counterparts are busy

[VII, 4, Autumn 1966. Copyright © 1966 by SNCC.]

doing the same thing with the recent history of the civil rights movement.

In 1964, for example, the National Democratic party, led by L. B. Johnson and Hubert H. Humphrey, cynically undermined the efforts of Mississippi's black population to achieve some degree of political representation. Yet, whenever the events of that convention are recalled by the press, one sees only that aversion fabricated by the press agents of the Democratic party. A year later the House of Representatives, in an even more vulgar display of political racism, made a mockery of the political rights of Mississippi's Negroes when it failed to unseat the Mississippi Delegation to the House which had been elected through a process which methodically and systematically excluded over 450,000 voting-age Negroes, almost one half of the total electorate of the state. Whenever this event is mentioned in print it is in terms which leave one with the rather curious impression that somehow the oppressed Negro people of Mississippi are at fault for confronting the Congress with a situation in which they had no alternative but to endorse Mississippi's racist political practices.

I mention these two examples because, having been directly involved in them, I can see very clearly the discrepancies between what happened and the versions that are finding their way into general acceptance as a kind of popular mythology. Thus the victimization of the Negro takes place in two phases—first it occurs in fact and deed, then, and this is equally sinister, in the official recording of those facts.

The "Black Power" program and concept which is being articulated by SNCC, CORE, and a host of community organizations in the ghettoes of the North and South has not escaped that process. The white press has been busy articulating their own analyses, their own interpretations, and criticisms of their own creations. For example, while the press had given wide and sensational dissemination to attacks made by figures in the civil rights movement—foremost among which are Roy Wilkins of the NAACP and Whitney Young of the Urban League—and to the hysterical ranting about black racism made by the political chameleon that now serves as vice-president, it has generally failed to give accounts of the reasonable and productive dialogue which is taking place in the Negro community, and in certain important areas in the white religious and intellectual community. A national committee of influential Negro churchmen affiliated with the National Council of Churches, despite their obvious respectability and responsibility, had to resort to a paid advertisement to articulate their position, while anyone shouting the hysterical yappings of "Black Racism" got ample space. Thus the American people have gotten at best a superficial and misleading account of the very terms and tenor of this debate. I wish to quote briefly from the statement by the national committee of churchmen which I suspect that the majority of Americans will not have seen. This statement appeared in *The New York Times* of July 31, 1966.

> *We an informal group of Negro Churchmen in America are deeply disturbed about the crisis brought upon our country by historic distortions of important human realities in the controversy about "black power." What we see shining through the variety of rhetoric is not anything new but the same old problem of power and race which has faced our beloved country since 1619.*
>
> *... The conscience of black men is corrupted because, having no power to implement the demands of conscience, the concern for justice in the absence of justice becomes a chaotic self-surrender. Powerlessness breeds a race of beggars. We are faced now with a situation where powerless conscience meets conscience-less power, threatening the very foundation of our Nation.*
>
> *... We deplore the overt violence of riots, but we feel it is more important to focus on the real sources of these eruptions. These sources may be abetted inside the Ghetto, but their basic cause lies in the silent and covert violence which white middleclass America inflicts upon the victims of the inner city.*
>
> *... In short, the failure of American leaders to use American power to create equal opportunity in life as well as law, this is the real problem and not the anguished cry for black power.*
>
> *... Without the capacity to participate with power, i.e., to have some organized political and economic strength to really influence people with whom one interacts—integration is not meaningful.*
>
> *... America has asked its Negro citizens to fight for opportunity as individuals, whereas at certain points in our history what we have needed most has been opportunity for the*

whole group, *not just for selected and approved Negroes.*
*... We must not apologize for the existence of this form of
group power, for we have been oppressed as a group and not
as individuals. We will not find our way out of that oppression
until both we and America accept the need for Negro Americans, as well as for Jews, Italians, Poles, and white Anglo-
Saxon Protestants, among others to have and to wield group
power.*

Traditionally, for each new ethnic group, the route to social
and political integration into America's pluralistic society has been
through the organization of their own institutions with which to
represent their communal needs within the larger society. This is
simply stating what the advocates of black power are saying. The
strident outcry, *particularly* from the liberal community, that has
been evoked by this proposal can only be understood by examining
the historic relationship between Negro and white power in this
country.

Negroes are defined by two forces, their blackness and their
powerlessness. There have been traditionally two communities in
America. The white community, which controlled and defined the
forms that all institutions within the society would take, and the
Negro community which has been excluded from participation in
the power decisions that shaped the society, and has traditionally
been dependent upon, and subservient to, the white community.

This has not been accidental. The history of every institution of
this society indicates that a major concern in the ordering and
structuring of the society has been the maintaining of the Negro
community in its condition of dependence and oppression. This
has not been on the level of individual acts of discrimination between individual whites against individual Negroes, but as total
acts by the white community against the Negro community. This
fact cannot be too strongly emphasized—that racist assumptions of
white superiority have been so deeply ingrained in the structure of
the society that it infuses its entire functioning, and is so much a
part of the national subconscious that it is taken for granted and is
frequently not even recognized.

Let me give an example of the difference between individual
racism and institutionalized racism, and the society's response to
both. When unidentified white terrorists bomb a Negro church

and kill five children, that is an act of individual racism, widely deplored by most segments of the society. But when in that same city, Birmingham, Alabama, not five but five hundred Negro babies die each year because of a lack of proper food, shelter, and medical facilities, and thousands more are destroyed and maimed physically, emotionally, and intellectually because of conditions of poverty and deprivation in the ghetto, that is a function of institutionalized racism. But the society either pretends it doesn't know of this situation, or is incapable of doing anything meaningful about it. And this resistance to doing anything meaningful about conditions in that ghetto comes from the fact that the ghetto is itself a product of a combination of forces and special interests in the white community, and the groups that have access to the resources and power to change that situation benefit, politically and economically, from the existence of that ghetto.

It is more than a figure of speech to say that the Negro community in America is the victim of white imperialism and colonial exploitation. This is in practical economic and political terms true. There are over twenty million black people comprising ten per cent of this nation. They for the most part live in well-defined areas of the country—in the shanty-towns and rural black belt areas of the South, and increasingly in the slums of northern and western industrial cities. If one goes into any Negro community, whether it be in Jackson, Mississippi, Cambridge, Maryland, or Harlem, New York, one will find that the same combination of political, economic, and social forces are at work. The people in the Negro community do not control the resources of that community, its political decisions, its law enforcement, its housing standards; and even the physical ownership of the land, houses, and stores *lie outside that community.*

It is white power that makes the laws, and it is violent white power in the form of armed white cops that enforces those laws with guns and nightsticks. The vast majority of Negroes in this country live in these captive communities and must endure these conditions of oppression because, and only because, *they are black and powerless.* I do not suppose that at any point the men who control the power and resources of this country ever sat down and designed these black enclaves and formally articulated the terms of their colonial and dependent status, as was done, for example, by the apartheid government of South Africa. Yet, one can not distinguish between one ghetto and another. As one moves from city to city it is as though some malignant racist planning unit had done precisely this—designed each one from the same master blueprint. And indeed, if the ghetto had been formally and deliberately planned, instead of growing spontaneously and inevitably from the racist functioning of the various institutions that combine to make the society, it would be somehow less frightening. The situation would be less frightening because, if these ghettoes were the result of design and conspiracy, one could understand their similarity as being artificial and consciously imposed, rather than the result of identical patterns of white racism which repeat themselves in cities as distant as Boston and Birmingham. Without bothering to list the historic factors which contribute to this pattern—economic exploitation, political impotence, discrimination in employment and education—one can see that to correct this pattern will require far-reaching changes in the basic power relationships and the ingrained social patterns within the society. The question is, of course, what kinds of changes are necessary, and how is it possible to bring them about?

In recent years, the answer to these questions which has been given by most articulate groups of Negroes and their white allies, the "liberals" of all stripes, has been in terms of something called "integration." According to the advocates of integration, social justice will be accomplished by "integrating the Negro into the mainstream institutions of the society from which he has been traditionally excluded." It is very significant that each time I have heard this formulation it has been in terms of "the Negro," the individual Negro, rather than in terms of the community.

This concept of integration had to be based on the assumption that there was nothing of value in the Negro community and that little of value could be created among Negroes, so the thing to do was to siphon off the "acceptable" Negroes into the surrounding middle-class white community. Thus the goal of the movement for integration was simply to loosen up the restrictions barring the entry of Negroes into the white community. Goals around which the struggle took place, such as public accommodation, open housing, job opportunity on the executive level (which is easier to deal with than the problem of semi-skilled and blue-collar jobs which involve more far-reaching economic adjustments), are quite simply middle-class goals, articulated by a tiny group of Negroes who had middle-class aspirations. It is true that the student demonstrations in the South during the early sixties, out of which SNCC came, had a similar orientation. But while it is hardly a concern of a black sharecropper, dishwasher, or welfare recipient whether a certain fifteen-dollar-a-day motel offers accommodations to Negroes, the overt symbols of white superiority and the imposed limitations on the Negro community had to be destroyed. Now, black people must look beyond these goals, to the issue of collective power.

Such a limited class orientation was reflected not only in the program and goals of the civil rights movement, but in its tactics and organization. It is very significant that the two oldest and most "respectable" civil rights organizations have constitutions which *specifically* prohibit partisan political activity. CORE once did, but changed that clause when it changed its orientation toward black power. But this is perfectly understandable in terms of the strategy and goals of the older organizations. The civil rights movement saw its role as a kind of liaison between the powerful white community and the dependent Negro one. The dependent status of the black community apparently was unimportant since—if the movement were successful—it would blend into the white community anyway. We made no pretense of organizing and developing institutions of community power in the Negro community, but appealed to the conscience of white institutions of power. The posture of the civil rights movement was that of the dependent, the suppliant. The theory was that without attempting to create any organized base of political strength itself, the civil rights movement could, by forming coalitions with various "liberal" pressure organizations in the white community —liberal reform clubs, labor unions, church groups, progressive civic groups—and at times one or the other of the major political parties—influence national legislation and national social patterns.

I think we all have seen the limitations of this approach. We have repeatedly seen that political alliances based on appeals to conscience and decency are chancy things, simply because institutions and political organizations have no consciences, outside their own special interests. The political and social rights of Negroes have been and always will be negotiable and expendable the moment they conflict with the interests of our "allies." If we do not learn from history, we are doomed to repeat it, and that is precisely the lesson of the Reconstruction. Black people were allowed to register, vote, and participate in politics because it was to the advantage of powerful white allies to promote this. But this was the result of white decision, and it was ended by other white men's decision before any political base powerful enough to challenge that decision could be established in the Southern Negro community. (Thus at this point in the struggle Negroes have no assurance—save a kind of idiot optimism and faith in a society whose history is one of racism—that if it were to become necessary, even the painfully limited gains thrown to the civil rights movement by the Congress would not be revoked as soon as a shift in political sentiments should occur.)

The major limitation of this approach was that it tended to maintain the traditional dependence of Negroes and of the movement. We depended upon the good-will and support of various groups within the white community whose interests were not always compatible with ours. To the extent that we depended on the financial support of other groups, we were vulnerable to their influence and domination.

Also, the program that evolved out of this coalition was really limited and inadequate in the long term and one which affected only a small select group of Negroes. Its goal was to make the white community accessible to "qualified" Negroes, and presumably each year a few more Negroes armed with their passports—a couple of university degrees—would escape into middle-class America and adopt the attitudes and life styles of that group; and one day the Harlems and the Wattses would stand empty, a tribute to the success of integration. This is simply neither realistic nor particularly desirable. You can integrate communities, but you assimilate individuals. Even if such a program were possible, its result would be, not to develop the black community as a functional and honorable segment of the total society, with its own cultural identity, life patterns, and institutions, but to abolish it—the final solution to the Negro problem. Marx said that the working class is the first class in history that ever wanted to abolish itself. If one listens to some of our "moderate" Negro leaders, it appears that the American Negro is the first race that ever wished to abolish itself. The fact is that what must be abolished is not the black community, but the dependent colonial status that has been inflicted upon it. The racial and cultural personality of the black community must be preserved and the community must win its freedom while preserving its cultural integrity. This is the essential difference between integration as it is currently practised and the concept of black power.

WHAT HAS THE MOVEMENT for integration accomplished to date? The Negro graduating from M.I.T. with a doctorate will have better job opportunities available to him than to Lynda Bird Johnson. But the rate of unemployment in the Negro community is steadily increasing, while that in the white community decreases. More educated Negroes hold executive jobs in major corporations and federal agencies than ever before, but the gap between white income and Negro income has almost doubled in the last twenty years. More suburban housing is available to Negroes, but housing conditions in the ghetto are steadily declining. While the infant mortality rate of New York City is at its lowest rate ever in the city's history, the infant mortality rate of Harlem is steadily climbing. There has been an organized national resistance to the Supreme Court's order to integrate the schools, and the federal government has not acted to enforce that order. Less than fifteen per cent of black children in the South attend integrated schools, and Negro schools, which the vast majority of black children still attend, are increasingly decrepit, overcrowded, under-staffed, inadequately equipped and funded.

This explains why the rate of school dropouts is increasing among Negro teenagers, who then express their bitterness, hopelessness, and alienation by the only means they have—rebellion. As long as people in the ghettoes of our large cities feel that they are victims of the misuse of white power without any way to have their needs represented—and these are frequently simple needs: to get the welfare inspectors to stop kicking down your doors in the middle of the night, the cops from beating your children, the landlord to exterminate the vermin in your home, the city to collect your garbage—we will continue to have riots. These are not the products of "black power," but of the absence of any organization capable of giving the community the power, the black power, to deal with its problems.

SNCC proposes that it is now time for the black freedom movement to stop pandering to the fears and anxieties of the white middle class in the attempt to earn its "good-will," and to return to the ghetto to organize these communities to control themselves.

This organization must be attempted in northern and southern urban areas as well as in the rural black belt counties of the South. The chief antagonist to this organization is, in the South, the overtly racist Democratic party, and in the North, the equally corrupt big city machines.

The standard argument presented against independent political organization is "But you are only ten per cent." I cannot see the relevance of this observation, since no one is talking about taking over the country, but taking control over our own communities.

The fact is that the Negro population, ten per cent or not, is very strategically placed because—ironically—of segregation. What is also true is that Negroes have never been able to utilize the full voting potential of our numbers. Where we could vote, the case has always been that the white political machine stacks and gerrymanders the political subdivisions in Negro neighborhoods so the true voting strength is never reflected in political strength. Would anyone looking at the distribution of political power in Manhattan, ever think that Negroes represented sixty per cent of the population there?

Just as often the effective political organization in Negro communities is absorbed by tokenism and patronage—the time honored practice of "giving" certain offices to selected Negroes. The machine thus creates a "little machine," which is subordinate and responsive to it, in the Negro community. These Negro political "leaders" are really vote deliverers, more responsible to the white machine and the white power structure than to the community they allegedly represent. Thus the white community is able to substitute patronage control for audacious black power in the Negro community. This is precisely what Johnson tried to do even before the Voting Rights Act of 1966 was passed. The National Democrats made it very clear that the measure was intended to register Democrats, not Negroes. The President and top officials of the Democratic party called in almost one hundred selected Negro "leaders" from the Deep South. Nothing was said about changing the policies of the racist state parties, nothing was said about repudiating such leadership figures as James Eastland and Ross Barnett in Mississippi or George Wallace in Alabama. What was said was simply "Go home and organize your people into the local Democratic party —then we'll see about poverty money and appointments." (Incidentally, for the most part the War on Poverty in the South is controlled by local Democratic ward heelers—and outspoken racists who have used the program to change the form of the Negroes' dependence. People who were afraid to register for fear of being thrown off the farm are now afraid to register for fear of losing their Head Start jobs.)

We must organize black community power to end these abuses, and to give the Negro community a chance to have its needs expressed. A leadership which is truly "responsible"—not to the white press and power structure, but to the community—must be developed. Such leadership will recognize that its power lies in the unified and collective strength of that community. This will make it difficult for the white leadership group to conduct its dialogue with individuals in terms of patronage and prestige, and will force them to talk to the community's representatives in terms of real power.

The single aspect of the black power program that has encountered most criticism is this concept of independent organization. This is presented as third-partyism, which has never worked, or a withdrawal into black nationalism and isolationism. If such a program is developed it will not have the effect of isolating the Negro community but the reverse. When the Negro community is able to control local office and negotiate with other groups from a position of organized strength, the possibility of meaningful political alliances on specific issues will be increased. That is a rule of politics and there is no reason why it should not operate here. The only difference is that we will have the power to define the terms of these alliances.

The next question usually is: "So—can it work, can the ghettoes in fact be organized?" The answer is that this organization must be successful, because there are no viable alternatives—not the War on Poverty, which was at its inception limited to dealing with effects rather than causes, and has become simply another source of machine patronage. And "Integration" is meaningful only to a small chosen class within the community.

The revolution in agricultural technology in the South is displacing the rural Negro community into northern urban areas. Both Washington, D.C., and Newark, New Jersey, have Negro majorities. One third of Philadelphia's population of two million people is black. "Inner city" in most major urban areas is already predominantly Negro, and, with the white rush to suburbia, Negroes will in the next three decades control the hearts of our great cities. These areas can become either concentration camps with a bitter and volatile population whose only power is the power to destroy, or organized and powerful communities able to make constructive contributions to the total society. Without the power to control their lives and their communities, without effective political institutions through which to relate to the total society, these communities will exist in a constant state of insurrection. This is a choice that the country will have to make.

By Power Possessed

A Commentary on Stokely Carmichael's
"Toward Black Liberation"

MILTON MAYER

ORRIS COHEN OF C.C.N.Y. was lecturing at Chicago in 1941 (prior to December 7), and his old friend Irving Salmon (like Cohen a Jew) was giving a reception for him at the University. The small talk was large and loud with the European war. Salmon, a rabid interventionist, was saying, "I just want to bash in a few Nazi heads before I die." "It seems to me, Irving," said Cohen, "that bashing heads is for the ninety-six per cent—not for the four per cent."

Now Stokely Carmichael is not for bashing in heads—though I don't suppose it's excluded, since White Power doesn't exclude it. And I think I comprehend what he means by Black Power. What I don't apprehend is how he thinks Black Power will be come by and what he thinks it will do. His counsel of desperation is no better counsel for being a reflexive response to a condition he and I find unendurable; any more than the starving man's theft of bread is a meaningful attack on *his* condition.

Nor do Stokely Carmichael's references (outside his essay) to Irish Power enlighten me. The Kennedys could shuck their Irish skins—even their Catholic skins, which, incidentally, put them into the twenty-five to thirty per cent Power bracket—and emerge as rich and beautiful young Americans with plenty of everything. Rich, young, beautiful—and white. The Negro has plenty of nothing, and when he has plenty of everything—jobs, houses, schools, votes—he will still be black: the one discernible *other* in a society whose Know-Nothings were never able to close the door altogether against the "Irish." The discriminable Negro is the uniquely irresistible object of discrimination.

The Kennedys represent a majority amalgam of special interests. The Carmichaels represent the Negro (who is poor) and nobody else; least of all the poor white. The Negro's is a special interest in which nobody else is interested. His special interest is, to be sure, *intelligible* to a rich society which rocks along without any consuming concern for the common good, but the small special interest (like the corner grocer's) is increasingly inconsequential in the age of amalgamation.

Irish Power never mobilized the white Anglo-Saxon Protestants, except sectionally and sporadically; and they were so sharply divided among themselves that they could not focus their hostility on the Irish. But Black Power mobilizes the whites in an ad hoc alliance in which (as is usual in such situations) they sink their differences and gang up. If Stokely Carmichael means to pit the ten per cent's Power against the ninety per cent's, the ninety per cent will be delighted to accommodate him and see what it can do against the ten in a fair and free contest. "It is white power that makes the laws," he says, as if he were somehow arguing *for* his position, "and it is violent white power in the form of armed white cops that enforces those laws with guns and nightsticks."

Let us suppose, contrary to likelihood, that the ten per cent comes out on top in the contest. What will it be and do then? It is not beyond a reasonable doubt that coercive triumph, over the centuries, has improved the triumphant Wasps. Nor has modern triumph over the Wasps much improved the Irish beyond putting lace curtains in their windows. Whatever the Wasps did in their day, the Irish (and the Portuguese, the Poles, and the Patagonians) do in theirs; and this is not necessarily improvement. Socrates, Acton, and Fulbright all seem to be saying that Power is not an unmixed blessing, and the statesman of ancient days said of the horrors of his triumphant Rome, "All that we do, we do because Power compels us."

What makes Stokely Carmichael think that the Negroes will use Power to better advantage than the whites have been able to use it? I know there is no great point in describing the disappointments of freedom to the untutored slave. But Stokely Carmichael is a tutored slave. He may hope that the Negro would master Power rather than be mastered by it, but his tutoring must have acquainted him with the dictum of Confucius: "He who says, 'Rich men are fools, but when I am rich I will not be a fool,' is already a fool."

I say "would," rather than "will," because I cannot see how Black Power, as I understand it, will come into its own until blacks are thirty, or forty, or fifty-one per cent of the whole society. It will elect a sheriff where it is fifty-one per cent of the electorate; but there are not many such counties, and still fewer states. White Power will fight for its commercial control of the "inner city"— where the Negro already has fifty-one (or eighty-five) per cent of the overnight populace; and when it surrenders what will we have then, except the ghetto unpolluted, with the Negro completing the wall the white began?

The exploitation of the huddled "nationality" neighborhoods, Irish, Italian, Jewish, German, Polish, Swedish, and Bohemian, tore our metropolitan communities to pieces three-quarters of a century ago. Their "leaders" delivered them en bloc to the boodlers and got them a statue of Kosciusko in exchange. Stokely Carmichael has to convince us that his high hope will be realized; that the Negroes will be an exception to the upper class pattern and their inner city serve the welfare of its inhabitants and the general welfare on which the particular ultimately depends. It will not be radical idealists like Stokely Carmichael or Martin King who will do what has always had to be done to win American elections. It is much more likely that the present congressman from Harlem will be the mayor of Stokely Carmichael's *new* New York.

Stokely Carmichael is righter than he is wrong. Integration does mean what he says it means—the assimilation of the psychologically suicidal Negro into the white man's society on the white man's intolerable and unenviable terms. And he is right in suggesting that the white's guilt is collective—I and all the other "friends of the Negro" have exploited him; and not through our grandfathers, either. We travel as effortlessly as we do because we, not our grandfathers, are riding on the black man's back.

Stokely Carmichael is righter than he is wrong; but he is mortally wrong. He is mortally wrong because he accepts the white definition of Power and ignores the demonstrable (if mystifying) fact that there is a kind of power that a majority (be it all men but one) cannot handily dispose of. I speak of nonviolent noncooperation, nonviolent resistance, and nonviolent action undertaken in a non-violent spirit.

Even on the white man's view of power, the Negro may get some mileage out of nonviolence. American society can live easier every year without menial labor, but for a few years or decades yet it cannot live in the manner to which it is accustomed without the

Negro ten per cent. They perform its filthiest jobs and return the profit on its filthiest property. At excruciating cost to themselves, but in solid self-interest, they can leave some of its filth unswept and unprofitable. They still have a small margin of muscle in non-cooperation, and by muscle I mean nothing more exalted than Stokely Carmichael or the white man means.

But the margin, in a society which cannot employ its whites, and does not need to, is shrinking. It is the powerlessness inherent in nonviolent noncooperation that the Negro can, perhaps—I say only "perhaps"—turn to account as a peculiar form of power. The whites are guilty. And they would rather fight than switch to expiation. If the Negro can find a weapon that will take the fight out of them, the whites' only remaining course may be justice, not only for the Negro but for every other oppressed minority.

In his *Massachusetts Review* statement, where he purports to present the essentials of the matter, Stokely Carmichael seems never to have heard of Martin King, or of Greensboro. Or of Rosa Parks —who brought Martin King and Greensboro *and Stokely Carmichael* into being. Rosa Parks had something less than ten per cent of the Power (as Stokely Carmichael reckons it) when she could not bring herself to move to the back of the bus in Montgomery. But without the strange power she exercised that day in 1955, Stokely Carmichael would not have the familiar power he has now.

Her power wasn't black. It was human (and, for all any of us know, divine by virtue of its being human). It was the power to heap coals of fire on the heads of the Powerful until they would *want* to do differently than they were doing. It was the power of redemption, and it came out of the most impotent segment of American society, the psalm-singing Southern Negro with his child-like power to believe that he would overcome some day. Out of that power came the Movement; out of the Movement came all that came in the next decade; and out of the deliquescence of the Movement, as it went North to the unbelieving Negro, comes the present vacuum into which Stokely Carmichael would proceed with hopeless weapons instead of none. The analogy with India is colossally imperfect, but it has this much application: We do not *know* that the American white man is less susceptible of being civilized than the British were at Amritsar.

Stokely Carmichael pointedly ignores the power that gave him birth, and he divides the Negroes into the unaccepting (like himself) and the acceptable "passers." He cannot possibly be unconscious of the singular phenomenon of our time and of all time—the power of one powerless person, neither murderer nor victim, neither combatant nor suppliant, to overcome; and, what is more, to win supporters from the ranks of the enemy. Until Montgomery nothing else had ever moved the white man's church at all. And without moved and uncoerced allies the ten per cent will never make it in the halls of Congress or the streets of Selma or any other center of Stokely Carmichael's kind of power.

The Movement is failing, if it is failing, because it has gone North, where the Negro is who doesn't see why he, of all people, should have to be better than the white man. The primitive Negro of the South sees why. Washed in the blood of the Lamb, he sees why he has to be responsible, not for the Negro, not for the white man, but for Man and the salvation of Man through sorrow and suffering and endurance to the end. But moving mountains is slow going, and Stokely Carmichael sounds like Marx's London businessman who would cut off his own right arm for a short-term profit. The short-term Negro will not even get the profit; he hasn't enough to invest.

The redemptive love to which men are called—and to which the psalm-singing Negro responded—is not assured of a profit either. Its prospect of short-term success is slight, but the slightest prospect is better than no prospect at all, and Stokely Carmichael's way has been tried (by the white man) again and again and again. It has failed.

Its very failure may be a sign that men are not bad, and that treating them (and oneself) as if they were is therefore inefficacious. "We have repeatedly seen," says Stokely Carmichael, "that political alliances based on appeals to conscience and decency are chancy things, simply because institutions and political organizations have no consciences outside their own special interests." ("Men are bad," says Machiavelli, "and if you do not break faith with them, they will break faith with you.") If Stokely Carmichael is right, his way is no worse than Martin King's, only more tiresome as a spectacle; except that Martin King's is directed to the refinement of our sensibilities and Stokely Carmichael's is not.

The issue between them is the issue of knowing. Stokely Carmichael knows, and Martin King doesn't. Martin King doesn't know what power may be within us, or working through us, or what we can and cannot do. William Penn was the first white man the Indians had ever seen without a gun. He went to them, saying to his followers, "Let us try what love will do, for if they see that we love them they will not want to injure us," and on that occasion, and as long as Penn and his successors governed Pennsylvania, and in Pennsylvania alone, the prospect proved to have been splendidly justified. But it was so slight that it took faith above all knowing.

Stokely Carmichael does not display that faith. For all the good his having become a Southern Negro has done him, he might as well have been a white man. He appropriates the white man's racism as the black's and adopts the white man's Power without either God *or* the big battalions. So far is he from supposing that there may be an omnipotence which empowers its votaries, that he has got to settle in the end, not for God, or even for man, but for brute. Count clubs or noses—and if men are brutes, it matters not which—coercion carries the day in the jungle. Whoever chooses the jungle had better be a lion.

Beyond Civil Rights

A Reply to the "Coalitionists"

NAT HENTOFF

I N ADOPTING THE ANTHEM of the civil rights movement, "We Shall Overcome," during his March, 1965, speech to Congress urging new legislation to enable more people to vote, Lyndon Johnson was trying to include "the movement" in his operative concept of consensus politics. There were immediate hosannas from such chronically sanguine whites as the editorial writers of the *New York Times* and the doughtily disoriented Max Lerner. Even a few Negro "leaders" applauded with some gusto. But others inside the churning pluralism that is now "the movement" were not impressed. Particularly not impressed were many of the young who, of course, provide the major dynamism in the current debate and action as "the movement" tries to find effectual methods of moving beyond civil rights to the fundamental barriers that keep the poor in the underclass—education, jobs, and housing.

On one side of the debate are such as Bayard Rustin and Michael Harrington. Watching the crowd of Northern liberals and the indigenous poor-and-black quarter-citizens of Alabama as they massed on the streets of Montgomery at the climax of the Selma-to-Montgomery march, Michael Harrington saw hope for "a new populism." Rustin agrees, and has been persistently calling for a broad-based coalition of "Negroes, trade unionists, liberals, and religious groups" to amass enough collective political power to so change the society that the opportunity to be equal will be more than rhetoric.

The essence of Rustin's position is contained in his article, "From Protest to Politics," in the February, 1965, *Commentary*. He is aware that the "consensus party" of Lyndon Johnson must be reorganized "along lines which will make it an effective vehicle for reconstruction." This can be done, he believes, by the coalition and also, hopefully, by an eventual clarification of national political lines during which Southern racists and those elements of Northern

"Big Business" which now support Johnson will move over to a solidly rightist Republican party, leaving the Democratic party a sturdy enclave of liberalism.

Unfortunately, Rustin has so far engaged more in wish-fulfill-ment than in realistic analysis. One hard fact is that while in 1940, thirty-eight per cent of the total adult voting population identified themselves as Republicans, now only twenty-five per cent do. If such Republican liberals (using the term relatively) as John Lind-say and Jacob Javits succeed to any extent in their goal of moving that party toward the center, the percentages of Republicans may rise, but what we will have is essentially a homogenization of present power and policies, because the Goldwater fundamentalists are correct in their complaint that there are a few basic ideological cleavages between "liberal" Republicans and the Johnson Demo-cratic consensus. If Rustin's hope that the Goldwaterites take over the Republican party is fulfilled, there will also be a homogenization of the vastly greater power of the consensus and the twenty-five per cent of self-declared Republicans may well diminish. Where Rustin, therefore, is heartened by the overwhelming Negro support of Johnson in 1964, I find enormous danger.

Dr. E. U. Essien-Udom, a Senior Lecturer in the Faculty of Political Science of Ibadan University in Nigeria, lived in the United States for several years and is an uncommonly astute analyst of the way this society is structured. In December, 1964, during a panel discussion in Lagos, Nigeria, Essien-Udom pointed out that John-son's election actually

> may manage to postpone the growing racial conflict in Amer-ica for some years. It is unlikely that Congress will appro-priate the kind of funds required or create the kind of state machinery necessary to bring about major changes. Above all, it is doubtful whether unplanned training in skills is of long-range importance, if it is not specifically related to anticipated skills which will be useful in an automated economy.

Rustin's answer would be that the "coalition" will force Johnson and Congress to undertake the requisite range and quality of planning, to provide funds for a radical restructuring of education, and to realize the need for a redefinition of work in the post-indus-trial Age of Cybernation. But let us look at this coalition. So far, what relatively cohesive Negro power blocs exist have minimal real

power. The men they send to Congress or to state and local legislatures are—with some exceptions—either co-opted by one or another
Democratic machine or insufficiently aware of the kind of legislation
that is acutely necessary if the gap between poor and non-poor in an
acceleratingly technological society is not to be further widened.

As for organized labor, aside from the grim resistance of craft
unions to open their suzerainties to Negroes, there is no evidence
that labor leadership recognizes how short-term and eventually inadequate are its customary demands for higher minimum wages,
extended unemployment compensation, massive public works ex-
penditures, and the like. These transitional demands are essential,
but leave unresolved the problem of what to do when, as RAND
estimates, two per cent of the present labor force will be able to
produce all present goods and services. Even if we allow for the
rise in goods and services required by a growing population, we
cannot assume that there will be nearly enough work—as work is
now defined—for the majority of the labor force a generation from
now. To talk, as organized labor does, of "full employment" requires a re-examination of the meaning of the term that labor has
not yet undertaken. Furthermore, labor is so closely annealed to the
Johnson politics of consensus—by short-term self-interest—that
there is no likelihood that it will push hard enough during the
foreseeable future to endanger its own alliance with the power
center. And, with very few exceptions, the secondary, younger
leadership in organized labor appears to be just as narrow of vision
and timid of radical action as do the present members of the
hierarchy.

The churches and the white liberals whom Rustin envisages as
vital elements of the "coalition" have been active, though belatedly,
in protesting discrimination in the South; but—again with few exceptions—they are not considered meaningful allies by the masses
of black poor in the Northern ghettos. These Negroes never do get
to hear the sermons of liberal churchmen nor do they attend the
symposia of white liberals; and since they see neither group in sustained protest against *local* compression (and/or in sustained political action against *local* compression), they regard talk of a "coalition" now as the fantasy it is.

Rustin, in *Commentary,* becomes simplistic when he writes: "The
objective fact is that *Eastland* and *Goldwater* are the main enemies

—they and the opponents of civil rights, of the war on poverty, of medicare, of social security, of federal aid to education, of unions, and so forth." But Eastland and Goldwater are only one kind of enemy; and they are diminishingly dangerous because the Johnson politics of consensus has largely limited their power and will limit it even more.

The more pervasive and more dangerous enemies, however, in the urban North where Negroes do have the vote but little else, are precisely those "liberal" politicians and administrators who are central to Johnson's power base and who consider themselves full-fledged members of the kind of coalition Rustin proposes. They are Mayor Robert Wagner of New York under whose pietistic platform speeches poverty in the city has deepened and widened. They are the "liberal" Congressmen who talk of the "real progress" the War on Poverty is making, ignoring its pyramid of hoaxes on the poor. (Job training for what? "Community action" without the poor being involved in decision making.) The cruel absurdity of much of the War on Poverty has been accurately distilled by Herbert Hill, Labor Secretary of the NAACP, when he applies to it the Talmudic saying: "If you don't know where you're going, any road will take you there."

And so, finally, instead of looking for a "coalition," New York CORE has declared it will no longer support Wagner for re-election. And in Brooklyn, a Brooklyn Freedom Democratic party is being formed to run its own people for offices. There *is* a coalition in Brooklyn, but it is a coalition of CORE and other Negro-led groups; and its targets are the discriminatory labor unions, and the "liberal" politicians who gutted such "pilot projects" as Mobilization for Youth on the Lower East Side because there was no patronage in it for them and because the previously apathetic poor in that area were actually beginning to go out on the streets and protest bad housing, bad education, and unemployment.

It is, in sum, too soon for the kind of "coalition" Rustin and Harrington are advocating (except in certain non-typical instances). Not enough of the labor leaders, the churchmen, and the white liberals yet realize that, as Joseph Lyford emphasizes,

> The demand of the civil rights movement cannot be fulfilled within the present context of society. The Negro is trying to

enter a social community and the tradition of work-income which are in the process of vanishing for even the hitherto privileged white worker.

What is needed—obviously—is a redistribution of power to change that tradition. There is no question that eventually a broad-based alliance will be essential, but to act as if it existed now is to act so unrealistically as to slow down possibilities of change.

The kind of power that might begin to make basic structural changes is going to come first, if it comes at all, from the ghettos. Later, there will be allies from labor as the unions continue to diminish in membership and as cybernation cuts more pitilessly into the lives and aspirations of white workers and *their* children. And even later, those in middle-management and in certain other kinds of doomed white-collar work will also be driven by painful self-interest to become allies. But an essential need now—as SNCC, the Northern Student Movement, the Brooklyn Freedom Democratic party, and such neighborhood groups in New York (with counterparts elsewhere around the country) as the Independent Action Committee for Social Progress on the Lower East Side and the Block Development Project in East Harlem know—is to start the poor organizing themselves. And in most cases, although Students for Democratic Society has had some success in integrated movements of local poor, the initial dynamism—if any—will be among the black poor because they hurt the most.

Admittedly this is an extraordinarily difficult route—beginning first by organizing around inflamed, specific, local issues; moving on to other problems as their interconnections become clear; linking up with other "community unions" throughout the country; and thereby amassing power, both political power in the narrow sense and the other kinds of power that can come from an informed, cohesive mass of people. It is true, after all, that more and more of the center cities contain growing percentages of blacks as whites move to the suburbs; and so long as these ghettos continue to grow, maximization of potential black power can work to end the ghettos. Bill Strickland of the Northern Student Movement makes the corollary point that as the cities grow—and as their needs multiply —it must become clearer that in many of their functions, state legislatures are anachronistic. "The movement," he asserts, "has to create new political forms in the city by which those in the city can deal much more directly with the federal government where the quantities of money exist that can help make change in the city." And, Strickland adds, in those cities in which black political power can be amassed in sufficient numbers, the planning and the expenditure of funds for the ghettos must be controlled by political leaders from—and directly responsible to—the black ghettos.

Admittedly again, these are infant movements now and have not yet become even strong enough to deal with a crucial problem, as described in *Studies on the Left:* "The problem of connecting up these issues with the consciousness of the need for an over-all transformation, in such a way that local power structures will not be able to co-opt the movements by granting parts or all of immediate demands. . . ."

I am not sure that this route will work, but I do not see any other in this decade despite Lyndon Johnson's rhetoric and Bayard Rustin's dream. What is somewhat encouraging is that most of the full-time workers toward these goals now in the ghettos are recognizing that they cannot bring in and try to superimpose sectarian ideologies or pre-set tactical glossaries on the poor as the poor find indigenous leaders and reason to move to action. This has to be an existential series of discoveries of the ways in which to begin real change.

Arthur Finch of the Boston Action Group (BAG), part of the Northern Student Movement, says: "There is a conflict among civil rights 'theoreticians' as to whether the movement is revolutionary or reformist in character. We, on the other hand, opt for what we can get and take." And Dick Flacks, an assistant professor at the University of Chicago, writes in the February, 1965, Students for a Democratic Society *Bulletin:*

> . . . there ARE times and places where local activists will see the need to work in and with liberal coalitions. One such time and place may be certain Southern areas right now. Or, putting it the other way, there are times and places where radicals must absolutely eschew top-down liberal coalition and organize radical constituencies—for example, cities like Chicago or New York right now.

Those civil rights groups who will have major roles in the movement beyond civil rights will be those who can get the poor to organize themselves. Martin Luther King is a charismatic presence, but his SCLC does not have a cohesive, on-going political program nor has it organized constituencies to implement a program in cities after King has left. The NAACP as a national body will probably continue to be an inadequate catalyst for political action on the basic issues—although valuable in other ways—but individual NAACP chapters are quite likely going to become increasingly a part of local, indigenous coalitions. More and more individual CORE chapters are planning in this direction; SNCC has already formed the Mississippi Freedom Democratic party and is encouraging independent political organizing in Georgia, Mississippi, Alabama, and Arkansas.

The crux of the division between such as SNCC, on the one hand, and Bayard Rustin and the "coalitionists," on the other, was dramatized at the Atlantic City Democratic Convention when the Freedom Democratic party (essentially SNCC), despite Rustin's efforts at persuasion, refused to accept a token compromise of two at-large seats. Those seats were not from Mississippi, and therefore, as Stanley Newman pointed out in his paper, *Atlantic City—Case Study in the New Politics,* the compromise did not acknowledge that the FDP represented the people in Mississippi. Secondly, the Credentials Committee—not the Freedom Democratic party—named the two delegates. And, Andrew Kopkind has pointed out in the *New Republic* ("New Radicals in Dixie," April 10, 1965), SNCC's "point was that they had no real interest in, or hope of assimilating into the Democratic establishment. They wanted to demolish it. It was rotten to the core, not just eroded here and there. They believed in their rights to political power, and they wanted them in 1964, not at some unnamed future date."

Yet Rustin writes in *Commentary:*

> . . . the difference between expediency and morality in politics is the difference between selling out a principle and making smaller concessions to win larger ones. The leader who shrinks from this task reveals not his purity but his lack of political sense.

That Rustin honestly could not comprehend so clear an illustration of compromise-as-selling-out-a-principle in Atlantic City, indicates that he and the new radicals in "the movement" have a basic disagreement on the definition of "political sense."

In the North, and increasingly in the South, political action by the poor will require decisions more complicated than in Atlantic

City, and there will be some wary participation in broader coalitions—as the objective situation requires. But the worth of the new radicals will be determined by the degree to which they force the liberals, the churchmen, and the union leaders in those tentative coalitions to prove themselves. The criteria will be whether each political action moves toward real change in the way the poor live. Any other kind of "political sense" is to turn the politics of poverty into the politics of delaying final despair.

Part Two

A Legacy of Creative Protest

LEONARD BASKIN *Henry David Thoreau, aet.44* [IV,I, Autumn 1962]

A Legacy of Creative Protest

THE REVEREND MARTIN LUTHER KING, JR.

During my early college days I read Thoreau's essay on civil disobedience for the first time. Fascinated by the idea of refusing to cooperate with an evil system, I was so deeply moved that I re-read the work several times. I became convinced then that non-cooperation with evil is as much a moral obligation as is cooperation with good. No other person has been more eloquent and passionate in getting this idea across than Henry David Thoreau. As a result of his writings and personal witness we are the heirs of a legacy of creative protest. It goes without saying that the teachings of Thoreau are alive today, indeed, they are more alive today than ever before. Whether pressed in a sit-in at lunch counters, a freedom ride into Mississippi, a peaceful protest in Albany, Georgia, a bus boycott in Montgomery, Alabama, it is an outgrowth of Thoreau's insistence that evil must be resisted and no moral man can patiently adjust to injustice.

SEPTEMBER 7, 1962

[IV, I, Autumn 1962]

Thoreau and American Nonviolent Resistance

WILLIAM STUART NELSON

IT IS YET TO DAWN FULLY upon the participants in sit-ins, freedom rides, and other recent forms of non-violent resistance in the United States how deeply indebted they are to Henry David Thoreau. Thoreau's name is mentioned upon occasion. Martin Luther King recalls that early in the 1955 bus boycott of Montgomery, Alabama, he reflected on Thoreau's essay on "Civil Disobedience" and was convinced that in Montgomery he and his followers were simply making clear, in the spirit of Thoreau, that they could no longer co-operate with an evil system.

Participants in this non-violent movement acknowledge a profound indebtedness to Mohandas K. Gandhi. Those who have not read the following words of Gandhi would profit in so doing:

> Why, of course, I read Thoreau. I read *Walden* first in Johannesburg in South Africa in 1906 and his ideas influenced me greatly. I adopted some of them and recommended the study of Thoreau to all my friends who were helping me in the cause of Indian independence. Why, I actually took the name of my movement from Thoreau's essay, "On the duty of Civil Disobedience," written about eighty years ago. Until I read that essay I never found a suitable English translation for my Indian word, *Satyagraha*. You remember that Thoreau invented and practised the idea of civil disobedience in Concord, Massachusetts, by refusing to pay his poll tax as a protest against the United States government. He went to jail too. There is no doubt that Thoreau's ideas greatly influenced my movement in India.[*]

The right to disobey government has been defended in literature and in practice for thousands of years, but Americans engaged in

[*] Quoted by George Hendrick, "Influence of Thoreau and Emerson on Gandhi's Satyagraha," *Gandhi Marg.*, III (July, 1959), 166.

or confronted by a civil resistance movement must above all understand Thoreau. He conceded that government is a present necessity
but held that governments by their very nature are prone to err.
The best of them are supported by majorities, indicating a victory of
numbers and not necessarily of justice. Law makers, as Thoreau
observed, too frequently serve the state with their heads and often
unintentionally serve the devil. What place, we may then inquire,
is left in such a government for conscience? If it is desirable to
develop a respect for law, it is essential to cultivate a respect for
conscience.

A genuine non-violent movement, therefore, includes the assertion of the right of conscience in the presence of the rule of law.
It is an appeal beyond government to the character of those whom
the government purports to represent.

Such an appeal, if it is responsible, has its laws. Civil resistance
is not necessarily invoked against every law which is regarded as bad.
It is obvious that a man cannot give himself to the eradication of
every wrong however great. He can, of course, disassociate himself
from it. Against what wrong of government, then, should he oppose
his conscience? In "Civil Disobedience" Thoreau has a formula: "If
the injustice is part of the necessary friction of the machine of government, let it go, let it go: perchance it will wear smooth—certainly the machine will wear out . . . but if it is of such a nature that
it requires you to be an agent of injustice to another, then, I say,
break the law. Let your life be a counter friction—friction to stop
the machine. What I have to do is to see, at any rate, that I do not
lend myself to the wrong which I condemn."

Civil disobedience requires also on the part of the resister the
willing subjection to the penalty exacted by the law. As Thoreau
states, "Under a government which imprisons any unjustly the true
place for a just man is also in prison." If the place of the fugitive
slave in Massachusetts is in prison, then the only place for her free
and just citizens is also in the prisons. This is in token of respect
for law as law. Moreover, it gives maximum force to protest, for as
Thoreau points out a just minority is irresistible when it acts with
its whole weight. The state will not place or keep all just men in
prison. Rather than this, it will abandon its evil practice.

The discussion of the civil disobedience aspect of non-violence
and non-violent resistance is of greatest importance, but it would
be extremely shortsighted and superficial to conclude that the mean-

ing of non-violence is exhausted merely by such a discussion. It is likewise unfortunate to separate Thoreau's doctrine of civil disobedience from other profound manifestations of his spirit. To persist in so doing is to miss the total message which he so forcefully epitomizes. It is only in the grasping of this total message that Negroes might possibly guarantee the fulfillment of Gandhi's fateful prophecy, namely, that it might be through them that the unadulterated message of non-violence would be made available to the world.

The roots of Thoreau's concept of civil resistance were deep. As a Transcendentalist he had turned away from economic royalism and was convinced that the purest insight commonly was not to be found in the person who accumulated property. His poverty he wore as a badge of honor and he preached eloquently against materialism, the disease of his century, reminding men that they err in laying up treasures which moths corrupt.

For him, living was the precious goal and the cost of a thing was "the amount of life it requires to be exchanged for it immediately and in the long run." Rebelling against acquisition, he was happy in the gift to him by the gods of years without an encumbrance. He was willing to live so Spartan-like as to put to flight all that was not life. He journeyed to Walden Pond not, as some may think, to flee from life but in the midst of this apparent privation to find it. One is reminded of Gandhi in our own time, who insisted that in the spirit of this self-denial he must reduce himself to zero. The Christ, the Buddha—all those who have found the secret of living in its noblest flowering—have seen the wisdom of finding the self by losing it. It cannot be expected that non-violent movements will be completely manned by such spirits as these. At the center, however, there must be those selfless, disinterested standard-bearers for whom fulness of life exists apart from material possessions.

There is a further quality without which no truly non-violent movement can be built. It is compassion—not simply sorrow for the suffering man but identification with him. This is the quality that led Gandhi to adopt his scant attire when he saw a woman in her one remaining sari, the remnant of a once adequate garment, and to declare that he would wear this minimum attire until somehow no longer would a woman of India be forced to such an embarrassing estate; or led Gandhi, when he could not abolish untouchability, to adopt an untouchable as his daughter and often to elect to live among untouchables.

Some may find it difficult to associate this quality with Thoreau. It was nonetheless present. His identification with the evil linked to the extension of slavery led him to prison; his unity in spirit with John Brown enabled Thoreau to defend him in the face of bitter hostility and threatened violence. Most men saw and judged John Brown from the outside. Thoreau knew and felt him from within. When the village postmaster was reported to have said of John Brown, "He died as the fool dieth," Thoreau said he should have been answered as follows: "He did not live as the fool liveth, and he died as he lived." Thoreau declared also: "It galls me to listen to the remarks of craven-hearted neighbors who speak disparagingly of Brown because he resorted to violence, resisted the government, threw his life away!—what way have they thrown their lives, pray?—neighbors who would praise a man for attacking singly an ordinary band of thieves or murderers. Such minds are not equal to the occasion. They preserve the so-called peace of their community by deeds of petty violence every day. . . . So they defend themselves and their hen roosts, and maintain slavery." Thoreau continued: "There sits a tyrant holding fettered four millions of slaves. Here comes their heroic liberator; if he falls, will he not still live?"

Thoreau saw through the crust of John Brown's violence, a violence which Brown had learned from thousands of years of pagan and Christian history and the practice of his own time. Thoreau, penetrating that crust, identified himself with the spirit of the man which sought the overthrow of an evil system.

The lesson here is that in a movement motivated by genuine non-violence, such as inspires the current resistance to racial injustice in America, men risk their lives not for beliefs but for *passionate* beliefs, beliefs in which intellectual accord has been deepened by spiritual identification.

These two threads—civil disobedience on the one hand and, on the other, capacity for divorcement from the material along with passionate identification with suffering—remained consistently interwoven throughout the life of Henry David Thoreau in spite of the urgings by others that he order his life otherwise. To illustrate, following the night in jail Thoreau completed his journey to the shoemaker interrupted by his arrest the day before. Having retrieved his shoe, he went huckleberrying. Emerson felt impatiently that Thoreau, instead of serving as the captain of huckleberry parties, should be employing his great gifts in leadership for all America. This, of course, would have proved a large responsibility even in Thoreau's and Emerson's time. Fortunately, Thoreau was not moved from his course. He remained true to himself. In our time, his life and thought, developed between and perhaps even during his jaunts through the woods in quest of huckleberries, move with increasing power upon America. Those who today assume the difficult role of removing certain of our country's weaknesses by non-violence, including civil disobedience, will do well to ponder Thoreau both as jail-goer and the voice of protest. Thoreau should also be remembered as one who resisted the temptation to permit things to ride in the saddle of his soul and who counted his life as none too precious a gift in testimony to his compassion for justice and for those who were willing to die in its behalf.

Thoreau in South Africa

A Letter to the Editors of The Massachusetts Review

THE REVEREND TREVOR N. W. BUSH

Y OUR LETTER, addressed to me at St. Andrew's College, Minaki, Tanganyika, reached me last week. As you know, I left South Africa as a political refugee after assisting the banned African National Congress to organize demonstrations of protest against the apartheid policies of the government. After spending a short time in East Africa I proceeded to Europe during March. At present I am working in a Welsh industrial parish but I expect to take up a teaching appointment in Cardiff during September.

I am deeply moved by your request for a tribute to Henry David Thoreau. His influence in South Africa has been extremely important and our struggle to win rights for the oppressed non-white population of our country has been assisted profoundly by the fearless liberal teachings and example of your great philosopher and prophet. It is therefore with pride that I wish to be associated with those who pay tribute to him during this one hundredth anniversary of his death.

If Thoreau were alive today he would certainly join forces with those who resist racial intolerance and the evils which flow from it. He would recognize, as we do, that although "the four million slaves" have been emancipated, many more millions of dark-skinned people continue to suffer unspeakable misery and indignities at the hands of allegedly Christian and democratic white people. Like the immortal John Brown who is the subject of so much of his writing, his example would be "to face his country herself, when she was in the wrong." We must not forget the courage which enabled him to campaign actively against slavery, the Mexican War, and the dispossession and despoiling of Indians. How much more would he direct his anger against the new and more diabolically subtle forms of slavery of the twentieth century, whether they take the guise of apartheid, Southern segregation, or the exploitation of people through neo-colonialism!

It is also opportune that we should remember Thoreau's attacks upon national leaders, pressmen, and church dignitaries who failed to give a lead in the struggle for justice: "Those who, while they disapprove of the character and measures of a government, yield to it their allegiance and support, and are thus undoubtedly its most conscientious supporters, and so frequently the most serious obstacles to reform." Talking and writing about abuses is not enough, he said, and there are times when it is patriotic to rise up in active revolt against a system which permits and encourages injustice by inertia and inaction. "The spirit of Harper's Ferry" must never be forgotten by those who are called to be reformers of the national life.

Recent history and the present time have produced campaigners for justice of Thoreau's calibre. Many have been profoundly influenced by his writings and can attribute their success in part to his compelling and inspiring lead. Gandhi, Martin Luther King, Albert Luthuli belong to this company, men who have sacrificed comfort and material advancement to win recognition for the rights of their fellow human beings. Like Thoreau they are fearless of the unpleasant labels their enemies have attempted to attach to them, and of the venomous retaliations of those whose selfish interests their activities have threatened.

I congratulate you on your plans to draw renewed attention to this outstanding American. Please accept my sincere good wishes and my earnest hope that you will succeed in persuading people in countries all over the world to take courage and inspiration from the message and work of your great fellow citizen.

June 13, 1962

John Brown, Jr. and the Haymarket Martyrs

LOUIS RUCHAMES, Editor

O N MAY 4, 1886, A BOMB EXPLODED in Haymarket
Square, Chicago, at a meeting which had been called to
protest the shooting by police of several workers outside
a strike-bound plant. Falling in the midst of a group of policemen,
the bomb killed or mortally wounded seven persons and injured
several others. Eight alleged anarchists were arrested by Chicago
police, charged with inciting the crime but not its commission, and
found guilty in one of the most shameful perversions of American
justice. Four were hanged, one committed suicide and three were
sentenced to life in prison, but were pardoned in 1893 by Illinois
Governor John Peter Altgeld, who was convinced of their innocence.

The hanging of.the four convicted men took place on November
11, 1887. On November 7, John Brown, Jr., the eldest of John
Brown's children, who was then living in Ohio, expressed his sympathy for the imprisoned men by sending each a box of Catawba
grapes accompanied by a warm and friendly letter. The letter to
the anarchists is here reproduced in a hitherto unpublished letter
to Franklin Sanborn,[1] a well known writer and editor, biographer
of John Brown, one of the "Secret Six" who helped finance Brown's
raid on Harpers Ferry and who, following Brown's hanging, remained a life-long friend of the family. The letter to Sanborn
throws important light on John Brown's vision of a better world
through co-operation and mutual help, and on the religious foundation of that vision. It is a poignant example of how Brown's devotion to social justice continued to be applied by his son almost

[v, 4, Summer 1964]
[1] The original letter is in the possession of Dr. Boyd B. Stutler, of
Charleston, West Virginia, who has provided a photostatic copy and
granted permission to publish it. I am also indebted to Dr. Stutler for
various items of information concerning John Brown, Jr.

thirty years later, in the face of a public opinion which heaped opprobrium upon those who either expressed sympathy for the anarchists in their plight or questioned the justness of the verdict.

Ottawa Co Ohio, Nov. 11th 1887.
Put-in-Bay Island Lake Erie,
4:00 A.M.

My Dear Friend:

I mailed letters to you yesterday, but owing to a gale from the northwest the Steamer Jay Cooke which carries the mail did not leave her dock.

Have this morning written to Mrs. Brann (sister of William Leeman)[2] informing her that I have sent to your care $5.00 in P.O. Money Order as my contribution towards relief of her necessities.

I now send you a number of letters, some of which you kindly enclosed for my perusal—the others, please return when read.

Have not seen the "International Record" of which you wrote Octo. 10th nor the paper from New Orleans you ordered sent. However, a young man of Put-in-Bay stopping a while at New Orleans kindly sent me the paper containing Hunter's article.[3] Possibly his statement of facts may balance his inaccuracies; his animating spirit is not commendable, but is not different from what should be expected. Today, I suppose, those Anarchists at Chicago must meet the demands of Illinois justice. Owing to the storm, have no late papers.

Last Sunday, I devoted the day to preparing for shipment to each of those men a basket of Catawba grapes as a token of my sympathy for them and their cause,—removal of the great burdens borne by the working, dependant class. I have socialistic tendencies, though my notions are not well defined,

[2] William Leeman was a member of John Brown's band who was slain at Harpers Ferry. Apparently, John Jr. helped Leeman's sister financially from time to time.

[3] Andrew Hunter was the Special Prosecutor at John Brown's trial. On September 5, 1887, the *New Orleans Times-Democrat* published his account of the trial. It was later reprinted with some revisions in *Southern History Association Papers* (Washington, D.C.), July, 1897, I, 3, 165–195.

for I have never met a "Socialist," to my knowledge, nor have I read much of any thing pertaining to their doctrines. Father's favorite theme was that of the *Community plan of cooperative industry,* in which all should labor for the Common good; "having all things in common" as did the disciples of Jesus in his day. This also has been, and still is, my Communistic or Socialistic faith. I cannot be an Anarchist, as I understand the meaning of the term Anarchy.—Would not resort to dynamite until I had exhausted all other means when "forbearance had ceased to be a virtue."

I expect to lose many friends in consequence of my small token of sympathy for those men, who have, according to the measure of their light and honest convictions, been *faithful to their highest ideas.* It will make no difference with me if such should be the result; for I have in this matter, been faithful to my highest sense of duty.

As a part of my last "Sabbath days journey," I wrote to each of those men a letter to accompany my gifts of the grapes, of which letter, the following is a *true copy.*

Put-in-Bay Island Lake Erie,
Ottawa Co. Ohio, 7th Nov. 1887

Brother:—

I send you by to day's Boat, a basket of Catawba grapes, pre-paid through, as per Express receipts enclosed. These grapes, I beg you to accept as a slight token of my sympathy for you, and for the cause which you represent.

Four days before his execution, my Father wrote to a friend, the following.

"Charleston, Va., Jail
Nov. 28th 1859.

It is a great comfort to feel assured that I am permitted to die for a cause,—not merely to pay the debt of nature, as all must.[4]

John Brown"

[4] Actually, this is but one sentence from a lengthy letter by John Brown to the Hon. D. R. Tilden. The letter is printed in its entirety in this writer's volume, *A John Brown Reader,* Abelard-Schuman, 1960, pp. 154–5.

That a like assurance may be a comfort to you, is the earnest desire of
Ever yours, for the cause of the faithful, honest laborer.—

John Brown, Jr.

To August Spies.
(Chicago Jail,)
Care, Sheriff of Cook County,
Chicago, Illinois.

If my letter to those men should not be published, or if published, should appear in any other words than the foregoing, you will do me a favor to publish in such a way as you choose.

It is nearly daylight once more, and I will go to the P.O. for the gale is not now so heavy and the Boat will probably leave this morning. Have much more to write you, but will resume another time.

All well, and would, I know, join me in sending regards to yourself and family, were they not still asleep.

Faithfully yours,
John Brown, Jr.

F. B. Sanborn, Esq.
Concord,
Mass.

How It, So Help Me, Was

JOSEPH LANGLAND

When I first went to Walden Pond
Alone in the afternoon of the last day of summer
In the centennial of his death
The woods rang with sparrows, squirrels, and crows.
Turning around the rockpile of Thoreau's hut
I discovered, also, that I had been born
In the centennial of his birth.
There in the lifted day, Icarian bird,
I circled the dark edge of an ancient dream
And started down to the water.

And the very first person I met upon my path
Was a tall young Negro.
He stood easily by the woodsy pond
With his white girl friend,
Casually linking their hands by a leaning birch.
Its leaves quivered in a light breeze
Wakening over the dark waters,
And under the random clouds in the deep sky
We smiled, and I went on.

And the very next person I met upon that path
Was a brown man from India
Lounging in mottled pebbles and blond sand
With a college sweatshirt hung on his shoulders.
Into the lake he dipped his golden hands;
He turned his palms in the common water
And lifted them, all spangled.
In the mystical geometry of light
Drops fell in a chain
And linked their circular furrows on the pond.
A frog plunked from the bank;

[IV, 1, Autumn 1962]

An autumn leaf swung down.
A bluejay screamed;
We smiled, and I went on.

And further along the brightly shadowed woods
The very next person I met upon that path
Was a wild white man
Running and leaping through the brush,
Mumbling some half-hummed song as he ran.
His jacket was flung open;
His face shone with light;
And a rumpled paisley muffler of rainbowing colors
Trailed from his torn pocket
And waved
In floating arcs among the aisles of trees,
Frightening the song sparrows into sudden answers
As he fled on.

And then, at a further turn, I met myself.
I smiled and stepped to the tall and weedy shades
At the small bay on the western edge,
Stripped to my native self
On brackish ground and shining sand
And, walking into the sun from tufted sedge
Past polliwogs and mudflats and water-spiders,
I strode those slippery shoals to the clear blue
And dove in calm delight
To thrash my limbs and throw my pale white arms
Around those springing waters.

Seeing the afternoon break from the woods
I heard the long dark tale of history flashing down
And rose in a clear dream.
Simply jeweled with all that pond
I put my homely raiment on
And rode the luminous hum of blue-grey twilight home.

A Negro Student at Harvard
at the End of the Nineteenth Century

W. E. B. DuBois

ARVARD UNIVERSITY in 1888 was a great institution of learning. It was two hundred and thirty-eight years old and on its governing board were Alexander Agassiz, Phillips Brooks, Henry Cabot Lodge, and Charles Francis Adams; and a John Quincy Adams, but not the ex-President. Charles William Eliot, a gentleman by training and a scholar by broad study and travel, was president. Among its teachers emeriti were Oliver Wendell Holmes and James Russell Lowell. Among the active teachers were Francis Child, Charles Eliot Norton, Justin Winsor, and John Trowbridge; Frank Taussig, Nathaniel Shaler, George Palmer, William James, Francis Peabody, Josiah Royce, Barrett Wendell, Edward Channing, and Albert Bushnell Hart. In 1890 arrived a young instructor, George Santayana. Seldom, if ever, has any American university had such a galaxy of great men and fine teachers as Harvard in the decade between 1885 and 1895.

To make my own attitude toward the Harvard of that day clear, it must be remembered that I went to Harvard as a Negro, not simply by birth, but recognizing myself as a member of a segregated caste whose situation I accepted. But I was determined to work from within that caste to find my way out.

The Harvard of which most white students conceived I knew little. I had not even heard of Phi Beta Kappa, and of such important social organizations as the Hasty Pudding Club, I knew nothing. I was in Harvard for education and not for high marks, except as marks would insure my staying. I did not pick out "snap" courses. I was there to enlarge my grasp of the meaning of the universe. We had had, for instance, no chemical laboratory at Fisk; our mathematics courses were limited. Above all I wanted to study philosophy! I wanted to get hold of the bases of knowledge, and explore foundations and beginnings. I chose, therefore,

Palmer's course in ethics, but since Palmer was on sabbatical that year, William James replaced him, and I became a devoted follower of James at the time he was developing his pragmatic philosophy.

Fortunately I did not fall into the mistake of regarding Harvard as the beginning rather than the continuing of my college training. I did not find better teachers at Harvard, but teachers better known, who had had wider facilities for gaining knowledge and lived in a broader atmosphere for approaching truth.

I hoped to pursue philosophy as my life career, with teaching for support. With this program I studied at Harvard from the fall of 1888 to 1890, as an undergraduate. I took a varied course in chemistry, geology, social science, and philosophy. My salvation here was the type of teacher I met rather than the content of the courses. William James guided me out of the sterilities of scholastic philosophy to realist pragmatism; from Peabody's social reform with a religious tinge I turned to Albert Bushnell Hart to study history with documentary research; and from Taussig, with his reactionary British economics of the Ricardo school, I approached what was later to become sociology. Meantime Karl Marx was mentioned, but only incidentally and as one whose doubtful theories had long since been refuted. Socialism was dismissed as unimportant, as a dream of philanthropy or as a will-o-wisp of hotheads.

When I arrived at Harvard, the question of board and lodging was of first importance. Naturally, I could not afford a room in the college yard in the old and venerable buildings which housed most of the well-to-do students under the magnificent elms. Neither did I think of looking for lodgings among white families, where numbers of the ordinary students lived. I tried to find a colored home, and finally at 20 Flagg Street I came upon the neat home of a colored woman from Nova Scotia, a descendant of those black Jamaican Maroons whom Britain had deported after solemnly promising them peace if they would surrender. For a very reasonable sum I rented the second story front room and for four years this was my home. I wrote of this abode at the time: "My room is, for a college man's abode, very ordinary indeed. It is quite pleasantly situated—second floor, front, with a bay window and one other window. . . . As you enter you will perceive the bed in the opposite corner, small and decorated with floral designs cal-

culated to puzzle a botanist. . . . On the left hand is a bureau with
a mirror of doubtful accuracy. In front of the bay window is a
stand with three shelves of books, and on the left of the bureau is
an improvised bookcase made of unpainted boards and uprights,
containing most of my library of which I am growing quite proud.
Over the heat register, near the door, is a mantel with a plaster
of Paris pug-dog and a calendar, and the usual array of odds and
ends. . . . On the wall are a few quite ordinary pictures. In this
commonplace den I am quite content."

Following the attitudes which I had adopted in the South, I
sought no friendships among my white fellow students, nor even
acquaintanceships. Of course I wanted friends, but I could not seek
them. My class was large—some three hundred students. I doubt
if I knew a dozen of them. I did not seek them, and naturally they
did not seek me. I made no attempt to contribute to the college
periodicals since the editors were not interested in my major interests. But I did have a good singing voice and loved music, so I
entered the competition for the Glee Club. I ought to have known
that Harvard could not afford to have a Negro on its Glee Club
travelling about the country. Quite naturally I was rejected.

I was happy at Harvard, but for unusual reasons. One of these
was my acceptance of racial segregation. Had I gone from Great
Barrington High School directly to Harvard, I would have sought
companionship with my white fellows and been disappointed and
embittered by a discovery of social limitations to which I had not
been used. But I came by way of Fisk and the South and there I
had accepted color caste and embraced eagerly the companionship
of those of my own color. This was of course no final solution.
Eventually, in mass assault, led by culture, we Negroes were going
to break down the boundaries of race; but at present we were
banded together in a great crusade, and happily so. Indeed, I
suspect that the prospect of ultimate full human intercourse, without reservations and annoying distinctions, made me all too willing
to consort with my own and to disdain and forget as far as was
possible that outer, whiter world.

In general, I asked nothing of Harvard but the tutelage of
teachers and the freedom of the laboratory and library. I was
quite voluntarily and willingly outside its social life. I sought only
such contacts with white teachers as lay directly in the line of my
work. I joined certain clubs, like the Philosophical Club; I was

a member of the Foxcroft Dining Club because it was cheap. James and one or two other teachers had me at their homes at meal and reception. I escorted colored girls to various gatherings, and as pretty ones as I could find to the vesper exercises, and later to the class day and commencement social functions. Naturally we attracted attention and the *Crimson* noted my girl friends. Sometimes the shadow of insult fell, as when at one reception a white woman seemed determined to mistake me for a waiter.

In general, I was encased in a completely colored world, self-sufficient and provincial, and ignoring just as far as possible the white world which conditioned it. This was self-protective coloration, with perhaps an inferiority complex, but with belief in the ability and future of black folk.

My friends and companions were drawn mainly from the colored students of Harvard and neighboring institutions, and the colored folk of Boston and surrounding towns. With them I led a happy and inspiring life. There were among them many educated and well-to-do folk, many young people studying or planning to study, many charming young women. We met and ate, danced and argued, and planned a new world.

Towards whites I was not arrogant; I was simply not obsequious, and to a white Harvard student of my day a Negro student who did not seek recognition was trying to be more than a Negro. The same Harvard man had much the same attitude toward Jews and Irishmen.

I was, however, exceptional among Negroes at Harvard in my ideas on voluntary race segregation. They for the most part saw salvation only in integration at the earliest moment and on almost any terms in white culture; I was firm in my criticism of white folk and in my dream of a self-sufficient Negro culture even in America.

This cutting of myself off from my white fellows, or being cut off, did not mean unhappiness or resentment. I was in my early manhood, unusually full of high spirits and humor. I thoroughly enjoyed life. I was conscious of understanding and power, and conceited enough still to imagine, as in high school, that they who did not know me were the losers, not I. On the other hand, I do not think that my white classmates found me personally objectionable. I was clean, not well-dressed but decently clothed. Manners I regarded as more or less superfluous and deliberately cultivated a certain brusquerie. Personal adornment I regarded as pleasant but not important. I was in Harvard, but not of it, and realized all the irony of my singing "Fair Harvard." I sang it because I liked the music, and not from any pride in the Pilgrims.

With my colored friends I carried on lively social intercourse, but necessarily one which involved little expenditure of money. I called at their homes and ate at their tables. We danced at private parties. We went on excursions down the Bay. Once, with a group of colored students gathered from surrounding institutions, we gave Aristophanes' *The Birds* in a Boston colored church. The rendition was good, but not outstanding, not quite appreciated by the colored audience, but well worth doing. Even though it worked me near to death, I was proud of it.

Thus the group of professional men, students, white-collar workers, and upper servants, whose common bond was color of skin in themselves or in their fathers, together with a common history and current experience of discrimination, formed a unit that, like many tens of thousands of like units across the nation, had or were getting to have a common culture pattern which made them an interlocking mass, so that increasingly a colored person in Boston was more neighbor to a colored person in Chicago than to a white person across the street.

Mrs. Ruffin of Charles Street, Boston, and her daughter, Birdie, were often hostesses to this colored group. She was widow of the first colored judge appointed in Massachusetts, an aristocratic lady, with olive skin and high-piled masses of white hair. Once a Boston white lady said to Mrs. Ruffin ingratiatingly: "I have always been interested in your race." Mrs. Ruffin flared: "Which race?" She began a national organization of colored women and published the *Courant,* a type of small colored weekly paper which was then spreading over the nation. In this I published many of my Harvard daily themes.

Naturally in this close group there grew up among the young people friendships ending in marriages. I myself, outgrowing the youthful attractions of Fisk, began serious dreams of love and marriage. There were, however, still my study plans to hold me back and there were curious other reasons. For instance, it happened that two of the girls whom I particularly liked had what was to me then the insuperable handicap of looking like whites, while they had enough black ancestry to make them "Negroes" in America. I could not let the world even imagine that I had married a white wife. Yet these girls were intelligent and companionable. One went to Vassar College, which then refused entrance to Negroes. Years later when I went there to lecture I remember disagreeing violently with a teacher who thought the girl ought not to have "deceived" the college by graduating before it knew of her Negro descent! Another favorite of mine was Deenie Pindell. She was a fine, forthright woman, blonde, blue-eyed and fragile. In the end I had no chance to choose her, for she married Monroe Trotter.

Trotter was the son of a well-to-do colored father and entered Harvard in my first year in the Graduate School. He was thick-set, yellow, with close-cut dark hair. He was stubborn and strait-laced and an influential member of his class. He organized the first Total Abstinence Club in the Yard. I came to know him and joined the company when he and other colored students took in a trip to Amherst to see our friends Forbes and Lewis graduate in the class with Calvin Coolidge.

Lewis afterward entered the Harvard Law School and became the celebrated center rush of the Harvard football team. He married the beautiful Bessie Baker, who had been with us on that Amherst trip. Forbes, a brilliant, cynical dark man, later joined with Trotter in publishing the *Guardian,* the first Negro paper to attack Booker T. Washington openly. Washington's friends retorted by sending Trotter to jail when he dared to heckle Washington in a public Boston meeting on his political views. I was not present nor privy to this occurrence, but the unfairness of the jail sentence led me eventually to form the Niagara movement, which later became the NAACP.

Thus I lived near to life, love, and tragedy; and when I met Maud Cuney, I became doubly interested. She was a tall, imperious brunette with gold-bronze skin, brilliant eyes, and coils of black hair, daughter of the Collector of Customs at Galveston, Texas. She had come to study music and was a skilled performer. When the New England Conservatory of Music tried to "jim-crow" her in the dormitory, we students rushed to her defense and we won. I fell deeply in love with her, and we were engaged.

Thus it is clear how in the general social intercourse on the campus I consciously missed nothing. Some white students made themselves known to me and a few, a very few, became life-long friends. Most of my classmates I knew neither by sight nor name. Among them many made their mark in life: Norman Hapgood, Robert Herrick, Herbert Croly, George Dorsey, Homer Folks, Augustus Hand, James Brown Scott, and others. I knew none of these intimately. For the most part I do not doubt that I was voted a somewhat selfish and self-centered "grind" with a chip on my shoulder and a sharp tongue.

Only once or twice did I come to the surface of college life. First I found by careful calculation that I needed the cash of one of the Boylston prizes in oratory to piece out my year's expenses. I got it through winning a second oratorical prize. The occasion was noteworthy by the fact that another black student, Clement Morgan, got first prize at the same contest.

With the increase at Harvard of students who had grown up outside New England, there arose at this time a certain resentment at the way New England students were dominating and conducting college affairs. The class marshal on commencement day was always a Saltonstall, a Cabot, a Lowell, or from some such New England family. The crew and most of the heads of other athletic teams were selected from similarly limited social groups. The class poet, class orator, and other commencement officials invariably were selected because of family and not for merit. It so happened that when the officials of the class of 1890 were being selected in early spring, a plot ripened. Personally, I knew nothing of it and was not greatly interested. But in Boston and in the Harvard Yard the result of the elections was of tremendous significance, for this conspiratorial clique selected Clement Morgan as class orator. New England and indeed the whole country reverberated.

Morgan was a black man. He had been working in a barber shop in St. Louis at the time when he ought to have been in school. With the encouragement and help of a colored teacher, whom he later married, he came to Boston and entered the Latin School. This meant that when he finally entered Harvard, he entered as freshman in the orthodox way and was well acquainted with his classmates. He was fairly well received, considering his color. He was a pleasant unassuming person and one of the best speakers of clearly enunciated English on the campus. In his junior year he had earned the first Boylston prize for oratory in the same contest where I won second prize. It was, then, logical for him to become class orator, and yet this was against all the traditions of America. There were editorials in the leading newspapers, and the South especially raged and sneered at the audience of "black washerwomen" who would replace Boston society at the next Harvard commencement.

Morgan's success was contagious, and that year and the next, in several leading Northern colleges, colored students became the class orators. Ex-President Hayes, as I shall relate later, sneered at this fact. While, as I have said, I had nothing to do with the plot, and was not even present at the election which chose Morgan, I was greatly pleased at this breaking of the color line. Morgan and I became fast friends and spent a summer giving readings along the North Shore to defray our college costs.

Harvard of this day was a great opportunity for a young man and a young American Negro and I realized it. I formed habits of work rather different from those of most of the other students. I burned no midnight oil. I did my studying in the daytime and had my day parceled out almost to the minute. I spent a great deal of time in the library and did my assignments with thoroughness and with prevision of the kind of work I wanted to do later. From the beginning my relations with most of the teachers at Harvard were pleasant. They were on the whole glad to receive a serious student, to whom extracurricular activities were not of paramount importance, and one who in a general way knew what he wanted.

Harvard had in the social sciences no such leadership of thought and breadth of learning as in philosophy, literature, and physical science. She was then groping and is still groping toward a scientific treatment of human action. She was facing at the end of the century a tremendous economic era. In the United States, finance was succeeding in monopolizing transportation and raw materials like sugar, coal, and oil. The power of the trust and combine was so great that the Sherman Act was passed in 1890. On the other hand, the tariff, at the demand of manufacturers, continued to rise in height from the McKinley to the indefensible Wilson tariff, making that domination easier. The understanding between the Industrial North and the New South was being perfected and, beginning in 1890, a series of disfranchising laws was enacted by the Southern states that was destined in the next sixteen years to make voting by Southern Negroes practically impossible. A financial crisis shook the land in 1893, and popular discontent showed itself in the Populist movement and Coxey's Army. The whole question of the burden of taxation began to be discussed.

These things we discussed with some clearness and factual understanding at Harvard. The tendency was toward English free trade and against the American tariff policy. We reverenced Ricardo and wasted long hours on the "Wages-fund." I remember Taussig's course supporting dying Ricardean economics. Wages came from what employers had left for labor after they had subtracted their own reward. Suppose that this profit was too small to attract the employer, what would the poor worker do but starve! The trusts and monopolies were viewed frankly as dangerous enemies of democracies, but at the same time as inevitable methods of industry. We were strong for the gold standard and fearful of silver. On the other hand, the attitude of Harvard toward labor was on the whole contemptuous and condemnatory. Strikes like that of the anarchists in Chicago and the railway strikes of 1886, the terrible Homestead strike of 1892 and Coxey's Army of 1894, were pictured as ignorant lawlessness, lurching against conditions largely inevitable.

Karl Marx was mentioned only to point out how thoroughly his theses had been disproven; of the theory itself almost nothing was said. Henry George was given but tolerant notice. The anarchists of Spain, the Nihilists of Russia, the British miners—all these were viewed not as part of political and economic development but as sporadic evil. This was natural. Harvard was the child of its era. The intellectual freedom and flowering of the late eighteenth and early nineteenth centuries were yielding to the deadening economic pressure which would make Harvard rich but reactionary. This defender of wealth and capital, already half ashamed of Sumner and Phillips, was willing finally to replace an Eliot with a manufacturer and a nervous war-monger. The social community that mobbed Garrison easily electrocuted Sacco and Vanzetti.

It was not until I was long out of college and had finished my first studies of economics and politics that I realized the fundamental influence man's efforts to earn a living had upon all his other efforts. The politics which we studied in college were conventional, especially when it came to describing and elucidating the current scene in Europe. The Queen's Jubilee in June, 1887, while I was still at Fisk, set the pattern of our thinking. The little old woman at Windsor became a magnificent symbol of Empire. Here was England with her flag draped around the world, ruling more black folk than white and leading the colored peoples of the earth to Christian baptism, and, as we assumed, to civilization and eventual self-rule. In 1885, Stanley, the traveling American reporter, became a hero and symbol of white world leadership in Africa. The wild, fierce fight of the Mahdi and the driving of the English out of the Sudan for thirteen years did not reveal their inner truth to me. I heard only of the martyrdom of the drunken Bible-reader and freebooter, Chinese Gordon.

After the Congo Free State was established, the Berlin Conference of 1885 was reported to be an act of civilization against the slave trade and liquor. French, English, and Germans pushed on in Africa, but I did not question the interpretation which pictured this as the advance of civilization and the benevolent tutelage of barbarians. I read of the confirmation of the Triple Alliance in 1891. Later I saw the celebration of the renewed Triple Alliance on the Tempelhofer Feld, with the new, young Emperor Wilhelm II, who, fresh from his dismissal of Bismarck, led the splendid pageantry; and, finally, the year I left Germany, Nicholas II became Czar of all the Russias. In all this I had not yet linked the political development of Europe with the race problem in America.

I was repeatedly a guest in the home of William James; he was my friend and guide to clear thinking; as a member of the Philosophical Club I talked with Royce and Palmer; I remember vividly once standing beside Mrs. Royce at a small reception. We ceased conversation for a moment and both glanced across the room. Professor Royce was opposite talking excitedly. He was an extraordinary sight: a little body, indifferently clothed; a big, red-thatched head and blazing blue eyes. Mrs. Royce put my thoughts into words: "Funny-looking man, isn't he?" I nearly fainted! Yet I knew how she worshipped him.

I sat in an upper room and read Kant's *Critique* with Santayana; Shaler invited a Southerner, who objected to sitting beside me, to leave his class; he said he wasn't doing very well, anyway. I became one of Hart's favorite pupils and was afterwards guided by him through my graduate course and started on my work in Germany. Most of my courses of study went well. It was in English that I came nearest my Waterloo at Harvard. I had unwittingly arrived at

Harvard in the midst of a violent controversy about poor English among students. A number of fastidious scholars like Barrett Wendell, the great pundit of Harvard English, had come to the campus about this time; moreover, New England itself was getting sensitive over Western slang and Southern drawls and general ignorance of grammar. Freshmen at this time could elect nearly all their courses except English; that was compulsory, with daily themes, theses, and tough examinations. But I was at the point in my intellectual development when the content rather than the form of my writing was to me of prime importance. Words and ideas surged in my mind and spilled out with disregard of exact accuracy in grammar, taste in word, or restraint in style. I knew the Negro problem and this was more important to me than literary form. I knew grammar fairly well, and I had a pretty wide vocabulary; but I was bitter, angry, and intemperate in my first thesis. Naturally my English instructors had no idea of, nor interest in, the way in which Southern attacks on the Negro were scratching me on the raw flesh. Tillman was raging like a beast in the Senate, and literary clubs, especially those of rich and well-dressed women, engaged his services eagerly and listened avidly. Senator Morgan of Alabama had just published a scathing attack on "niggers" in a leading magazine, when my first Harvard thesis was due. I let go at him with no holds barred. My long and blazing effort came back marked "E"—not passed!

It was the first time in my scholastic career that I had encountered such a failure. I was aghast, but I was not a fool. I did not doubt but that my instructors were fair in judging my English technically even if they did not understand the Negro problem. I went to work at my English and by the end of that term had raised it to a "C." I realized that while style is subordinate to content, and that no real literature can be composed simply of meticulous and fastidious phrases, nevertheless, solid content with literary style carries a message further than poor grammar and muddled syntax. I elected the best course on the campus for English composition—English 12.

I have before me a theme which I submitted on October 3, 1890, to Barrett Wendell. I wrote: "Spurred by my circumstances, I have always been given to systematically planning my future, not indeed without many mistakes and frequent alterations, but always with what I now conceive to have been a strangely early and deep appreciation of the fact that to live is a serious thing. I determined while in high school to go to college—partly because other men did, partly because I foresaw that such discipline would best fit me for life. . . . I believe, foolishly perhaps, but sincerely, that I have something to say to the world, and I have taken English 12 in order to say it well." Barrett Wendell liked that last sentence. Out of fifty essays, he picked this out to read to the class.

Commencement was approaching, when, one day, I found myself at midnight on one of the swaggering streetcars that used to roll out from Boston on its way to Cambridge. It was in the spring of 1890, and quite accidentally I was sitting by a classmate who would graduate with me in June. As I dimly remember, he was a nice-looking young man; well-dressed, almost dapper, charming in manner. Probably he was rich or at least well-to-do, and doubtless belonged to an exclusive fraternity, although that did not interest me. Indeed I have even forgotten his name. But one thing I shall never forget and that was his rather regretful admission (which slipped out as we gossiped) that he had no idea as to what his life work would be, because, as he added, "There's nothing in which I am particularly interested!"

I was more than astonished—I was almost outraged to meet any human being of the mature age of twenty-one who did not have his life all planned before him, at least in general outline, and who was not supremely, if not desperately, interested in what he planned to do.

In June, 1890, I received my bachelor's degree from Harvard *cum laude* in philosophy. I was one of the five graduating students selected to speak at commencement. My subject was "Jefferson Davis." I chose it with the deliberate intent of facing Harvard and the nation with a discussion of slavery as illustrated in the person of the president of the Confederate States of America. Naturally, my effort made a sensation. I said, among other things: "I wish to consider not the man, but the type of civilization which his life represented: its foundation is the idea of the strong man— individualism coupled with the rule of might—and it is this idea that has made the logic of even modern history, the cool logic of the Club. I made of a naturally brave and generous man, Jefferson Davis, one who advanced civilization by murdering Indians; then a hero of a national disgrace, called by courtesy the Mexican War; and finally, as the crowning absurdity, the peculiar champion of a people fighting to be free in order that another people should not be free. Whenever this idea has for a moment escaped from the individual realm, it has found an even more secure foothold in the policy and philosophy of the State. The strong man and his mighty right arm has become the strong nation with its armies. However, under whatever guise a Jefferson Davis may appear as man, as race, or as a nation, his life can only logically mean this: the advance of a part of the world at the expense of the whole; the overwhelming sense of the I, and the consequent forgetting of the Thou. It has thus happened that advance in civilization has always been handicapped by shortsighted national selfishness. The vital principle of division of labor has been stifled not only in industry, but also in civilization; so as to render it well-nigh impossible for a new race to introduce a new idea into the world except by means of the cudgel. To say that a nation is in the way of civilization is a contradiction in terms, and a system of human culture whose principle is the rise of one race on the ruins of another is a farce and a lie. Yet this is the type of civilization which Jefferson Davis represented: it represents a field for stalwart manhood and heroic character, and at the same time for moral obtuseness and refined brutality. These striking contradictions of character always arise when a people seemingly become convinced that the object of the world is not civilization, but Teutonic civilization."

A Harvard professor wrote to *Kate Field's Washington,* then a leading periodical: "Du Bois, the colored orator of the commencement stage, made a ten-strike. It is agreed upon by all the people I have seen that he was the star of the occasion. His paper was on 'Jefferson Davis,' and you would have been surprised to hear a colored man deal with him so generously. Such phrases as a 'great man,' a 'keen thinker,' a 'strong leader,' and others akin occurred in the address. One of the trustees of the University told me yesterday that the paper was considered masterly in every way. Du Bois is from Great Barrington, Massachusetts, and doubtless has some white blood in his veins. He, too, has been in my classes the past year. If he did not head the class, he came pretty near the head, for he is an excellent scholar in every way, and altogether the best black man that has come to Cambridge."

Bishop Potter of New York wrote in the *Boston Herald:* "When at the last commencement of Harvard University, I saw a young colored man appear . . . and heard his brilliant and eloquent address, I said to myself: 'Here is what an historic race can do if they have a clear field, a high purpose, and a resolute will.' "

Already I had now received more education than most young white men, having been almost continuously in school from the age of six to twenty-two. But I did not yet feel prepared. I felt that to cope with the new and extraordinary situations then developing in the United States and the world I needed to go further and that as a matter of fact I had just well begun my training in knowledge of social conditions.

I revelled in the keen analysis of William James, Josiah Royce, and young George Santayana. But it was James with his pragmatism and Albert Bushnell Hart with his research method who turned me back from the lovely but sterile land of philosophic speculation to the social sciences as the field for gathering and interpreting that body of fact which would apply to my program for the Negro. As an undergraduate, I had talked frankly with William James about teaching philosophy, my major subject. He discouraged me, but not by any means because of my record in his classes. He used to give me "A's" and even "A-plus," but as he said candidly, there is "not much chance of anyone earning a living as a philosopher." He was repeating just what Chase of Fisk had said a few years previously.

I knew by this time that practically my sole chance of earning a living combined with study was to teach, and after my work with Hart in United States history I conceived the idea of applying philosophy to an historical interpretation of race relations. In other words, I was trying to take my first steps toward sociology as the science of human action. It goes without saying that no such field of study was then recognized at Harvard or came to be recognized for twenty years after. But I began with some research in Negro history and finally at the suggestion of Hart, I chose the suppression of the African slave trade to America as my doctor's thesis. Then came the question as to whether I could continue study in the graduate school. I had no resources in wealth or friends. I applied for a fellowship in the graduate school of Harvard, was appointed Henry Bromfield Rogers Fellow for a year, and later the appointment was renewed; so that from 1890 to 1892, I was a fellow in Harvard University, studying history and political science and what would have been sociology if Harvard had yet recognized such a field.

I finished the first draft of my thesis and delivered an outline of it at the seminars of American history and political economy December 7, 1891. I received my master's degree in the spring. I was thereupon elected to the American Historical Society and asked to speak in Washington at their meeting in December, 1892. The *New York Independent* noted this among the "three best papers presented," and continued:

> The article upon the "enforcement of the Slave Laws" was written and read by a black man. It was thrilling when one could, for a moment, turn his thoughts from listening to think that scarcely thirty years have elapsed since the war that freed his race, and here was an audience of white men listening to a black man—listening, moreover, to a careful, cool, philosophical history of the laws which had not prevented the enslavement of his race. The voice, the diction, the manner of the speaker were faultless. As one looked at him, one could not help saying, "Let us not worry about the future of our country in the matter of race distinctions."

I had begun with a bibliography of Nat Turner and ended with a history of the suppression of the African slave trade to America; neither would need to be done again, at least in my day. Thus in my quest for basic knowledge with which to help guide the American Negro, I came to the study of sociology, by way of philosophy and history rather than by physics and biology. After hesitating between history and economics, I chose history. On the other hand, psychology, hovering then on the threshold of experiment under Muensterberg, soon took a new orientation which I could understand from the beginning.

Already I had made up my mind that what I needed was further training in Europe. The German universities were at the top of their reputation. Any American scholar who wanted preferment went to Germany for study. The faculties of Johns Hopkins and the new University of Chicago were beginning to be filled with German Ph.D.'s, and even Harvard, where Kuno Frank had long taught, had imported Muensterberg. British universities did not recognize American degrees and French universities made no special effort to encourage American graduates. I wanted then to study in Germany. I was determined that any failure on my part to become a recognized American scholar must not be based on lack of modern training.

I was confident. So far I had met no failure. I willed and lo! I was walking beneath the elms of Harvard—the name of allurement, the college of my youngest, wildest visions! I needed money; scholarships and prizes fell into my lap—not all I wanted or strove for, but all I needed to keep me in school. Commencement came, and standing before governor, president, and grave, gowned men, I told them certain truths, waving my arms and breathing fast! They applauded with what may have seemed to many as uncalled-for fervor, but I walked home on pink clouds of glory! I asked for a fellowship and got it. I announced my plan of studying in Germany, but Harvard had no more fellowships for me. A friend, however, told me of the Slater Fund and that the Board was looking for colored men worth educating.

No thought of modest hesitation occurred to me. I rushed at the chance. It was one of those tricks of fortune which always seem partly due to chance. In 1882, the Slater Fund for the education of Negroes had been established and the board in 1890 was headed by ex-President R. B. Hayes. Ex-President Hayes went down to Johns Hopkins University, which admitted no Negro students, and told a "darkey" joke in a frank talk about the plans of the fund. The *Boston Herald* of November 2, 1890, quoted him as saying: "If there is any young colored man in the South whom we find to have a talent for art or literature or any special aptitude for study, we are willing to give him money from the education funds to send him to Europe or give him advanced education." He added that so far they had been able to find only "orators." This seemed to me a nasty fling at my black classmate, Morgan, who had been Harvard class orator a few months earlier.

The Hayes statement was brought to my attention at a card party one evening; it not only made me good and angry but inspired me to write ex-President Hayes and ask for a scholarship. I received a pleasant reply saying that the newspaper quotation was incorrect; that his board had some such program in the past but had no present plans for such scholarships. I responded referring him to my teachers and to others who knew me, and intimating that his change of plan did not seem to me fair nor honest. He wrote again in apologetic mood and said that he was sorry the plan had been given up, that he recognized that I was a candidate who might otherwise have been given attention. I then sat down and wrote Mr. Hayes this letter:

May 25, 1891

Your favor of the 2nd. is at hand. I thank you for your kind wishes. You will pardon me if I add a few words of explanation as to my application. The outcome of the matter is as I expected it would be. The announcement that any agency of the American people was willing to give a Negro a thoroughly liberal education and that it had been looking in vain for men to educate was to say the least rather startling. When the newspaper clipping was handed me in a company of friends, my first impulse was to make in some public way a categorical statement denying that such an offer had ever been made known to colored students. I saw this would be injudicious and fruitless, and I therefore determined on the plan of applying myself. I did so and have been refused along with a "number of cases" beside mine.

As to my case, I personally care little. I am perfectly capable of fighting alone for an education if the trustees do not see fit to help me. On the other hand the injury you have—unwittingly I trust—done the race I represent, and are not ashamed of, is almost irreparable. You went before a number of keenly observant men who looked upon you as an authority in the matter, and told them in substance that the Negroes of the United States either couldn't or wouldn't embrace a most liberal opportunity for advancement. That statement went all over the country. When now finally you receive three or four applications for the fulfillment of that offer, the offer is suddenly withdrawn, while the impression still remains.

If the offer was an experiment, you ought to have had at least one case before withdrawing it; if you have given aid before (and I mean here toward liberal education—not toward training plowmen) then your statement at Johns Hopkins was partial. From the above facts I think you owe an apology to the Negro people. We are ready to furnish competent men for every European scholarship furnished us off paper. But we can't educate ourselves on nothing and we can't have the moral courage to try, if in the midst of our work our friends turn public sentiment against us by making statements which injure us and which they cannot stand by.

That you have been looking for men to liberally educate in the past may be so, but it is certainly strange so few have heard it. It was never mentioned during my three years stay at Fisk University. President Price of Livingstone [then a leading Negro spokesman] has told me that he never heard of it, and students from various other Southern schools have expressed great surprise at the offer. The fact is that when I was wanting to come to Harvard, while yet in the South, I wrote to Dr. Haygood [Atticus G. Haygood, a leader of Southern white liberals], for a loan merely, and he never even answered my letter. I find men willing to help me thro' cheap theological schools, I find men willing to help me use my hands before I have got my brains in working order, I have an abundance of good wishes on hand, but I never found a man willing to help me get a Harvard Ph.D.

Hayes was stirred. He promised to take up the matter the next year with the board. Thereupon, the next year I proceeded to write the board: "At the close of the last academic year at Harvard, I received the degree of Master of Arts, and was reappointed to my fellowship for the year 1891–92. I have spent most of the year in the preparation of my doctor's thesis on the suppression of the Slave Trade in America. I prepared a preliminary paper on this subject and read it before the American Historical Association at its annual meeting at Washington during the Christmas holidays. . . . Properly to finish my education, careful training in a European university for at least a year is, in my mind and the minds of my professors, absolutely indispensable." I thereupon asked respectfully "aid to study at least a year abroad under the direction of the graduate department of Harvard or other reputable auspices" and if this was not practicable, "that the board loan me a sufficient sum for this purpose." I did not of course believe that this would get me an appointment, but I did think that possibly through the influence of people who thus came to know about my work, I might somehow borrow or beg enough to get to Europe.

I rained recommendations upon Mr. Hayes. The Slater Fund Board surrendered, and I was given a fellowship of seven hundred and fifty dollars to study a year abroad, with the promise that it might possibly be renewed for a second year. To salve their souls, however, this grant was made half as gift and half as repayable loan with five per cent interest. I remember rushing down to New York and talking with ex-President Hayes in the old Astor House, and emerging walking on air. I saw an especially delectable shirt in a shop window. I went in and asked about it. It cost three dollars, which was about four times as much as I had ever paid for a shirt in my life; but I bought it.

Overcoming the
White Man's History

HOWARD N. MEYER

E VERY PHASE of the movement for equal rights has produced
results that have been of benefit to *all* Americans, white
and non-white. The struggle to defend freedom of speech
and press for abolitionists not only won converts to their cause but
aided all dissenters. The neglected education of the children of
the poor whites was ended by the fine work of the biracial
Reconstruction legislatures. The process of restoring the Fourteenth
Amendment to the dimensions originally envisaged by its framers
(a process that has been unfairly called "expansion" even by liberals
who should know better) is one that helps to protect white as well
as black against all forms of legal lynching. The battle of Selma
has contributed not only to the fight for voting rights, but also
to advance the cause of protection for all peaceful protest, on any
subject, by any group.

There has been a thaw of late in one seemingly less dramatic
area that has a far wider potential than its significance to the Negro
alone. Until recent years the mainstream of American history has
appeared to have a frozen white surface. There was a kind of
shadow history underneath, a truth that all Negro scholars knew
and that the uneducated sensed. All but a tiny handful of whites
knew nothing about their real heritage. After the ice was broken in
the fight for justice to the Negro, there began to surface other important and neglected aspects of the indigenous American radical
tradition.

The whole truth about the whole of our past is needed as much
outside the schools as within. The impotence of a minority to
achieve social justice, even when aroused and militant, has recently
prompted talk of "neo-Populism." Yet, one cannot adapt the idea
of Populism to the needs of the present without a fuller understanding of the faults as well as the virtues of the mass insurgency of the

nineties. The gains made by the partisans of the "Negro History" movement open the door to a new hearing for the forgotten rebel voices of the American past. "You realize," as James Baldwin said, "that if *you* are not in the history books, a great many other things must be left out of the history books too."

This was a figure of speech, as Baldwin would be the first to admit, for the grievance has not been merely, or even primarily, the simple *absence* of the Negro from the pages of history. It is a measure of the connection of our educational systems with the forces making for rationalization and perpetuation of racism that primers, science books, and histories long excluded dark faces from the very illustrations. When civil rights became *chic,* it was seriously suggested by one convert that sticker-pictures be provided for insertion, as if this would make things right until the next printing. With respect to American history, the evils that have to be remedied go far beyond the addition of pictures and achievements. It is important that students and the adult mis-educated learn more, much more, than the catalogue of omitted items: such as that Elijah McCoy, whose 1872 invention of an advanced lubricating system fathered the phrase "it's the real McCoy," was the son of fugitive slaves, or that the valor of a black regiment saved Teddy Roosevelt and his Rough Riders from ignominious defeat at San Juan Hill. The omission of such items is more instructive than their content.

The breadth and depth of the idea of "Negro History," as agitated for half a century by a Negro-led organization that never made a front page headline in the white press, is a challenge to the foundation and structure of an entire academic discipline. The Establishment has now blandly but only nominally accepted it. It hopes, perhaps, to contain it and to restrict it to the notion of finding a "place" for the "contribution" of this "minority" to the American heritage. There are other important facets to the Negro History idea that must be integrated within the framework of American History—enough to require a complete overhaul.

The year 1965 marked the Golden Anniversary of the Association for the Study of Negro Life and History, an organization concerning which, I suspect, most white liberals and radicals know very little. Those who have encountered the name of the organization are likely to have pigeon-holed and dismissed it as a purely intra-racial and rather exotic sort of affair, of no more concern to them than is the African Methodist Episcopal Church. One wonders how many university libraries (let alone those of secondary schools) subscribe to its principal publication, the *Journal of Negro History;* one suspects that, at least until relatively recently, even holders of the Ph.D. in history ignored it or failed fully to utilize it. It is also to the point to suggest that few of the popular writers, award-winning or otherwise, of the recent cascade of books on "the problem" had consulted its pages.

The *Journal* is a quarterly publication, produced on a low budget. It has appeared regularly for five decades and its bound volumes, by now, constitute a storehouse crammed with the contributions of Negro and white scholars. There are several broad headings under which this work can be grouped, long neglected in past United States historical writing and still omitted in text writing and most popularizations. These categories would include:

(a) the extent to which the "American heritage" consists of the oppression of the Negro—a picture that must be drawn in all its grim details to understand the residual effects of that oppression on both Negro and white;

(b) the scope and character of the resistance to that oppression, both within and without the ranks of its victims; and especially the advantages to all Americans of the struggle for the equality of the Negro;

(c) the degree to which the work of the white historian of the past—in some cases of the present—has itself been a tool of oppression (One may include in this category some fascinating passages of legal history, such as found in an exposé in one *Journal* piece, of the fraudulent miscitation of authorities in the prevailing opinion in *Plessy* v. *Ferguson.*);

(d) the fact, in all of its ramifications, that Africa is our mother country as much as England and Europe; that there is blended in our culture, in varying degrees in every branch, an African heritage that is no less significant than that of the "West"; that there is as much to be recalled with pride in the histories of the African tribes as in the European.

The Association for the Study of Negro Life and History, the *Journal* and a younger, less scholarly, *Bulletin,* as well as many other publications of the Association, were all launched by one man, Carter G. Woodson. Holder of the Ph.D. from Harvard

('12), this son of slaves had worked in coal mines in his native West Virginia as a boy and entered his first formal school at the age of twenty, before embarking on an academic career that was to win him the post of Dean in two colleges. The promise of a career of advancement within the ranks of the black bourgeoisie did not tempt him further, after he had become possessed of a sense of his mission. The year that saw the unveiling of *The Birth of a Nation* as the dramatic embodiment and permanent symbol of the sins of our historiography produced, as it were, the prescription for the antidote.

The point that Woodson perceived was that racism, as the product of an aggregate of false beliefs about a people, could be combatted best by the proof and publication of the truths that would dispel those beliefs. The dedicated energy that almost single-handedly seemed to sustain the A.S.N.L.H. during its early years was nourished by his inspired perception that he was forging an instrument of his people's fight for freedom. There are some intelligent and articulate "civil rights" leaders who do not quite understand this, and who neglect the tool he bequeathed them.

Some scholars and intellectuals, even today, will raise their eyebrows in skeptical disapproval of the suggestion that the white American historian has been a "tool of oppression." Most of these do understand, looking overseas, why the rewriting of history begins, as an implement of thought control, almost immediately after the broadcasting stations have been taken over and the Secret Police reorganized following a power shift. They cannot bring themselves to believe, however, that their own colleagues and predecessors at home have been employed in an indigenous American "Ministry of Truth." Erich Fromm, for one, in discussing Orwell's *1984,* correctly insists that those who see in its treatment of the abuses of history "only another denunciation of Stalinism" are missing the point. The process, Fromm suggests, of distorting the past in an effort to control the future is one that has been taking place continuously in the West. Somehow those who have welcomed a Fulbright's exposure of the self-created myths that imprison popular thinking about foreign affairs are not ready to confront the origin of the stereotypes that inhibit genuine unity among the masses of the poor and that impede an alliance between the poor and lower middle class.

As more and more legislation is enacted with the stated purpose of eliminating discrimination in the way people treat each other, little is done to change the way people think about each other. The moral dividends of direct non-violent action are not at all to be underestimated; one may still validly insist that effects be tackled with some understanding of their causes. Roy Wilkins once pointed out that the caricature of the Negro bequeathed us by *The Birth of a Nation* haunts many of those who react hysterically to the threat of token desegregation in the South or intrusions upon "neighborhood" school patterns in the North. Those who discuss "next steps" in the civil rights revolution are sometimes inattentive to the causes of the backward steps occurring in their presence.

The activity of the lay section of the Negro History movement—which may be described as centered within the chapters of the A.S.N.L.H., augmented by an active Chicago-based group called the Amistad Society (after a slave ship whose cargo mutinied and won) as well as a number of NAACP and CORE chapters—has consisted in transmuting the work of scholars to an agitational level. They have battled the belief in Negro inferiority that is rooted in the concept of an inferior past performance. The principal source of the documentation, by fact and analysis, that has equipped the movement to challenge school boards and text book manufacturers has been the publication of papers in the *Journal of Negro History.* These provide as well the material and much of the inspiration for the current neo-revisionist school of American historiography. What tends to distinguish historians of this new school from their predecessors and colleagues is a willingness to accept the premise that the Negro is and always has been entirely human.

Until the "new" school began to develop in the last two decades, the work that Woodson and his followers (able scholars like Charles H. Wesley, Saunders Redding, Rayford W. Logan, Lawrence D. Reddick, Benjamin Quarles, John Hope Franklin, and others less well-known) did was to create a "Negro History" that was itself an involuntarily segregated product—separate from the American history of which it was entitled to be an integral part. The white school administrator and teacher, editor and publisher—all conspired to force this artificially separate development of what was obviously not a separate discipline. This co-existence of "two histories" has survived almost completely on the secondary school level, whence the dropouts and high school graduates who enter adult life, even today, with racist notions.

The injustices, the inaccuracies, the distortions, the omissions that have been the targets of the Negro History movement have by no means been confined to the period of the First Reconstruction. They are, and long have been, focused on the 1865–77 period for functional reasons that make the analogy to Orwell painfully valid. The perfectly ghastly course that race relations took in the United States, from about 1875 onward, required nothing less than the nullification of the Fourteenth and Fifteenth Amendments. Even the Thirteenth Amendment had been violated in spirit, for as Clarence Darrow suggested in a speech six decades ago (and the SNCC kids are even finding in some backwaters today), the condition of the Negro had become worse by 1900, in some ways, than it was in 1860.

For a society to condone what is evil is inconceivable; it must be disguised and perhaps portrayed as a positive good. To induce a nation to accept the non-enforcement of the Fifteenth Amendment, its people had to be led to believe that enfranchisement had been unfortunate, even vicious. When inequality was being institutionalized, in violation of the Fourteenth Amendment's assurances of equality, the architects of the Fourteenth Amendment had to be denigrated. This was effectively done by white historians from Rhodes to Bowers (and even later) who depicted the Republican radicals in the language of their foes of the sixties: vindictive, self-seeking, and unscrupulous, or vain theorists who were windbags to boot. They compounded their offense by making Orwellian unpersons of Frederick Douglass and the Southern Negro statesmen who emerged after the Civil War, and the black regiments that helped win the war amendments.

Never had such twin images of evil as the abolitionist and the carpetbagger been created by historians. This was an essential part of establishing that the Negro was unfit to be a participant in a democracy and of perpetuating that exclusion. Even the bright, young, and somewhat "radical" historians who are now helping to demolish the myths about the history of our race relations cannot quite bring themselves to admit that their predecessors were bigots. They indulge in a variety of ingenious speculation and psychologizing in attempted explanation of the injustices that are being eroded by current revisionism.

Justice not only to the Negro but to the white man of integrity and conscience has been the object of the research and agitation of the Negro History Movement. The battle against anti-Negro history turned the corner with the publication in 1935 of W. E. B. DuBois's *Black Reconstruction,* a book that had a shattering impact in its day, and that still has a passionate freshness and vitality that make the current neo-revisionists look pallid. One wonders whether it was a McCarthyite hang-over that prevented the reviewers of a most notable recent work, *The Peculiar Institution,* from mentioning DuBois (the old man joined the Communist Party at ninety-three after a flirtation of some years). Furthermore, it was unjust of Kenneth Stampp, the author of that work, to dismiss *Black Reconstruction* as "naive" and "disappointing."[1]

The Rosenwald Fund aided DuBois's work in the thirties. For the most part, however, even now when everybody wants to be seen in the act, the wealthy foundations that like to be thought of as the "angels" of the Movement and that have been prodigal in grants to way-out poets and the like have not supported the efforts of the A.S.N.L.H. One is prompted to suggest that the reason for the abstention is the truly radical character of the search for the truth in race relations history. The men who control the coffers are likely to conclude that their institutions are not threatened as much by direct action street demonstrations as they would be by a widespread revelation that as a nation we have been living on lies; that what has until now been accepted as the American heritage is permeated with falsehood and mendacity.

In the recent decades of the developing Civil Rights Revolution, the National Association for the Advancement of Colored People,

[1] One of the most satisfactory evaluations is that of John Hope Franklin in an address, as yet unpublished, delivered at a February, 1964, memorial meeting to DuBois that was held at Carnegie Hall: "Since the publication of *Black Reconstruction* American historiography has not been the same and the study of reconstruction can never be the same again. The mark he left is indeed indelible. One sees in it the beginning of the estrangement that was to become complete before his death. One suspects that the review of this period of the nation's history revealed to him a depth of human perfidy here that left him with a sense of helplessness and hopelessness." *Black Reconstruction* was added to the "model" White House library at the suggestion of this writer and has been re-issued in paperback by Meridian Books.

the American Council on Education, the Anti-Defamation League, and others joined the fight that had at the beginning been waged virtually alone by the A.S.N.L.H. (One should say that the street demonstrations and other protests launched by NAACP against the original distribution of *The Birth of a Nation* were a phase of the "Negro History" fight.) The academic community did not respond very promptly, nor did the school administrators, whose faults were the most grievous, and whose twin problems—revising curricula and re-training teachers—were almost insuperable. The resistance to change could not last indefinitely in the face of the pressures of national self-criticism.

The pitch of protest from local and state organizations began to break into the white press in the 1960's. In Chicago, in August, 1963, a new note in street demonstrations was struck as the Amistad Society sponsored the picketing of the Chicago Board of Education by one hundred students and teachers. Their slogans: "Include the Negro in History," "Is History White?" "We've all been brainwashed." Said one demonstrator: "We want Negro history as part of American history, not as a separate unit." The Berkeley chapter of CORE sponsored a study by six University of California historians whose findings were that the school textbooks most widely used in California contained distortions of history that "help perpetuate and intensify the pattern of racial discrimination." The result, they declared, is to "reinforce notions among whites of their superiority." Carter G. Woodson was about to become a man who overcame, fifteen years after his death.

Recognition of the evils has been followed, ever so slowly, by grudging concessions to some of the demands of the protesters. One notable initial breakthrough was the publication, in response to the protests of the Detroit NAACP chapter, of a seventh-grade pamphlet supplement, "The Struggle for Freedom and Rights: Basic Facts About the Negro in American History." This was followed by the appearance during 1964 of identically titled, lengthy booklets *for teachers* in New York City and the District of Columbia: "The Negro in American History." Patchwork changes have been noted in the new editions of the thick, expensive, hardbound publications that provide the profit that explains Wall Street's interest in the textbook industry. (One editor in a top company told me, "We don't call them books; we call them products.")

I have published elsewhere a more detailed critique of the initial three pamphlet supplements, particularly the New York School Board's effort, which questions why and by whom a sentence was inserted praising existing texts, and of the separate and not very equal quality of the effort to date.[2] The principal deficiency of the response until now is the failure to face up to the necessary restructuring (not merely reconstruction) of basic thinking on the subject of what our history is about: a sample of what I mean is that we must look upon Charles Sumner, not Webster/Clay/Calhoun, as the focus of attention for the middle of the nineteenth century.

In the Introduction to his recent *The Anti-Slavery Vanguard,* Martin Duberman found it "depressing" to note that the contemporary writers he presents have often quoted "from past writings and speeches which repeat almost word for word arguments and attitudes still current today." I do not think he would have found it depressing so much as instructive if he had a full sense of the scope and the potential of the "Negro History" idea as an instrument of liberation from the fetters of prejudice produced by past scholarly malpractice. Similarly, I do not find it "depressing" that Charles Edward Russell emphasized, writing in 1910, that poverty was difficult to arouse people about because of its invisibility: "Year in and year out, unless I go to seek them," wrote Russell, "I shall see practically no persons that do not have enough to eat, enough to wear, and are not comfortably housed; for so is the world arranged." His book was entitled *Why I Am a Socialist.* There are significant conclusions to be drawn from the fact that so few liberals or radicals are aware that the concept of the invisibility of poverty is not a recent, sensational discovery.

The thoroughgoing re-excavation of our past that the Negro History lesson should inspire can extend, too, to the virtually unanimous agreement of all the good writers of the country, who united a decade before Russell's book was published, as Van Wyck Brooks has told us, to argue "that America had no right to hold subject states, or to crush a republic—or to take over the title of a dispossessed tyrant." Those who question the involvement of civil rights leaders in the effort to turn toward peace need to be reminded

[2] See "Tokens of Truth," *Integrated Education,* #13 (February/March 1965), Integrated Education Associates, Chicago, Ill., 60604. The same journal carried the six-Professor Berkeley CORE report, #11, October/November 1964.

of the militant response of the surviving abolitionists at the turn of the century, in joining the one-hundred per cent American "Anti-Imperialist League" that came into being to fight the suppression of the Philippine Insurrection.[3]

One of the finest personal portraits in the *New York Times* "Man in the News" series was published on March 26, 1965, during the march from Selma to Montgomery. Selected to symbolize the marchers and the Alabama Freedom Fighters who may have begun the ending of the nullification of the Fifteenth Amendment was a Negro named Albert Turner, who had given up a fairly prosperous situation as a bricklayer to go into voter registration work. Interviewed by the *Times*, Mr. Turner was more relevant than I could be in summarizing the need for the truthful integration of America's heritage.

"In school I learned the white man's history," Mr. Turner says.

Reconstruction was presented as a bad thing and the fact that there were Negro voters and Negro officials in the Alabama of the eighteen-seventies was not mentioned. The youth learned that by outside reading, although he "sort of knew it was true all the time."

"You can learn a lot from history," Mr. Turner says. "We know now that you can't change the political system from above, because it produces leaders that are always trying to sell you wooden nickels. The movement has got to be rooted in the people."

[3] As instructive as their protest was the response of a Massachusetts pro-Imperialist of 1900 who defended the slaughter of the natives because of the strategic importance of control of the Southeast Asian region in relation to "the richest prize . . . the vast markets of China." His name was Henry Cabot Lodge.

The Pulitzer Prize
Treatment of Charles Sumner

LOUIS RUCHAMES

THE SUBVERSION of the character of a founding father of American civil equality should not be taken lightly—especially during the era of the Freedom Riders. When such subversion is honored by a Pulitzer award, there is great cause for concern.

At the end of the Civil War, Charles Sumner of Massachusetts was regarded by many as one of the nation's foremost statesmen, perhaps, as George F. Hoar described him, "the greatest American statesman since the Revolutionary time." Scholar, humanitarian, and senator from 1851 to his death in 1874, Sumner contributed magnificently to some of the most important social causes of his day: the abolition of slavery, prison reform, public education, and international peace. His arguments in 1849 before the Supreme Court of the Commonwealth on behalf of integration in the public schools of Boston anticipated the reasoning of the Supreme Court of the United States in 1954. He helped to organize the antislavery Whigs and to found the Republican Party. He was the chief spokesman for the slave in the Senate during the years immediately preceding the Civil War. During the war he was the recognized leader of the radical Republicans in the Senate; as chairman of the Senate Foreign Relations Committee, no one played a more important role in preventing embroilment with England and France. After the war he was the principal architect of Congressional Reconstruction in the South. He was one of the early proponents of the eight-hour day. He was a key figure in the acquisition of Alaska and gave that territory its name. "No death," wrote Edward L. Pierce, his foremost biographer, "except that of Lincoln—it was a common remark at the time—had for a long period so touched the popular heart."

Despite these achievements, Sumner's reputation has grown dim. The passage of fifty years since his last biography provides a measure of his declining status in American history. Even when he is discussed, his virtues are transformed into their opposites. The outspoken enemy of every form of injustice, the advocate of international peace, the devoted friend of the slave and the free Negro, has become in the writings of some modern historians an "eerie, evil genius . . . spinning tenuous spider-webs of far-fetched theory about Negro equality"—a "complete doctrinaire." Yet these judgments are unable to wipe out the contrary opinions of many outstanding men of his day—of Emerson, who said of him, "I never knew so white a soul"; or of Theodore Parker, who saw him as "the senator with a conscience." A contemporary historian of American law has called him "New England's greatest Senator."

The appearance of David Donald's *Charles Sumner and the Coming of the Civil War,** a study employing new sources of information which have been made public during the past half century, offers a fresh opportunity to reappraise the conflicting claims concerning Sumner's life and his role in American history. Donald brings to his task notable qualifications. He is a historian of note, and professor of history at Princeton University. His knowledge of Sumner's life is based upon years spent in diligent study of thousands of letters and other manuscripts in the Sumner Collection at Harvard and elsewhere. Yet as one studies his work there comes to mind the caution sounded by another historian, Arthur Reed Hogue, who a decade ago edited Carl Schurz's unfinished biography of Sumner: "An objective view of Sumner was, and still is, difficult to obtain. The embers of those Civil War controversies still glow in the United States affecting, among others, the judgments of trained historians. The issues which men of Sumner's day argued can still, on occasion, become current issues, arousing century-old prejudices whenever they come into debate. Such prejudices are often, in fact, so deeply ingrained as to go unrecognized by those who possess them. The result is that when men like Sumner are introduced for discussion their real personalities are completely obscured in the smoke and dust raised by conflicting prejudices. . . . Charles Sumner . . . needs to be studied without prejudice. . . ."

Donald, unfortunately, is both prejudiced and apparently unaware of his prejudice. "Certainly I started my research without conscious preconceptions or partialities"—so he assures the reader

* Alfred A. Knopf, New York, 1960. This is the first volume of a projected two-volume biography.

in the preface to the present work. A glance at his biography of William Herndon, Lincoln's law partner, published in 1948, as he began his research into Sumner's life, reveals the opposite. There he characterizes Sumner as "the pompous Massachusetts senator with his ornate oratory and his affectation of grandeur," "the arrogant Massachusetts solon," and he observes about the address for which the Southerner Brooks assaulted Sumner in the Senate that "In spite of its perfumed quotations from the classics, the speech reeked of the sewer."

Joined to this initial antipathy toward Sumner is an attitude toward slavery which fails to perceive its horrors and which renders it difficult for him to understand the deep hostility of Sumner and other antislavery leaders toward the "peculiar institution." Apparently Donald had some pangs of conscience in the matter, for in the book before us he feels impelled to assure the reader on this score. "In particular," he writes, "I hope that no one will accuse me of sympathizing with Negro slavery because I have not interjected a little moral discourse after each of Sumner's orations to the effect that he was on the side of the angels. Surely in the middle of the twentieth century there are some things that do not need to be said." If so, one wonders about those earlier comments in the Herndon biography in which he condemns Herndon's "intolerance" toward slavery: "But for the most part Herndon had the intolerance of a man whose knowledge comes entirely from books. He knew all about slavery. . . . But did he really know slavery? . . . It never occurred to him that slavery was something more than organized oppression, that the plantation was a way of life." Although Donald is not nearly so frank on this subject in his current biography, his judgments of the antislavery leaders and of various issues in which they were involved seem to stem from his inability to share their abhorrence of slavery as an indefensible evil.

A third significant characteristic of Donald's thinking is his concept of the ideal statesman. This concept, an inarticulate major premise of the present volume, is explicitly set forth in his collection of essays entitled *Lincoln Reconsidered,* published in 1956, where he notes that "Perhaps the secret of Lincoln's continuing vogue is his essential ambiguity. He can be cited on all sides of all questions. 'My policy,' he used to say, 'is to have no policy.' " This "fundamental opportunism," Donald asserts approvingly, "is characteristic of major American political leaders from Jefferson to Franklin D. Roosevelt. Our great Presidents have joyously played the political piano by ear, making up the melody as they went." The proper answer to the demand that historians teach "American values," he characteristically affirms, is to heed the "nonideological approach" of Abraham Lincoln, "whose one dogma was an absence of dogma." One may well take issue with Donald's characterization of Jefferson, Lincoln, and Roosevelt as opportunists. But the crucial question is: How can a historian whose standards of statesmanship are the apotheosis of opportunism do justice to a statesman, the essence of whose life was a rejection of opportunism and a devotion to principle? To make plain that Donald does considerable injustice to Sumner and in many ways distorts the meaning of his life is the object of the following remarks.

DONALD ENTITLES THE FIRST CHAPTER of his book "A Natural Coldness," and attributes that quality to the young Sumner. In his zeal to demonstrate coldness, he does some curious things to the facts. One example will suffice. Referring to the death of Sumner's twin sister, Matilda, he observes that when she died Sumner "coolly recalled the anecdote of the Persian matron, who, told by her monarch that she could 'save from death *one* of her family and relatives,' chose to sacrifice husband and children in order to save her old and decrepit father, 'saying that another husband and other children she might have, *but another father never.*'" When read apart from their context in the letter in which they originally appeared and in conjunction with the paragraph which follows them in Donald's book, these words seem to show Sumner's heartless disregard for his twin sister. The meaning of the letter, however, is quite different. For it was written to Charlemagne Tower in reply to a letter of condolence on the death of Matilda, which had in turn revealed the death of Charlemagne's father. In trying to console his friend, Sumner wrote:

> Permit me to join with you in grief. I offer you my sincere sympathies. The loss of a father I can only imagine: may God put far distant the day when that affliction shall come over me. . . .
>
> You kindly mentioned my sister. I owe every one thanks and regard who speaks of her with respect. But my grief, whatever it may be, has not the source that yours has. A

Persian matron, oppressed by a tyrant king, had the leave of the monarch to save from death *one* of her family and relatives. She had many children and a husband; but she had also a father, old and decrepit. Him she selected and saved, saying that another husband and other children she might have, *but another father never.* I have lost a sister; but I still have other sisters and brothers, entitled to my instructions and protection. I strive to forget my loss in an increased regard for the living. . . .

The reader may judge whether these words reflect a "natural coldness" in Sumner's character. A more representative description of Sumner's personality as a youth (not cited by Donald) is that of the Reverend Dr. Samuel M. Emery of Newburyport, Sumner's schoolmate, who wrote: "He was cordial to all, having a kind word for all, and ready for a joke with any one whom he chanced to meet. . . . He was more dignified than most young students, but genial at all times; and would perpetrate a joke with as much gusto as any others of his class."

Donald's attitude toward Sumner is clearly shown in his interpretation of Sumner's relationship toward a succession of older men who allegedly served as father substitutes, and whom he supposedly adored and slavishly imitated. These were Justice Joseph Story, the Reverend William Ellery Channing, and John Quincy Adams. That Sumner had a warm relationship with each of these men is true, and that each loved him as a father would a son is no less true. But Donald perverts this relationship into a caricature when he portrays Sumner as capable only of aping each of these men, echoing their words whenever he spoke, and incapable of independent thought or action not patterned after something that one of them had said or done.

In describing Sumner's relationship to Judge Story, his teacher at the Harvard Law School, Donald offers several examples of such slavish imitation. Of Sumner's enthusiasm for Fanny Kemble, he declares that when "Story was charmed by Fanny Kemble, the young English actress who moved Boston to flurries of tears," Sumner "promptly dropped his law studies to attend the theater." One finds no indication here that perhaps the actress had an especial appeal for students generally and for Sumner in particular, that she had entranced many of Sumner's friends, and that Sumner always had a strong interest in the art of public declamation, for which she was justly renowned. That his enthusiasm was hardly a flunkey's response to Judge Story's opinion is obvious in a comment made in later years by Professor William C. Russell of Cornell University, a friend of Sumner's in the early thirties, who wrote that Sumner "was, as much as any of us, infatuated by her acting; and I remember his one day stopping me in the street, and drawing me out of the thoroughfare, and saying, 'Come, Russell, tell me something about Fanny Kemble,' with all the interest of a lover."

Disregarding Sumner's passionate fondness for literature since early childhood, Donald mistakenly ascribes this interest, too, to Judge Story's law school influence. Concerning Sumner's trip to Washington in 1834, he writes that "Sumner obediently made his first visit to Washington in 1834" at the suggestion of Judge Story and Professor Greenleaf of the Harvard Law School. If one recalls Sumner's lifetime hunger for travel, which began in his junior year in college, it is difficult to think of the trip to Washington as the result of a puppet's response. Pierce's explanation that "the love of travel was with Sumner an inherited passion," and that "he had for some time felt a strong desire to visit the national Capital . . . to see and hear the eminent statesmen of the time, and particularly to attend a session of the Supreme Court . . . to see Judge Story, whom he had known so well as professor," is a far more judicious explanation. Not only does Donald insist that Sumner aped Judge Story, he even manages to ascribe their disagreements to a similar cause: Sumner's inability to abandon certain of Story's earlier opinions which the latter no longer believed in. Even Sumner's trip to Europe, in December, 1837, over Judge Story's opposition, was taken, according to Donald, only because the latter had once suggested it. A more reasonable view of their disagreements is that Sumner, as an independent thinker, never permitted his esteem for any person to stand in the way of his own judgment. He accepted what he thought was true in Judge Story's opinions, but never hesitated to reject what he thought was untrue.

During the winter of 1837, Sumner sailed for Europe and remained there several years. Donald's animus toward Sumner is exposed by his comments upon Sumner's views of European life and thought. The Sumner who appears in this part of Donald's portrait is a two-faced character adapting his opinions to what he thinks his correspondent wants to hear, frequently condemning and praising the very same things to different friends. Concerning Sumner's assessment of European jurisprudence, Donald writes that he was "favorably predisposed toward continental jurisprudence" and "was impressed by what he saw. To his older friends at home, to be sure, he reported his opinions on the French law with circumspection." While condemning French law and lawyers to Judge Story, who had a poor view of the French legal system, to his lawyer friend, George Hillard, "Sumner wrote his true opinion that the French Code, so grossly calumniated in America, offered 'much greatly to admire.' " The fact is that this alleged differentiation between older and younger friends, and between Story and Hillard, is nowhere apparent in Sumner's letters. The comments to Hillard which Donald quotes are made in a letter of April, 1838. In this same letter, while praising the French Code, Sumner speaks harshly of Dupin, a leading French lawyer. True it is that at the end of March he had written to Story that a French court is "a laughable place," yet at the end of April, in still another letter to Story, he concludes: "I have attended court every day, and am delighted with the operation of the French penal code. There are many particulars in which they have immeasurably the start of us. . . ."

In view of Donald's tendency to misinterpret Sumner's views by failing to read his letters carefully, another example may be cited in passing. At one point he writes that, when in England, Sumner "thought poorly of Lord John Russell, who reminded him of a pettifogging attorney, since he wriggled as he spoke, 'played with his hat [and] seemed unable to dispose of his hands or his feet.' " The opinion in question occurs in a letter written to Story in June, 1838. When read in context quite the opposite emerges: "Lord John Russell rose in my mind the more I listened to him. In person diminutive and rickety, he reminded me of a pettifogging attorney who lives near Lechmere Point. He wriggled round, played with his hat, seemed unable to dispose of his hands or his feet; his voice was small and thin, but notwithstanding all this, a house of upwards of five hundred members was hushed to catch his slightest accents. You listened, and you felt that you heard a man of mind, of thought, and of moral elevation."

Donald's almost willful lack of insight into Sumner's character is revealed in his attempt to explain Sumner's popularity during his European trip. The reasons given are various: "He had come to England at a most opportune time." ". . . the English were in a receptive mood . . . Sumner's letters of introduction initially opened doors for him . . . his own social resources. . . ." The last of these, according to Donald, consisted of Sumner's English descent, his "handsome and personable" appearance, the fact that "everything was delightfully new to him," his "naïveté," which delighted everyone, his quickness in adopting English social conventions, his enthusiasm in doing whatever his English hosts planned for him, his reserve, his discreetness, his interest in promoting the books of his American friends, and almost unreflecting anti-American Anglophilism. Can these reasons account for the lifelong affection which Sumner evoked among the leading statesmen and writers of England? A more plausible explanation of his popularity was given by an Englishwoman, the wife of John Stuart Wortley: "I never knew an American who had the degree of social success he had; owing, I think, to the real elevation and truth of his character, his *genuine* nobleness of thought and aspiration, his kindliness of heart, his absence of dogmatism and oratorical display, his general amiability, his cultivation of mind, and his appreciation of England without any thing approaching to flattery of ourselves or depreciation of his own country."

The months and early years following his return from Europe were unhappy ones for Sumner. Donald attributes this unhappiness in part to Sumner's financial worries and to his "comparative failure at the bar." But most important of all, he suggests, was the fact that "for the first time in his life he was obliged to stand alone, without the guidance and support from some older man who could give direction to his career." Now it is Samuel Gridley Howe who becomes the father figure. Although Sumner and Howe, the prominent humanitarian, became the most intimate of friends during these years, Donald explains that "Howe could not quite fill the place that Sumner's father and later Judge Story had played in his life." Moreover, Howe's marriage and departure for Europe in April, 1843, left Sumner "without that paternal counsel he needed to direct his life."

Amateur psychoanalysis is a dangerous pastime. In this instance, Donald's assumption that the key to an understanding of Sumner's early life is his almost desperate need of a father leads him to an unfortunate juggling of the facts. Thus he writes that "Sumner tried to imitate his friend in his career of bettering society." While it is true that as a result of this friendship Sumner grew interested in

Howe's work with the blind and deaf, Donald is in error when he asserts that "Howe called Sumner's attention to the important work Horace Mann was doing to rejuvenate the public schools of the Commonwealth. . . ." Sumner first met Howe in June, 1837, and their friendship blossomed only after Sumner's return from Europe in 1840. However, Sumner and Mann occupied law offices in the same building as early as 1834. They saw one another frequently, and Sumner undoubtedly knew of Mann's work before he met Howe. As early as June, 1836, Sumner commended Mann in writing as "the President of the Senate of Massachusetts, and a distinguished member of our profession." During the fall of 1837, Mann wrote in his journal: "Dined with C. Sumner to-day, who is going to Europe soon. When he goes, there will be one more good fellow on that side, and one less on this." In Europe, after visiting Victor Cousin at the Sorbonne in March, 1838, Sumner wrote in his Journal: "I described to him Mann's labors and character; he seemed grateful to hear of them, and asked particularly about Mr. Mann."

After insisting that Sumner sought to lean upon Howe as a father substitute, Donald concludes that "Howe resolutely refused to be an older man directing a young friend's career. On the contrary, he insisted that it was he who derived inspiration from Sumner. 'It has never been my lot to know a man more perfectly loyal to truth, right, and humanity,' he assured his friend. 'You are my junior by many years, but to you I owe many of the feeble aspirations which I feel for progress upwards and onwards in my spiritual nature.' " The truth is that Howe never refused to direct Sumner's career, since he was never asked to do so. When he insisted that it was he who derived inspiration from Sumner, he was not pretending, as Mr. Donald seems to imply, but simply stating a fact. A look at the letter from which the above quotation is taken—it was written by Howe on November 7, 1846—indicates the extent of Howe's dependence upon Sumner. The truth is that they were deeply devoted friends whose influence upon one another, despite Howe's greater age, was mutual.

When Donald discusses the relationship between Sumner and William Ellery Channing, the Unitarian minister with whom Sumner formed a close friendship after his return from Europe, he again falls into a pit of his own digging. Applying his dogma of Sumner's extreme imitativeness, he writes: "Where Channing led, Sumner followed. He adopted all of the minister's arguments; he shared his concern over prison reform, education, international peace, and Negro slavery." But Sumner's concern with the above issues and many of his arguments were formed before he had the opportunity to be influenced by Channing's personality. Indeed, Donald's extremism in describing Sumner's so-called aping of Channing is revealed when he insists that from Channing Sumner "borrowed unquestioningly the postulates that 'states and nations . . . were amenable to the same moral law as individuals' and, therefore, that *what is wrong for an individual is wrong for a state.'*" One would expect that such a judgment as "he borrowed unquestioningly" would be bolstered by documentation. Yet the footnote to this remark simply refers to a speech by Sumner, a scrutiny of which reveals that the words attributed to him are simply his approval of Channing's belief. From nothing in the speech could anyone conclude that Sumner had received the idea *unquestioningly* from Channing.

Nor does Donald offer any substantiation, other than the fact that their views coincided, for such statements as, "From Channing . . . Sumner derived his view of the proper role of the reformer," or "[Sumner was] convinced by Channing" that "'man, as an individual, is capable of indefinite improvement, so long as he lives.'" Indeed, the latter remark is a quotation from Sumner's address of 1848 on "The Law of Human Progress." It is significant that nowhere in this address does Sumner mention Channing, although he quotes others who contributed to the idea of progress—Pascal and Turgot, for instance.

In 1845, Sumner, delivering Boston's annual Fourth of July oration, entitled "The True Grandeur of Nations," discussed the theme of international peace, and created a national and international sensation by his denunciation of war and preparations for war. In his obsession with Sumner's "extremism," Donald refers to this address as "the earliest public demonstration of Sumner's propensity for what might be called illogical logicality, his tendency to extend a principle to its utmost limits. Given the assumption that war is bad, Sumner thought it followed that all wars are equally bad." Again the biographer fails to give a balanced analysis of Sumner's position. He omits, for instance, Sumner's basic argument, which takes its point of departure from the nature of modern war: "Whatever may have been its character in periods of barbarism, or when invoked to repel an incursion of robbers or pirates—the enemies of the human race—War becomes in our day, *among all the nations who are parties to the existing International Law,* simply a mode of litigation, or of deciding a Lis Pendens, between these nations. It is a mere TRIAL OF RIGHT. It is an appeal for justice to Force." As Sumner further notes, his argument "excludes the question, so often agitated, of the right of revolution, and that other question, on which the friends of Peace sometimes differ, the right of personal self-defence. It does not in any way involve the question of the right to employ force in the administration of justice, or in the conservation of domestic quiet." Had Donald remembered this point, he would not have stated that "When war came in 1861, America's foremost peace advocate solidly supported the military measures of the Union government," as though Sumner had abandoned his earlier peace principles in supporting the war measures of the North. At no time would the suppression of a slaveholders' rebellion against a legally and democratically constituted government have been, in Sumner's opinion, other than "the right to employ force in the administration of justice, or in the conservation of domestic quiet."

Although much more might be said about Donald's evaluation of Sumner's arguments against war, there is space here for only one additional comment—upon Sumner's address of 1849, "The War System of the Commonwealth of Nations." Referring to this address, Donald grudgingly admits that "If Sumner made any contribution to the ideas of the peace movement, it was his theory that war should be outlawed through international law." But he then qualifies this admission with the remark that "The difficulties involved in changing international law or in yielding national sovereignty to some international organization never occurred to Sumner. He was concerned with principles not with mechanics." The error here is twofold. Several times during this address Sumner alludes to the difficulties involved in changing international law and in persuading nations to yield their sovereignties. Moreover, he emphasizes the idea that the study of history reveals great obstacles to his plan: "In our aspirations let us not be blind to the lessons of history, or to the actual condition of men, so long accustomed to brute force, that, to their imperfect natures, it seems the only means by which injustice can be crushed." Sumner, indeed, cites the complexity of the task as an argument for setting forth the practical steps required for achieving world peace: ". . . unhappily we cannot—in the present state of human error—expect large numbers to appreciate its [war's] true character, and to hate it with that perfect hatred, which shall cause them to renounce its agency, unless we can offer an approved and practical mode of determining the controversies of nations, as a *substitute* for the imagined necessity of an appeal to the sword. This we are able to do. . . ." He then devotes a substantial part of the address to the presentation of such proposals as a Congress of Nations, a High Court of Judicature, and the establishment of arbitration through formal treaties between nations as a way of eliminating conflict and, in the process, creating a new system of international law.

Following "The True Grandeur of Nations" address and his growing dedication to the causes of peace, prison reform and anti-slavery, Sumner came to be ostracized by Boston's conservative leaders of public opinion and by many others of its higher social and economic strata with whom he had previously been intimate. Donald places the blame for this estrangement on Sumner's personality, suggesting that it was due primarily to his alleged inability to accept criticism and hardly at all to ideological differences: "He started by holding ideas most New Englanders shared. . . . Once he appeared before the public, he was attacked, and the more he was criticized, the more inflexible his opinions became. Carrying his ideas to extremes, he alienated moderate opinion and placed himself, as George Ticknor announced, 'outside the pale of society.'" But Donald does not explain why, if Sumner shared the ideas of most New Englanders, these ideas were initially criticized when Sumner expressed them publicly. Actually, most leaders of society and opinion in Boston did not share Sumner's views on slavery and other issues when he first expressed them in the 1840's. Leonard W. Levy, in his perceptive study, *The Law of the Commonwealth and Chief Justice Shaw,* suggests, using Charles Francis Adams as his source, "that while a shallow veneer of antislavery sentiment had been fashionable among them," this veneer was "without roots either in conviction or in material interests,"—as Adams put it, "mere sentiment." Levy concludes that by mid-century "a great majority of Boston's 'best people' no longer concealed their warmness toward Southern interests."

The difference between Sumner and most of the leaders of New England society was that the latter generally expressed privately any aversion they had to slavery; their public expression was cautiously phrased so as not to offend the slaveholder. On specific issues, as for instance the Fugitive Slave Act of 1850, they were willing to compromise with slavery even where compromise meant increasing its strength. Sumner's opposition, however, was always forthright, on specific as well as on theoretical issues, since his basic aim was to weaken and overthrow the institution. His course could do no other than arouse the enmity of those Bostonians who really wished to maintain the status quo.

Donald's bias is disclosed when he views the conflict between Sumner and the elite of Boston society from the point of view of George Ticknor, the literary historian, an arch-conservative in his political and economic views. Donald suggests, in Ticknor's phrase, that Sumner "placed himself" outside of high society. The implications is that Sumner's exclusion was due to his "extremism" and alleged rigidity rather than to the intolerance of a stratum of society which could brook no opposition to its views. A more likely explanation is suggested by Pierce when he notes that Ticknor, who was an important arbiter of opinion in Boston, "was firm in his conviction against antislavery agitation." "In a society where public opinion governs," Ticknor wrote to Hillard, "unsound opinions must be rebuked; and you can no more do that while you treat their apostles with favor, than you can discourage bad books at the moment you are buying and circulating them." Through failure to discern the ideological source of the conflict between Sumner and Boston's conservatives, or to recognize the aggressive ostracism practiced by many of the latter toward non-conformists, Donald is led to explain the conflict as the result of Sumner's irascibility and rigidity. These he attributes to the "personal disasters and professional failures during the early 1840's" which

> had turned Sumner against the Boston society he once so admired. His inner state of mind was reflected in the rhetoric of his orations, in the frequent images of destruction and mutilation which occurred in his speeches. His references to "Nations, now prostrate on the earth with bloody streams running from their sides," to "Blood! blood! . . . on the hands of the representative from Boston," to the "blood which spurts

from the lacerated, quivering flesh of the slave," are ample, if unintentional, evidence of the deep anger that drove him on.

The intimation of these remarks, that Sumner's strong response to slavery and the war against Mexico was abnormal, to be adequately accounted for by his personal bitterness, is perhaps an index of Donald's insensitivity to the evils of slavery and the unjustness of the Mexican War. For in that speech Sumner was referring to the fact that Robert C. Winthrop, Congressman from Boston, had voted for arms to carry on the war against Mexico. One wonders what was spilt during that war, if not blood? As to blood flowing from the "quivering flesh of the slave," Donald may be referred to the autobiographies of Frederick Douglass and other escaped slaves for evidence as to whether this was hyperbole or fact.

By attributing Sumner's conflict with Boston's conservatives to personal frustrations culminating in hatred and anger, rather than to ideological differences, Donald is unable to explain why Sumner's broken friendships were with those who condemned the anti-slavery agitation or wished to compromise the issue for reasons of economic or political expediency, while his unbroken and deepening friendships for the most part were with those who did not. Nor does he deal with the fact that Sumner sought to maintain friendship with many who disagreed with his views, as, for instance, with Edward Everett, Judge William Kent, Louis Agassiz, and William Prescott. How incorrect he is in his interpretation of this matter is revealed in a passage from the biography of Richard Henry Dana, Jr., by Charles Francis Adams, who writes that at the time

feeling also ran high; and in Boston it ran all one way. . . . An abolitionist was looked upon as a sort of common enemy of mankind; a Free-Soiler was only a weak and illogical abolitionist. . . . The few representatives of the unfashionable side—and in number they were a mere handful—who had a recognized standing in the drawing-rooms of Summer, Park, and Beacon streets were made to feel in many ways the contempt there felt for the cause they espoused. Sumner and Dana, for instance, had long been frequent and favored guests in the house of Mr. Ticknor. After they became pronounced Free-Soilers they soon ceased to be seen there; and, indeed, things went so far that all social relations between them and the family of their former host were broken off. So it was generally.

Sumner became a close friend of John Quincy Adams during the years immediately preceding the ex-President's death in 1848. Donald remarks that Adams "had apparently hardly known Sumner before he delivered 'The True Grandeur of Nations' " in July, 1845. Yet almost two years earlier, in September, 1843, Sumner had written to Lord Morpeth in England: "I have seen old Mr. Adams lately several times. He is very well; and indeed he is strong and more intense than ever in his hatred of slavery. I enclose a recent letter from him on the subject." In discussing Adams's praise of Sumner's "The True Grandeur of Nations," Donald remarks:

> Always responsive to praise, Sumner became Adams's adoring admirer. He had always extolled the ex-President's "unquestioned purity of character, and remarkable attainments, the result of constant industry," but in earlier years, when under the influence of Beacon Hill, he had objected "most strenuously to his manner, and to some of his expressions and topics, as unparliamentary and subversive of the rules and order of debate." Now he rejoiced in the very violence and vituperation with which Adams conducted his congressional campaign against slavery. Whenever the old President was in Quincy, Sumner came out to sit at his feet, and he undiscriminatingly adopted all of Adams's opinions, from his enthusiastic nationalism to his injunction that a statesman should "*Never accept a present.*"

These comments exaggerate both Sumner's early criticism of Adams and his alleged discipleship in later years. The criticism cited above, contained in a letter to Francis Lieber in February, 1842, was not particularly due to the influence of Beacon Hill but to Sumner's belief that the rules of debate in Congress, which he felt that Adams had violated, were "among the great safeguards of liberty, and particularly of freedom of speech." And in the same letter it is more than Adams's "purity of character, and remarkable attainments" that are praised: "His cause was grand. If I had been in the House, I should have been proud to fight under his banners. He has rallied the North against the South; has taught them their rights, and opened their eyes to the 'bullying' (I dislike the word as much as the thing) of the South." In December, 1842, Sumner wrote to Longfellow: "Send, if you have not already, a copy of your 'Slavery Poems' to John Quincy Adams. He deserves the compliment for his earnest advocacy of freedom, and the rights of the North. God bless every champion of the truth! And may man bless the champion also." These are hardly the sentiments of someone writing under the antagonistic influence of Beacon Hill.

Nor did Sumner adopt "undiscriminatingly" in later years "all of Adams's opinions." In 1846, for instance, when, according to Donald, Sumner had already become Adams's intellectual sycophant, Sumner disagreed strongly with Adams's nationalist position in the Oregon dispute. In a letter to Lord Morpeth in March he commented that "Among the persons who have lost character in the Oregon discussions is J. Q. Adams. His course has been eccentric, claiming the whole 54° 40′ . . . and I have been not a little pained to be obliged to withdraw my sympathies from the revered champion of freedom. . . ." In passing, it may be noted that Donald tars Adams with the same brush he uses upon Sumner, when he attributes Adams's praise of Sumner's "The True Grandeur of Nations" and later addresses to Adams's "sheer love of combat," a "suspicious hostility toward State Street," and "bad temper and stubborn disposition." Not a word about Adams's feeling for the suffering of the slave, or for the democracy endangered by the slaveholders and their Northern sympathizers.

Donald offers a detailed study of the efforts of Sumner and other antislavery members of the Whig party, known as Conscience Whigs, to form an antislavery party for the 1848 Presidential election. After the Democrats had nominated proslavery Lewis Cass and the Whigs slaveholder Zachary Taylor, the Conscience Whigs, through Sumner and Charles Francis Adams, issued a call for a convention at Worcester, to which all opposed to both Taylor and Cass were invited. In describing Sumner's hopes for the convention, Donald quotes as his own the opinion of George Hillard, who because of his conservative political views, devotion to the Whig party, and attachment to George Ticknor, had grown somewhat estranged from Sumner: "Sumner, as Hillard cynically observed, expected the union of antislavery factions to produce 'a new political Jerusalem. . . .'" About Sumner's suggestion at the convention that it was time to abandon both old parties and form a new one based upon sincere antislavery convictions, Donald comments: "It was well for Sumner that he had the power of self-deception, for the great crusading army he thought he was organizing was, even in Massachusetts, a mongrel assortment of disgruntled Conscience Whigs, a few Webster followers, furious that their chief had been spurned at Philadelphia, assorted Liberty men, and other disaffected. . . . None of these discords and inconsistencies troubled Sumner; he was marching to Zion."

It may be noted, first, that no one, according to Donald, seems to have been present at the convention out of concern for the slave or for democracy. All were there for personal reasons: they were "disgruntled," "patronage-hungry," and "disaffected." Nor is it true, as Donald suggests, that Sumner expected the convention to march quickstep to Zion. He realized the difficulties which the new movement faced. In his speech at the convention he discussed the likelihood that the new party would fail to elect its candidates. He emphasized that the party was being organized not for immediate but for ultimate political victory. "But it is said," he remarked,

> that we shall throw away our votes, and that our opposition will fail. Fail, sir! No honest, earnest effort in a good cause can fail. It may not be crowned with the applause of men; it may not seem to touch the goal of immediate worldly success, which is the end and aim of so much in life. But it is not lost; it helps to strengthen the weak with new virtue, to arm the irresolute with proper energy, to animate all with devotion to duty, which in the end conquers all. . . . Our example will be the mainspring of triumph hereafter.

When one remembers that out of this convention there ultimately emerged the victorious Republican Party, the reader may decide as to whose judgment is superior: the biographer's or his subject's.

Donald, at one point, assesses the impact of Sumner's increasing antislavery activities during the 1840's upon his early friendship with Charles Felton and George Hillard. Describing their increasing estrangement, he chides Sumner, who, he says, became "increasingly rabid" on antislavery and peace. The characterization of Sumner as "rabid" indicates the biographer's prejudice; one need only say that Sumner was no more rabid in his opposition to slavery than were Boston's leaders of public opinion in their insistence upon compromise with slavery. Indeed, Sumner's views on slavery did not change perceptibly after 1845. His basic political goal was to prevent slavery from spreading to the Territories, and to prohibit it wherever the national government held political power, as in Washington, D.C. Hillard, on the other hand, came increasingly under Ticknor's influence. In 1850, he supported the Fugitive Slave Law and in 1860, the Bell-Everett ticket. It was not that Sumner became increasingly fanatical but that the two friends grew to have less and less in common as their political paths diverged. Yet even here Donald exaggerates the break between the two when he says that Hillard kept up only a "thin, formal relationship" with Sumner. Indeed, since he makes Sumner out to be something of a monster—"In the spring of 1847, when Hillard was seriously ill and confined to his house for eight days, Sumner did not take time to visit him"—it may be noted, as Donald fails to do, that just before Hillard sailed for Europe in 1847 he confided to Sumner his will and other papers while Sumner in turn gave Hillard letters of introduction to English friends. In later years they continued to exchange letters, and their last meeting, in 1873, reveals their deep affection for one another despite their differences.

In describing Sumner's political activities after the election of 1848, Donald attributes to him a demagoguery in his desire to court the favor of the Democrats, which, he implies, was motivated by political ambition. "Shortly after the election of 1848," he writes, "Sumner began making statements he once would have condemned as Jacksonian demagoguery. . . . He grew enthusiastic about the European revolutions of 1848 . . . and hoped that they would destroy the outrageous social and economic injustices that had, to tell the truth, seemed anything but outrageous to him only a few years earlier when he visited England." But the contrary is true. That Sumner had been outraged by the injustices which he had seen ten years earlier in Europe is plain in a letter written to Judge Story in 1838, wherein he describes "the state of things which I find here, where wealth flaunts by the side of the most squalid poverty, where your eyes are constantly annoyed by the most disgusting want and wretchedness. . . ." It is similarly expressed after his return from Europe in 1842 in a letter written to his brother, George, then in London. "Those who know my opinions," Sumner wrote, "know that I saw and felt the plague-spots of England as much as anybody. The government is an oligarchy,—the greatest and most powerful in the history of the world. There is luxury the most surprising side by side with poverty the most appalling. I never saw this in England, I never think of it now, without a shock."

SUMNER WAS ELECTED to the Senate in 1851. During his early months in office he hesitated to take the floor against slavery, although speaking on other issues, to prove to his colleagues and others that his interests extended beyond antislavery. As his silence continued it elicited a growing criticism from his antislavery constituents in Massachusetts. Finally, Sumner did secure the floor and in August, 1852, delivered a powerful antislavery address entitled "Freedom National, Slavery Sectional," which pleased his critics and evoked great praise from antislavery circles. The criticism was resumed during the next session when he again seemed unable to attack slavery. During this period, Donald holds, "Sumner became petulant under these strictures." Strangely enough, the one remark by Sumner which is cited as evidence indicates that Sumner bore the criticism with stoicism rather than petulance. "If among my discouragements," Donald quotes him as writing, "shall be alienation or distrust at home, I will try to bear this, and keep on in my duty." Indeed, because his devotion to the antislavery movement transcended personal considerations, Sumner exercised unusual forbearance toward his most violent critics. To Theodore Parker he wrote on March 28, 1853: "If Phillips, whom I love as an early comrade and faithful man, or Pillsbury, rail at me for my small work in antislavery, I will not reply. To me the cause is so dear that I am unwilling to set myself against any of its champions. I would not add to their burdens by any word of mine." Several other letters written during this period indicate a similar attitude.

Donald's attempt to depict Sumner as testy is intended to prove that a conflict with the political scientist Lieber, which took place at this time, was provoked by Sumner's so-called viciousness. The cause of the conflict is described as follows: "Sore and sensitive, Sumner did not re-examine his own course to see whether he might possibly have been at fault. . . . Nor did he reply directly to his critics. Characteristically, he vented his anger upon a bystander, much as a child in a temper tantrum will beat the wall or the floor." "The bystander" was Francis Lieber, a South Carolina professor originally from Germany, whom Sumner had met in

Washington in 1834, and with whom, from then on, he carried on an intensive correspondence. How, according to Donald, did Sumner vent his anger? Apparently Lieber had protested to Sumner in 1853 against the latter's practice of sending him antislavery material which told of the ill-treatment of Southern slaves by their masters. Sumner replied, says Donald, "that Lieber had no right to complain, as he had become 'the apologist of slavery.'" Lieber retorted with a denial that he was such an apologist and Sumner in turn "replied curtly that he was 'right glad' if indeed Lieber was not a slavery apologist." Lieber, continues Donald, "refused to answer so offensive a communication and broke off the correspondence and the friendship."

There are several points to be made about Donald's narration. First, it seems an exaggeration to refer to Sumner's two replies to Lieber as the venting of "wrath." Nor was there anything of the "innocent" bystander in Lieber's relationship to Sumner. They had been drifting apart for years as a result of their antithetical positions on the subject of slavery, and their final exchange of letters was simply the climax of an ideological conflict of several years' standing. Indeed, Sumner had shown great forbearance in not breaking off the friendship long before 1853, for as Donald admits, when Sumner was elected to the Senate Lieber wrote to Hillard that the victory was "bad for Sumner, for Boston . . . for Congress, for the Union, for the country." He also wrote to Sumner, "I do not rejoice at your election"—hardly the comment of a friend. Moreover, when Sumner, in private correspondence, accused Lieber of being "the apologist of slavery," he was not calumniating an innocent man but simply speaking the truth. Lieber was a slaveholder, and in the letter to Hillard in which he regretted Sumner's election he also wrote, "I detest this whole business and really think that if people must have slaves it is their affair to keep them." When the Liebers visited the Longfellows in 1849, Sumner was present and a very vigorous discussion ensued in which Lieber defended the physical treatment of the Southern Negro. Lieber also condemned any public agitation for the abolition of slavery. If these facts do not constitute an apology for slavery, it is difficult to conceive what would.

Sumner's election in 1851 had come about through a coalition of antislavery Democrats and Conscience Whigs who had formed the

Free-Soil Party. In the election of November, 1853, the coalition that had elected Sumner to office was defeated. The most important issue of this election was the adoption of a revised state constitution, formulated at a convention which had assembled in May of that year. The demand for a new constitution was initiated by the anti-slavery coalition that had elected Sumner; if passed, the new constitution would have weakened the political domination of the Boston conservatives. Among those who opposed it were Charles Francis Adams and Robert Gorham Palfrey, who had been Conscience Whigs and supporters of the coalition. Their attacks helped to defeat the constitution and resulted in a rift with the Free-Soil Party leaders which continued for years. Donald, in discussing this election, remarks that "The recent campaign caused many of the old Conscience Whig group to doubt, as did Adams and Palfrey, Sumner's political morality and to suspect that he lacked 'the main requisite, sagacity and penetration.' "

It is indicative of Donald's one-sidedness that he does not mention existing evidence that Sumner emerged not with diminished but with augmented popularity. While some Conscience Whigs did leave the Free-Soil Party in the wake of Palfrey's and Adams's defection, it is also true that a public reference to Sumner by Adams, which Sumner felt to be derogatory, harmed Adams more than it did Sumner. Referring to certain mutual friends, Adams wrote to Sumner: "They think you unjustly attacked, and they pour out all their indignation against me for it. . . . But the feeling thus engendered may stand you in stead in the career you have before you." Senator Salmon Chase of Ohio thought that Sumner had emerged with greater prestige. "I mourn our loss in Massachusetts," he wrote, "but you individually acquitted yourself most nobly. That is a great consolation to your friends." Mr. Robert Carter, a journalist and scholar then living in Cambridge, wrote to Sumner: "Your popularity was never greater here than now. Everybody applauds your efforts in the late campaign; and the men who were most angry with you in 1852, are foremost in praising your course and your speech on the Constitution."

THE REMAINDER OF THIS biography abounds in other errors of fact and interpretation. In discussing the events preceding the passage of the Kansas-Nebraska Act in 1854, Donald states that following the introduction of the bill by Stephen Douglas, Sumner proposed an amendment reaffirming the Missouri Compromise ban on slavery in the Nebraska territory. He suggests that the amendment "may have inadvertently been a disservice to freedom, as it also alerted Southern senators to the ambiguities of Douglas's proposal." To understand Sumner's purpose, it is necessary to know that immediately following the introduction of the bill by Douglas, and prior to Sumner's amendment, Senator Dixon of Kentucky, a Whig, offered an amendment which explicitly annulled the Missouri Compromise prohibition of slavery in the Territory and legalized slavery there. The amendment was offered because Douglas's bill was believed by Dixon to be ambiguous, and it was to counter Dixon's amendment, as well as the implied pro-slavery provisions of the original bill, that Sumner offered his amendment which affirmed the prohibition against slavery. Nor is Donald fair when he cites only Sumner and Chase as being opposed to the immediate consideration of Douglas's bill. There were others who thought Douglas's haste in requesting almost immediate debate upon his bill unseemly and unjustified. These included Senator Norris of New Hampshire, who was the first to ask for delay with the explanation that "Senators have not yet had time to examine the substitute which he reported from the committee yesterday." Senators Jones of Tennessee and Cass of Michigan, who were hardly political associates of Sumner and Chase, also called for postponement, the latter remarking that "just comity requires" an avoidance of "precipitancy."

Donald's treatment of the discussion of Kansas affairs in the Senate, which began in March, 1856, is replete with so many half-truths that it would take a book to refute them all. The key to his presentation is a refusal to attribute any guilt to the South for the outrages, murders and invasions which were committed in the Territory by ruffians and politicians from Missouri and other Southern states. "Disorder there was," he writes, "and some bloodshed, but up to 1856 there had been scarcely more of either than was normal on any frontier." He arrives at this conclusion by omitting to mention the invasion of Kansas in 1854 by about 1700 Missourians who voted for a delegate to Congress; another invasion in March, 1855 by 5000 armed Missourians who voted for a pro-slavery legislature and terrorized anti-slavery legislators and voters; and a third in November, 1855 by more than 1200 Missourians. The result was a pro-slavery legislature that voted a code of laws which Oswald Garrison Villard has called "one of the foremost monuments of legislative tyranny and malevolence in the history of this country," and which a pro-slavery leader in Kansas praised as being "more efficient to protect slave property than [the code] of any state in the Union." Only pro-slavery men could hold office or serve as jurors; it was a felony punishable by at least two years' imprisonment to deny the legality of slavery in Kansas, and death was the penalty for creating dissatisfaction among slaves. To say that all this was no more than normal on any frontier is a travesty of the truth.

Donald, in closing his eyes to the repeated pro-slavery invasions of Kansas, is unable, apparently, to believe that the Republicans were serious in charging that the pro-slavery legislature had been elected by fraudulent means, for he remarks that the difference on the Kansas issue between the Democrats and the Republicans was in their respective attitudes toward popular sovereignty. The Democrats, he asserts, favored popular sovereignty while the Republicans opposed it. Yet the basic charge of the Republicans was that popular sovereignty had never been exercised and that both the legislature and its legislation were fraudulent. The result is that Donald is unable to understand the sense of outrage which overwhelmed Sumner and other Republicans when they were confronted with the Kansas facts and which led them to speak as they did during the debate. To him they were simply hysterical extremists and fanatics and the only way he can account for their attitudes, as in Sumner's case, is to attribute them to personal frustrations of various kinds. The result is neither biography nor history.

During the course of this critique, the concentration has been on the faults of Donald's book rather than on its virtues. This has been done because there has thus far been no really critical evaluation of the volume. Those who have reviewed it have accepted Donald's facts and interpretations and have been led by a certain surface reasonableness into believing it to be a judicious biography. This, joined to the fact that its pages are well written, has resulted in the encomia which have greeted it and, remarkably, in its author's receipt of a Pulitzer award. That the book is well written is true. But it does not present the real Charles Sumner. One does not find in it the indefatigable scholar, the humanitarian willing to lay down his life for his fellow man regardless of color, the warm human being never too busy to help his friends or forgive his enemies, the orator and statesman who ranks with the founding fathers of American democracy.

Through the Prism of Folklore
The Black Ethos in Slavery

STERLING STUCKEY

I T IS NOT EXCESSIVE to advance the view that some historians, because they have been so preoccupied with demonstrating the absence of significant slave revolts, conspiracies, and "day to day" resistance among slaves, have presented information on slave behavior and thought which is incomplete indeed. They have, in short, devoted very little attention to trying to get "inside" slaves to discover what bondsmen thought about their condition. Small wonder we have been saddled with so many stereotypical treatments of slave thought and behavior.[1]

Though we do not know enough about the institution of slavery or the slave experience to state with great precision how slaves felt about their condition, it is reasonably clear that slavery, however draconic and well supervised, was not the hermetically sealed monolith—destructive to the majority of slave personalities—that some historians would have us believe. The works of Herbert Aptheker, Kenneth Stampp, Richard Wade, and the Bauers, allowing for differences in approach and purpose, indicate that slavery, despite its brutality, was not so "closed" that it robbed most of the slaves of their humanity.[2]

[IX, 3, Summer 1968]

[1] Historians who have provided stereotypical treatments of slave thought and personality are Ulrich B. Phillips, *American Negro Slavery* (New York, 1918); Samuel Eliot Morison, and Henry Steele Commager, *The Growth of the American Republic* (New York, 1950); and Stanley Elkins, *Slavery: A Problem in American Institutional and Intellectual Life* (Chicago, 1959).

[2] See Herbert Aptheker, *American Negro Slave Revolts;* Kenneth M. Stampp, *The Peculiar Institution* (New York, 1956); Richard Wade, *Slavery in the Cities* (New York, 1964); and Alice and Raymond Bauer, "Day to Day Resistance to Slavery," *Journal of Negro History,* XXVII No. 4, October, 1942.

It should, nevertheless, be asserted at the outset that blacks could not have survived the grim experience of slavery unscathed. Those historians who, for example, point to the dependency complex which slavery engendered in many Afro-Americans, offer us an important insight into one of the most harmful effects of that institution upon its victims. That slavery caused not a few bondsmen to question their worth as human beings—this much, I believe, we can posit with certitude. We can also safely assume that such self-doubt would rend one's sense of humanity, establishing an uneasy balance between affirming and negating aspects of one's being. What is at issue is not whether American slavery was harmful to slaves but whether, in their struggle to control self-lacerating tendencies, the scales were tipped toward a despair so consuming that most slaves, in time, became reduced to the level of "Sambos."[3]

My thesis, which rests on an examination of folk songs and tales, is that slaves were able to fashion a life style and set of values—an ethos—which prevented them from being imprisoned altogether by the definitions which the larger society sought to impose. This ethos was an amalgam of Africanisms and New World elements which helped slaves, in Guy Johnson's words, "feel their way along the course of American slavery, enabling them to endure. . . ."[4] As Sterling Brown, that wise student of Afro-American culture, has remarked, the values expressed in folklore acted as a "wellspring to which slaves" trapped in the wasteland of American slavery "could return in times of doubt to be refreshed."[5] In short, I shall contend that the process of de-

[3] I am here concerned with the Stanley Elkins version of "Sambo," that is, the inference that the overwhelming majority of slaves, as a result of their struggle to survive under the brutal system of American slavery, became so callous and indifferent to their status that they gave survival primacy over all other considerations. See Chapters III through VI of *Slavery* for a discussion of the process by which blacks allegedly were reduced to the "good humor of everlasting childhood." (p. 132).

[4] I am indebted to Guy Johnson of the University of North Carolina for suggesting the use of the term "ethos" in this piece, and for helpful commentary on the original paper which was read before the Association for the Study of Negro Life and History at Greensboro, North Carolina, on October 13, 1967.

[5] Professor Brown made this remark in a paper delivered before The Amistad Society in Chicago, Spring, 1964. Distinguished poet, literary critic, folklorist, and teacher, Brown has long contended that an aware-

humanization was not nearly as pervasive as Stanley Elkins would have us believe; that a very large number of slaves, guided by this ethos, were able to maintain their essential humanity. I make this contention because folklore, in its natural setting, is of, by, and for those who create and respond to it, depending for its survival upon the accuracy with which it speaks to needs and reflects sentiments. I therefore consider it safe to assume that the attitudes of a very large number of slaves are represented by the themes of folklore.[6]

II

FREDERICK DOUGLASS, commenting on slave songs, remarked his utter astonishment, on coming to the North, "to find persons who could speak of the singing among slaves as evidence of their contentment and happiness."[7] The young DuBois, among the first knowledgeable critics of the spirituals, found white Americans as late as 1903 still telling Afro-Americans that "life was joyous to the black slave, careless and happy." "I can easily believe this of some," he wrote, "of many. But not all the past South, though it rose from the dead, can gainsay the heart-touching witness of these songs."

> They are the music of an unhappy people, of the children of disappointment; they tell of death and suffering and unvoiced longing toward a truer world, of misty wanderings and hidden ways.[8]

---

ness of Negro folklore is essential to an understanding of slave personality and thought.

[6] I subscribe to Alan Lomax's observation that folk songs "can be taken as the signposts of persistent patterns of community feeling and can throw light into many dark corners of our past and our present." His view that Afro-American music, despite its regional peculiarities, "expresses the same feelings and speaks the same basic language everywhere" is also accepted as a working principle in this paper. For an extended treatment of these points of view, see Alan Lomax, *Folk Songs of North America* (New York, 1960), Introduction, p. xx.

[7] Frederick Douglass, *Narrative of the Life of Frederick Douglass* (Cambridge, Massachusetts: The Belknap Press, 1960), p. 38. Originally published in 1845.

[8] John Hope Franklin (ed.), *Souls of Black Folk* in *Three Negro Classics* (New York, 1965), p. 380. Originally published in 1903.

Though few historians have been interested in such wanderings and ways, Frederick Douglass, probably referring to the spirituals, said the songs of slaves represented the sorrows of the slave's heart, serving to relieve the slave "only as an aching heart is relieved by its tears." "I have often sung," he continued, "to drown my sorrow, but seldom to express my happiness. Crying for joy, and singing for joy, were alike uncommon to me while in the jaws of slavery."[9]

Sterling Brown, who has much to tell us about the poetry and meaning of these songs, has observed: "As the best expression of the slave's deepest thoughts and yearnings, they (the spirituals) speak with convincing finality against the legend of contented slavery."[10] Rejecting the formulation that the spirituals are mainly otherworldly, Brown states that though the creators of the spirituals looked toward heaven and "found their triumphs there, they did not blink their eyes to trouble here." The spirituals, in his view, "never tell of joy in the 'good old days'. . . . The only joy in the spirituals is in dreams of escape."[11]

Rather than being essentially otherworldly, these songs, in Brown's opinion, "tell of this life, of 'rollin'' through an unfriendly world!" To substantiate this view, he points to numerous lines from spirituals: "Oh, bye and bye, bye and bye, I'm going to lay down this heavy load"; "My way is cloudy"; "Oh, stand the storm, it won't be long, we'll anchor by and by"; "Lord help me from sinking down"; and "Don't know what my mother wants to stay here fuh, Dis ole world ain't been no friend to huh."[12] To those scholars who "would have us believe that when the Negro sang of freedom, he meant only what the whites meant, namely freedom from sin," Brown rejoins:

> Free individualistic whites on the make in a prospering
> civilization, nursing the American dream, could well have felt
> their only bondage to be that of sin, and freedom to be reli-

---

[9] Douglass, *Narrative,* p. 38. Douglass's view adumbrated John and Alan Lomax's theory that the songs of the folk singer are deeply rooted "in his life and have functioned there as enzymes to assist in the digestion of hardship, solitude, violence (and) hunger." John A. and Alan Lomax, *Our Singing Country* (New York: The Macmillan Co., 1941), Preface, p. xiii.

[10] Sterling Brown, "Negro Folk Expression," *Phylon,* October, 1953, p. 47.

[11] Brown, "Folk Expression," p. 48.

[12] *Ibid.,* p. 47.

gious salvation. But with the drudgery, the hardships, the auction block, the slave-mart, the shackles, and the lash so literally present in the Negro's experience, it is hard to imagine why for the Negro they would remain figurative. The scholars certainly did not make this clear, but rather take refuge in such dicta as: "the slave never contemplated his low condition."[13]

"Are we to believe," asks Brown, "that the slave singing 'I been rebuked, I been scorned, done had a hard time sho's you bawn,' referred to his being outside the true religion?" A reading of additional spirituals indicates that they contained distinctions in meaning which placed them outside the confines of the "true religion." Sometimes, in these songs, we hear slaves relating to divinities on terms more West African than American. The easy intimacy and argumentation, which come out of a West African frame of reference, can be heard in "Hold the Wind."[14]

When I get heaven, gwine be at ease,
Me and my God *gonna do as we please.*

Gonna chatter with the Father, argue with the Son,
Tell um 'bout the world I just come from.[15] (Italics added.)

If there is a tie with heaven in those lines from "Hold the Wind," there is also a clear indication of dislike for the restrictions imposed by slavery. And at least one high heavenly authority might have a few questions to answer. *Tell um 'bout the world I just come from* makes it abundantly clear that some slaves—even when released from the burdens of the world—would keep alive painful memories of their oppression.

If slaves could argue with the son of God, then surely, when

[13] *Ibid.,* p. 48.

[14] Addressing himself to the slave's posture toward God, and the attitudes toward the gods which the slave's African ancestors had, Lomax has written: "The West African lives with his gods on terms of intimacy. He appeals to them, reviles them, tricks with them, laughs at their follies. In this spirit the Negro slave humanized the stern religion of his masters by adopting the figures of the Bible as his intimates." Lomax, *Folk Songs of North America,* p. 463.

[15] Quoted from Lomax, *Folk Songs of North America,* p. 475.

on their knees in prayer, they would not hesitate to speak to God
of the treatment being received at the hands of their oppressors.

> Talk about me much as you please, (2)
> Chillun, talk about me much as you please,
> Gonna talk about you when I get on my knees.[16]

That slaves could spend time complaining about treatment received from other slaves is conceivable, but that this was their only
complaint, or even the principal one, is hardly conceivable. To be
sure, there is a certain ambiguity in the use of the word "chillun"
in this context. The reference appears to apply to slaveholders.

The spiritual, *Samson*, as Vincent Harding has pointed out,
probably contained much more (for some slaves) than mere
Biblical implications. Some who sang these lines from *Samson*,
Harding suggests, might well have meant tearing down the edifice
of slavery. If so, it was the ante-bellum equivalent of today's "burn
baby burn."

> He said, 'An' if I had-'n my way,'
> He said, 'An' if I had-'n my way,'
> He said, 'An' if I had-'n my way,
> I'd tear the build-in' down!'

> He said, 'And now I got my way, (3)
> And I'll tear this buildin' down.'[17]

Both Harriet Tubman and Frederick Douglass have reported
that some of the spirituals carried double meanings. Whether most
of the slaves who sang those spirituals could decode them is another matter. Harold Courlander has made a persuasive case against
widespread understanding of any given "loaded" song,[18] but it

[16] Quoted from Brown, Sterling A., Davis, Arthur P., and Lee, Ulysses,
The Negro Caravan (New York: The Dryden Press, 1941), p. 436.

[17] Vincent Harding, *Black Radicalism in America*. An unpublished
work which Dr. Harding recently completed.

[18] See Harold Courlander, *Negro Folk Music, U.S.A.* (New York:
Columbia University Press, 1963), pp. 42, 43. If a great many slaves did
not consider Harriet Tubman the "Moses" of her people, it is unlikely that
most failed to grasp the relationship between themselves and the Israelites,
Egypt and the South, and Pharaoh and slavemasters in such lines as:
"Didn't my Lord deliver Daniel / And why not every man"; "Oh Mary
don't you weep, don't you moan / Pharaoh's army got drowned / Oh Mary

seems to me that he fails to recognize sufficiently a further aspect of the subject: slaves, as their folktales make eminently clear, used irony repeatedly, especially with animal stories. Their symbolic world was rich. Indeed, the various masks which many put on were not unrelated to this symbolic process. It seems logical to infer that it would occur to more than a few to seize upon some songs, even though created originally for religious purposes, assign another meaning to certain words, and use these songs for a variety of purposes and situations.

At times slave bards created great poetry as well as great music. One genius among the slaves couched his (and their) desire for freedom in a magnificent line of verse. After God's powerful voice had "Rung through Heaven and down in Hell," he sang, "My dungeon shook and my chains, they fell."[19]

In some spirituals, Alan Lomax has written, Afro-Americans turned sharp irony and "healing laughter" toward heaven, again like their West African ancestors, relating on terms of intimacy with God. In one, the slaves have God engaged in a dialogue with Adam:

> 'Stole my apples, I believe.'
> 'No, marse Lord, I spec it was Eve.'
> Of this tale there is no mo'
> Eve et the apple and Adam de co'.[20]

Douglass informs us that slaves also sang ironic seculars about the institution of slavery. He reports having heard them sing: "We raise de wheat, dey gib us de corn; We sift de meal, dey gib us de huss; We peel de meat, dey gib us de skin; An dat's de way dey take us in."[21] Slaves would often stand back and see the tragicomic aspects of their situation, sometimes admiring the swiftness of blacks:

> Run, nigger, run, de patrollers will ketch you,
> Run, nigger, run, it's almost day.

---

don't you weep"; and "Go down Moses / Way down in Egypt-land / Tell old Pharaoh / To let my people go."

[19] Quoted from Lomax, *Folk Songs of North America*, p. 471.

[20] *Ibid.*, p. 476.

[21] Frederick Douglass, *The Life and Times of Frederick Douglass* (New York: Collier Books, 1962), p. 146.

> Dat nigger run, dat nigger flew;
> Dat nigger tore his shirt in two.[22]

And there is:

> My ole mistiss promise me
> W'en she died, she'd set me free,
> She lived so long dat 'er head got bal'
> An' she give out'n de notion a-dyin' at all.[23]

In the ante-bellum days, work songs were of crucial import to slaves. As they cleared and cultivated land, piled levees along rivers, piled loads on steamboats, screwed cotton bales into the holds of ships, and cut roads and railroads through forest, mountain, and flat, slaves sang while the white man, armed and standing in the shade, shouted his orders.[24] Through the sense of timing and coordination which characterized work songs well sung, especially by the leaders, slaves sometimes quite literally created works of art. These songs not only militated against injuries but enabled the bondsmen to get difficult jobs done more easily by not having to concentrate on the dead level of their work. "In a very real sense the chants of Negro labor," writes Alan Lomax, "may be considered the most profoundly American of all our folk songs, for they were created by our people as they tore at American rock and earth and reshaped it with their bare hands, while rivers of sweat ran down and darkened the dust."

> Long summer day makes a white man lazy,
> Long summer day.
> Long summer day makes a nigger run away, sir,
> Long summer day.[25]

Other slaves sang lines indicating their distaste for slave labor:

> Ol' massa an' ol' missis,
> Sittin' in the parlour,
> Jus' fig'in' an' a-plannin'
> How to work a nigger harder.[26]

[22] Brown, "Folk Expression," p. 51.
[23] Brown, *Caravan,* p. 447.
[24] Lomax, *Folk Songs of North America,* p. 514.
[25] *Ibid.,* p. 515.
[26] *Ibid.,* p. 527.

And there are these bitter lines, the meaning of which is clear:

> Missus in the big house,
> Mammy in the yard,
> Missus holdin' her white hands,
> Mammy workin' hard (3)
> Missus holdin' her white hands,
> Mammy workin' hard.

> Old Marse ridin' all time,
> Niggers workin' round,
> Marse sleepin' day time,
> Niggers diggin' in the ground, (3)
> Marse sleepin' day time,
> Niggers diggin' in the ground.[27]

Courlander tells us that the substance of the work songs "ranges from the humorous to the sad, from the gentle to the biting, and from the tolerant to the unforgiving." The statement in a given song can be metaphoric, tangent or direct, the meaning personal or impersonal. "As throughout Negro singing generally, there is an incidence of social criticism, ridicule, gossip, and protest."[28] Pride in their strength rang with the downward thrust of axe—

> When I was young and in my prime, (hah!)
> Sunk my axe deep every time, (hah!)

Blacks later found their greatest symbol of manhood in John Henry, descendant of Trickster John of slave folk tales:

> A man ain't nothing but a man,
> But before I'll let that steam driver beat me down
> I'll die with my hammer in my hand.[29]

[27] Courlander, *Negro Folk Music,* p. 117.

[28] *Ibid.,* p. 89.

[29] Brown, "Folk Expression," p. 54. Steel-driving John Henry is obviously in the tradition of the axe-wielding blacks of the ante-bellum period. The ballad of John Henry helped spawn John Henry work songs:

> Dis ole hammer—hunh
> Ring like silver—hunh (3)
> Shine like gold, baby—hunh
> Shine like gold—hunh

Though Frances Kemble, an appreciative and sensitive listener to work songs, felt that "one or two barbaric chants would make the fortune of an opera," she was on one occasion "displeased not a little" by a self-deprecating song, one which "embodied the opinion that 'twenty-six black girls not make mulatto yellow girl,' and as I told them I did not like it, they have since omitted it."[30] What is pivotal here is not the presence of self-laceration in folklore, but its extent and meaning. While folklore contained some self-hatred, on balance it gives no indication whatever that blacks, as a group, liked or were indifferent to slavery, which is the issue.[31]

To be sure, only the most fugitive of songs sung by slaves contained direct attacks upon the system. Two of these were associated with slave rebellions. The first, possibly written by ex-slave Denmark Vesey himself, was sung by slaves on at least one island off the coast of Charleston, South Carolina, and at meetings convened by Vesey in Charleston. Though obviously not a folksong, it was sung by the folk.

> Hail! all hail! ye Afric clan,
> Hail! ye oppressed, ye Afric band,

Dis ole hammer—hunh
Killt John Henry—hunh (3)
Twon't kill me baby, hunh
Twon't kill me. (Quoted from Brown, "Folk Expression," p. 57.)

[30] Frances Anne Kemble, *Journal of a Residence on a Georgia Plantation, 1838–1839* (New York: Alfred Knopf), pp. 260–61. Miss Kemble heard slaves use the epithet "nigger": "And I assure you no contemptuous intonation ever equalled the prepotenza (arrogance) of the despotic insolence of this address of these poor wretches to each other." Kemble, *Journal,* p. 281. Here she is on solid ground, but the slaves also used the word with glowing affection, as seen in the "Run, Nigger, Run" secular. At other times they leaned toward self-laceration but refused to go the whole route: "My name's Ran, I wuks in de sand, I'd rather be a nigger dan a po' white man." Brown, "Folk Expression," p. 51. Some blacks also sang, "It takes a long, lean, blackskinned gal, to make a preacher lay his Bible down." Newman I. White, *American Negro Folk Songs* (Cambridge, 1928), p. 411.

[31] Elkins, who believes Southern white lore on slavery should be taken seriously, does not subject it to serious scrutiny. For a penetrating—and devastating—analysis of "the richest layers of Southern lore" which, according to Elkins, resulted from "an exquisitely rounded collective creativity," see Sterling A. Brown, "A Century of Negro Portraiture in American Literature," *The Massachusetts Review* (Winter, 1966).

> Who toil and sweat in slavery bound
> And when your health and strength are gone
> Are left to hunger and to mourn,
> Let independence be your aim,
> Ever mindful what 'tis worth.
> Pledge your bodies for the prize,
> Pile them even to the skies![32]

The second, a popular song derived from a concrete reality, bears the marks of a conscious authority:

> You mought be rich as cream
> And drive you coach and four-horse team,
> But you can't keep de world from moverin' round
> Nor Nat Turner from gainin' ground.
>
> And your name it mought be Caesar sure,
> And got you cannon can shoot a mile or more,
> But you can't keep de world from moverin' round
> Nor Nat Turner from gainin' ground.[33]

The introduction of Denmark Vesey, class leader in the A.M.E. Church, and Nat Turner, slave preacher, serves to remind us that some slaves and ex-slaves were violent as well as humble, impatient as well as patient.

It is also well to recall that the religious David Walker, who had lived close to slavery in North Carolina, and Henry Highland Garnett, ex-slave and Presbyterian minister, produced two of the most inflammatory, vitriolic, and doomed-bespeaking polemics America has yet seen.[34] There was theological tension here, loudly proclaimed, a tension which emanated from and was perpetuated by American slavery and race prejudice. This dimension of ambiguity must be kept in mind, if for no other reason than to place in bolder relief the possibility that a great many slaves and free

---

[32] Quoted from Archie Epps, "A Negro Separatist Movement," *The Harvard Review,* IV, No. 1 (Summer-Fall, 1956), 75.

[33] Quoted in William Styron, "This Quiet Dust," *Harpers,* April 1965, p. 135.

[34] For excerpts from David Walker's *Appeal* and Henry H. Garnett's *Call to Rebellion,* see Herbert Aptheker (ed.), *A Documentary History of the Negro People in the United States.* 2 vols. (New York: Citadel Press, 1965). Originally published in 1951.

Afro-Americans could have interpreted Christianity in a way quite different from white Christians.

Even those songs which seemed most otherworldly, those which expressed profound weariness of spirit and even faith in death, through their unmistakable sadness, were accusatory, and God was not their object. If one accepts as a given that some of these appear to be almost wholly escapist, the indictment is no less real. Thomas Wentworth Higginson came across one—". . . a flower of poetry in that dark soil," he called it.[35]

> I'll walk in de graveyard, I'll walk through de graveyard,
>   To lay dis body down.
> I'll lie in de grave and stretch out my arms,
>   Lay dis body down.

Reflecting on "I'll lie in de grave and stretch out my arms," Higginson said that "Never, it seems to me, since man first lived and suffered, was his infinite longing for peace uttered more plaintively than in that line."[36]

There seems to be small doubt that Christianity contributed in large measure to a spirit of patience which militated against open rebellion among the bondsmen. Yet to overemphasize this point leads one to obscure a no less important reality: Christianity, after being reinterpreted and recast by slave bards, also contributed to that spirit of endurance which powered generations of bondsmen, bringing them to that decisive moment when for the first time a real choice was available to scores of thousands of them.

When that moment came, some slaves who were in a position to decide for themselves did so. W. E. B. DuBois re-created their mood and the atmosphere in which they lived.

> There came the slow looming of emancipation. Crowds and
> armies of the unknown, inscrutable, unfathomable Yankees;
> cruelty behind and before; rumors of a new slave trade, but
> slowly, continuously, the wild truth, the bitter truth, the magic
> truth, came surging through. There was to be a new freedom!

[35] Thomas Wentworth Higginson, *Army Life in a Black Regiment* (New York: Collier, 1962), p. 199.
[36] *Ibid.*

And a black nation went tramping after the armies no matter what it suffered; no matter how it was treated, no matter how it died.[37]

The gifted bards, by creating songs with an unmistakable freedom ring, songs which would have been met with swift, brutal repression in the ante-bellum days, probably voiced the sentiments of all but the most degraded and dehumanized. Perhaps not even the incredulous slavemaster could deny the intent of the new lyrics. "In the wake of the Union Army and in the contraband camps," remarked Sterling Brown, "spirituals of freedom sprang up suddenly. . . . Some celebrated the days of Jubilo: 'O Freedom; O Freedom!' and 'Before I'll be a slave, I'll be buried in my grave!', and 'Go home to my lord and be free.'" And there was: "'No more driver's lash for me. . . . Many thousand go.'"[38]

DuBois brought together the insights of the poet and historian to get inside the slaves:

There was joy in the South. It rose like perfume—like a prayer. Men stood quivering. Slim dark girls, wild and beautiful with wrinkled hair, wept silently; young women, black, tawny, white, and golden, lifted shivering hands, and old and broken mothers, black and gray, raised great voices and shouted to God across the fields, and up to the rocks and the mountains.[39]

Some sang:

Slavery chain done broke at last, broke at last, broke at last,
Slavery chain done broke at last,
Going to praise God till I die.

I did tell him how I suffer,
In de dungeon and de chain,
And de days I went with head bowed down,
And my broken flesh and pain,
Slavery chain done broke at last, broke at last, broke at last.[40]

[37] W. E. B. DuBois, *Black Reconstruction* (Philadelphia: Albert Saifer), p. 122. Originally published in 1935 by Harcourt, Brace and Company.
[38] Brown, "Folk Expression," p. 49.
[39] DuBois, *Reconstruction,* p. 124.
[40] Quoted in Brown, *Caravan,* pp. 440–41. One of the most tragic scenes of the Civil War period occurred when a group of Sea Island freedmen,

Whatever the nature of the shocks generated by the war, among those vibrations felt were some that had come from Afro-American singing ever since the first Africans were forcibly brought to these shores. DuBois was correct when he said that the new freedom song had not come from Africa, but that "the dark throb and beat of that Ancient of Days was in and through it."[41] Thus, the psyches of those who gave rise to and provided widespread support for folk songs had not been reduced to *tabulae rasae* on which a slave-holding society could at pleasure sketch out its wish-fulfillment fantasies.

We have already seen the acute degree to which some slaves realized they were being exploited. Their sense of the injustice of slavery made it so much easier for them to act out their aggression against whites (by engaging in various forms of "day to day" resistance) without being overcome by a sense of guilt, or a feeling of being ill-mannered. To call this nihilistic thrashing about would be as erroneous as to refer to their use of folk lore as esthetic thrashing about.[42] For if they did not regard themselves as the

---

told by a brigadier-general that they would not receive land from the government, sang, "Nobody knows the trouble I've seen." DuBois, *Souls,* p. 381.

[41] DuBois, *Reconstruction,* p. 124.

[42] If some slavemasters encouraged slaves to steal or simply winked at thefts, then slaves who obliged them were most assuredly *not acting against their own interests,* whatever the motivation of the masters. Had more fruitful options been available to them, then and only then could we say that slaves were playing into the hands of their masters. Whatever the masters thought of slaves who stole from them—and there is little reason to doubt that most slaves considered it almost obligatory to steal from white people —the slaves, it is reasonable to assume, were aware of the unparalleled looting in which masters themselves were engaged. To speak therefore of slaves undermining their sense of self-respect as a result of stealing from whites—and this argument has been advanced by Eugene Genovese—is wide of the mark. Indeed, it appears more likely that those who engaged in stealing were, in the context of an oppressor-oppressed situation, on the way to realizing a larger measure of self-respect. Moreover, Genovese, in charging that certain forms of "day to day" resistance, in the absence of general conditions of rebellion, "amounted to individual and essentially nihilistic thrashing about," fails to recognize that that which was possible, that which conditions permitted, was pursued by slaves in preference to the path which led to passivity or annihilation. Those engaging in "day to day" resistance were moving along meaningful rather than nihilistic lines, for their activities were designed to frustrate the demands of the authority-system. For a very suggestive discussion of the dependency

equals of whites in many ways, their folklore indicates that the generality of slaves must have at least felt superior to whites morally. And that, in the context of oppression, could make the difference between a viable human spirit and one crippled by the belief that the interests of the master are those of the slave.

When it is borne in mind that slaves created a large number of extraordinary songs and greatly improved a considerable proportion of the songs of others, it is not at all difficult to believe that they were conscious of the fact that they were leaders in the vital area of art—giving protagonists rather than receiving pawns. And there is some evidence that slaves were aware of the special talent which they brought to music. Higginson has described how reluctantly they sang from hymnals—"even on Sunday"—and how "gladly" they yielded "to the more potent excitement of their own 'spirituals.' "[43] It is highly unlikely that the slaves' preference for their own music went unremarked among them, or that this preference did not affect their estimate of themselves. "They soon found," commented Alan Lomax, "that when they sang, the whites recognized their superiority as singers, and listened with respect."[44] He might have added that those ante-bellum whites who listened probably seldom understood.

What is of pivotal import, however, is that the esthetic realm was the one area in which slaves knew they were not inferior to whites. Small wonder that they borrowed many songs from the larger community, then quickly invested them with their own economy of statement and power of imagery rather than yield to the temptation of merely repeating what they had heard. Since they were essentially group rather than solo performances, the values inherent in and given affirmation by the music served to strengthen bonds-

complex engendered by slavery and highly provocative views on the significance of "day to day" resistance among slaves, see Eugene Genovese, "The Legacy of Slavery and the Roots of Black Nationalism," *Studies on the Left*, VI, No. 6 (Nov.–Dec. 1966), especially p. 8.

[43] Higginson, *Black Regiment*, p. 212. Alan Lomax reminds us that the slaves sang "in leader-chorus style, with a more relaxed throat than the whites, and in deeper-pitched, mellower voices, which blended richly." "A strong, surging beat underlay most of their American creations . . . words and tunes were intimately and playfully united, and 'sense' was often subordinated to the demands of rhythm and melody." Lomax, *Folk Songs of North America*, Introduction, p. xx.

[44] Lomax, *Folk Songs*, p. 460.

men in a way that solo music could not have done.[45] In a word, slave singing often provided a form of group therapy, a way in which a slave, in concert with others, could fend off some of the debilitating effects of slavery.

The field of inquiry would hardly be complete without some mention of slave tales. Rich in quantity and often subtle in conception, these tales further illumine the inner world of the bondsmen, disclosing moods and interests almost as various as those found in folksongs. That folk tales, like the songs, indicate an African presence, should not astonish; for the telling of tales, closely related to the African griot's vocation of providing oral histories of families and dynasties, was deeply rooted in West African tradition. Hughes and Bontemps have written that the slaves brought to America the "habit of storytelling as pastime, together with a rich bestiary." Moreover, they point out that the folk tales of slaves "were actually projections of personal experiences and hopes and defeats, in terms of symbols," and that this important dimension of the tales "appears to have gone unnoticed."[46]

[45] Commenting on the group nature of much of slave singing, Alan Lomax points out that the majority of the bondsmen "came from West Africa, where music-making was largely a group activity, the creation of a many-voiced, dancing throng. . . . Community songs of labour and worship (in America) and dance songs far outnumbered narrative pieces, and the emotion of the songs was, on the whole, joyfully erotic, deeply tragic, allusive, playful, or ironic rather than nostalgic, withdrawn, factual, or aggressively comic—as among white folk singers." Lomax, *Folk Songs,* pp. xix and xx of Introduction. For treatments of the more technical aspects of Afro-American music, see Courlander, *Negro Folk Music,* especially Chapter II; and Richard A. Waterman, "African Influences on the Music of the Americas," in *Acculturation in the Americas,* edited by Sol Tax.

[46] Arna Bontemps and Langston Hughes (ed.), *The Book of Negro Folklore* (New York: Dodd, Mead & Company, 1965), Introduction, p. viii. Of course if one regards each humorous thrust of the bondsmen as so much comic nonsense, then there is no basis for understanding, to use Sterling Brown's phrase, the slave's "laughter out of hell." Without understanding what humor meant to slaves themselves, one is not likely to rise above the superficiality of a Stephen Foster or a Joel Chandler Harris. But once an effort has been made to see the world from the slave's point of view, then perhaps one can understand Ralph Ellison's reference to Afro-Americans, in their folklore, "backing away from the chaos of experience and from ourselves," in order to "depict the humor as well as the horror of our living." Ralph Ellison, "A Very Stern Discipline," *Harpers* (March, 1967), p. 80.

Possessing a repertoire which ranged over a great many areas, perhaps the most memorable tales are those of Br'er Rabbit and John.[47] Br'er Rabbit, now trickster, ladies' man and braggart, now wit, joker and glutton, possessed the resourcefulness, despite his size and lack of strength, to outsmart stronger, larger animals. "To the slave in his condition," according to Hughes and Bontemps, "the theme of weakness overcoming strength through cunning proved endlessly fascinating."[48] John, characterized by a spiritual resilience born of an ironic sense of life, was a secular high priest of mischief and guile who delighted in matching wits with Ole Marster, the "patterollers," Ole Missy, and the devil himself. He was clever enough to sense the absurdity of his predicament and that of white people, smart enough to know the limits of his powers and the boundaries of those of the master class. While not always victorious, even on the spacious plane of the imagination, he could hardly be described as a slave with an inferiority complex. And in this regard it is important to note that his varieties of triumphs, though they sometimes included winning freedom, often realistically cluster about ways of coping with everyday negatives of the system.[49]

Slaves were adept in the art of storytelling, as at home in this area as they were in the field of music. But further discussion of the scope of folklore would be uneconomical, for we have already seen a depth and variety of thought among bondsmen which embarrasses stereotypical theories of slave personality. Moreover, it should be clear by now that there are no secure grounds on which to erect the

[47] For additional discussions of folk tales, see Zora Neale Hurston, *Mules and Men* (Philadelphia: J. B. Lippincott, 1935); Richard Dorson, *American Negro Folktales* (Greenwich, Connecticut: Fawcett, 1967); and B. A. Botkin, *Lay My Burden Down* (Chicago: University of Chicago Press, 1945).

[48] Bontemps and Hughes, *Negro Folklore,* Introduction, p. ix.

[49] The fact that slaveowners sometimes took pleasure in being outwitted by slaves in no way diminishes from the importance of the trickster tales, for what is essential here is how these tales affected the slave's attitude toward himself, not whether his thinking or behavior would impress a society which considered black people little better than animals. DuBois's words in this regard should never be forgotten: "Everything Negroes did was wrong. If they fought for freedom, they were beasts; if they did not fight, they were born slaves. If they cowered on the plantation, they loved slavery; if they ran away, they were lazy loafers. If they sang, they were silly; if they scowled, they were impudent. . . . And they were funny, funny—ridiculous baboons, aping men." DuBois, *Reconstruction,* p. 125.

old, painfully constricted "Sambo" structure.[50] For the personalities which lay beneath the plastic exteriors which slaves turned on and off for white people were too manifold to be contained by cheerful, childlike images. When it is argued, then, that "too much of the Negro's own lore" has gone into the making of the Sambo picture "to entitle one in good conscience to condemn it as 'conspiracy',"[51] one must rejoin: Only if you strip the masks from black faces while refusing to read the irony and ambiguity and cunning which called the masks into existence. Slave folklore, on balance, decisively repudiates the thesis that Negroes *as a group* had internalized "Sambo" traits, committing them, as it were, to psychological marriage.

III

IT IS ONE OF THE CURIOSITIES of American historiography that a people who were as productive esthetically as American slaves could be studied as if they had moved in a cultural cyclotron, continually bombarded by devastating, atomizing forces which denuded them of meaningful Africanisms while destroying any and all impulses toward creativity. One historian, for example, has been tempted to wonder how it was ever possible that "*all* this (West African) native resourcefulness and vitality have been brought to such a point of *utter* stultification in America."[52] (Italics added.) This sadly misguided view is, of course, not grounded in any recognition or understanding of the Afro-American dimension of American culture. In any event, there is a great need for students of American slavery to attempt what Gilberto Freyre tried to do for Brazilian civilization—an effort at discovering the contributions of

[50] Ralph Ellison offers illuminating insight into the group experience of the slave: "Any people who could endure all of that brutalization and keep together, who could undergo such dismemberment and resuscitate itself, and endure until it could take the initiative in achieving its own freedom is obviously more than the sum of its brutalization. Seen in this perspective, theirs has been one of the great human experiences and one of the great triumphs of the human spirit in modern times, in fact, in the history of the world." Ellison, "A Very Stern Discipline," p. 84.

[51] Elkins sets forth this argument in *Slavery*, p. 84.

[52] *Ibid.*, p. 93.

slaves toward the shaping of the Brazilian national character.[53] When such a study has been made of the American slave we shall probably discover that, though he did not rival his Brazilian brother in staging bloody revolutions, the quality and place of art in his life compared favorably. Now this suggests that the humanity of people can be asserted through means other than open and widespread rebellion, a consideration that has not been appreciated in violence-prone America. We would do well to recall the words of F. S. C. Northrop who has observed:

During the pre-Civil War period shipowners and southern landowners brought to the United States a considerable body of people with a color of skin and cultural values different from those of its other inhabitants. . . . Their values are more emotive, esthetic and intuitive . . . (These) characteristics can become an asset for our culture. For these are values with respect to which Anglo-American culture is weak.[54]

These values were expressed on the highest level in the folklore of slaves. Through their folklore, black slaves affirmed their humanity and left a lasting imprint on American culture. No study of the institutional aspects of American slavery can be complete, nor can the larger dimensions of slave personality and style be adequately explored, as long as historians continue to avoid that realm in which, as DuBois has said, "the soul of the black slave spoke to man."[55]

In its nearly two and one half centuries of existence, the grim system of American slavery doubtless broke the spirits of uncounted numbers of slaves. Nevertheless, if we look through the prism of folklore, we can see others transcending their plight, appreciating the tragic irony of their condition, then seizing upon and putting

[53] Gilberto Freyre, *The Masters and the Slaves* (New York: Alfred A. Knopf, 1956). Originally published by Jose Olympio, Rio de Janeiro, Brazil.

[54] F. S. C. Northrop, *The Meeting of East and West* (New York: The Macmillan Co., 1952), pp. 159–60.

[55] DuBois, *Souls,* p. 378. Kenneth M. Stampp in his *The Peculiar Institution* (New York: Alfred A. Knopf, 1956), employs to a limited extent some of the materials of slave folklore. Willie Lee Rose, in *Rehearsal for Reconstruction* (New York: The Bobbs-Merrill Company, 1964), makes brief but highly informed use of folk material.

to use those aspects of their experience which sustain in the present and renew in the future. We can see them opposing their own angle of vision to that of their oppressor, fashioning their own techniques of defense and aggression in accordance with their own reading of reality and doing those things well enough to avoid having their sense of humanity destroyed.

Slave folklore, then, affirms the existence of a large number of vital, tough-minded human beings who, though severely limited and abused by slavery, had found a way both to endure and preserve their humanity in the face of insuperable odds. What they learned about handling misfortune was not only a major factor in their survival as a people, but many of the lessons learned and esthetic standards established would be used by future generations of Afro-Americans in coping with a hostile world. What a splendid affirmation of the hopes and dreams of their slave ancestors that some of the songs being sung in ante-bellum days are the ones Afro-Americans are singing in the freedom movement today: "Michael, row the boat ashore"; "Just like a tree planted by the water, I shall not be moved."

Part Three

Blues and Jazz

The Duality of Bygone Jazz

MAX MARGULIS

A MUSICAL SPEECH of the American Negro people, having undergone many qualitative changes, culminated for a brief spell in the veritable jazz idiom. Because of factors inherent in its begetting, the jazz idiom already contained the deadly seed that was to corrupt it even at the moment of its greatest flourishing —its two irreconcilable elements of creative expression and self-caricature.

Conditions operating in every part of the South gave rise to this special kind of music and nourished its creative side. The duality embodied in it, however, had been characteristic of all Negro musical expression for a century before jazz came into being. How this interplay of antagonistic elements permeated the musical mani-festations of the nineteenth century and persisted into the jazz medium will throw light upon the real sources of the new music and explain the crucial historical directions which changed jazz trends, until the music exhausted its possibilities of development and was supplanted by a new jazz medium.

I

LONG BEFORE THE CIVIL WAR, talented "ear" musicians on the slave plantations were groomed to entertain the "Big House" folks, and at times they were even exhibited in a semi-professional capacity on a limited circuit of neighboring Big Houses. To entertain meant to arouse laughter, and the music was necessarily subordinated to clowning. A parody of religious plantation songs was broadened into outright self-caricature. Lyrics ridiculed Negro ways, and the language was ostentatiously comic. This forced perversion of their songs by the plantation entertainers set up a new style with wide appeal, and it was not long before white imitators in "blackface" began to exploit the novelty. They parodied at second hand the

Negro's self-caricature, counterfeiting the more obvious structural patterns of the music and the ensemble effects—singing style, banjo, bones, etc.—which accompanied the comic song and dance. In this manner, isolated elements of the Negro's basic expressive idiom were abstracted and used out of context, being thus deprived of their organic meaning.

"Blackface" minstrel shows were known in 1830. Audiences did not think of them as musical shows: primarily they were displays of rough clowning, with the music only incidental to the comedy, or they were modified stage adaptations of the type of plantation entertainments which used Negro impersonations as their comic base. The shows, which fathered the most stubborn of stereotypes in American theatre history, had established themselves by 1840 as a basic form of American entertainment, the earliest of the popular forms. Performers toured the length and breadth of the United States and were favorably received in Europe.

The religious plantation songs, folk products of slavery, grew out of the emotional outpourings of revival meetings, and expressed, through Scriptural symbols, the longing for freedom (the children of bondage would pass out of the wilderness of slavery over into the land of freedom). In some sections of the South even religious meetings were forbidden; the persistent worshippers had to "steal away to Jesus" secretly in the dead of night. In such circumstances, the singing was forced to resort to a protective dualism. It gave two different emotional colorings to the same text, or it introduced an alternate or substitute set of words whenever whites were within earshot. The slave owners could not counter this effectively, although they took no chances: during the war years, Negroes were jailed for singing such songs as "It Won't Be Long" and "Poor Sinners Suffer Here."

Much later, secular songs echoed the same sense of protective dualism:

Bossman call me nigger I jes' laugh
He kick the seat of my pants and that ain't half
You don't know, you don't know my mind
When you see me laughin', jes' laughin' to keep from cryin'
and

Got one mind for white folks to see
'Nother for what I know is me

Drawing room ballads became very popular during the fifties. Against the unbuttoned burlesque which marked the ordinary idiom of the minstrelsy, the sweet and romantic ballad offered an interesting counter. This appeal carried it over into the minstrel show itself, where the "plantation" song was typical of these ballads. The fifties was the decade which produced the first of many "plantation" songs written by white composers resident in the North, whose idyllic Southland was an unabashed fantasy. The most talented of these white writers—and perhaps the finest of all American song writers—was Stephen Foster, who lived in Pittsburgh. His charming songs idealized plantation noblemen, but their sentimentalized subjects reflected neither the Negro nor the old South.

To this day, as a matter of fact, the nostalgia for the "romantic" South remains one of the mainstays of the popular music turned out in the workshops of Tin Pan Alley, and present-day songsmiths continue to capitalize upon the Swanee subjects and themes.

After the Civil War, plantation music and slavery were so interwoven in the minds of the new generation that it was difficult to dissociate them. At that time the Negroes reacted with marked resentment against the traditional folk music. Besides, the war had scattered the Negroes from the plantations. The influx of Negroes into Northern cities and the gradual growth of the industrial and urbanized "New South" had definitely dispersed the old Negro community and broken its ties. The conditions in which the group songs of the original folk pattern had flourished disappeared.

In the rural areas, the making of music was passing from the folk in general and becoming the activity of specialized musicians. A growing number of talented, though untrained, musicians were at work refurbishing the folk tradition. They were social pariahs, entertaining for a handout. Their precarious and unrespected calling reduced their status to that of vagrants and "idlers." They were wanderers, following the great migratory movements of their people throughout the South, to the West and to the North. They came and went on freight cars, and they sang at railroad stations for people waiting for trains. A basic symbol and theme was the railroad and its melancholy train whistle. Another was the wanderer or hobo, homeless, moneyless, friendless ("I look down dat lonesome road and cry") in a world still hostile, wracked by the survivals of slavery.

In the cities of the South, the prevailing popular music was

European dance music, light and relaxing. During slavery most of the dance music had been played by Negroes, whose skilled "ear" fiddling had kept pace with the fashions in reels, jigs, *contredanses,* cotillions, and other dance modes. Now, after the war, there was a renewed demand for Negro dance musicians. And with this went a demand for Negro entertainment, which fused with the dance music, and transformed its character.

In New Orleans, a new generation of musicians among the liberated Negroes learned, as had their fiddling forebears, to play by ear. Many acquired battered but standard wind instruments and castoff stringed instruments, and took up the dance vogues, the melodies and harmonies of city culture. Ear-playing groups predominated at dance and band functions, and soon they were hired even on Mississippi River boats, where they supplemented their nightly entertaining as musicians and buffoons by working as porters, waiters, and deckhands by day.

When the Negroes themselves entered the professional minstrel field in the sixties, the sentimental ballad was already beginning to lose favor, and the fast, comic dance rhythms were again coming into vogue. From the double shuffle, jig, clog, and other clowning and self-caricaturing dances, arose a formula for what Negro music was supposed and expected to be. Increasingly, the duality which had originally been merely a protective panoply became a real duality of personality, and out of it evolved the main outward features of all subsequent popular music intended to accompany dancing.

The Negroes who remained in the cities playing odd jobs were quick to adopt the musical recipes exploited by their minstrel-show colleagues. At dances, they played quadrilles and polkas, which they had learned by ear. Being remote from the traditional way of feeling of these dances, they gave them a new twist, hybridizing them with comic, rural elements—stylized effects which, coming by way of the laughter-evoking minstrel dances, echoed the antebellum entertainment music they now identified with slavery. Thus a new stage of self-caricature was embodied in the dance music.

It is a far cry from the "exercise of the nigger heel in the African fashion," as the irrepressible folk dance was called, to the double shuffle of the minstrel shows. Self-ridiculing Negro buffoonery extracted the marketable spectacle from the social activity and was instrumental as well in producing such forms of entertainment as the "coon song" of mid-century minstrelsy. Negro minstrelsy, like earlier plantation entertainment, became in its essence a caricature, then a ridiculing of Negro life and ways. Persistence in the form developed rigid patterns, grotesque and set imitations in undeviating molds. By sheer force of talent, the Negro musicians who entered the field added musical qualities to the established clowning. The true strength of the minstrels' music did not lie in the words of the songs—which were the staple stage dialect about chickens, watermelons, and razors—or in the miming of the dance, both of these being generally without distinction. It lay rather in isolated musical elements, distinctive in themselves, abstracted from the original expressive Negro musical language, but still retaining some sparkle even in their vulgar new setting.

Negro music thus achieved wide public acceptance, at the cost of debasement. So the irony continued its spiralling cycle: minstrelsy began by being self-caricature; the white comedian then parodied the Negro's self-caricature; the cycle prolonged its travesty by becoming a Negro imitation of the white man's parody of him. And social insistence on the self-caricature went so far even as to require the Negro entertainer himself to appear in "blackface"!

II

THE END OF THE CENTURY brought the popular enthusiasm for ragtime—a good index of the new urban spirit. The ragtime movement as such did not introduce a new kind of popular music. Its musical ingredients were the same ones that had for half a century been familiar in stage minstrelsy. The activity of expanding and thriving cities no longer found its expressive echo in the European dances or in the sentimental, nostalgic ballads of which only Stephen Foster's survive. The new era brought with it the "two step," and an unprecedented participation in couple dancing. The couple dance was replacing the group dance, and bringing into favor as its accompanying music all the Negro-inspired rhythmic elements of previous popular music, abstracted from their "blackface" setting. So ragtime emerged in the early nineties as a definitely instrumental music, a working up of the stage and entertainment music of preceding decades into a utilitarian music for the accompaniment of couple dancing. The closeness of ragtime to its origins in the comic "coon song" and lively cakewalk is evident in the minstrel-show tune, "Old Zip Coon," sometimes known as "Turkey in the Straw," which was popular as far back as the 1830's. No clear-cut demarcation existed between ragtime and the music of the minstrel-show bands. Ragtime as music for instruments was being played long before its commercial exploitation in sheet music form for the piano. So, when ragtime music was first printed for piano solo, the playing of the bands was in no way affected. Ragtime achieved at least a partial independence by dropping the elements of content associated with the stage, such as the human voice and words, pantomime, and dialogue development.

On the other hand, ragtime did not dissociate itself completely from the minstrel show. Cakewalk performers danced to ragtime, and singing comedians fitted their comic ditties to a synthetic ragtime rhythm. Now, bands of accomplished musicians were a prominent feature of the minstrel companies, and the musicians at the turn of the century often owed their musical training to the Negro regimental bands in which they had been enrolled during the Spanish-American War. The skilled alumni of the army bands, virtuosi on the cornet and other instruments, in displaying their technical prowess in the accompaniment of the cakewalk, were creating the contours of modern dance style. These were the full professionals among Negro musicians and the pioneers in the development of instrumental technique. They constituted a small minority, however, playing with the large minstrel companies that toured the whole country.

The instrumentation of the ragtime era bands was not confined to brass, nor did it resemble the divided and sectionalized groupings which marked the later jazz bands. It had a folk character: it informally combined whatever instruments were readily available. For example, besides saxophones, trumpets, trombones, and drums, Will Marion Cook's twenty-piece band, the Memphis Students, also numbered mandolins, banjos, guitars, violins, and string bass.

Ragtime pieces at that time were published in many cities all over the country—in St. Louis, Chicago, Denver, San Francisco—mainly as sheet music for the piano. It does not follow from this fact that ragtime was a peculiarly pianistic art. It is true that the best-known ragtime composers (such as Tom Turpin, who wrote "Harlem Rag" and "St. Louis Rag"; Scott Joplin, who wrote "Maple Leaf Rag"; and Louis Chauvin, who wrote many favorite rags which were credited to others) were themselves pianists. Indeed the main instrument of the time was the piano. It competed to advantage with the phonograph, which was then in its crude early form. It was used to accompany the moving picture, then an emerging phenomenon. Around it as center, however, other instruments gathered to play music for couple dancing. The rags were frankly written for dancing, not singing. The music of the good rags was written without accompanying words—the melodies could not suitably be sung. The sheet music publications reflected an era when player-pianos were in every home, piano "professors" in every brothel, and popular music writers in every city. No doubt the title "ragtime band" covered a multitude of sins against the best musical standards established by pianists, but since all dance bands played the piano rags (i.e., rags *published* as piano solos), it is fair to presume that ragtime was a general instrumental art. The note-reading bands played the rags in moderate tempo, in accordance with the literal sheet music notation. The ear-playing bands played them as fast stomps, handling them freely. Emphasis on the place of the piano in ragtime is justified in one respect: ragtime proved to be the medium which brought the piano forward for the first time with a unique, independent solo technique for dance accompaniment.

When ragtime was enjoying its greatest popularity, by about 1910, the hack song writers had learned the working formulas for turning out the rags almost by rote. These mechanical methods of composition suited the policies of the large publishers. But however much the publication of the debased product was multiplied, its extinction could not be postponed for long.

The changes that were occurring throughout the South reached their peak points in New Orleans. The popular error that New Orleans is the place of origin of jazz can be simply explained. New Orleans, as the commercial center and chief seaport of the South, served as a delta upon which converged all the contributions of the rest of the South. The extravagant character of New Orleans as a metropolis and entertainment center, its bordellos and renowned carouses, was the product of an exuberant economy and a mingling of cultures. This rich flowering drew its sustenance ultimately from its roots in the hinterlands of the South. Jazz came out of the hinterlands along with the cotton and the tobacco. To this city of more than a quarter of a million population, holding out the prospect of lucrative work, were attracted musicians from all over the South. The chief service of New Orleans to jazz was that it provided a cultural center, facilitating the contact between numerous musicians, and it integrated their diverse gifts.

By the beginning of the twentieth century, one quarter of the population of New Orleans was Negro, but relatively few Negroes were musicians. Actually, the Negro musician was sometimes tolerated but more often avoided and despised by his people. As an entertainer it was his business to represent by broad clowning the ludicrous scarecrow that most white audiences preferred to believe was the typical Negro. As a dance musician—dance music was the only field for Negro professionals—he had no social status: he had to live precariously in a field that gave no steady pay, and he had to work in disreputable dives.

W. C. Handy records the contempt in which "respectable" Negroes everywhere held the musical profession, when he describes his father's reaction to his first purchase of a musical instrument: "Son, I'd rather see you in a hearse. I'd rather follow you to the graveyard than to hear that you had become a musician."

The white musicians of the time, also low in social status, were forced, like the Negroes, to live precariously. Those white musicians especially who chose, in the manner of the enterprising white minstrels, to play in the Negro style, in the dives where the patrons did not object to it, were regarded with scorn and derision. The ragtime pieces that were played by these musicians, both Negro and white, were viewed with more respect than the musicians themselves; generally held in high regard, these pieces were to be found in the typical household library of mechanical piano rolls.

IN THE URBAN DISTRICTS to which bands and "professors" were relegated, many dives which could not afford to employ musicians regularly depended for their entertainment upon itinerants who played for tips and drinks. These nondescript musicians—singers, above all, with accompanying pianists, guitarists, fiddlers—who played neither strictly popular music nor wholly genuine country music, were not new in the cities. For half a century after 1865, vagrant musicians of their sort had been wandering in and out of cities up and down the Mississippi River and across the Gulf Coast, performing music not sophisticated enough to combat the widespread prejudice against country folk music. They were folk musicians insofar as their music adhered to an oral tradition common to the rural Negro population of the South. But they differed from folk musicians in that they carried their folk material beyond the confines of regional folk music, adapting it to an urban point of view and commercial forms. Thus, although their efforts contributed fundamentally to the later development of jazz, they fell between the two stools and so proved to be pariahs in a double sense.

While urban taste favored popular music, which served to entertain or to accompany dancing, the music of the itinerant musicians owed whatever tang it had to folk music. It was not a part of the original folk tradition of group songs, where one person took the chant lead, as in work songs of the levees and cotton fields, or songs of plantation meetings and revivals. Their music was, in fact, an embodiment of folk experience, combining folk poetry with folk music, yet somewhat paralleling in its voice and accompaniment respectively the group leader or soloist of the early songs and the chorus with its function of commentator, interpreter, and creator of formal antiphony to the voice.

This music's core was an expressive vocal lament, issuing out of the relation of the singer to his harsh environment. Its mood was a mingling of grief, irony, and disillusionment. Its form was a mold for convenient improvising, for easy filling and refilling. It found an ear among the waterfront workers and the whimsical idlers who frequented the honky-tonks and occupied a place on the fringe of city life.

For all that, this music, which was later to become the mainspring of creativity among the instrumentalists in the bands, was utterly remote from the life and background of other Negro musicians, and was not at first viewed sympathetically by them. Handy, for example, states, in his *Father of the Blues,* that it was not until 1903, when he was thirty, that he began to feel any awareness of the *blues:* " . . . I was leading the orchestra in a dance program when someone sent up an odd request. Would you play some of 'our native music,' the note asked. This baffled me." He describes how a blues singer, repeating a line three times, accompanied himself on the guitar with "the weirdest music I had ever heard." He says frankly, "I hasten to confess that I took up with low folk forms hesitantly."

Given these original antipathies to the country blues, the ultimate absorption of blues elements into the dance tradition can be explained only by an analysis of the process by which the absorption took place.

During the nineteenth century, folk music was accompanied by guitar, banjo, mandolin, fiddle, and other instruments associated with typical rural music. As it repeatedly invaded the city, however, it began to be accompanied—in the shape of the blues—also by piano, which was already used in urban ragtime. By the turn of the century, a number of blues singers with a theatrical flair—women as well as men—had entered the entertainment field and were making professional appearances not only in tent shows and minstrel shows, but in city cabarets. Under such conditions, the untutored ragtime bands began accompanying the blues. With the participation of piano, cornet, clarinet, trombone, and drums, the blues was urbanized and fused with ragtime. In the course of devising and working out a style of playing suitable to the accompaniment of the blues, the ragtime musicians rediscovered their own instruments and gained entirely new insights into their relation to one another in the band.

The rags had been tirelessly rehearsed and memorized note for note, and then were played over and over, with admirable propulsion. But the blues demanded a continuous, inspired act of creation from the band, and expressive performance in place of simple jauntiness. Expressive performance logically presupposed an underlying musical language with immediate, communicable points of reference. Such a musical language, with its vocabulary of *typical* or immediately apprehended relationships, was conceivable only in terms of a tradition issuing from the experience and consciousness of many people. It was the blues, therefore, which, in demanding expressive performance from band musicians, introduced fundamental, significant, emotional values into dance music.

The rhythmic aspects of jazz in this early stage had in it, even after the devastating dilutions of half a century of minstrel comic dances, something of the impulse of Negro folk dance. The expressive aspect of jazz had in it the vocal impulse of plantation folk music, with modifications which reflected the turbulent, continuing industrialization of the Southern scene.

Being a vocal and a lament, the blues had a slow or deliberate tempo; its phrases, set off by the large and small caesuras, were pithy and declamatory. Obviously, the headlong staccato beat of prevailing dance music was not suited to the tempo, the mood or the form of the blues. The blues as an art of singing, with an emotional content conveyed by subtle alteration of melodic intervals, by its perverse rhythmic cadence and complex variations in quality of tone and dynamic shading, required an accompaniment peculiar to its traditions and standards.

This instrumental rapport with the way of feeling of the sung blues was achieved gradually, feature by feature, by the renownless, self-taught musicians attached to cabarets and saloons in Southern cities. Stirred by the fluidly contoured, infinitely suggestive vocal phrase, they were impelled to strive for a singing style; exploring the resources of their instruments, they approximated the inflections and intonations of blues vocal style.

The vocalized instrumental style gradually attained consistency, stabilizing and making familiar by repetition a number of new expressive cadences, figures, and textures, each indicating an equivalent emotional context. It was an instrumental solo style, exercised in the band by all the melodic instruments playing independent parts simultaneously.

III

ALTHOUGH INSTRUMENTAL BLUES had been played throughout the first decade of the century, the earliest phonograph records of jazz by Negro musicians did not appear until 1922 or 1923. The record companies shunned Negro artists and held aloof from the authentic jazz idiom. The catalogue of Victor records for May, 1913, for example, lists Turkey Trots as well as Rag Time Music, Cakewalks, Clog Dances, One Steps, and Two Steps. All are played, alas, by Pryor's Band, the Victor Military Band, and similar organizations. Scott Joplin's celebrated "Maple Leaf Rag" is played by the United States Marine Band, while Tom Turpin's "Buffalo Rag" appears as a novelty banjo solo by Mr. Vess L. Ossman. "Coon Songs," a subject-heading in the catalogue, are described as "up-to-date comic songs in negro [*sic*] dialect," and are performed by such popular contemporary white comedians as Arthur Collins, Billy Golden, Eddie Morton, and Billy Murray. The Fisk University Jubilee Quartet is the only Negro group in the Victor Company's artist listing. The catalogue comments thus on the folk songs introduced by the original Fisk Jubilee Singers: "Some touch the heart with their pathos; and some although intensely religious, sometimes excite to laughter by their quaint conceptions of religious ideas or Biblical facts."

The Victor Record Catalogue of 1918 continues to list Rag Time music and the older dances, but now includes Fox Trots. Performances are still predominantly by conventional brass bands, although the sedate ballroom aggregations are represented by Joseph C. Smith and his Orchestra. The word "jazz" is noted in the band titles: Original Dixieland Jazz Band and Fuller's Famous Jazz Band. The catalogue's final innovation is a listing of " 'Blue' Records." The Victor Record Catalogue of 1923 introduces Paul Whiteman's Orchestra and numerous other "society" orchestras, which challenge the sway of the brass bands over recorded dance music. "Blue" titles or blues are listed as in 1918, and a brief note explains that " 'Blues' fox-trot records are in slow time as a rule, with grotesque effects."

Authentic, idiomatic jazz was first recorded about 1923 by the Negro musicians Joseph "King" Oliver, Ferdinand "Jelly Roll" Morton, and others who, having emigrated to the North years before, made their records in Northern cities. The twenty-odd years of musical activity that preceded them had no recorded examples.

The first records of any jazz whatever were made in 1917 and for several years thereafter by the so-called Original Dixieland Jazz Band, a group of five white musicians. These records probably supply the link between the unrecorded early-century jazz and that introduced on records in 1923 by Negro bands. Their music shows, in the first place, that the ragtime mode, even at that late date, was still vigorously alive. Furthermore, it reveals a preoccupation with the rhythmic element of Negro musical style—that which was earliest abstracted from the Negro musical language by white minstrels and which developed steadily as a dance mode. It has a minimum of vocalized phrasing; its original motives had a history in caricature and comedy, although it also acquired a limited, formal language of its own.

The Original Dixieland Jazz Band was one characteristic product of the New Orleans environment. Its non-note-reading members, playing cornet, clarinet, trombone, drums, and piano respectively, were contemporaneous with the very Negro musicians who were to make the 1923 records. Like other New Orleans Negro and white musicians, they had ventured to Chicago in response to attractive offers, and in 1917 had moved on to jobs in New York. They had little which set them apart from other bands; their importance lies in their typical and passably idiomatic expression, rather than in any extraordinary qualities. These white musicians at this time caught some of the rhapsodic, improvisatory character of the folk-derived music in its urban locale, and adopted its outward expressive norms. "We played from the heart, what we felt," is the frequently quoted statement of Nick La Rocca, cornettist of the Original Dixieland Jazz Band.

But while most of the Negro dance musicians immersed themselves completely in the expressive content of the folk-derived *vocal* music, the Southern white musicians seemed at this stage to be satisfied with a more superficial borrowing. Negro vocal music, directly or by way of Negro dance instrumentalists, stimulated the white musicians, but the latter proved incapable of absorbing its content. The predominant Negro tendency in jazz, founded on the vocal blues, was, at its simplest and starkest, a lament. The predominant tendency among the white musicians was more eclectic.

In addition to ragtime there was another strong influence affecting them, that of the military brass band, which had dominated popular music for more than fifty years after the Civil War. During the war, in both the North and the South, folk and urban tunes were adapted to the march structure, which, in the most erratic way, was absorbing the phrasing peculiar to American music. Thus, the song "Dixie," a pre-war composition of a white minstrel, Dan Emmett, became the battle march of the Confederacy, although it had originally been intended as "Negro" music, and its first title had been "Dixie-land: Ethiopian Walk'round."

Not only was the march inherently stirring, but it had unrivalled opportunities for presenting its appeal to the whole population. It was outdoor music. There was no price of admission. It was simple in structure and demanded little concentration. The uniformed band held a firm place in the local scene; it became easily the leading popular music institution in the country.

The Spanish-American War completed the democratization of the march. Small brass bands of assorted ear-players could now be seen everywhere in the streets. They played marches at carnival parades, funeral parades, lodge and society parades, and the instrumental parts were so familiar that note-reading was not necessary. At about that time marches began to be used as dance music. Both were played by the one class of musician in all Southern cities, and the single style they adapted to both is one of the sources of the so-called "New Orleans style" of jazz performance. The dance modes—the two step and the one step of succeeding decades as well as the fox trot—developed from the rag *and* the march.

The brass band flourished in the ragtime era; dance music players were also march music players, and dance music, until it assimilated the blues-derived vocalized style, sounded like march music. The early jazz musicians in New Orleans and elsewhere who failed to assimilate the vocal blues were victims of the limitations imposed by the march as well as by the rag. To be sure, the character of the march and the rag made them suitable for retaining the comic effects without absorbing the true expressiveness of Negro music. It is no wonder, then, that in the heyday of the Original Dixieland Jazz Band, most white musicians played music that lacked the inner life and implication of the genuinely vocalized style.

Negro musicians at the turn of the century, in adapting the vocal blues to the brass band style of the march as well as to the standard dance tune, were transcending the march mentality in both. But the brass band itself, with its characteristic march, was proving a survival of the dying era. As early as the 1890's, economic depression and the closing of the banks had created a new generation of wanderers and hoboes, and set into motion migratory movements of people to the Northern industrial centers. Beginning with the First World War and the demand for labor in the war industries, large-scale city migration became inevitable. The demand for industrial labor did not abate after the war, while inflation, oppressive living standards, and chronic farm crisis in the cotton and tobacco country of the South continued to drive people off the land. Expanding industry was completing the urbanization of Northern cities and producing a community that could find little cultural sustenance on the model provided by the more atomized life of the semi-urban, provincial cities of an earlier time. The march had seen its best days during the semi-urbanity of cities; now its outdoor optimism jarred on a generation still living in the disillusionments that followed the war.

Now, the vocalized style predominated in dance music, and the march itself sounded like the new dance music, with delayed or anticipated stresses and free phrasing. With the rise of this vocalized style, precision in performance was no longer a desideratum, and the playing of unison passages and the persistent repetition of motives, inoffensive in a utilitarian dance accompaniment or march, became meaningless devices. Popular marches served, along with jumps, stomps, struts, and shuffle steps, as early Negro jazz dances. The march "High Society," which still survives, is of this vintage. But where the vocalized style was absent, the dances sounded noticeably like conventional marches. In short, the introduction of emotional values into dance music created the idiom and the communicable way of feeling now generally known as the "New Orleans style." This music, jazz, was music of a special kind; it was a popular music, neither blues, ragtime nor march. It was a vernacular speech in music.

IV

FROM THIS POINT ON, the development of jazz is seen to be a series of crises and compromises. Thus the history of the blues is a history of far-reaching urban adaptations. In the rural locale of its origin, its folk tradition was carried on by a rapidly dwindling body of middle-aged singers. Until about 1940, the record companies catalogued the rural blues as "race" records. Suspect from its first influx into cities because of its rural origins—its emotion was in direct and continuous line with the original religious plantation songs—the blues was compelled to adopt a few of the tricks of the trade of popular music. Its subsequent transformation into jazz, or the vocalized style of instrumental playing, representing the most consummate of all its adaptations, led to the early urban, or provincial urban, style of hot jazz. This music which converged upon, and matured in, New Orleans, became of necessity sophisticated and professional in delivery, since it was urban now, competing to some extent with city popular music.

But another kind of compromise was immediately required. No sooner did the honky-tonks and cabarets pay wages to musicians than they demanded popular music. To survive, the improvisers of expressive jazz played the commercial dance numbers, but not without recasting them by covertly maintaining the vocalized style. Jazz as entertainment or as utilitarian dance music provided the protective integument behind which jazz as expressive lament might continue to find a voice. This protectiveness passed into the modern era of dance music; the "dance" front was retained to house and hide the feeling that lay obscured behind the bright surface.

These were the halcyon days of jazz, when it was still the artistic expression of an invisibly linked but indivisible group that played according to a common tradition, and was equally a means of concrete emotional communication apprehended by a mass of people. Yet, rural blues subject matter, overlapping into this period, was sung by sophisticated singers with sophisticated accents. The chief vocal and instrumental interpreters of this time carried their style into the wholly urban decade of the 1920's.

Large numbers of Negro and white musicians came North in the early 1920's, in response to attractive offers from musical agents. The honky-tonks and cabarets of Chicago, the musicians soon discovered, were no less disreputable and sordid than those of New Orleans and other Southern cities, but the money, so it seemed, flowed like water. By this time, the "New Orleans style" had many white as well as Negro performers. In somewhat the same way that the pre-Civil War Negro slaves sang and assimilated the spirituals of white revivalists, the white honky-tonk musicians of the South had by now assimilated the Negro blues, finding it congenial to their situation and their temperament and gratifyingly expressing their own relations to an oppressive environment. Moreover, its style, replete with complex innuendos and subtle inflections, was for them a richer medium for musical expression than any they had known before.

But small compromises by the New Orleans style with popular music and its fashions foreshadowed a cumulative series of crises in jazz. More frequently, adaptations away from the blues were made imperative by the need for constant variation and protective coloring as jazz met changing musical and social conditions.

A sweeping adaptation took place in the middle 1920's, and its fruit was the full urban, or Chicago, style of jazz. At this time, all roads led not to New Orleans but to Chicago where, too, great wealth converged. The city was the literary capital of America, home of Floyd Dell, Carl Sandburg, and the poetry revival, as as well as the legendary high spot of racketeering. Chicago's particular infamy, moreover, had a quality of romantic recklessness resembling that of early-century New Orleans.

The ascendancy of big "name" bands was one aspect of the

corrupt Prohibition era of fluid money, while semi-commercial music indulged tastes based on easy-money values. There was a relative economic security in big bands, and the best of the jazz players were drawn to them. Some, like the gifted cornettist Leon "Bix" Beiderbecke, joined Paul Whiteman's commercial dance band. Others, like Louis Armstrong, joined Fletcher Henderson's "hot" band.

Prohibition also hatched the speak-easy, the small dimensions of which could accommodate only a small band of musicians. Since such a band earned more from customers' tips than from wages, it had to be alert to up-to-the-minute popular tunes. For the sake of bigger tips, it played the tunes "straight," using for that purpose large-band clichés derived originally from its own small-band patterns. Almost at once, a new generation of white jazzmen arose to renovate the New Orleans musical language, making it an equivalent of their own sensibility. This speak-easy elite simply played the popular tunes "hot," imparting to these tunes an almost incredible degree of earnestness and sincerity. The Chicago style that they founded was erratic, embodying a rueful, perverse adultera-tion of the expressive style with the trivial themes of Tin Pan Alley. The best Chicago music was wry and unsweet, frenetic, angular-phrased, and percussive. Its emotion was desperate, sometimes repressed and self-conscious, always unconsoled and unconsolable. It was an authentic postwar expression, revealing alternate flashes of despair, disillusion, and revolt. Ironically, Tin Pan Alley, with its whole stock-in-trade of false emotion, vulgar publicity, and big money manipulation, was the source of the Chicago style.

BY THE THIRTIES, small-band hot jazz had reached its artistic zenith. Whether in the spirit represented by Louis Armstrong and his Hot Five, or by the combinations that played in Chicago style, it was effective expression and communication, both a musical and a social manifestation. The music was played allusively, behind a façade of commercial songs. Often it had to be played "after hours," or, as it were, in concealment, without audience or re-muneration. Lacking a paying audience, spurred on only by their own self-consuming zeal, its executants kept it alive at a bitter cost. The repeal of Prohibition in 1933, and the abrupt disappearance of speak-easies uprooted it, and it faced extinction.

V

JAZZ MUSIC HAD BURST on the ears of the post-war generation in the twenties with extraordinary effect. In a general sense the term "jazz" was applied to popular dance music. Specifically, it denoted a musical idiom which, rooted in the history of the American Negro people, had come to flower as the musical expression of an entire generation. At its best, it was a creative and expressive music, often known as "hot" jazz. This music, which drew little response from the academic musicians, expressed emotions in a new way, and, to the audience that loved it, it seemed to be the only expression in music of their own experience.

The jazz artists were out to make a living. Only incidentally were they concerned to find an expressive voice or to create an art form. They molded forms out of whatever contingencies their immediate environment offered, socially or musically. Musically the forms that they generated arose out of the marches of the brass bands, from the worksongs and songs of lamentation heard everywhere in the plantation South, and from Tin Pan Alley tunes. Socially the maturity of the musicians stemmed from equally diverse influences—the rural South and its travails, and the frenzied and perfervid atmosphere of the twenties. These circumstances gave a shape to their exuberance or their pain, even as the expressive element in their music was forced to undergo more and more hybridization and thinning down. In this welter, their genius snagged odds and ends, using any resources at hand.

The original ideal of the small band's "collective improvisation" was an expressive anonymity, such a congruity of instruments playing independent parts simultaneously that no single solo was heard apart from the others. Although the music had a recognizable body of melodic material, it did little with it, but was a mold for creative interpretation. Jazz was creative or "hot," as it was called, not in terms of its melody or improvisation, but in terms of instrumental temperament. The player was judged by the canniness of his ensemble sense, and by the *authenticity* of his style: his phrasing, intonation, timing, and even his virtuosity had to be typical and characteristic of the New Orleans musical language.

But anonymity as an ideal carried the seeds of its own destruction: from the outset, the typical teemed with elements of the unique, and even as the collective style became more fluent, the musician's individuality became more conspicuous and loomed in the foreground. Emerging solo styles, with accompaniment, deep-rooted in the ensemble solo style, were to prove the vehicle for *both* the greatest nostalgic typicalness and the greatest individuality in all subsequent jazz.

A few musicians who epitomized the different jazz trends succeeded, only for golden moments, in fashioning beauty out of their ordeal:

> O caught like pennies beneath soot and steam,
> Kiss of our agony thou gatherest . . .

Especially because their idiom functioned as an accompaniment for dancing, their art was ephemeral: it gave way before the needs of repetitive commercial formulas. The unconscious and unreasoned ways in which moments of vision rose out of their art spells a certain triumph. But it exposes their limitations: their art was incapable of perpetuating itself into a lasting tradition.

In that company of musicians who conceived the culminating expressions of jazz, Louis Armstrong was pre-eminent. All the experience of the bold New Orleans lyrical style of jazz, whose eloquence derived directly from the vocalized style of playing, was concentrated in the *bravura* expression of this trumpeter. His phrases, intonations, and expressive devices became part of jazz tradition, adopted not only by other instrumentalists but by singers as well. It need only be pointed out that Armstrong's contributions are the pith of the "hot" idiom; because of their extensiveness and breadth, they came close to exhausting what could be accomplished within the limits of the New Orleans solo style.

The cornettist Leon "Bix" Beiderbecke was reared in the Dixieland style. The shaping force in the unique style he made his own—despite its accrued indebtedness to Joe Oliver, Louis Armstrong, Bessie Smith, and the others, and his grateful emulation of their practice—is dance rhythm. But he ultimately transcended its small range of emotional values. Although he drew incompletely from the vocalized style, the result was nonetheless a music like eloquent mellifluous speech, lyrical and intense. Beiderbecke's mature style, as molded by this inflected musical speech, was defined by a deliberately narrowed pitch range. Within this area he could create nuances of phrasing and dynamics by means of fluid and shimmering tone, alternating them with "breaks" and *sforzandi* of flashing brilliance. In the employment of such color, shade, and tint he has no peer in jazz.

Beiderbecke was defenseless against the stultifying effects of routine work in the commercialized bands. His Negro colleagues at least could indulge their private meanings in the disguised symbolism of their intonation. That relief was to a frustrating extent denied Beiderbecke.

A musician whose labor in a byway of the jazz idiom proved to be no limitation upon his achievement is Meade "Lux" Lewis, known as a boogiewoogie pianist. The boogiewoogie style is as old as blues piano and has the same twelve-bar structural and harmonic form as the blues. Outwardly, the style is based on the pianist's independent use of the two hands—an unflagging *ostinato* figure in the bass against free improvisation in the right hand. The interplay of these flexible and inflexible factors provides the basis for its expressiveness. The music combined a strong blues feeling with a relentless percussive accent, while it faintly suggested ragtime and player pianos. It was severely unsentimental, making no compromise with fashions in popular music, yet it was nostalgic. The style was an offshoot; its environment amid the low life of the honky-tonks promised it no commercial future.

Lewis's celebrated "Honky-Tonk Blues" (recorded in several versions), an apostrophe to the motive of the lonesome railroad train, is a concentration of the sum and substance of the boogie-woogie musical outlook. "The Blues (parts 1–4)," probably the longest of all improvised piano blues, is a personal, inviolable world of boogiewoogie as well as blues, wherein the nostalgia is fortified by austerity and compression, and the honky-tonk train appears shadow-like as one demotic symbol in a severely enclosed existence. Strange for Lewis's medium are the tone color and the elegance, and the awareness of the subtle aspects of keyboard resonance. But Lewis was an eccentric in the adaptation history of jazz, and boogie-woogie remained a mutation without progeny.

The full Chicago style, only starting to emerge in the world of Beiderbecke, reached the most poignant expression of its unrest and agony in the wildly reckless, almost self-flagellating playing of the clarinettist Frank Teschmaker. Indifferent to the vulgarity of the new style's origins in blatant commercialism, Teschmaker probed it boldly and searchingly. Out of the Tin Pan Alley musical banality he elaborated an odd discourse. The Chicago style with which his name is identified contributed neither shoddy novelty nor extravagant sensation; it was a true innovation which preserved the integrity of the jazz emotion. The innovation was creative, superior to the existing forms which it replaced. In this medium Teschmaker was an inspired musician. His best solos (as in "Nobody's Sweetheart") are dissonant and calculatedly unpretty, and the emotion is frenzied and impulsive. He played erratically, but while some solos were listless, his invention and feeling never flagged for long.

Beiderbecke dissipated his young manhood during the twenties; Teschmaker died in an automobile accident at the age of twenty-six. Both were products of their unhappy environment. Lewis, who was brought out of obscurity by a brief boogiewoogie revival, returned to obscurity. Armstrong, a prodigy of adaptation, survived only by suiting his talents to ever new fashions in showmanship and comedy.

The careers of these heroes were paralleled in the blues singers. The period of full urban jazz discovered a generation of sumptuous- and full-voiced entertainers led by Gertrude "Ma" Rainey, and including Sara Martin, Edith Johnson, and Ida Cox, singing semi-blues or strophic songs in blues moods. Even Bessie Smith, whose singing was the peak expression of all poignant blues, was obliged to sing a preponderance of synthetic blues and of popular songs. She contributed grandeur to the semi-blues, but in the thirties her singing became out-of-date and hastened the wane of her popularity. The concrete communicable aspect of the blues language was becoming blurred while its early-century feeling-connotations were becoming anachronistic.

The blues singers, like the instrumentalists, maintained their blues language allusively, singing with magnetic eloquence only the imitations of their own singing, now appropriated and conventionalized by the popular vocalists. Behind the worthless words was a residual musical speech, still controlled and impressive. The best-known singers, and notably Bessie Smith, developed a classical, austere manner of singing the popular song, and turned it into a kind of abstract musical ritual. In the very act of keeping alive their integrity, the blues singers created the monster that was to destroy them. And curiously, the process of decline of the vocal blues reversed the earlier process of jazz growth which had culminated in the vocalized instrumental style. Instrumental music had acquired its significance from the sung blues, but now the singer tried to sound like an instrument, abstracting the purely tonal elements of jazz expression and sacrificing the *human* qualities of the voice.

At this stage, those artists in whose interpretations jazz achieved its unquestioned moments of greatness actually were agents of its degeneration. By now their instrumental brilliance represented a high point in technical resourcefulness, but it was concealing the vocal source of their music, while their refinement of style inevitably foreshadowed the decline of their own medium. Even as the idiom received widespread recognition as a *métier,* it was becoming increasingly formalistic, the musical elements detached and elaborated far from the primary emotional context.

In the late twenties, the expanding entertainment industries had already begun to dominate the production of dance music. The development of large commercial jazz orchestras gave prominence to arranged music, which reduced solo improvisation to a minimum. Such arrangements emphasized the dance or rhythmic elements at the expense of the vocal or expressive. The "swing" movement of the middle thirties was a development of this trend, in which arranged music was defined by "riffs," i.e., repeated rhythmic figures, and distinctive "styling" to provide a trade mark for each particular band. In this situation, the periodic wide detours of jazz from its early idiom, and its successive compromises with Tin Pan Alley, while often necessary for its bare survival, resulted in the indiscriminate accumulation of certain meretricious trappings from commercial music. Commercial music, on the other hand, has always disguised its poverty by filching effects from the jazz idiom. The two tended in this way to have ever larger overlapping areas, while the blurred and undefined forms of the jazz idiom lent themselves to parody. For a while, an earnest small-band activity, guided by the jazz critics, tried to revive the playing styles from the twenties. But that only bespoke the impasse that jazz was in. Grown decadent by divorce from its origins, it tried to feed on the past and brought no new grist to the mill. When the conditions expired which gave this musical language its justification as authentic lament, the medium died too, and no latter-day exhuming could breathe back into Lazarus that which the needs of time and history had abandoned.

IN THE FORTIES, the majority of Negro musicians were in full flight from the expressive wellspring of the old jazz idiom. In their deliberate turning away from the blues, there was a conscious rejection of the element of self-caricature and self-derision with which they associated it. A new idiom was unavoidable if any kind of jazz at all was to survive.

Rather late, the jazz musicians discovered some of the harmonic innovations of modern art music, and they experienced the same elation as the art composers who, inversely, had responded to the rhythms and timbre effects of jazz two decades earlier. Self-conscious and technique-centered, the jazz players at first created phrases and phrase-patterns that were recitative-like and complex, dramatic with a kind of musical prose. The Negro musicians, in particular, reveling in the elaboration of cunning arabesques, saw themselves at last as worthy of being judged as equals, on their merits, in the fraternity of all musicians. Moreover, in a frank reaching after bizarre effects, all the players were learning to combine a calculated grotesqueness of phrase with the harmonic novelty of unresolved progresssions. A new jazz idiom was in the making and no other was possible. It was established during the war years by the innovators of modern jazz. Rooted in a gathering dissatisfaction with the poverty of jazz expression, it revealed novel attitudes of irony and sophistication. It retained from the idiom it supplanted only the bare musical elements abstracted from their primary musical context. Upon these elements it was founding a body of harmonic, coloristic, and textural conventions peculiar to itself. This still experimental idiom, which shapes present-day jazz trends, requires a full discussion in its own right.

Mississippi Ham Rider

TONI CADE

I'LL BE HERE TOMORROW for my early morning coffee fix. If you gonna meet me, sister, bring your own dime."

He swiveled away from the counter and stomped out past the juke-box, huddling his greatcoat about him. I flipped my notebook open and wrote: Mississippi Ham Rider can best be described as a salty stud. We had talked for nearly an hour—or rather I had talked, he had merely rolled his eyes and stared into his cup as he swirled the watery coffee revealing the grinds—and still I had nothing to write up really except that there was no humor about the man, and, at seventy, he was not particularly interested in coming to New York to cut records for the new blues series.

The waitress had wiped the counter menacingly and was leaning up against the pie display with her hands on her hips. I was trying to figure out whether I should follow Rider, put Neil on his trail, or try to scrounge up a story from the townsfolk. The waitress was tapping her foot. And the cook, a surly looking bastard in white cap, was peeping over the edge of the kitchen counter, his head kind of cocked to the side so that the sweat beaded around his nostril. I was trying to get myself together, untangle my legs from the stool and get out of there. It was obvious that these particular sinister folks were not going to fill my dossier with anything printable. I moved. But before I even reached the door I was in the third person absentular.

"So what's this high yaller Northern bitch doin' hittin' on evil ole Ham?"

There was only one Rider in the ten-page directory, an Isabele Rider, the address typed in the margin. I folded myself into Neil's Volkswagen and tried to find it. The town itself was something out of Alice or Poe, the colored section was altogether unbelievable—outhouses, corner hard-heads, a predominance of junkyards with people in them, poverty with all the usual trimmings. And Isabele

Rider ran one of those time-immemorial stores—love potions and dream books and star charts and bleaching creams and depilatory powders, and mason jars of ginger roots and cane shoots. A girl of about sixteen was sitting on a milk box reading a comic book and eating a piece of sweet potato pie.

"Mrs. Isabele Rider around?" I asked.

"No." She went right on reading and eating.

"I'm Inez Williams," I said. "The people I work for are trying to persuade Mr. Ham Rider to record some songs. They want him to come to New York and bring his guitar. He's a great blues singer," I said.

She looked me over and closed the book. "You want some pie?"

"No thanks, just Mrs. Rider. She around?"

"No. Just me. I'm Melanie. My mother says Ham ain't going nowhere nor me either. Lady before asked me to sit-in somewhere. My mother says I ain't going nowhere, Ham neither."

I leaned on the counter and unbuttoned my sweater. A badly drawn zodiac chart was right in front of me. I traced the orbits looking for Aries the Ram to give me the high sign. He looked like a very sick dog in the last stages of sickle-cell anemia. I tried to figure out the best way to run it down to this girl right quick that they didn't have to live in this town and hang around in this store and eat sweet potato pie for lunch and act like throwbacks, before I totally distracted myself with the zodiac or considerations of abnormal hemoglobins and such like.

"Look," I said, "back in the twenties a lot of record companies put out a series called race records. And a lot of blues singers and country singers and some flashy show business types made a lot of records. Some made a lot of money. But when the depression came, the companies fell apart and these singers went on home. Some stuck around and mopped floors and ran elevators. Now this jive mother who is my boss thinks he can make some bread by recording some of the old-timers. And they can make some bread too. So what I want is to get your grand-daddy to come with us and sing awhile. You see?"

"You best speak to Ham himself," she said.

"I did. But he thought I was just trying to get into his business. All I do is write up a thing about the singers, about their life, and the company sticks this onto the album cover."

She licked the last of the pie from her fingers and stood up. "What you wanna know?"

I whipped out my notebook. "What does he like, where does he come from, who're his friends. Stuff like that."

"We three all what's left. His landlady, Mama Teddy, looks out for him when he gets drinking and can't help himself. And I look out of his way when he gets raffish." She shrugged.

"Any chance of us all getting together? My partner, Mr. Neil McLoughlin, is the one who handles the business and all. I'd like you all to meet him."

"This some fay cat?"

"Uh . . . yeh."

"Uh-hunh." She ripped off the edge of the calendar and wrote an address. "This here is where we eat, Mama Teddy's. You be there at six."

Neil was going into one of his famous crouches by the time I got to the park. He had spent the day trying to find quarters for us both which was a lost cause. There was not even a diner where we could trade notes without incident, so I fell in beside him on the bench, jostling the bottle in his pocket.

"I'm beat and burnt-out, I mean it," he wailed, rolling his eyes up to the heavens. "This is the most unfriendly town. I escaped from an unbelievable little rooming house down the road just as an incredible act of hospitality was about to be committed."

"Yeh, well look, pull yourself together and let's deal with the Rider character first. He's quite a sketch—jack boots, the original War-One bespoke overcoat, razor scar, gravel voice and personality to match and—you ready?—he'll be damned if he's going North. Says he was badly mistreated up there. Froze his behind off one winter in Chicago. And in New York, the Negro artists had to use a drafty freight elevator to get to the recording studio."

"Not like the swell conditions here."

"He wasn't an artist here. I think the best thing to do is just tape him here and let him sign whatever release one signs."

"But old man Lyons, dearheart, wants him in the flesh to allow the poor folkway-starved sophisticates to, through a out-rageous process of osmosis, which in no way should suggest miscegenation— to absorb their native—"

"Alright, alright, calm down. The thing is, his last offer was to sing obscene songs for party records. He damned near committed mayhem. In short, the man don't wanna leave, buddy."

"But wasn't he at least knocked out by your superior charms, not to mention your long, lean gams?"

"Those are my superior and singular charms. He was totally unimpressed. But the man's seventy something, keep in mind."

Neil slouched over into his hands. "This is hard work, I mean it. And I feel a mean and nasty spell coming on. I never had so much trouble and complication in my life before. I've got consumption of the heart and—"

"Neil, my nerves."

"They were always pretty easy to find. Mobile, Auburn, just a sitting there in a beat-up room in a beat-up town in a beat-up mood, just sitting there waiting for an angel of mercy, me. Doing nothing but a moaning and a hummin' and a strummin'—"

"Alright, cut it out. We're in trouble. The man don't wanna budge and all you can do is indulge in these theatrical and most unnerving, irritating fits of—"

"Dearheart, recall," he demanded, shoving his spread hand in my face. "There was old man Supper, a real nice old supper man. Kinda quiet like and easy going, just dipping his snuff and boiling his supper. And then ole Jug Henderson, the accident-prone saint of white lightning, fiddling away and sipping that bad stuff out of a mayonnaise jar. And—"

"Neil, my nerves."

"And ole Blind Grassy Wilson from Lynchburg, only one leg left by the time I arrived, but swinging still and real nice about talking into the machine to tell how his best gal slapped a razor across his chops."

"Enough, you're running amok." I got up and stretched my legs. "We've got to find a place called Mama Teddy's. And please, Neil, let me do the talking. I'm tired of eating sandwiches out of paper bags. Just be quiet till after we eat. And no wise cracks. We might get killed."

"Good Lord," he jumped up, "I'm not insured. One false move and the man's liable to cut me, beat me up, starve me to death, and then poison me." He grabbed himself by the throat and rolled around atop the mailbox. A truck passed, I stepped aside and acted like I wasn't with the lunatic.

"Amazing how your race has deteriorated under segregation, Neil. If only you'd had an example to follow, you might have been a halfway decent dancer."

He smoothed his hair back and walked quite business-like to the car.

"Get in, woman."

MAMA TEDDY'S was a store front thing. Fried chicken legs and bar-b-qued ribs were painted on the window pane. And scrawled across the top of the glass in fussy little curlicues were the various price-fixed meals. In the doorway were three large jugs with soapy, brown something or other in them, rag wicks stuffed into the necks and hanging over the sides to the floor. But you could see that the place was clean, sort of. I was starving. Neil was dragging along the tape recorder mumbling statistics about hernia and prostate damage.

"You see that pick-up truck over there," he whispered. "It's full of angry blacks with ugly sticks who're gonna whip my head 'cause they think you're my woman."

"Never mind, let's go find Mr. Ethnic-Authentic."

Neil tripped over the jugs and a whiff of chit'lins damn near knocked me over. A greasy smell from the kitchen had jammed up my breathing before I even got into the place.

"Somebody's dying," whispered Neil.

"Soul food," I gasped, eyes watering.

"What?"

"You wouldn't understand, my boy."

The large, jovial woman who shuffled out of the kitchen with what only looked like great speed was obviously Mama Teddy.

"Hi, little honey," she said squashing me into her bosom. "Little Melanie told me all about you and you're surely welcome. You too," she said swallowing up Neil's hand in her fist. She hustled us over to a table with cloth and flowers.

"Mr. Rider'll be in directly less'n he's in his cups. And Miss Isabele's expected soon. Just rest yourself. We're going to have a fine southern dinner. Your folks from here?" she asked me.

"Mother's from Atlanta and my father was born in Beaufort, South Carolina."

"Mmmm-huh," she nodded, agreeing that these were certainly geographically fine folks.

"My people hail from Galway Bay," offered Neil.

"Well I'm sure they're mighty fine people too," she winked. "Now, is it for true," she whispered, setting the silverware, "you taking Mr. Ham to New York to sing?"

"We'd like to. But he doesn't seem very interested."

"Oh," she laughed, snapping the dishcloth across the table. "All that huffin' and puffin' don't signify. You know what he and Melanie been doing all day? Writing out the songs, the words. She's very smart, that girl. Make a fine secretary. I bet you could use a fine secretary with all that writing you do. There must be a lot of jobs. . . ."

Neil saw it coming. He slouched in his seat and pushed his glasses up. He sat all the while rubbing his eyes. I fingered the soup spoon, vaguely attentive to Mama Teddy's monologue. It was perfectly clear what kind of game she was running. And why not? Along with the numerous tapes of chats and song-fests, Neil had collected from the Delta and the Carolinas a volume of tales that didn't go into the album catalogues, things he was saving for some sensational book he'd never write. The payoffs, bribes, bargains, and deals, interviews in jail cells, drug wards, wino bins. Things apart from the usual folksy atrocity story. The romance had long since gone out of the job. Neil's first trauma occurred last spring when he finally smoked Bubba Mabley out of a corner. The sixty-year-old card shark had insisted on taking his "little woman" along to New York. This sloe-eyed youngster of fifteen turned out to be his illegitimate daughter by his niece. It knocked Neil out though he told it now with a certain rehearsed nonchalance.

"Mr. Rider wouldn't think of traveling without his family," the big woman was saying. "They're a very devoted family."

Neil had worked his eyes into a feverish red. But I was perfectly content. One good exploitive act deserved another. And what was the solitary old blues singer going to do after he had run the coffee-house circuit and scared the living shit out of the college kids? It was grotesque no matter how you cut it. I wished I was in films instead. Ole Ham Rider besieged by well-dressed coffee drinkers wanting his opinion on Miles Davis and Malcolm X was worth a few feet of film. And the quaint introduction some bearded fool in tight-across-the-groin pants would give would justify more footage. No amount of drunken thinking could convince me that Mr. Lyons could groom this character for popular hootenannies. On the other hand, if the militant civil liberties unions got hold of him, Mr. Charlie was a dead man.

"Here's Miss Isabele," the woman announced.

She looked real enough to upset Lyons's plans. She shook hands and sat down, crossed her legs, and lit up a cigarette. She was good looking in a way—plucked eyebrows, clinging wool dress, scary make-up. You knew she'd been jitterbugging since kindergarten, but she looked good anyhow.

"So you want the old man to sing," she said, sniffing in the curls of smoke. "Sits in the window sometimes to sing, but that don't cut no greens, don't make no coins." She swerved around in her chair and kicked Neil's foot. "The man needs money, mister. He's been needing for a long time. Now what you gonna do for him?"

"We're going to give him a chance to sing," Neil said, catapulting a cigarette butt across the room with the tablespoon.

She looked dissatisfied. "He needs," she said simply, sending up a smoke screen.

The image of the great old artist fallen on bad times, holing up in a stuffy rooming house drinking bad home brew out of a jelly jar and howling blues out the window appealed to my grade-B movie-ruined mind.

"Now when he gets here," Miss Isabele instructed me with her cigarette, "you get him to do 'Evil Landlord.' That's his best."

"Will he bring his guitar?" Neil asked.

"He mostways do."

"To the dinner table?" Neil persisted.

"To the dinner table," she said, one eyebrow already on its way to a threatening arch. "And I need a cigarette."

Mississippi Ham Rider brought his guitar and his grand-daughter. He had on a white shirt and had left the greatcoat at home. He mumbled his greetings and straddled a chair, dislocating my leg in the process.

"You got a long pair of legs, sister."

I had no clever retort so we all just sat there while Mama Teddy heaved big bowls of things onto the table. There were collard greens and black-eye peas and ham hocks and a long pan of corn bread. And there were a whole lot of things I'd never even seen, even in my household.

"Bet you ain't ate like this in long time," Rider said. "Most people don't know how to cook nohow, 'specially you Northerners."

"Jesus Christ," said Neil, leaning over to look into the bowls on the far side of the table. "What's that that smells?"

"That's the South, boy," said Rider.

Melanie smiled and I supposed the old man had made a joke. Neil leaned back and got quiet.

"I don't sing no cotton songs, sister," he said, picking up a knife. "And I ain't never worked in the fields or shucked corn. And I don't sing no nappy-head church songs neither. And no sad numbers about losing my woman and losing my mind. I ain't never lost no woman and that's the truth." He sliced the corn bread with a ceremonial air.

"Good," I said for no particular reason.

He looked up and for one rash moment I thought he was going to smile. I lost my head. But he really looked like he was going to work that bony, old, ashen skull in that direction.

"Well what else is there?" Neil finally asked. "I mean just what kind of songs do you sing?"

"My kind."

Melanie smiled again and Miss Isabele laughed on her cigarette. But I was damned if I could get hold of this new kind of humor.

After we had eaten, Mama Teddy put coffee on the table and then tended to her customers. I stretched my legs into the aisle and relaxed, watching the old man work up his pipeful. He was impressive, the way a good demolition site can be, the way horror movies from the thirties are now. I was tempted to ask him how many people he had killed in his lifetime, thinking I had at last gotten hold of his vein of humor. But I sat and waited for him to sing. I was sure that on the first job he'd turn the place out and maybe do somebody in just for the fun that was in it. And then a really weird thing came over me. I wanted to ask him a lot of dumb things about the South, about what he thought of the sit-ins and all. But he had already taken on a legendary air and was simply not of these times. I cursed Mr. Lyons's fairy-tale mentality and quietly indulged in fabricating figures from whole cloth.

"First I'm gonna sing you my birthday song," he said, pushing the coffee cups to the side. "And then I'm going to do this number about a little lady with long legs."

"Then what?" I smiled, putting my cup down.

"Then I'm gonna get drunk directly and pack my things. My bad suspenders and my green hat," he said. "One jar of Noxzema and my stocking cap."

Melanie laughed straight out and Neil began gagging on Miss Isabele's cigarette smoke.

"And I gotta get a brand new jug of Gallo," he sighed. "I don't never do no heavy traveling without my loving spoonful."

"Then you're coming with us?" I asked.

"We all going to New York and tear it up," he said.

"Damn," coughed Neil.

Rider grabbed his guitar by the neck and swung it over the dishes. He gave Neil a terrible look that only aggravated the coughing.

"But first I think Mr. Somebody best go catch himself some air."

"I can take it," Neil growled, hooking up the tape recorder. He climbed over customers to get to the outlet. "It's on, man," he said. "Go ahead and sing your song."

He looked up at Neil and then he did smile. I wouldn't ever want him to smile at me.

"I can take it," said Neil again, pushing up his glasses.

"See that you do, boy. See that you do." He plucked at the strings, grinning from ear to ear.

Written after Hearing Ellington in Concert, July 1961

JOHN MACKAY

Ellington, sixty-two years old, handsomer than ever, oversized-collared, square-shouldered, Ellington, getting unhip crowd with him after one sentence into microphone.

Making it very clear right from the beginning who runs the Ellington band as he sits workmanlike at piano and bangs out opening chords of 1931, Cotton Club, beautiful, Creole Rhapsody.

Instrumentalists rising from their seats to step forward to single center-stage mike and blow lovely solos then slip back into band, cooler than any hard boppers.

Ellington at end of tune practically leaping from piano, after final slash at keyboard, gliding big wide-cuffed, suede-shoed stride out to mike and in refreshingly confident (he knows by now that he is a great man) cultured voice winding audience around his finger.

Then from 1930 Harlem to 1960 "Theme from Asphalt Jungle," showing us where Mingus came from (which Charlie knows better than anyone) with big dissonant horn sections, and Duke pounding out Monk-like, no, Ellington-like chords from his driver's seat.

Getting up from his piano as band still plays and saying something in bass player's ear at which they both laugh, both of them grooving along all the while, until Duke brings tune to a close with big two-fisted, wheeling, jump.

[III, 3, Spring 1962]

Next with swingingest yet "Just A-Settin' and A-Rockin'," and
drummer Sam Woodyard showing that he's not afraid of any
backbeat (this band that's played a thousand dances) while
Ellington at the piano makes all kinds of noises from somewhere down in his throat.

Trombonist Lawrence Brown, feet spread like a boxer, reminding
us with funny wa-wa mute that "Tricky Sam" is gone from the
band, but not forgotten.

Lean Gonsalves, crouching, slightly hunched over, and looking like
in great pain, squeezing out cruising tenor solo, then sneaking
sort of slyly back to his chair.

Harry Carney, who looks like he *ought* to play a baritone saxo-
phone, and Ray Nance, very hip, very cool, singing "It Don't
Mean a Thing If It Ain't Got That Swing," and Duke, finger
popping, looking like he still digs Ray after all these years.

Johnny Hodges, older, but still no one besides himself, blowing
lovely, perfect, alto so that you can hear the breath slipping
across the reed and you know that's the only way Johnny
ever wants to play horn.

And Duke himself in ivory-colored silk suit playing incredibly sad
"Don't Get Around Much Anymore" while behind him the
saxophones are saying they know just how he feels.

Big, Duke-ish, fourteen manpower, Ellington machine, within
whose ranks once sat Blanton, and Cootie, and "Tricky Sam,"
and big, bedroomy, Ben Webster, and Greer (if you could
see him behind all those cymbals) and oh so sensitive, so fine,
Ivie Anderson.

And Duke, at night's end, receiving applause, arms upstretched in
characteristic Ellington gesture, grinning proudly, like a man
who rides the "A" train all the way up to Sugar Hill every
night of the week.

The Blues as a Literary Theme

GENE BLUESTEIN

THE USE OF FOLKLORE by American writers is a subject that has been discussed only briefly. Daniel Hoffman's *Form and Fable in American Fiction* is the most successful attempt to understand the impact on our early writers of themes and techniques related to folk tradition, and he has gone far toward correcting the view that folklore has counted for little in our literary developments. My concern here will be with the use of Negro folklore and folksong in more recent works which reflect both the ideological and technical implications of folklore as a basis for literary expression. One area of special interest is jazz and themes related to its origin and development.

It has been widely noted that there is a special relationship between the Negro and the American experience in general. For one thing, it is important to recall that of all the diverse groups who came to this country only the Negro came in large numbers against his will and under conditions of chattel slavery. David Brion Davis has pointed out that while slavery posed a general moral problem for all of Western culture, it had a special relevance in the New World. His major conclusion in *The Problem of Slavery in Western Culture* is that the central patterns of slavery in all cultures have been more like than unlike, yet there is a sense in which slavery came close to defining the very meaning of the "American mission." He observes that "Americans have often been embarrassed when reminded that the Declaration of Independence was written by a slaveholder and that Negro slavery was a legal institution in all thirteen colonies at the beginning of the revolution." Critics of America's national aspirations have made the most of what is an obvious contradiction and inconsistency in our equalitarian ideology, and Davis shows in his study how widely spread were the rationalizations utilized to justify the existence of slavery within the context of a democratic society such as the United States claimed to be. His explorations stop short of the abolitionist period in this country, concluding with the prophecy of Quaker John Woolman that "if Americans continued to be unfaithful to their high destiny, their descendants would face the awful retribution of God's justice." In general, and to the present day, Americans have relied on standard rationalizations to justify either slavery or the separation of Negroes from the mainstream of American life. Several of our major folklorists (Constance Rourke, and John and Alan Lomax), on the other hand, have attempted to find a central position for the Negro and his accomplishments within the framework of American civilization, emphasizing the seminal influence of Negro folk materials. Most academic folklorists, however, tended to place Negro tradition outside the main lines of American development, identifying it either as African or as mere imitation of white traditions.

Our formal writers have often taken a rather different approach. Mark Twain, for example, used Jim in *Huckleberry Finn* as a way of expressing strong opposition to the hypocrisy of middle class American society. Hoffman has pointed out that Jim rises above the stereotyped notion of the fearful slave to become "a source of moral energy," though he also recognizes that "Mark Twain's triumph here is incomplete: despite the skillful gradation of folk beliefs and other indications of Jim's emergent stature, what does come through for many readers is, as Mr. Ellison remarks, Jim's boy-to-boy relationship with Huck, 'a violation of our conception of adult maleness.' We remember that Mark Twain himself admired Uncle Remus extravagantly, and much as he means for us to admire Jim —much as he admires Jim himself—the portrait, though drawn in deepest sympathy, is yet seen from the outside." I shall return later to Ralph Ellison's comments about Negro folklore and American literature. But it is interesting to see what the outsider's view of the Negro has meant not only for the characterization of Negroes in our literature, but also for the uses of Negro folklore as well. Curiously, one of the main purposes of employing Negro materials by many of our writers has been ideological—as a way of establishing some sense of the world view of non-Negro characters in fiction.

Some obvious examples from the period after World War I come to mind, and they illustrate the general approach. Most of them take place in the context of the "jazz age," and they provide a good contrast between white writers who know little about the history or meaning of jazz and those later writers whose knowledge of jazz and its folk sources are more sophisticated. F. Scott Fitzgerald limns a scene early in *The Great Gatsby* (1925) which is calculated to dramatize the opulence and emptiness of American society in the twenties. At one of Gatsby's wild parties the orchestra leader announces: " 'At the request of Mr. Gatsby we are going to play for you Mr. Vladimir Tostoff's latest work which attracted so much attention at Carnegie Hall last May. If you read the papers, you know there was a big sensation.' He smiled with jovial condescension, and added: 'Some sensation!' Whereupon everybody laughed. 'The piece is known,' he concluded lustily, 'as Vladimir Tostoff's *Jazz History of the World.*' " Fitzgerald's narrator comments that the nature of the piece eluded him, but notices that when it was over, "girls were putting their heads on men's shoulders in a puppy-ish, convivial way, girls were swooning over backward playfully into men's arms, even into groups, knowing that some one would arrest their falls . . .," though Gatsby himself remains aloof from the activities. Despite the fact that we get no description of the work, it is easy to piece together the nuances of the passage. The performance of the work was a sensation—apparently a scandalous occasion in the major hall associated with symphonic music and recitals. The composer's name 'suggests why: it is a piece simply tossed off, which is a close approximation of the main criticism of jazz, namely that it is not carefully or consciously composed but simply a kind of musical fling. (The less pejorative term would be *improvised,* which is an accurate way of defining one of the essential elements in jazz performances.) A *Jazz History of the World* would have been an assault on the very idea of history itself, expressing the lack of order with an equally shocking disregard of conventional musical sound—cacophonous, perhaps polyrhythmic, and above all sensual in its appeal, as the orchestra leader's "lusty" introduction and the following aphrodisiacal effects reveal. (Fitzgerald may have been referring to one of Igor Stravinsky's early works which were received with great hostility in the first part of this century precisely because they contained innumerable innovations, including techniques borrowed from jazz.) The important point is that jazz is defined in essentially negative terms as a way of identifying the chaos and libertinism of Gatsby's world, and although the composer is obviously a Russian, the controlling elements of his work depend on their relationship to jazz, a Negro music.

Fitzgerald's interest in what he calls jazz as well as in popular music reminds us how rarely American writers use music thematically in their work, unlike European writers (Mann, for example) who often derive major elements of their form and content through conscious analogies with music. (Whitman, as has been widely noted, is an exception and so is Eliot.) There are, however, a number of references to popular songs in *The Great Gatsby* and they generally reflect the uncommitted, lackadaisical attitudes of Fitzgerald's characters—other than Gatsby, of course, who pays little attention to the surface atmosphere which he has caused to be created. The tunes include "The Sheik of Araby," "Ain't We Got Fun," "Three O'Clock in the Morning," and "The Love Nest," several of these performed by Gatsby's boarder, Mr. Klipspringer. In a flashback which details Gatsby's early involvement with Daisy in Louisville, Fitzgerald wrote: "For Daisy was young and her artificial world was redolent of orchids and pleasant, cheerful snobbery, and orchestras which set the rhythm of the year, summing up the madness and suggestiveness of life in new tunes. All night long the saxophones wailed the hopeless comment of the *Beale Street Blues* while a hundred pairs of golden and silver slippers shuffled the shining dust." Shortly thereafter Fitzgerald announces Daisy's decision to marry Tom Buchanan. Again it is apparent that the music reflects the hollowness of Daisy's environment and although Fitzgerald identifies the pop tunes with sadness as well as the possibilities of new life, the clinching reference is to the "hopeless comment" of the blues. All of these statements amount to an ideological position which appears regularly in American literature thereafter, probably through the influence of Fitzgerald, though he was familiar with Eliot's similar approach in *The Waste Land* (1922): "When lovely woman stoops to folly and / Paces about her room again, alone, / She smoothes her hair with automatic hand, / And puts a record on the gramophone." On the one hand, we might define this position as the use of popular songs to provide incidental music for the decline of man's vitality and sensibility in the modern world. The pop tune works marvelously in this manner, for it is technically slight (a simple formula defines almost all the compositions) and its diction illustrates perfectly a cloying, sentimental tone that contrasts obviously with the achievements of "serious" poetry.

But even as we identify these elements of commercial, popular music, it is apparent that it contributes something else to the values asserted by writers such as Fitzgerald—and we might add Hemingway, Dos Passos, and Faulkner, among others. However trite and barbaric the music appears to be, it functions nevertheless as a lever against the cultural pretensions of conventional middle-class society. And it does so, I would suggest, not so much for its own sake as for its association with a tradition of which it is a heavily watered-down version—namely, Negro jazz and its folk sources. Despite their limited awareness of the nature and sources of American music, some sense of what underlay the popular songs leaked through in the work of writers like Fitzgerald. Jazz carried clear associations with a level of culture decidedly outside the stream of middle-class white morality and rooted essentially in the attitudes and expression of the Negro. For the writers of the twenties and thirties, jazz carried strong sexual connotations and was associated with stereotypes of the Negro as fantastically virile and barbarously effective in his sexual life. Attempts to pinpoint the etymology of the word have failed to produce a clear explanation, but all discover a primary use of jazz (sometimes *jass*) as a verb meaning to fornicate. The Jazz Age (the coinage seems in fact to have been Fitzgerald's) picked up all these nuances: the disillusionment with the Great War, the reaction to Prohibition and associated "puritanical" restrictions of the period, the wide open life of speak-easies with their flow of bootleg liquor and promiscuous women—though the latter are always underplayed in our nostalgic recreations of the period, in films particularly. Although Negroes appear occasionally (as musicians), the Jazz Age is presented to us in literature from the disaffected white's point of view; what it suggests to us about the Negro himself is a form of sentimental primitivism: jazz is his music and the white listener uses it as a way of making some small contact with the jungle madness which its beat suggests. The sense of distance is important, for while jazz is conceived to be a threat to the values of the sick world in the period after World War I, it is also the fitting accompaniment for its impending demise. Tostoff's composition is ironically only the other side of Tom Buchanan's assertion: "Civilization's going to pieces. . . . I've gotten to be a ter-rible pessimist about things. Have you read 'The Rise of the Colored Empires' by this man Goddard? . . . Well it's a fine book, and everybody ought to read it. The idea is if we don't look out the white race will be—will be utterly submerged. It's all scientific stuff; it's been proved." The *Jazz History of the World* is the finale for the last act.

William Faulkner's response to music is in general very much like Fitzgerald's. But occasionally he gives us a view of Negro music (and folklore) which is much less patronizing than that of his contemporaries, and at times he comes close to folkloristic precision. Ralph Ellison has noted in *Shadow and Act* (1964) that, despite his ambivalence and his willingness to accept major stereotypes of the Negro, Faulkner "has explored perhaps more successfully than anyone else, either white or black, certain forms of Negro humanity." In part this is due to his remarkably prolific exploration of the South in general, but Ellison observes that Faulkner's central quest is for human truth rather than regional or racial insights. Because the social order of the South "harms whites no less than blacks, the sensitive Southerner, the artist, is apt to feel its effects acutely—and within the deepest levels of his personality. For not only is the social division forced upon the Negro by the ritualized ethic of discrimination, but upon the white man by the strictly enforced set of anti-Negro taboos. The conflict is always within him. Indeed, so rigidly has the recognition of Negro humanity been tabooed that the white Southerner is apt to associate any form of personal rebellion with the Negro. So that for the Southern artist the Negro becomes a symbol of his personal rebellion, his guilt, and his repression of it. The Negro is thus a compelling object of fascination, and this we see very clearly in Faulkner." Since Faulkner has also recognized how inextricably the Negro is involved in the meaning of America itself, he has often taken an approach somewhat different from Fitzgerald's. At the same time, like many of our Southern writers, he is closer to the roots of Negro folk tradition and often reproduces elements from it with great accuracy, as we can see from some descriptions of Negro music in his novels. *Sartoris* (1929) was Faulkner's third novel but the first in which he found his distinctive voice and most of his major themes. It abounds in Negro stereotypes—"his race's fine feeling for potential theatrics," "the grave and simple pleasure of his race." But it also contains some prime examples of the quality, style, and range of Negro music. Elnora, the house servant, sings snatches of spirituals "as she soused her mop into the pail and thumped it on the floor again.

> Sinner riz fum de moaner's bench,
> Sinner jump to de penance bench;
> When de preacher ax 'im whut de reason why,

Say, "Preacher got de women jes' de same ez I."
    Oh, Lawd, oh, Lawd!
Dat's whut de matter wid de church today."

On other occasions Elnora's voice floats "in meaningless minor suspense," or wells "in mellow falling suspense"—a description which catches nicely the melismatic quality of Negro singing as it moves from tone to tone, rarely stopping squarely on a given pitch.

In another section young Bayard puts together a Negro trio to provide an evening serenade: "They stopped here, in shadow. The Negroes descended and lifted the bass viol out, and a guitar. The third one held a slender tube frosted over the keys upon which the intermittent moon glinted in pale points, and they stood with their heads together, murmuring among themselves and touching plaintive muted chords from the strings. . . . The tunes were old tunes. Some of them were sophisticated tunes and formally intricate, but in the rendition this was lost and all of them were imbued instead with a plaintive similarity, a slurred and rhythmic simplicity; fading, dying in minor reiterations along the treacherous vistas of the moon." The performance ends with "Home, Sweet Home" and a rendition of "Good Night, Ladies," sung in the "true, oversweet tenor" of one of the white men who accompany the Negroes. (Faulkner refers to the rich *minor* of "Home, Sweet Home" although it is actually in a major key. Yet the rendition of this standard sentimental tune by a Negro group could easily give it a minor tonality.) But as in much of his work, Faulkner is perhaps more accurate than he knew, because the description of Negroes appropriating materials from the general culture into their own style is a precise illustration of that hybridization of diverse materials which defines the quality of American folksong. (As Alan Lomax has pointed out, the major elements in American folksong derive from West African and British sources combined uniquely in the United States.)

Finally there is Bayard's response to the movements of country Negroes through the town at noon: "—Negroes slow and aimless as figures of a dark placid dream, with an animal odor, murmuring and laughing among themselves; there was in their consonantless murmuring something ready with mirth, in their laughter something grave and sad. . . ." Bayard continues to watch: "Against the wall, squatting, a blind Negro beggar, with a guitar and a wire frame holding a mouth organ to his lips, patterned the background of smells and sounds with a plaintive reiteration of rich, monotonous chords, rhythmic as a mathematical formula, but without music. He was a man of at least forty and his was that patient resignation of many sightless years. . . ." Bayard groped for a coin in his pocket "and the beggar sensed his approach and his tune became a single repeated chord, but without a break in the rhythm, until the coin rang into the cup, and still without a break in the rhythm and the meaningless strains of the mouth organ, his left hand dropped groping a little, to the cup and read the coin in a single motion; then once more guitar and mouth organ resumed their monotonous pattern." What Faulkner has caught here is the central tradition of Negro folksong—the blues. In fact one of the main sources of its dispersion in the South was through the agency of blind street singers such as the one described in the passage, and Faulkner is incredibly accurate in his description of what the music sounded like; it is indeed a heavily rhythmic, formulaic repetition of standard motifs, though more complex than Faulkner suggests. The combination of guitar and mouth organ is a traditional one—in the South the harmonica is more likely to be called a French harp, I think because it is tongued and hence by analogy from French kiss. In any case, the style associated with blues harmonica is a major innovation of Southern Negroes. It is accomplished by playing the instrument in a key different from the one in which it is tuned, which results in a striking blues tonality ordinarily not possible on the instrument, which is non-chromatic and has a very limited range. As in some of his other comments about Negro music and singing, Faulkner refers to meaningless strains, and of course, having omitted any reference to the singing which would accompany the blues, he misses the verbal comment as well as the complex relationships between instrumental and vocal styles that is inherent in the country blues. In other words, Faulkner is still far from understanding fully the meaning or the function of blues in Negro tradition, and he uses the music to underscore the disaffection of his lost generation protagonist, Bayard Sartoris. Yet he comes closer to the materials than any writer up to his time, just as in *The Sound and the Fury* he gives us one of the best descriptions of a Negro singing-sermon which has ever been presented in American literature. The Reverend Shegog begins in the standard speech of educated Southerners and then suddenly breaks into a country dialect: " 'Breddren en sistuhn!' His voice rang again, with the horns. He removed his arm and stood erect and raised his hands. 'I got de ricklickshun en de blood of de lamb!' They did not mark just when his intonation, his pronunciation became negroid, they just sat swaying a little in their seats as the voice took them into itself." It is a perceptive insight into the pluralistic pattern of American Negro life, and when the disguise is lifted Shegog fits immediately into the pattern of call and response which is basic to Negro folksong and folk sermons, the preacher half-speaking and half-singing, in concert with the occasional cries and melodic intonations of the congregation.

BUT WHILE FAULKNER'S is a significant accomplishment, it yet falls short of fulfilling the possibilities of Negro materials for their own sake as well as for what they can tell us of American life in general. We can see this best by looking closely at Ralph Ellison's *Invisible Man* (1952), which defines the ideological and technical possibilities of American Negro materials more accurately and effectively than any work in our literary history. Ellison is valuable also because he is one of those writers whose criticism is as carefully crafted as his fiction—it is a virtue we often associate with poets (from Dryden to Eliot) but which, with the major exception of Henry James, seems less prevalent among fiction writers.

To begin with, it is important to recognize that Ellison does not conceive the book as a "Negro novel" in any sense of the term. What he has learned from Faulkner is that the relationships between black and white are central to the meaning of *American* development. That does not prevent him from understanding the unique qualities of Negro life and culture, but it does mark him from the tendency discernible in some of our Negro writers (Leroi Jones and James Baldwin, for example) to associate themselves with separatism or Black Nationalism. Ellison explains his position partly from the fact that his roots are in the Southwest rather than in the deep South, though it seems to me he could have arrived at a similar conclusion even if he had been brought up in the Black Belt. Still it is important for him to recall that as a boy he and his companions felt little of the pressure to move inwardly toward the ghetto and away from the possibilities of American life: "Contrary to the notion currently projected by certain specialists in the 'Negro problem' which characterizes the Negro American as self-hating and defensive, we did not so regard ourselves. We felt, among ourselves at least, that we were supposed to be whoever we would and could be and do anything and everything which other boys did, and do it better. Not defensively, because we were ordered to do so; not because it was held in the society at large that we were naturally, as Negroes, limited—but because we demanded it of ourselves. Because to measure up to our own standards was the only way of affirming our notion of manhood." This is in line with Ellison's general conception of the meaning of American life which, as I think can be made clearer from the novel, is closest to the ideas of Emerson. Consequently, he points out, it was perfectly logical for him and his companions to think of themselves as Renaissance men, just as white Southerners viewed themselves as ancient Greeks or Cavaliers: "Surely our fantasies have caused far less damage to the nation's sense of reality, if for no other reason than that ours were expressions of a more democratic ideal. Remember, too, as William Faulkner made us so vividly aware, that the slaves often took the essence of the aristocratic ideal (as they took Christianity) with far more seriousness than their masters, and that we, thanks to the tight telescoping of American history, were but two generations from that previous condition." Ellison's point is that the Negro has never really been out of the mainstream of the American experience, despite continuing assertions that the Negro is best understood as a man without a past: his African inheritance stripped away, this argument insists, there was nothing capable of replacing it in a society which consciously kept him hermetically sealed in the ghetto.

But Ellison uses just this circumstance to point out how closely the Negro's experience reproduces that of the American's. In response to a critic's attempt to define the Negro as a primitive "trickster," Ellison argues that the Negro uses the mask precisely as all Americans have, in the context of "the old American problem of identity." For the American, as Constance Rourke had pointed out, was always defined as a "barbarian" who had left his claim to culture in the Old World. The idea of "the smart man playing dumb" is a strategy hardly limited to Negroes. "Actually," Ellison notes, "it is a role which Negroes share with other Americans, and it might be more 'Yankee' than anything else. It is a strategy common to the culture. . . . The white American has charged the Negro American with being without past or tradition (something which strikes him with nameless horror), just as he himself has been so charged by European and American critics with a nostalgia for the stability of European cultures; and the Negro knows that both were 'mammy-made' right here at home. What's more, each secretly believes that he alone knows what is valid in the American experience, and the other knows he knows, but will not admit it, and each suspects the other of being at bottom a phony." This is a version of what I have called "The Arkansas Traveler" strategy of humor, in which the American faces his critic by pretending to be even dumber than he is expected to be, all the while undercutting his opponent by a play of witty *double entendre.* (The classic encounter is between a farmer and a city slicker, but a close look at the opposing values reveals that the antagonists symbolize the New World and the Old.)

But Ellison goes even farther along folkloristic lines. As he has suggested, one of his essential interests is in the revelation of the peculiarly American problem of identity. Many of our writers and critics have turned to folklore as a way of answering some of the questions that problem raises; and Ellison takes the same tack, though here we are in a position to see how the strategy will work in the context of Negro folk tradition. The general approach, however, is the same one that I have traced to the German folklorist and historian, J. G. von Herder. It uses folk tradition as the basis for an understanding of the national character, and in this case it becomes possible to examine closely the roots of Negro folklore in order to trace the elements that have formed major segments of American Negro expression. (At the same time, Ellison understands the Negro to represent some essential qualities of the American himself—as Constance Rourke and the Lomaxes had already argued in their own versions of Herderian folk ideology.) Yet another major connection is apparent when Ellison notes that his major interest is literary and he explains that his concern with folklore is primarily for what it will allow him to do as a writer: "I use folklore in my work not because I am Negro, but because writers like Eliot and Joyce made me conscious of the literary value of my folk inheritance. My cultural background, like that of most Americans, is dual (my middle name, sadly enough, is Waldo) . . . . My point is that the Negro American writer is also an heir of the human experience which is literature, and this might well be more important to him than his living folk tradition. For me, at least, in the discontinuous, swiftly changing and diverse American culture, the stability of the Negro American folk tradition became precious as a result of an act of literary discovery." Ralph Waldo Ellison is a lot closer politically and esthetically to his namesake than he has admitted. More importantly, and despite his valid objection to being construed as a folk writer, he has given us a major illustration of how the American writer uses folk materials to create a distinctly national expression which yet speaks in broadly human rather than racial or regional terms. These are the values I have examined in previous sections of this study; Ellison not only brings us up to date; he is an effective and impressive heir to what has gone before, filling in outlines of crucial areas that had only been sketched before.

Ellison's central concern in *Invisible Man* is to provide a portrait of the American, and his focusing on a Negro hero raises at once that peculiarly American formulation which we have encountered earlier. The American is conceived to be a man without a past or anterior folklore which will serve to define his national values and literary expression. If this is true for the American in general, it is especially true for the Negro—and Ellison's point is that his situation is the same as his white counterpart's. But the circumstances of his attempt to define his identity will be framed by his relationships to the white world, which functions in relation to the Negro as the European world operated in regard to the white American. The hero, in short, is *peau rouge* whatever the actual color of his skin. And he is also the American barbarian, although the source of barbarism in this case is not the frontier but the jungle heritage of Africa. In the face of this collection of stereotypes, the hero assumes the mask as a means of undercutting the assumptions of his adversaries. The next step is predictable: as the American needs to show that his tradition is rich and meaningful, so the American Negro needs to convince himself and his critics that Negro folk tradition is more than mumbo-jumbo or the cacophony that jazz is usually taken to be. The dynamic of the novel stems from the hero's struggle with himself to acknowledge the legitimacy of his heritage in the face of constant attacks by the white community or its allies in the society of Negroes. Nothing is simple, and the virtue of Ellison's comic strategy is that it cuts both ways, undermining the stereotypes of the whites and exposing the insecurities of the Negroes. But the progression of values is clear: in order to acknowledge his existence as a man, the hero must first accept the folk legacy of his people; having attained this position, he will discover his identity as an American; but then he must move to the next stage, which expresses the universal values of humanity. The progression is from folk to national and finally international values.

But everything depends on the identification of the folk culture as rich and sufficiently sophisticated to pass the test of the self-appointed superior culture which judges it to be innately inferior. In order to satisfy these demands, Ellison must first establish the legitimacy of Negro folk tradition, and his argument runs along lines already familiar to us. The anterior folklore of the Negro (like all folklore) is not simple-minded or barbaric but operates on a level very close to that of formal art. The central question can be resolved in terms of the richness of folk diction, and Ellison gives us several scenes which make the point well. After the narrator arrives in New York he encounters a junk man one morning singing a blues as he pushes his cart along: " 'She's got feet like a monkey / Legs like a frog—Lawd, Lawd! / But when she starts to loving me / I holler Whoooo, God-dog / Cause I loves my baabay, / Better than I do myself. . . .' " The junk man asks the narrator if he's "got the dog," and the narrator plays "The Arkansas Traveler," pretending he doesn't understand the reference:

> I laughed nervously and stepped back. He watched me out of shrewd eyes. "Oh, goddog, daddy-o," he said with a sudden bluster, "who got the damn dog? Now I know you from down home, how come you trying to act like you never heard that before! Hell, ain't nobody out here this morning but us colored—why you trying to deny me?"

The narrator is uncomfortable in the face of this attempt to make him acknowledge his country background, but he cannot resist the junk man's spiel and his relish for language:

> "Well, daddy-o, it's been good talking with a youngster from the old country but I got to leave you now. This here's one of them good ole downhill streets. I can coast a while and won't be worn out at the end of the day. . . . I thought you was trying to deny me at first, but now I be pretty glad to see you. . . ."

"I hope so," I said. "And you take it easy."

"Oh, I'll do that. All it takes to get along in this here man's town is a little shit, grit and mother-wit. And man, I was bawn with all three. In fact, I'maseventhsonofaseventhson-bawnwithacauloverbotheyesandraisedonblackcatboneshighjohn theconquerorandgreasygreens—" he spieled with twinkling eyes, his lips working rapidly. "You dig me, daddy?"

"You're going too fast," I said, beginning to laugh.

"Okay, I'm slowing down. I'll verse you but I won't curse you—my name is Peter Wheatstraw, I'm the Devil's only son-in-law, so roll 'em. You a southern boy, ain't you?" he said, with his head to one side like a bear's.

"Yes," I said.

"Well, git with it! My name's Blue and I'm coming at you with a pitchfork. Fe Fi Fo Fum. Who wants to shoot the devil one, Lord God Stingeroy!"

He had me grinning despite myself. I liked his words though I didn't know the answer. I'd known the stuff from childhood, but had forgotten it; had learned it back of school. . . .

This is only one of several scenes in which the issues of identity, name, and Negro tradition are brought together. (Joyce has a similar motif in *A Portrait of the Artist* in which a play of language is associated with Stephen's name and relationship to Ireland.) Ellison's nameless narrator is prodded by the junk man to acknowledge his roots as a Southern Negro and though he has been trained to look down his nose at the country people and their culture, he has nevertheless intimations that there is something rich and valuable in their expression. The combination of blues and folk speech appears in several other sequences where the same point is made.

The Jim Trueblood episode, which is one of the best drawn scenes (and to judge from the critics, one of the most problematical), moves along similar lines. The narrator is ordered by one of the white trustees to show him the countryside, and by mistake they arrive at Trueblood's. Mr. Norton is a New Englander who represents the legacy of abolitionism and there are several pointed references to Emerson—"I am a New Englander," Mr. Norton says, "like Emerson. You must learn about him, for he was important to your people. He had a hand in your destiny." Ellison is reacting against the white liberal's patronizing attitude toward the Negro and, as in a later scene involving a young man actually named Emerson, the tone is ironic and pejorative. At the same time, Mr. Norton becomes nostalgic over the memory of his dead daughter, for whom he had an unnatural affection. All this is fore-shadowing for the interview with Trueblood, a sharecropper "who told the old stories with a sense of humor and a magic that made them come alive. He was also a good tenor singer, and sometimes when special guests visited the school he was brought up along with members of a country quartet to sing what the officials called 'their primitive spirituals' when we assembled in the chapel on Sunday evenings." Ellison's handling of this situation reveals how well he can utilize the materials of folk tradition to expose the full range of their ideological and technical meaning. To begin with, it gives him a chance to undercut the conventional image of the Negro folk character whose major reference for most readers is the kindly Uncle Remus. Norton is ready to receive the impression of a fascinating spinner of tales in the quaint and curious diction of the country folk. What he gets is Trueblood's incredibly effective recital of incest. Norton reveals the basis for his own interest in the story when he comments, " 'You did and are un-harmed!' . . . his blue eyes blazing into the black face with something like envy and indignation." This leads into a little dialogue that employs the strategy of "The Arkansas Traveler":

> "You have looked upon chaos and are not destroyed!"
> "No suh! I feels all right."
> "You do? You feel no inner turmoil, no need to cast out the offending eye?"
> "Suh?"
> "Answer me!"
> "I'm all right suh," Trueblood said uneasily. "My eyes is all right too. And when I feels po'ly in my gut I takes a little soda and it goes away."

The contrast between Norton's stilted diction and Trueblood's folk speech (which is one of the technical achievements of "The Ar-kansas Traveler" motif) works as well as ever. Ellison has pointed out that the "Negro stereotype is really an image of the unorgan-ized, irrational forces of American life, forces through which, by projecting them in forms of an easily dominated minority, the white individual seeks to be at home in the vast unknown world of America. Perhaps the object, of the stereotype is not so much to crush the Negro as to console the white man." It is just this kind of psychological projection that the Trueblood incident illustrates, and it accounts for the compulsion Norton has to hear the tale to the end, relishing every tabooed nuance that Trueblood narrates.

Having punctured the stereotype of the kindly old folk character, Ellison pursues the implications of the scene. Like many of Ellison's characters, Trueblood's name carries much of the meaning. Incest is literally being true to one's blood and though Trueblood does not know it, the practice is an ancient and often honorable one, re-served indeed for the aristocracy. It is, in short, an old folkway and Ellison can thereby indicate his rejection of the sentimental notion that folklore will reveal the naïveté and innocence of the common people. The white trustee anticipates a version of pastoral inno-cence and agrarian antisepsis, quite unaware that for the Negro, pastoral carries major associations with the horror and brutality of slavery. (Ellison clearly identifies Emerson with just such a simple-minded optimism, although as I have noted earlier, Emerson oc-casionally recognized that the reliance on folk diction might dredge up some materials that would shock genteel society.) In another, more fundamental sense, however, Jim is true to his blood as a man, that is, he experiences the possibility of sin which inheres in the human condition. (Trueblood's dream in the midst of his sexual relations with his daughter invokes images suggesting the fires of hell.) What counts most heavily is Trueblood's reaction after his sin—and after he barely manages to escape the wrath of his wife. (It is true that sex figures prominently in certain areas of Negro folklore, but that should not lead to the dangerous and erroneous conception that Negroes are generally promiscuous. Trueblood's wife makes the point with an axeblade!) The old man is rejected by his family, his preacher, and the Negro community, but the whites take a great interest in him, encouraging him to tell the story over and over again. Finally he is forced back on his own resources:

> "I leaves tryin' to pray, but I can't. I thinks and thinks until
> I thinks my brain go'n bust, 'bout how I'm guilty and how I
> ain't guilty. I don't eat nothin' and I don't drink nothin' and

cain't sleep at night. Finally, one night, way early in the mornin', I looks up and sees the stars and I starts singin' I don't know what it was, some kinda church song, I guess. All I knows is I *ends up* singin' the blues. I sings me some blues that night ain't never been sang before, and while I'm singin' them blues I makes up my mind that I ain't nobody but myself and ain't nothin' I can do but let whatever is gonna happen happen. I made up my mind that I was goin' back home and face Kate; yeah, and face Matty Lou too."

It will take the rest of the book for Ellison's hero to learn the lesson, but ultimately he comes to the same understanding that "a man ain't nothin' but a man." Unlike Norton, who represses the knowledge of his deep instinct, Trueblood owns up to his sin —it is another sense in which his name is symbolic.

BUT IT IS IMPORTANT to emphasize that the catharsis occurs through a creative act which Ellison accurately relates to a Negro folk tradition, the blues. As much as the spirituals, the blues is susceptible of ideological interpretation, though its definition was much later in coming. Yet the form easily takes on esthetic, political, and historical meanings. As one of the major forms of Negro music, the blues has defined a central tradition in American music at large. The tonality comes from an indeterminacy in several crucial intervals of the scale, the third, fifth, or seventh degrees, which are the so-called blues notes. But actually something more complicated is involved and this is compounded by the fact that one of the characteristics of Negro folk music is that in performance it sounds very different from what any notation can describe. (This is true of all music, but it seems unusually so in Negro styles which depend on highly complex vocal effects and extensive ornamentation.) The sources of these effects are still not entirely known; some are clearly African, but the "blue notes" themselves do not seem to have African sources.

Although the form is often described as three lines in a twelve bar framework, there is in fact almost an unlimited number of variations possible, with a strong tendency toward improvisation in most authentic performances. But blues suggests sadness, an awareness of trouble or a general lament, and that meaning of the term goes back to Elizabethan usage. The poetry of the blues reveals the ability of the folk to create striking and impressive imagery, and in this case it exposes the remarkable range of Negro folk expression. The themes are often love, death, the sense of loss and at the same time a hope for release and fulfillment. The imagery is often frankly sexual but in highly metaphorical terms which contribute a joy in language and the possibility for a witty humor based on *double entendre*. Ellison's definition of the blues expresses succinctly and effectively the ideological implications of the form: "The blues is an impulse to keep the painful details and episodes of a brutal experience alive in one's aching consciousness, to finger its jagged grain, and to transcend it, not by the consolation of philosophy but by squeezing from it a near-tragic, near-comic lyricism. As a form, the blues is an autobiographical chronicle of personal catastrophe expressed lyrically." We can see how far this is from earlier conceptions of Negro music as an expression of hopelessness and chaos. What emerges is an artistic form that makes possible the catharsis we usually associate with tragedy. Ellison pointedly emphasizes that the blues does not skirt the painful facts of human experience, but works through them to an artistic transcendence. We have already seen that this is the formula of Emerson's prescription for achieving the epiphanic moment— to work through the natural fact in order to express the spiritual truth that underlies it. But this similarity is less important than the fact that Ellison recognizes both the force of folk tradition and its close relationship to a sophisticated literary expression. Inevitably such an approach will move against the idea of isolated literary genres (such as tragedy) and in the direction of those mixed modes which seem to define American literary tendencies. The blues is not the "power of positive thinking" but a transformation of catastrophe through the agency of art. This esthetic, like Emerson's, will not allow a poetry of abstract generalization, for the "jagged grain" is valued in its own terms—it is roughly comparable to Emerson's natural facts which make it possible for the low but vital levels of diction to make themselves felt. And because of its close association with Negro folk culture, it is an esthetic which will also resist a movement toward expression for its own sake. There is, in short, the same balance of natural facts and spiritual truths which pervades a good deal of, the literature in America that has been influenced by the Emerson-Whitman tradition.

This is precisely what Trueblood accomplishes with his blues. But

Ellison extends this possibility to jazz as well, for if, on the one hand, the blues is a stage forward from earlier Negro musical expression (work songs, field cries, and spirituals), it is also a major link with jazz; and Ellison's use of jazz as a literary theme is one of his most impressive accomplishments. He raises the issue first in the Prologue, after a reference that comes close to reproducing Emerson's transparent eyeball image: "Nor is my invisibility exactly a matter of bio-chemical accident to my epidermis. That invisibility to which I refer occurs because of a peculiar disposition of the eyes of those with whom I come in contact. A matter of the construction of their *inner* eyes, those eyes with which they look through their physical eyes upon reality." The mass of men are blind to the spiritual truths, and Ellison's narrator explains that "Without light I am not only invisible, but formless as well; and to be unaware of one's form is to live a death." To be free is a function of the awareness of form, that is to say, it is closely related to the creative act, and the analogue of that combination is best defined by jazz: "I'd like to hear five recordings of Louis Armstrong playing and singing 'What Did I Do to Be so Black and Blue'—all at the same time. . . . Perhaps I like Louis beause he's made poetry out of being invisible. I think it must be because he's unaware that he *is* invisible. And my own grasp of invisibility aids me to understand his music. . . . Invisibility, let me explain, gives one a slightly different sense of time, you're never quite on the beat. Sometimes you're ahead and sometimes behind. Instead of the swift imperceptible flowing of time, you are aware of its nodes, those points where time stands still or from which it leaps ahead. And you slip into the breaks and look around. That's what you hear vaguely in Louis' music." Appropriately it is a jazz performance of a blues that the narrator responds to and it is not accidental that the selection has strong social overtones. Ellison's knowledge of the sources of jazz helps him to pinpoint the meaning of Armstrong's music. He knows, for example, that Louis plays cornet (later trumpet), an instrument associated with military bands, and that the marching band was one of the musical traditions absorbed and adapted by early New Orleans jazz groups. What Armstrong does with the military tradition is related to what he makes of his invisibility: he bends the inflexible lock-step militarism into a lyrical sound as he turns the condition of invisibility into poetry. It is an affirmation of the ability to overcome oppression through the creation of art, and it is another example of Ellison's tendency to associate the idea of freedom with the awareness of form.

In more positive terms, jazz provides one with a new sense of time; again it is not the rhythm of a military march in which everyone must be in step; for despite the regular pulsing beat of a jazz band, there is always the offbeat, or offbeats, which are characteristic of jazz style. Even the drummer, who establishes the fundamental beat, will be more valued if he pushes it a bit, and the instrumentalists will take their solos either slightly behind or ahead of the other musicians. (The ultimate source of this is in Negro folk tradition where the leader and chorus patterns are strong, but overlapping of the relationship between the two is a standard device —it is what one critic has called "over-lapping antiphony.") Instead of a mechanical rhythm, then, jazz demands an awareness of the nodes, those moments within the heart of pulsation which are static or which provide the occasion for a leap to another level of rhythmic awareness. This is an effective description of those essential qualities of jazz syncopation which are difficult to notate but which we recognize as fundamental to the jazz performance. But the rhythmic awareness that Ellison is concerned with also provides an analogy to the recognition of spiritual truths, the opening of the inner eye. The musician slips into the breaks and looks around; he enters into the center of meaning and creates his own statement, which is precisely what the jazz soloist must do. Ellison puts this also in terms of "The Arkansas Traveler" motif. The narrator describes a prize fight between a professional boxer and a yokel: "The fighter was swift and amazingly scientific. His body was one violent flow of rapid rhythmic action. He hit the yokel a hundred times while the yokel held up his arms in stunned surprise. But suddenly the yokel, rolling about in the gale of boxing gloves, struck one blow and knocked science, speed, and footwork as cold as the well-digger's posterior. The smart money hit the canvas. The long shot got the nod. The yokel had simply stepped inside of his opponent's sense of time." This is precisely what the Squatter does, and in both cases, the opponent never knows what hit him.

The difference between Armstrong and the narrator is important. Louis is not aware of his invisibility because he is positively and deeply associated with the cultural sources of his art. For if jazz provides an outlet for individual expression it also demands an allegiance to the group as well, and Ellison employs this circumstance thematically as a way of defining the relationship of the individual to his society, thus raising the issue from a purely esthetic to a political level as well. It seems to me the best explanation for the denouement of the book in which the narrator affirms his resolve to emerge from underground. "I'm shaking off the old skin," he says, "and I'll leave it here in the hole. I'm coming out, no less invisible without it, but coming out nevertheless. And I suppose it's damn well time. Even hibernation can be overdone, come to think of it. Perhaps that's my greatest social crime, I've overstayed my hibernation, since there's a possibility that even an invisible man has a socially responsible role to play." Louis Armstrong figures prominently in the final decision: "With Louis Armstrong one half of me says, 'Open the window and let the foul air out,' while the other says, 'It was good green corn before the harvest.' Of course Louis was kidding, *he* wouldn't have thrown old Bad Air out, because it would have broken up the music and the dance, when it was the good music that came from the bell of old Bad Air's horn that counted." This is another formulation of Ellison's definition of blues, that transformation of brutal experience into the language of art—the bad air transmitted through Louis' horn becomes the remarkable achievement that we call jazz. And if one part of it is foul, another reflects the green corn, the folk roots of jazz itself. (Foul air is reminiscent of a Jelly Roll Morton tune, "Buddy Bolden's Blues," which is based on the theme of expelling ugly and obnoxious characters; the green corn reference may be to any number of Southern folksongs which use the expression, in dance or play-party tunes, as an image of vitality.)

Ellison reveals his relationship to the folk ideology that I have considered earlier in his awareness that the individual talent draws on the well of tradition from which the art form is derived. This is handled indirectly in the novel, though it counts heavily in the narrator's sense of social responsibility. Ellison develops the idea, however, in one of his essays where he explains what jazz has meant to him as an aritst: "Now, I had learned from the jazz musicians I had known as a boy in Oklahoma City something of the discipline and devotion to his art required of the artist. . . . These jazzmen, many of them now world famous, lived for and with music intensely. Their driving motivation was neither money nor fame, but the will to achieve the most eloquent expression of idea-emotions through the technical mastery of their instruments (which, incidentally, some of them wore as a priest wears the cross) and the give and take, the subtle rhythmical shaping and blending of idea, tone, and imagination demanded of group improvisation. The delicate balance struck between strong individual personality and the group during those early jam sessions was a marvel of social organization. I had learned too that the end of all this discipline and technical mastery was the desire to express an affirmative way of life through its musical tradition and this tradition insisted that each artist achieve his creativity within its frame. He must learn the best of the past, and add it to his personal vision. Life could be harsh, loud, and wrong if it wished, but they lived it fully, and when they expressed their attitude toward the world it was with a fluid style that reduced the chaos of living to form." This is the antithesis of the earlier attitude toward jazz as the very apex of confusion, but it is also important to note that Ellison's affirmation enables him to solve problems usually considered insoluble by the American writer. In Negro folklore and the music which issued from it, Ellison finds his sense of the past, and also the basis for his commitment to technical and artistic competence. But the technical accomplishment of the jazz musician is never strictly an individual phenomenon, however much improvisation and personal vision are valued. For underlying it is the folk tradition from which it emerged and hence, as Herder had pointed out, there is a communal base which the folk themselves provided as a legacy to the individual artist. That delicate balance which Ellison describes between the individual and the group in a jam session becomes as well a description of what the society as a whole might be. The political implications of Ellison's folk ideology begin to emerge as inevitably as in the approaches of the writers I have discussed earlier. For jazz is a uniquely American expression and when we understand it as Ellison does, it encompasses just that sense of individualism directed toward communal concerns which we have already encountered in Emerson and Whitman. The metaphor of the jazzman illustrates the relationship better than any analogy we have seen to this point. Jazz values improvisation, personal vision, an assault on the conventional modes of musical expression, but it will not allow the individual to forget what he owes to tradition—not the tradition of a great man, but the legacy shaped by a whole people. It is precisely what folk ideologues have always argued: the authentic sources of a nation's culture lie in the lower levels and if they are developed sensitively, not only the poet speaks but his nation also finds its expression.

Hence the narrator is finally able to unravel the meaning of his grandfather's advice: "I want you to overcome 'em with yeses, undermine 'em with grins, agree 'em to death and destruction, let 'em swoller you till they vomit or bust open." At first he takes this to mean accepting the values of the white world, playing the good Negro, all the while making the most of his opportunities for himself. But ultimately he understands that the grandfather's plea for affirmation was toward something else: "Could he have meant— hell he *must* have meant the principle, that we were to affirm the principle on which the country was built and not the men, or at least not the men who did the violence. Did he mean say 'yes' because he knew that the principle was greater than the men, greater than the numbers and the vicious power and all the methods used to corrupt its name? Did he mean to affirm the principle, which they themselves dreamed into being out of the chaos and darkness of the feudal past, and which they had violated and compromised to the point of absurdity even in their own corrupt minds? Or did he mean that we had to take the responsibility for all of it, for the men as well as the principle because no other fitted our needs? Not for the power or for vindication, but because we, with the given circumstances of our origin, could only thus find transcendence?" For all his awareness of evil and his contempt for an easy optimism, the narrator reveals himself to be essentially an Emersonian "yea sayer." He has tried all the versions of the American dream, beginning with the tradition that hard work and prudence will lead to material success. "Though invisible, I am in the great American tradition of tinkers," the narrator explains at the outset. "That makes me kin to Ford, Edison, and Franklin. Call me, since I have a theory and a concept, a 'thinker-tinker.'" But what he finally learns is to accept his humanity (as his grandfather and Louis Armstrong always have) and the idea of self-reliance: "But my world has become one of infinite possibilities. What a phrase— still it's a good phrase and a good view of life, and a man shouldn't accept any other; that much I've learned underground. Until some gang succeeds in putting the world in a strait jacket, its definition is possibility. Step outside the narrow borders of what men call reality and you step into chaos—ask Rinehart, he's a master of it— or imagination. That too I've learned in the cellar, and not by deadening my sense of perception; I'm invisible, not blind." This is essentially what one strand of Emerson's thought has come to suggest—that the reality of our life needs to be held constantly to the demands of the American dream; and when it fails to measure up to the standard, it is the individual's responsibility to say so. But Emerson's individualism was balanced by an awareness of national requirements, which would be best expressed esthetically in the creation of a truly American art. The principle that Ellison's narrator affirms is best defined as non-conformity, but it contains also a commitment to that balance between individualism and communal responsibility which we noted in Whitman's concern with both the "I and the en-masse"; the danger is still that the balance will be tilted in the extreme of either direction: "Now I know that men are different and all life is divided and that only in division is there true health. . . . Whence all this passion toward conformity anyway?—diversity is the word. Let man keep his many parts and you'll have no tyrant states. Why if they follow this conformity business they'll end up forcing me to become white, which is not a color but the lack of one. Must I strive toward color-lessness? But seriously, and without snobbery, think of what the world would lose if that should happen. America is woven of many strands; I would recognize them and let it so remain. It's 'winner take nothing' that is the great truth of our country or of any country. Life is to be lived, not controlled; and humanity is won by continuing to play in face of certain defeat. Our fate is to become one, yet many—This is not prophecy but description."

The character who symbolizes the idea of possibilities as a way of life is Rinehart, ideologically the most important figure in the book, though dramatically just a sketch. In response to a question about Rinehart, Ellison recalled that the name appeared in one of blues singer Jimmy Rushing's songs and was not a conscious play on Django Rhinehardt, the great jazz guitarist. The line from the blues was haunting, "and as I was thinking of a character who was a master of disguise, of coincidence, this name with its suggestion of inner and outer came to mind. Later I learned that it was a call used by Harvard students when they prepared to riot, a call to chaos. Which is very interesting, because it is not long after Rinehart appears in my novel that the riot breaks out in Harlem. Rinehart is my name for the personification of chaos. He is also intended to represent America and change. He has lived so long with chaos that he knows how to manipulate it. It is the old theme of *The Confidence Man.* He is a figure in a country with no solid or stable past or stable class lines; therefore he is able to move about easily from one to the other." The reference to Melville is interesting because it seems to me that stylistically Ellison is closer to him than any other source, and this seems the more evident if we recall Melville's use of Emerson's esthetic and his insistence on seeing the darker implications of Emerson's political philosophy. But Rinehart's ability to manipulate chaos also suggests that he is a symbol of the artist. He is a Proteus, and Ellison himself has made this analogy with the artist: "For the novelist, Proteus stands for both America and the inheritance of illusion through which all men must fight to achieve reality. . . ." Encountering Rinehart in an evangelical mission, the narrator finally understands his function: "I had heard it before but I'd never come so close. Still, could he be all of them: Rine the runner and Rine the gambler and Rine the briber and Rine the lover and Rinehart the Reverend? Could he himself be both rind and heart? What is real anyway? But how could I doubt it? He was a broad man, a man of parts who got around. Rinehart the rounder. It was true as I was true. His world was possibility and he knew it. He was years ahead of me and I was a fool. I must have been crazy and blind. The world in which we lived was without boundaries. A vast, seething, hot world of fluidity, and Rine the rascal was at home in it. It was unbelievable, but perhaps only the unbelievable could be believed. Perhaps the truth was always a lie." Yet although Rinehart is closest to the truth he has a major fault; he is in danger of tipping the scales too far in the direction of selfish exploitation of the world's possibilities. He is irresponsible in not acknowledging the communal sources of that artistic power which enables him to master illusion. (It is the analogue of art for art's sake and Ellison is as uncomfortable as Emerson at the prospect.) Rinehart, to recall Mather's metaphor, is like a man pulling only one oar; he has forgotten his social responsibilities.

Hence, although Rinehart is attractive, he cannot provide the narrator with a complete world view. And Ellison has resented inferences that his narrator will remain an anti-hero, simply a version of Dostoievsky's underground man. "The final act of *Invisible Man,*" he notes, "is not that of a concealment in darkness in the Anglo-Saxon connotation of the word, but that of a voice issuing

its little wisdom out of the substance of its own inwardness—
after having undergone a transformation from ranter to writer.
. . . And in keeping with the reverse English of the plot, and with
the Negro American conception of blackness, his movement ver-
tically downward (not into a 'sewer,' Freud notwithstanding, but
into a coal cellar, a source of heat, light, power, and, through
association with the character's motivation, self-perception) is a
process of *rising* to an understanding of his human condition."
That underground suggests as well the substratum of folk culture
upon which an American art can be built, and Ellison's hero plays
a variation on the Marxist dictum: "All boundaries down, freedom
was not only the recognition of necessity, it was the recognition of
possibility."

The narrator will not give up his color because that would
mean rejecting as well the heritage of Negro culture which, as
Ellison has argued, is a major contribution to America as well.
But the force of Negro culture (in folklore and jazz) is to remind
us of the principle especially appropriate for American development—that the roots of high culture lie in the expression of the
common people. Ellison modifies the optimism of Emerson's ideology with his blues formulation; it is what he means by "continuing to play in face of certain defeat"—play refers not just to the
game, but also to Louis Armstrong playing his music, though conscious that he is black and blue. What Ellison has in mind in his
formulation of equality recalls Herder's conception of the equal
validity of incommensurable cultures. The aim is not to make the
Negro white, or the white Negro, but to allow for the fullest development of each strand which will ultimately contribute to the
definition of America. It is not Black Nationalism Ellison is after,
but American nationalism as the Emerson-Whitman tradition had
defined it. For the Negro it means first accepting his folk heritage
in order to be an American; then he can acknowledge his status
as a man. (Ellison knows that "in the United States when traditions are juxtaposed they tend, regardless of what we do to prevent
it, irresistibly to merge," and he adds: "Those who know their
native culture and love it unchauvinistically are never lost when
encountering the unfamiliar.") Meanwhile the familiar strategy
continues to work. It is the seeming barbarian whose level of culture defines the highest values of our civilization, while his language revitalizes our literary expression.

This has been the central motif of this study and Ellison has defined even more accurately what it has meant for his own career as an artist. The Negro's experience, he noted, "is that of America and the West, and is as rich a body of experience as one can find anywhere. We can view it narrowly as something exotic, folksy, or 'low-down,' or we may identify ourselves with it and recognize it as an important segment of the larger American experience— not lying at the bottom of it, but intertwined, diffused in its very texture." The irony is that Americans at large still need to be convinced that it is so.

Tell Martha not to Moan

S. A. WILLIAMS

M Y MAMMA A BIG WOMAN, tall and stout and men like her cause she soft and fluffy looking. When she round them it all smiles and dimples and her mouth be looking like it couldn't never be fixed to say nothing but darling and honey.

They see her now, they sho see something different. I should not even come today. Since I had Larry things ain't been too good between us. But—that's my mamma and I know she gon be there when I need her. And sometime when I come, it okay. But this ain't gon be one a them times. Her eyes looking all ove me and I know it coming. She snort cause she want to say god damn but she don't cuss. "When it due, Martha?"

First I start to say, what. But I know it ain't no use. You can't fool old folks bout something like that, so I tell her.

"Last part of November."

"Who the daddy?"

"Time."

"That man what play piano at the Legion?"

"Yeah."

"What he gon do bout it?"

"Mamma, it ain't too much he can do, now is it? The baby on its way."

She don't say nothing for a long time. She sit looking at her hands. They all wet from where she been washing dishes and they all wrinkled like you hands be when they been in water too long. She get up and get a dish cloth and dry 'em, then sit down at the table. "Where he at now?"

"Gone."

"Gone? Gone where?" I don't say nothing and she start cussing then. I get kinda scared cause mamma got to be real mad foe she cuss and I don't know who she cussing—me or Time. Then she start talking to me. "Martha, you just a fool. I told you that man wan't no good first time I seed him. A musician the worst kind of man you can get mixed up with. Look at you. You ain't even eighteen years old yet, Larry just barely two and here you is pregnant again." She go on like that for a while and I don't say nothing. Couldn't no way. By the time I get my mouth fixed to say something, she done raced on so far ahead that what I got to say don't have nothing to do with what she saying right then. Finally she stop and ask, "What you gon do now? You want to come back here?" She ain't never liked me living with Orine and when I say no, she ask, "Why not? It be easier for you."

I shake my head again. "If I here, Time won't know where to find me, and Time coming; he be back. He gon to make a place for us, you a see."

"Hump, you just played the fool again, Martha."

"No mamma, that not it at all; Time want me."

"Is that what he say when he left?"

"No, but. . . ."

Well, like the first night we met, he come over to me like he knowed me for a long time and like I been his for awmost that long. Yeah, I think that how it was. Cause I didn't even see him when we come in the Legion that first night.

Me and Orine, we just got our checks that day. We went downtown and Orine bought her some new dresses. But the dress she want to wear that night don't look right so we go racing back to town and change it. Then we had to hurry home and get dressed. It Friday night and the Legion crowded. You got to get there early on the week-end if you want a seat. And Orine don't want just any seat; she want one right up front. "Who gon see you way back there? Nobody. They can't see you, who gon ask you to dance? Nobody. You don't dance, how you gon meet people? You don't meet people, what you doing out?" So we sit up front. Whole lots a people there that night. You can't even see the bandstand cross the dance floor. We sharing the table with some more people and Orine keep jabbing me, telling me to sit cool. And I try cause Orine say it a good thing to be cool.

The set end and people start leaving the dance floor. That when I see Time. He just getting up from the piano. I like him right off cause I like men what look like him. He kind of tall and slim. First time I ever seed a man wear his hair so long and it nappy—he tell me once it an African Bush—but he look good anyway and he know it. He look round all cool. He step down from the bandstand and start walking toward me. He come over to the table and just look. "You," he say, "you my Black queen." And he bow down most to the floor.

Ah shit! I mad cause I think he just trying to run a game. "What you trying to prove, fool?" I ask him.

"Ah man," he say and it like I cut him. That the way he say it. "Ah man. I call this woman my Black queen—tell her she can rule my life and she call me a fool."

"And sides what, nigga," I tell him then, "I ain't black." And I ain't, I don't care what Time say. I just a dark woman.

"What's the matter, you shamed of being Black? Ain't nobody told you Black is pretty?" He talk all loud and people start gathering round. Somebody say, "Yeah, you tell her bout it, soul." I embarrassed and I look over at Orine. But she just grinning, not saying nothing. I guess she waiting to see what I gon do so I stand up.

"Well if I is black, I is a fine black." And I walk over to the bar. I walk just like I don't know they watching my ass, and I hold my head up. Time follow me right on over to the bar and put his arm round my shoulder.

"You want a drink?" I start to say no cause I scared. Man not supposed to make you feel like he make me feel. Not just like doing it—but, oh, like it right for him to be there with me, touching me. So I say yes. "What's your name?" he ask then.

I smile and say, "They call me the player." Orine told a man that once in Berkley and he didn't know what to say. Orine a smart woman.

"Well they call me Time and I know yo mamma done told you Time ain't nothin to play with." His smile cooler than mine. We don't say nothing for a long while. He just stand there with his arm round my shoulder looking at us in the mirror behind the bar. Finally he say, "Yeah, you gon be my Black queen." And he look down at me and laugh. I don't know what to do, don't know what to say neither, so I just smile.

"You gon tell me your name or not?"

"Martha."

He laugh. "That a good name for you."

"My mamma name me that so I be good. She name all us kids from the Bible," I tell him laughing.

"And is you good?"

I nod yes and no all at the same time and kind of mumble cause I don't know what to say. Mamma really did name all us kids from the Bible. She always saying, "My mamma name me Veronica after the woman in the Bible and I a better woman for it. That why I name all my kids from the Bible. They got something to look up to." But mamma don't think I'm good, specially since I got Larry. Maybe Time ain't gon think I good neither. So I don't answer, just smile and move on back to the table. I hear him singing soft-like, "Oh Mary don't you weep, tell yo sister Martha not to moan." And I kind of glad cause most people don't even think bout that when I tell em my name. That make me know he really smart.

We went out for breakfast after the Legion close. Him and me and Orine and German, the drummer. Only places open is on the other side of town and at first Time don't want to go. But we finally swade him.

Time got funny eyes, you can't hardly see into em. You look and you look and you can't tell nothing from em. It make me feel funny when he look at me. I finally got used to it, but that night he just sit there looking and don't say nothing for a long time after we order.

"So you don't like Black?" he finally say.

"Do you?" I ask. I think I just ask him questions, then I don't have to talk so much. But I don't want him to talk bout that right then, so I smile and say, "Let's talk bout you."

"I am not what I am." He smiling and I smile back, but I feel funny cause I think I supposed to know what he mean.

"What kind of game you trying to run?" Orine ask. Then she laugh. "Just cause we from the country don't mean we ain't hip to niggas trying to be big-time. Ain't that right, Martha?"

I don't know what to say, but I know Time don't like that. I think he was going to cuss Orine out, but German put his arm round Orine and he laugh. "He just mean he ain't what he want to be. Don't pay no mind to that cat. He always trying to blow some shit." And he start talking that talk, rapping to Orine.

I look at Time. "That what you mean?"

He all lounged back in his seat, his legs stretched way out under the table. He pour salt in a napkin and mix it up with his finger. "Yeah, that's what I mean. That's all about me. Black is pretty, Martha." He touch my face with one finger. "You let white people make you believe you ugly. I bet you don't even dream."

"I do too."

"What you dream?"

"Huh?" I don't know what he talking bout. I kind of smile and look at him out the corner of my eye. "I dreams bout a man like you. Why, just last night, I dream—"

He start laughing. "That's all right. That's all right."

The food come then and we all start eating. Time act like he forgot all bout dreams. I never figure out how he think I can just sit there and tell him the dreams I have at night, just like that. It don't seem like what I dream bout at night mean as much as what I think bout during the day.

We leaving when Time trip over this white man's feet. That man's feet all out in the aisle but Time don't never be watching where he going no way. "Excuse me," he say kind of mean.

"Say, watch it buddy." That white man talk most as nasty as Time. He kind of old and maybe he drunk or an Okie.

"Man, I said excuse me. You the one got your feet in the aisle."

"You," that man say, starting to get up, "you better watch yourself, boy."

And what he want to say that for? Time step back and say real quiet, "No, motherfucker. You the one. You better watch yourself and your daughter too. See how many babies she gon have by boys like me." That man get all red in the face, but the woman in the booth with him finally start pulling at him, telling him to sit down, shut up. Cause Time set to kill that man.

I touch Time's arm first, then put my arm round his waist. "Ain't no use getting messed behind somebody like that."

Time and that man just looking at each other, not wanting to back down. People was gon start wondering what going on in a few minutes. I tell him, " 'Got something for you, baby,' " and he look down at me and grin. Orine pick it up. We go out that place singing, " 'Good loving, good, good lovin, make you feel so clean.' "

"You like to hear me play?" he ask when we in the car.

"This the first time they ever have anybody here that sound that good."

"Yeah," Orine say. "How come you all staying round a little jive-ass town like Ashley?"

"We going to New York pretty soon," Time say kind of snappy.

"Well, shit, baby, you—"

"When you going to New York?" I ask real quick. When Orine in a bad mood, can't nobody say nothing right.

"Couple of months." He lean back and put his arm round me. "They doing so many things with music back there. Up in the City, they doing one maybe two things. In L.A. they doing another one, two things. But, man, in New York, they doing everything. Person couldn't never get stuck in one groove there. So many things going on, you got to be hip, real hip to keep up. You always growing there. Shit, if you 'live and playing, you can't help but grow. Say, man," he reach and tap German on the shoulder, "let's leave right now."

We all crack up. Then I say, "I sorry but I can't go, got to take care of my baby."

He laugh, "Sugar, you got yo baby right here."

"Well, I must got two babies then."

We pull up in front of the partment house then but don't no one move. Finally Time reach over and touch my hair. "You gon be my Black queen?"

I look straight ahead at the night. "Yeah," I say. "Yeah."

We go in and I check first on Larry cause sometimes that girl don't watch him good. When I come in some nights, he be all out the cover and shivering but too sleepy to get back under em. Time come in when I'm pulling the cover up on Orine two kids.

"Which one yours?" he ask.

I go over to Larry bed. "This my baby," I tell him.

"What's his name?"

"Larry."

"Oh, I suppose you name him after his daddy?"

I don't like the way he say that, like I was wrong to name him after his daddy. "Who else I gon name him after?" He don't say nothing and I leave him standing there. I mad now and I go in the bedroom and start pulling off my clothes. I think, that nigga can stand up in the living room all night, for all I care; let Orine talk to German and him, too. But Time come in the bedroom and put his arms round me. He touch my hair and my face and my tittie, and it scare me. I try to pull away but he hold me too close. "Martha," he say, "Black Martha." Then he just stand there holding me, not saying nothing, with his hand covering one side of my face. I stand there trembling but he don't notice. I know a woman not supposed to feel the way I feel bout Time, not right away. But I do.

He tell me things nobody ever say to me before. And I want to tell him that I ain't never liked no man much as I like him. But sometime you tell a man that and he go cause he think you liking him a whole lot gon hang him up.

"You and me," he say after we in bed, "we can make it together real good." He laugh. "I used to think all I needed was that music, but it take a woman to make that music sing, I think. So now stead of the music and me, it be the music and me and you."

"You left out Larry," I tell him. I don't think he want to hear that. But Larry my baby.

"How come you couldn't be free?" he say real low. Then, "How you going when I go if you got a baby?"

"When you going?"

He turn his back to me. "Oh, I don't know. You know what the song say, 'When a woman take the blues, She tuck her head and cry. But when a man catch the blues, He grab his shoes and slide.' Next time I get the blues," he laugh a little, "next time the man get too much for me, I leave here and go someplace else. He always chasing me. The god damn white man." He turn over and reach for me. "You feel good. He chasing me and I chasing dreams. You think I'm crazy, huh? But I'm not. I just got so many, many things going on inside me I don't know which one to let out first. They all want out so bad. When I play—I got to be better, Martha. You gon help me?"

"Yes, Time, I help you."

"You see," and he reach over and turn on the light and look down at me, "I'm not what I am. I up tight on the inside but I can't get it to show on the outside. I don't know how to make it come out. You ever hear Coltrane blow? That man is together. He showing on the outside what he got on the inside. When I can do that, then I be somewhere. But I can't go by myself. I need a woman. A Black woman. Them other women steal your soul and don't leave nothing. But a Black woman—" He laugh and pull me close. He want me and that all I care bout.

Mamma came over that next morning and come right on in

the bedroom, just like she always do. I kind of shamed for her to see me like that, with a man and all, but she don't say nothing cept scuse me, then turn away. "I come to get Larry."

"He in the other bedroom," I say starting to get up.

"That's okay; I get him." And she go out and close the door.

I start to get out the bed anyway. Time reach for his cigarettes and light one. "Your mamma don't believe in knocking, do she?"

I start to tell him not to talk so loud cause mamma a hear him, but that might make him mad. "Well, it ain't usually nobody in here with me for her to walk in on." I standing by the bed buttoning my house coat and Time reach out and pull my arm, smiling.

"I know you ain't no tramp, Martha. Come on, get back in bed."

I pull my arm way and start out the door. "I got to get Larry's clothes together," I tell him. I do go to get them clothes together cause when mamma come for Larry like that on Sadday morning, she want to keep him for the rest of the weekend. But—I don't know. It just don't seem right for me to be in the bed with a man and my mamma in the next room.

I think Orine and German still in the other bedroom. But I don't know; Orine don't too much like for her mens to stay all night. She say it make a bad impression on her kids. I glad the door close anyway. If mamma gon start talking that "why don't you come home" talk the way she usually do, it best for Orine not to hear it.

Orine's two kids still sleep but mamma got Larry on his bed tickling him and playing with him. He like that. "Boy, you sho happy for it to be so early in the morning," I tell him.

Mamma stop tickling him and he lay there breathing hard for a minute. "Big mamma," he say laughing and pointing at her. I just laugh at him and go get his clothes.

"You gon marry this one?" Every man I been with since I had Larry, she ask that about.

"You think marrying gon save my soul, Mamma?" I sorry right away cause mamma don't like me to make fun of God. But I swear I gets tired of all that. What I want to marry for anyway? Get somebody like daddy always coming and going and every time he go leave a baby behind. Or get a man what stay round and beat me all the time and have my kids thinking they big shit just cause they got a daddy what stay with them, like them saddity kids at school. Shit, married or single they still doing the same thing when they goes to bed.

Mamma don't say nothing else bout it. She ask where he work. I tell her and then take Larry in the bathroom and wash him up.

"The older you get, the more foolish you get, Martha. Them musicians ain't got nothing for a woman. Lots sweet talk and babies, that's all. Welfare don't even want to give you nothing for the one you got now, how you gon—" I sorry but I just stop listening. Mamma run her mouth like a clatterbone on a goose ass sometime. I just go on and give her the baby and get the rest of his things ready.

"So your mamma don't like musicians, huh?" Time say when I get back in the bedroom. "Square-ass people. Everything they don't know about, they hate. Lord deliver me from a square-ass town with square-ass people." He turn over.

"You wasn't calling me square last night."

"I'm not calling you square now, Martha."

I get back in the bed and he puts his arm round me. "But they say what they want to say. Long as they don't mess with me things be okay. But that's impossible. Somebody always got to have their little say about your life. They want to tell you where to go, how to play, what to play, where to play it—shit, even to fuck and how to fuck em. But when I get to New York—"

"Time, let's don't talk now."

He laugh then, "Martha, you so Black." I don't know what I should say so I don't say nothing, just get closer and we don't talk.

That how it is lots a time with me and him. It seem like all I got is lots little pitchers in my mind and can't tell nobody what they look like. Once I try to tell him bout that, bout the pitchers, and he just laugh. "Least you head ain't empty. Maybe now you got some pictures, you get some thoughts." That make me mad and I start cussing, but he laugh and kiss me and hold me. And that time, when we doing it, it all—all angry and like he want to hurt me. And I think bout that song he sing that first night bout having the blues. But that the only time he mean like that.

Time and German brung the piano a couple days after that. The piano small and all shiny black wood. Time cussed German when German knocked it against the front door getting it in the house. Time want to put it in the bedroom but I want him to be thinking bout me, not some damn piano when he in there. I tell him he put it in the living room or it don't come in the house. Orine don't want it in the house period, say it too damn noisy—that's what she tell me. She don't say nothing to Time. I think she half-way scared of him. He pretty good bout playing it though. He don't never play it when the babies is sleep or at least he don't play loud as he can. But all he thinking bout when he playing is that piano. You talk to him, he don't answer; you touch him, he don't look up. One time I say to him, "pay me some tention," but he don't even hear. I hit his hand, not hard, just playing. He look at me but he don't stop playing. "Get out of here, Martha." First I start to tell him he can't tell me what to do in my own self's house, but he just looking at me. Looking at me and playing and not saying nothing. I leave.

His friends come over most evenings when he home, not playing. It like Time is the leader. Whatever he say go. They always telling him how good he is. "Out of sight, man, the way you play." "You ought to get out of this little town so somebody can hear you play." Most times, he just smile and don't say nothing, or he just say thanks. But I wonder if he really believe em. I tell him, sometime, that he sound better than lots a them men on records. He give me his little cool smile. But I feel he glad I tell him that.

When his friends come over, we sit round laughing and talking and drinking. Orine like that cause she be playing up to em all and they be telling her what a fine ass she got. They don't tell me nothing like that cause Time be sitting right there, but long as Time telling me, I don't care. It like when we go to the Legion, after Time and German started being with us. We all the time get in free then and get to sit at one a the big front tables. And Orine like that cause it make her think she big time. But she still her same old picky self; all the time telling me to "sit cool, Martha," and "be cool, girl." Acting like cool the most important thing in the world. I finally just tell her. "Time like me just the way I am, cool or not." And it true; Time always saying that I be myself and I be fine.

Time and his friends, they talk mostly bout music, music and New York City and white people. Sometime I get so sick a listening to em. Always talking bout how they gon put something over on the white man, gon take something way from him, gon do this, gon do that. Ah shit! I tell em. But they don't pay me no mind.

German say, one night, "Man, this white man come asking if I want to play at his house for—"

"What you tell him, man, 'Put money in my purse?' " Time ask. They all crack up. Me and Orine sit there quiet. Orine all swole up cause Time and them running some kind of game and she don't know what going down.

"Hey man yo all member that time up in Frisco when we got fired from that gig and wan't none of our old ladies working?" That Brown he play bass with em.

"Man," Time say "all I remember is that I stayed high most of the time. But how'd I stay high if ain't nobody had no bread? Somebody was putting something in somebody's purse." He lean back laughing a little. "Verna's mamma must have been sending her some money till she got a job. Yeah, yeah man, that was it. You remember the first time her mamma sent that money and she gave it all to me to hold?"

"And what she wanna do that for? You went out and gambled half a it away and bought pot with most of the rest." German not laughing much as Time and Brown.

"Man, I was scared to tell her, cause you remember how easy it was for her to get her jaws tight. But she was cool, didn't say nothing. I told her I was going to get food with the rest of the money and asked her what she wanted, and—"

"And she say cigarettes," Brown break in laughing, "and this cat, man, this cat tell her, 'Woman, we ain't wasting this bread on no non-essentials!' " He doubled over laughing. They all laughing. But I don't think it that funny. Any woman can give a man money.

"I thought the babe was gon kill me, her jaws was so tight. But even with her jaws tight, Verna was still cool. She just say, 'Baby, you done fucked up fifty dollars on non-essentials; let me try thirty cents.' "

That really funny to em. They all cracking up but me. Time sit there smiling just a little and shaking his head. Then, he reach out and squeeze my knee and smile at me. And I know it like I say; any woman can give a man money.

German been twitching round in his chair and finally he say, "Yeah, man, this fay dude want me to play at his house for fifty cent." That German always got to hear hisself talk. "I tell him take his fifty cent and shove it up his ass—oh scuse me. I forgot that baby was here—but I told him what to do with it. When I play for honkies, I tell him, I don't play for less than two hundred dollars and he so foolish he gon pay it." They all laugh, but I know German lying. Anybody offer him ten cent let lone fifty, he gon play.

"It ain't the money, man," Time say. "They just don't know what the fuck going on." I tell him Larry sitting right there. I know he ain't gon pay me no mind, but I feel if German can respect my baby, Time can too. "Man they go out to some little school, learn a few chords, and they think they know it all. Then they come round to the clubs wanting to sit in with you. Then, if you working for a white man, he fire you and hire him. No, man, I can't tie shit from no white man."

"That where you are wrong," I tell him. "Somebody you don't like, you supposed to take em for everything they got. Take em and tell em to kiss yo butt."

"That another one of your pictures, I guess," Time say. And they all laugh cause he told em bout that, too, one time when he was mad with me.

"No, no," I say. "Listen, one day I walking downtown and this white man offer me a ride. I say okay and get in the car. He start talking and hinting round and finally he come on out and say it. I give you twenty dollars, he say. I say okay. We in Chinatown by then and at the next stop light he get out his wallet and give me a twenty dollar bill. 'That what I like bout you colored women,' he say easing all back in his seat just like he already done got some and waiting to get some more. 'Yeah,' he say, 'you all so easy to get.' I put that money in my purse, open the door and tell him, 'Motherfucker, you ain't got shit here,' and slam the door."

"Watch your mouth," Time say, "Larry sitting here." We all crack up.

"What he do then?" Orine ask.

"What could he do? We in Chinatown and all them colored folks walking around. You know they ain't gon' let no white man do nothing to me."

Time tell me after we go to bed that night that he kill me if he ever see me with a white man.

I laugh and kiss him. "What I want with a white man when I got you?" We both laugh and get in bed. I lay stretched out waiting for him to reach me. It funny, I think, how colored men don't never want no colored women messing with no white mens but the first chance he get, that colored man gon be right there in that white woman's bed. Yeah, colored men sho give colored womens a hard way to go. But I know if Time got to give a hard way to go, it ain't gon be for no scaggy fay babe, and I kinda smile to myself.

"Martha—"

"Yeah, Time," I say turning to him.

"How old you—eighteen?—what you want to do in life? What you want to be?"

What he mean? "I want to be with you," I tell him.

"No, I mean really. What you want?" Why he want to know I wonder. Everytime he start talking serious-like, I think he must be hearing his sliding song.

"I don't want to have to ask nobody for nothing. I want to be able to take care of my own self." I won't be no weight on you, Time, I want to tell him. I won't be no trouble to you.

"Then what you doing on the Welfare?"

"What else I gon do? Go out and scrub somebody else's toilets like my mamma did so Larry can run wild like I did? No. I stay on Welfare a while, thank you."

"You see what the white man have done to us, is doing to us?"

"White man my ass," I tell him. "That was my no good daddy. If he'd got out and worked, we woulda been better off."

"How he gon work if the man won't let him?"

"You just let the man turn you out. Yeah, that man got yo mind."

"What you mean?" he ask real quiet. But I don't pay no tention to him.

"You always talking bout music and New York City, New York City and the white man. Why don't you forget all that shit and get a job like other men? I hate that damn piano."

He grab my shoulder real tight. "What you mean, 'got my mind?' What you mean?" And he start shaking me. But I crying and thinking bout he gon leave.

"You laugh cause I say all I got in my mind is pitchers but least they better than some old music. That all you ever think bout, Time."

"What you mean? What you mean?"

Finally I scream. "You ain't going no damn New York City and it ain't the white man what gon keep you. You just using him for a scuse cause you scared. Maybe you can't play." That the only time he ever hit me. And I cry cause I know he gon leave for sho. He hold me and say don't cry, say he sorry, but I can't stop. Orine bamming on the door and Time yelling at her to leave us lone and the babies crying and finally he start to pull away. I say, "Time. . . ." He still for a long time, then he say, "Okay. Okay, Martha."

No, it not like he don't want me no more, he—

"Martha. Martha. You ain't been listening to a word I say."

"Mamma." I say it soft cause I don't want to hurt her. "Please leave me lone. You and Orine—and Time too, sometime—yo all treat me like I don't know nothing. But just cause it don't seem like to you that I know what I'm doing, that don't mean nothing. You can't see into my life."

"I see enough to know you just get into one mess after nother." She shake her head and her voice come kinda slow. "Martha, I named you after that woman in the Bible cause I want you to be like her. Be good in the same way she is. Martha, that woman ain't never stopped believing. She humble and patient and the Lord make a place for her." She lean her hands on the table. Been in them dishes again, hands all wrinkled and shiny wet. "But that was the Bible. You ain't got the time to be patient, to be waiting for Time or no one else to make no place for you. That man ain't no good. I told you—"

Words coming faster and faster. She got the cow by the tail and gon on down shit creek. It don't matter though. She talk and I sit here thinking bout Time. "You feel good . . . You gon be my Black queen? . . . We can make it together . . . You feel good . . ." He be back.

Part Four

Black Portraits

The Negro in the Art of
Homer and Eakins

SIDNEY KAPLAN

W INSLOW HOMER'S portraits of the American Negro fall into two major groups: the Civil War and the Reconstruction. Ten years after Appomattox, Homer locked up his studio in New York and boarded a train south for Petersburg, Virginia—where earlier he had sketched the siege in which Grant had crippled Lee in the final crisis of the war. Why this decision to carry his brushes south instead of north to Glouces-ter seascapes or the Adirondacks? Was it that the Negro's "color" fascinated Homer, as one critic has put it? Or was there, perhaps, somewhere in his mind a vague disquiet about certain aspects of his rendering of the war—as reporter-artist for *Harper's* and in the canvases worked up from his sketches—during the days of the fighting?

Despite the classic claim that Homer was the supreme realist of the war, it cannot in truth be said that his image of the Negro soldier, aside from its technical virtuosity, differed remarkably from the image seen by lesser artists at the front. The white soldier in blue or gray he saw plain. But the stalwart black in blue—who was present in strength at Petersburg and elsewhere, and to whose critical force Lincoln ascribed the triumph of the Union—is notably absent. Although in Homer's notebook there is a powerful field-drawing of a bearded, black teamster in the saddle, it is, regrettably, the two jolly, Jim Crow-jumping, saucer-lipped, kinky-haired cooks and kitchen police—the old vulgarizations—that are for the most part painfully present in the finished work of this time. Indeed, Lloyd Goodrich makes an overgenerous case, perhaps, for this phase of Homer's Civil War work, when he writes: "Although his attitude reflected some of the typical Northern idea that the Negro was primarily a humorous object, his sense of colored character and physiognomy was already more realistic than the average artist's minstrel-show conception."

A decade later, in the paintings of his Reconstruction group—the outcome of the Virginia trips of 1875 and 1876—the Negro is no longer "primarily a humorous object." When Homer managed to get that bromide out of his head, he was able to apply his great and growing powers to seeing the Negro plain. "Here for the first time in American art," says Goodrich rightly, "was a mature understanding of Negro character."

In Petersburg, Homer set up his easel in the dooryards of the Negro shanties. When a local lyncher ordered the "damned nigger-painter" out of town—so Homer wrote his brother—the artist, sitting on his hotel porch, "looked him in the eyes, as mother used to tell us to look at a wild cow." Here he worked furiously, painting especially women and boys—who neither grin nor prance—and sent to the Paris Universal Exposition of 1878 *The Visit of the Old Mistress** and *Sunday Morning in Virginia.** When, a few years later at the National Academy of Design, he exhibited the same two paintings, a reviewer told a story that revealed part of Homer's attitude toward his subjects: " 'Why don't you paint our lovely girls instead of those dreadful creatures?' asked a First-Family belle when he was in Virginia . . . 'Because they are the purtiest,' he said, in his gruff, final way."

The Visit of the Old Mistress, in theme and structure, recalls Homer's best painting of the war days, his *Prisoners from the Front.* The issue of *Prisoners* is a confrontation: like two columns without an architrave, separated by an ocean of air and idea, the officer of the blue faces the officer of the gray. In *The Visit* the columnar figures are black and white—again a tense confrontation without sentimentality. The blonde, curled mistress, with parasol and lace, seems to expect "friendship" from her former slaves, but the black matriarch, her great arms at her sides, stands like a coffer-dam. She is scarcely a Jemima—not even a Faulknerian Dilsey. Her glance is rejection, a withering of the white delusion of her simplicity, while the eyes and mouths of her family shadow forth nuances of her dignity, scorn, and restraint.

Sunday Morning in Virginia uses the same backdrop of worn planks and patched door—but not as an Eastman Johnson ruin.

* Paintings here reproduced are marked by an asterisk.

Although the columnar feeling is gone, there is still a confrontation, although quite properly no face-to-face tension—the old
woman is the past, too late; the young matron and the children
focus on the pages of the future.

There are two figures in *Sunday Morning* that Homer delighted
to paint again and again—the comely woman and the lovely boy
on her right—and they are never victims of genre jollity. (Even in
Carnival* a sad stillness pervades the central group—it is a rather
unhilarious carnival, only the children smile, unraucously.) The
black angel, who, in a small water-color, is *Taking a Sunflower to
Teacher,** is surely one of the happier realizations of the artist who
never tired of painting the ragged American country boy. Romantic
in the best sense, not naturalistic or darling, the boy's bright face
repeats the sunflower in his hand, while a butterfly, the old emblem
of Psyche and Resurrection, flutters like a wing on his shoulder. In
various settings the face of the strong-bodied young woman, por-
tending the heroic forms of Tynemouth, is studied in the shifting
moods of a free and troubled soul. In *Captured Liberators** Homer
takes her back to the war, a firm if trembling statue framed in a
doorway, her apprehensive hands clutching her apron, as hope
passes her by. She will appear again in the defiant features of a girl
in *The Cotton Pickers,* her dark restless face a commentary on the
white fluffs that surround her.

These then are some of the works of that "damned nigger-
painter" Winslow Homer, who portrayed the whole history of
the hope and failure of Reconstruction on the eve of its compromise. They look forward to the shining Caribbeans of his late
water-colors and to that masterpiece of the black image—the death-
less Negro waiting stoically, Homerically, for his end between
waterspout and white-bellied shark in *The Gulf Stream*—the picture, which, says Alain Locke, broke "the cotton-patch-and-back-
porch tradition" and marked "the artistic emancipation of the
Negro in American art."

IN 1914, when he was seventy, the painter of *The Gross Clinic*
modestly told an inquiring reporter that Winslow Homer, who had
died four years before, had been the best American painter of his
time. Homer, oddly enough, never painted his Negro townsmen of
New York or Maine but found his black subjects at the front, in
Virginia, in the West Indies. Did Homer ever really give his mind

deeply in a social way to the Negro's plight? Or is it rather our great good luck that a granite honesty, like one of his Maine ledges, dashed into spray the white wave of hatred that surged about him and his sitters in Virginia?

Thomas Eakins, a humanist of broader culture, painted a few of his Philadelphia Negro friends and neighbors—a nearby family, a pupil, a rhythmic line of shad fishermen, a few hunting companions, a woman in a red shawl—with as much dedication to what he termed "the character of things" as he lavished on his white friends. Only a handful of pictures, to be sure, but in them he sought facets of the Negro's inmost being that Homer could not reach. "Eakins is not a painter," his friend Walt Whitman—whom he had portrayed as a wild bard—once said, "He is a force."

One of his youthful works, a nude *Negress*** with coral earrings —painted from life during his student days under Gérôme at the Beaux-Arts in Paris—is both warmly exotic and brownly real, quite unlike his teacher's overfinished Moorish slavegirls and "plaster Cleopatras," as Zola once described them. Eight years after his return from France, with his *Negro Boy Dancing,*** which was originally called, simply, *The Negroes,* Eakins, for the first time in American genre, sharply questioned the slavophile iconography of banjo, grin, and jig when he depicted a serious, lyric family drawn together by music—oblivious to the vaudeville public—quickened and entranced by themselves. On the bare wall behind them hangs the fourth head of the family—a framed oval of Lincoln and his son. How much loving care Eakins gave to his dancing boy may be seen in the spirited oil sketch for the final work. As scrupulous in its justice to the face without a film is the dynamically modeled head of the black hunter in *Whistling for Plover,*** who squats and towers like a pyramid on the marshy flats. There is a similar scene of about the same time, *Will Schuster and Blackman Going Shooting,* in which the Negro hunter, his punting-pole like a javelin stretching from top to bottom of the canvas, has a majesty like Jocelyn's *Cinqué* and Mount's spearwoman. (In still another picture of the hunt, Eakins painted himself in the black's place.) Even minor appearances of the Negro in large, complex works—as, for instance, the correct coachman of *The Fairman Rogers Four-in-Hand* or the discreet chaperone of the later version of *William Rush*—show persons rather than props.

Only in Eakins's black commoners, the "divine average" of

Whitman's century, do we have a visual evocation of the life-caresser's chant on a Negro teamster:

> His glance is calm and commanding, he tosses the slouch
>   of his hat away from his forehead,
> The sun falls on his crispy hair and mustache, falls
>   on the black of his polish'd and perfect limbs.

"Whitman never makes a mistake," Eakins liked to say.

But no image like that of the young mulatto woman of *The Red Shawl** exists in *Leaves of Grass,* nor, to be sure, among the Reconstruction figures of Homer. Eakins painted her—we do not know her name—in the same year as his marvelous *Clara;* yet I would rank her unsurpassed head—let lesser adjectives go—with that crowning jewel of American portraiture, his *Edith Mahon.* (All three with their matchless eyes and throats.)

In that single portrait of a Negro woman and in the troubled countenance of his Negro pupil, *Henry Ossawa Tanner** of Pittsburgh, Eakins helped show the way to what he called "a great and distinctively American art." What, indeed, is more "American" than the racial tragedy—the mastered grief, the outraged stillness, the polite cynicism—that Eakins discerned in Tanner's hypersensitive face?

WINSLOW HOMER, *Captured Liberators,* oil, 1875, Edward Eberstadt and Sons, New York

WINSLOW HOMER, *Taking a Sunflower to Teacher*, water-color, 1875, Georgia Museum of Art

WINSLOW HOMER, *The Visit of the Mistress*, oil, 1876, National Collection of Fine Arts, Smithsonian Institution, Washington

WINSLOW HOMER, *Carnival*, oil, 1877, Metropolitan Museum of Art, New York (Lazarus Fund, 1922)

WINSLOW HOMER, *Sunday Morning in Virginia*, oil, 1877, The Cincinnati Art Museum

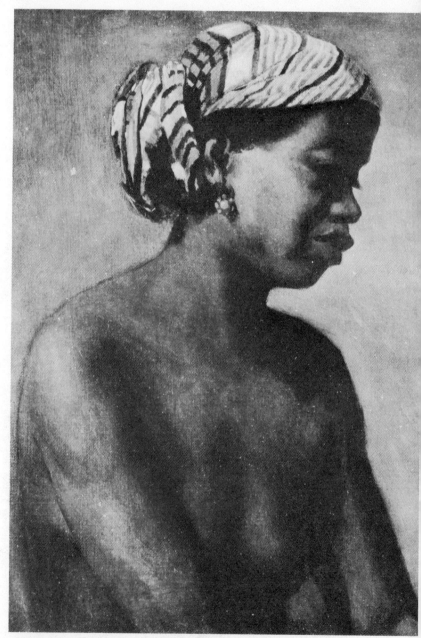

THOMAS EAKINS, *Negress,* oil, ca. 1867-69, M. Knoedler and Company, New York

THOMAS EAKINS, *Whistling for Plover*, water-color, 1874, The Brooklyn Museum

THOMAS EAKINS, *Negro Boy Dancing,* oil sketch, ca. 1878,
Collection of Mr. and Mrs. Paul Mellon

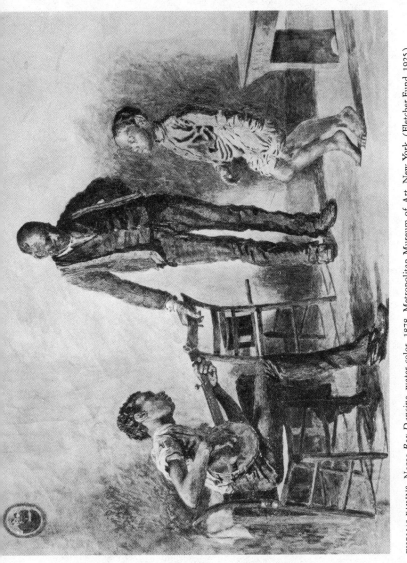

THOMAS EAKINS, *Negro Boy Dancing*, water-color, 1878, Metropolitan Museum of Art, New York, (Fletcher Fund, 1925)

THOMAS EAKINS, *The Red Shawl*, oil, ca. 1890, Philadelphia Museum of Art

THOMAS EAKINS, *Portrait of Henry O. Tanner,* oil, ca. 1900, The Hyde Collection, Glens Falls, New York

The notes on the artists and the
reproductions of their paintings
originally appeared in the catalogue of
an exhibition of
The Portrayal of the Negro
in American Painting 1710-1963
at the Bowdoin College Museum of Art
during the summer of 1964.
The exhibition of eighty paintings was
organized by Marvin S. Sadik,
Director of the Museum, who prepared
the catalogue.

By permission of the President and
Trustees of Bowdoin College.

Black Mutiny on
the Amistad

SIDNEY KAPLAN

On June 28, 1839 a Spanish schooner, ironically named *La Amistad*, sailed from Havana for Port Principe with a cargo of fifty-four African slaves. Four nights later, headed by one Joseph Cinqué, the slaves rose up, killed the captain and three of the crew, and tried to steer the vessel to the coast of Africa. But the Spaniard they had spared to serve as navigator played them false. Two months later, after ascertaining that they were in a "free country," the Africans surrendered to the United States Navy off Montauk Point on Long Island.

The *Amistad* affair quickly became a *cause célèbre* of the antislavery movement. In the North, where the newspapers printed every detail of the case, there was sympathy for the black mutineers and hostility against the Spanish slavetraders, who claimed indemnity for their lost slaves—"pirates who, by revolt, murder, and robbery, had deprived" the owners of their property. The abolitionists, who defended the blacks in and out of the courts, sent Kale, one of the mutineers, on a speaking tour. On the stage at Niblo's in New York the mutiny was dramatized in *The Black Schooner*, whose hero was Cinqué, a planter of rice in the Mendi country of Sierra Leone, son of a prince, "of magnificent physique, commanding presence, forceful manners and commanding oratory." A talented young artist, William H. Townsend, drew the faces of some twenty of the Africans; wax figures of the group, "taken from the life," were exhibited here and there; and Nathaniel Jocelyn of New Haven painted a noble portrait of Cinqué. Two years after the mutiny, in a long and masterful argument, the aged ex-President John Quincy Adams, won from the Supreme Court the historic opinion that black men, abducted from their African homeland, had the right in seeking their liberty to kill anyone who stood in their way. By the following year, aided by the abolitionist Lewis Tappan and the American Missionary Association, Cinqué and his friends were back in their own country.

The *History of the Amistad Captives,* a rare, illustrated pamphlet here reprinted in facsimile, was written by John W. Barber, a Connecticut historian who interviewed the Africans while their struggle for freedom was still in process. It is the basic source for our knowledge of the *Amistad* affair, and unlike most narratives of slave mutiny, is rich not only in detail about the revolt and the legal defense, but also in the full treatment given to the characters and histories of the mutineers as unique human beings and Africans.

The fame of the mutiny on the *Amistad* is apt to obscure the fact that it was but one of hundreds, perhaps thousands, of black mutinies—led by many Cinqués—that occurred during four centuries of the slave trade. (Herman Melville based his *Benito Cereno* on one of them.) For this reason, I append below a few passages culled from firsthand accounts of mutinies that bloodied the decks of blackbirds more than a hundred years before Cinqué broke his shackles:

1699

WILLIAM BOSMAN, Chief Factor of the Dutch West India Company at the Castle of St. George d'Elmina: "*We are sometimes sufficiently plagued with a parcel of slaves which come from a far in-land country, who very innocently persuade one another, that we buy them only to fatten and afterwards eat them as a delicacy. When we are so unhappy as to be pestered with many of this sort, they resolve and agree together (and bring over the rest of their party) to run away from the ship, kill the Europeans, and set the vessel à-shore . . . I have twice met with this misfortune . . . the first time . . . the up roar was timely quashed by the master of the ship and my self, by causing the abettor to be shot through the head, after which all was quiet. But the second time it fell heavier on another ship, by the carelessness of the master, who having fished up the anchor of a departed English ship, had laid it in the hold where the male slaves were lodged; who, un known to any of the ships crew, possessed themselves of a hammer; with which, in a short time, they broke all their fetters in pieces upon the anchor: after this they came above deck and fell upon our men; some of whom they grievously wounded, and would certainly have mastered the ship, if a French and English ship had not very fortu-*

nately happened to lye by us . . . and drove the slaves under deck . . . twenty of them were killed. The Portuguese have been more unlucky in this particular than we; for in four years time they lost four ships in this manner."[1]

1701

JAMES BARBOT, JR., English slavetrader: *"About one in the afternoon, after dinner . . . many of them provided with knives, which we had indiscreetly given them . . . others had pieces of iron they had torn off our forecastle door . . . they had also broken off the shackles . . . Thus arm'd, they fell in crouds and parcels on our men . . . and stabb'd one of the stoutest . . . Next they assaulted our boatswain, and cut one of his legs . . . others cut our cook's throat to the pipe, and others wounded three of the sailors, and threw one of them over-board . . . we stood in arms, firing on the revolted slaves, of whom we kill'd some, and wounded many: which so terrify'd the rest, that they gave way . . . many of the most mutinous, leapt over board, and drown'd themselves in the ocean with much resolution, shewing no manner of concern for life . . . for an example we caused thirty of the ringleaders to be very severely whipt."*[2]

1721

WILLIAM SNELGRAVE, Captain of an English blackbird: *". . . sometimes we meet with stout stubborn People among them, who are never to be made easy; and these are generally some of the Cormantines, a Nation of the Gold Coast . . . We were obliged to secure them very well in Irons, and watch them narrowly. Yet they nevertheless mutinied, tho' they had little prospect of succeeding . . . After we had secured these People, I called the Linguists, and ordered them to bid the Men-Negroes between Decks to be quiet; (for there was a great noise amongst them.) On their being silent, I asked, 'What had induced them to mutiny?' They answered, 'I was a great Rogue to buy them, in order to carry them away from their own Country, and they were resolved to regain their Liberty*

[1] *A New and Accurate Description of the Coast of Guinea . . .* (London, 1705), 363–5.

[2] "An Abstract of a Voyage to Congo River . . ." in Churchill, *Voyages*, 518–9.

*if possible.' I replied, 'That they had forfeited their Freedom before
I bought them, either by Crimes or by being taken in War, according to the Custom of their Country, and they being now my Property, I was resolved to let them feel my Resentment, if they abused
my Kindness . . .' This served my purpose, and they seemed to be
convinced of their Fault, begging, 'I would forgive them, and
promising for the future to be obedient . . .' However, a few days
after this, we discovered they were plotting again, and preparing to
mutiny. For some of the Ringleaders proposed to one of our
Linguists, If he could procure them an Ax, they would cut the
Cables . . . get out of our hands, and then become his Servants."[3]*

1721

JOHN ATKINS, Surgeon in the Royal Navy: ". . . *I had every day
the Curiosity of observing their Behaviour* [in a slave-pen of Sierra
Leone], *which with most of them was very dejected . . . I could not
help taking notice of one Fellow among the rest, of a tall, strong
Make, and bold, stern aspect. As he imagined we were viewing
them with a design to buy, he seemed to disdain his Fellow-Slaves
for their Readiness to be examined, and as it were scorned looking
at us, refusing to rise or stretch out his Limbs, as the Master commanded; which got him an unmerciful Whipping . . . all of which
the Negro bore with Magnanimity, shrinking very little, and shed-
ding a Tear or two, which he endeavoured to hide as tho' ashamed
of. All the Company grew curious at his Courage . . . this same
Fellow, called Captain Tomba, was a leader in some Country
Villages that opposed them and their Trade, at the River Nunes;
killing our Friends there . . .* [we] *surprized, and bound him in the
Night . . . he having killed two in his Defence . . .* [later] *we met
the* Robert *of Bristol, Captain Harding, who sailed from Sierraleon
before us, having purchased thirty slaves, whereof Captain Tomba
was one; he gave us the following melancholly Story. That this
Tomba, about a Week before, had combined with three or four of
the stoutest of his Country-Men to kill the Ship's Company, and
attempt their Escapes, while they had a Shore to fly to, and had
near effected it by means of a Woman-Slave, who being more at
large, was to watch the proper Opportunity. She brought him word*

[3] *A New Account of some Parts of Guinea, and the Slave Trade*
(London, 1734), 164.

*one night that there were no more than five white Men upon the
Deck, and they asleep, bringing him a Hammer at the same time
(all the Weapons she could find) to execute the Treachery. He
encouraged the Accomplices what he could, with the Prospect of
Liberty, but could now at the Push, engage only one more and the
Woman to follow him opn Deck. He found three Sailors sleeping
on the Fore-castle, two of which he presently dispatched, with
single Strokes upon the Temples; the other rouzing with the
Noise, his Companions seized; Tomba coming soon to their Assistance, and murdering him in the same manner. Going after to finish
the work . . . their Defence soon awaked the Master [who] took a
Hand-spike [and] redoubling his Strokes home upon Tomba, laid
him at length flat upon the Deck, securing them all in Irons. The
Reader may be curious to know their Punishment: Why, Captain
Harding weighing the Stoutness and Worth of the two Slaves, did,
as in other Countries they do by Rogues of Dignity, whip and
scarify them only; while three other, Abettors, but not Actors, nor
of Strength for it, he sentenced to cruel Deaths; making them first
eat the Heart and Liver of one of them killed, the Woman he
hoisted up by the Thumbs, whipp'd, and slashed her with Knives,
before the other Slaves till she died."*[4]

The uprising on the *Amistad* was by no means the last instance
of black mutiny. Two years later, during the fall of 1841, the brig
Creole set sail from Hampton Roads for New Orleans with a cargo
of tobacco and one hundred thirty-five slaves. One Sunday night,
nineteen of the slaves led by the Afro-American Madison Washington—a fugitive from Virginia who had returned from Canada to
rescue his wife, had been captured, and was being returned to
bondage—rose up, killed a slavedealer on board, wounded the
captain, cowed the passengers, and forced the crew to sail to free
Nassau. The indignation of Southerners in Congress was boundless,
and Daniel Webster, then Secretary of State, supported them, for
which Garrison, Channing and Sumner assailed him roundly. Some
years later, Frederick Douglass would write a short story, its hero
Madison Washington.

[4] *A Voyage to Guinea, Brasil, and the West-Indies . . .* (London, 1735),
181.

Pencil portraits of four of the *Amistad* Africans
by William H. Townsend (1822–1851).
(Courtesy of Yale University Library).

MARQU

MALHUE

LITTLE KALE

PONA

CINQUÉ
portrait by Nathaniel Jocelyn (1796–1881)
(Courtesy of New Haven Colony Historical Society)

A

HISTORY

OF THE

AMISTAD CAPTIVES:

BEING A

CIRCUMSTANTIAL ACCOUNT

OF THE

CAPTURE OF THE SPANISH SCHOONER AMISTAD,

BY THE AFRICANS ON BOARD;

THEIR VOYAGE, AND CAPTURE

NEAR LONG ISLAND, NEW YORK; WITH

BIOGRAPHICAL SKETCHES

OF EACH OF THE SURVIVING AFRICANS

ALSO, AN ACCOUNT OF

THE TRIALS

HAD ON THEIR CASE, BEFORE THE DISTRICT AND CIRCUIT COURTS OF THE
UNITED STATES, FOR THE DISTRICT OF CONNECTICUT.

COMPILED FROM AUTHENTIC SOURCES,
BY JOHN W. BARBER,
MEM. OF THE CONNECTICUT HIST. SOC.

NEW HAVEN, CT.:
PUBLISHED BY E. L. & J. W. BARBER.
HITCHCOCK & STAFFORD, PRINTERS.

1840.

PREFACE.

THE capture of the Amistad with her cargo of native Africans, and the peculiar circumstances of the case, have excited an unusual degree of interest in this country, and in Europe. A correct statement of the facts of this extraordinary case, is deemed desirable, and the compiler has availed himself of the facilities at his command, for the attainment of this object. Free use has been made of what Professor GIBBS, of Yale College, and others, have published respecting the Africans. The compiler has also had the opportunity of personal conversation with them, by means of James Covey, the Interpreter, and has confined himself to a bare relation of facts.

J. W. B.

NEW HAVEN, CT., May, 1840.

HISTORY

AMISTAD CAPTIVES, &c.

DURING the month of August, 1839, the public attention was somewhat excited by several reports, stating that a vessel of suspicious and piratical character had been seen near the coast of the United States, in the vicinity of New York. This vessel was represented as a "long, low, black schooner," and manned by blacks. The United States steamer Fulton, and several Revenue Cutters, were dispatched after her, and notice was given to the Collectors at various sea ports.

The following, giving an account of the capture of this vessel, and other particulars, is taken from the "New London Gazette."

"The suspicious looking schooner" captured and brought in this port.

Much excitement has been created in New York for the past week, from the report of several Pilot Boats having seen a clipper-built schooner off the Hook, full of negroes, and in such condition as to lead to the suspicion that she was a pirate. Several Cutters and naval vessels are said to have been dispatched in pursuit of her, but she has been most providentially captured in the Sound, by Capt. Gedney, of the surveying Brig Washington. We will no longer detain the reader, but subjoin the official account of the capture, very politely furnished to us by one of the officers.

"U. S. Brig Washington,
NEW LONDON, Aug. 26th, 1839.

"While this vessel was sounding this day between Gardner's and Montauk Points, a schooner was seen lying in shore off Culloden Point, under circumstances so suspicious as to authorize Lieut. Com. Gedney to stand in to see what was her character—seeing a number of people on the beach with carts and horses, and a boat passing to and fro, a boat was armed and dispatched with an officer to board her. On coming along side, a number of negroes were discovered on her deck, and twenty or thirty more were on the beach—two white men came forward and claimed the protection of the officer. The schooner proved to be the 'Amistad,' Capt. Ramonflues, from the Havanah, bound to Guanajah, Port Principe, with 54 blacks and two passengers on board; the former, four nights after they were out, rose and murdered the captain and three of the crew—they then took possession of the vessel, with the intention of returning to the coast of Africa. Pedro Montez, passenger, and Jose Ruiz, owner of the slaves and a part of the cargo, were only saved to navigate the vessel. After boxing about for four days in the Bahama Channel, the vessel was steered for the Island of St. Andrews, near New Providence—from thence she went to Green Key, where the blacks laid in a supply of water. After leaving this place the vessel was steered by Pedro Montez, for New Providence, the negroes being under the impression that she was steering for the coast of Africa—they would not however permit her to enter the port, but anchored every night off the coast. The situation of the two whites was all this time truly deplorable, being treated with the greatest severity, and Pedro Montez, who had charge of the navigation, was suffering from two severe wounds, one on the head and one on the arm, their lives being threatened every instant. He was ordered to change the course again for the coast of Africa, the negroes themselves steering by the sun in the day time, while at night he would alter their course so as to bring them back to their original place of destination. They remained three days off Long Island, to the eastward of Providence, after which time they were two months on the ocean, sometimes steering to the eastward, and whenever an occasion would permit, the whites would alter the course to the northward and westward, always in hopes of falling in with some vessel of war, or being enabled to run into some port, when they would be relieved from their horrid situation. Several times they were boarded by vessels; once by an American schooner from Kingston; on these occasions the whites were ordered below, while the negroes communicated and traded with the vessels; the schooner from Kingston supplied them with a demijon of water for the moderate sum of one doubloon—this schooner, whose name was not ascertained, finding that the negroes had plenty of money, remained lashed alongside the 'Amistad' for twenty-four hours, though they must have been aware that all was not right on board, and probably suspected the character of the vessel—this was on the 18th of the present month ; the vessel was steered to the northward and westward, and on the 20th instant, distant from New York 25 miles, the Pilot Boat No. 3 came alongside and gave the negroes some apples. She was also hailed by No. 4 : when the latter boat came near, the negroes armed themselves and would not permit her to board them ; they were so exasperated with the two whites for bringing them so much out of their way, that they expected every moment to be murdered. On the 24th they made Montauk Light and steered for it in the hope of running the vessel ashore, but the tide drifted them up the bay and they anchored where they were found by the Brig Washington, off Culloden Point. The negroes were found in communication with the shore, where they laid in a fresh supply of water, and were on the point of sailing again for the coast of Africa. They had a good supply of money, some of which it is likely was taken by the people on the beach. After disarming and sending them on board from the beach, the leader jumped overboard with three hundred doubloons about him, the property of the Captain, all of which he succeeded in loosing from his person, and then submitted himself to be captured. The schooner was taken in tow by the brig and carried into New London.''

"*Tuesday*, 12 *o'clock*, *M.*"

We have just returned from a visit to the Washington and her prize, which are riding at anchor in the bay, near the fort. On board the former we saw and conversed with the two Spanish gentlemen, who were passengers on board the schooner, as well as owners of the negroes and most of the cargo. One of them, Jose Ruiz, is a very gentlemanly and intelligent young man, and speaks English fluently. He was the owner of most of the slaves and cargo, which he was conveying to his estate on the Island of Cuba. The other, Pedro Montez, is about fifty years of age, and is the owner of four of the slaves. He was formerly a ship master and has navigated the vessel since her seizure by the blacks. Both of them, as may be naturally supposed, are most unfeignedly thankful for their deliverance. Jose Pedro is the most striking instance of complacency and unalloyed delight we have ever witnessed, and it is not strange, since only yesterday his sentence was pronounced by the chief of the bucaniers, and his death song chanted by the grim crew, who gathered with uplifted sabres around his devoted head, which, as well as his arms, bear the scars of several wounds inflicted at the time of the murder of the ill-fated captain and crew. He sat smoking his Havana on the deck, and to judge from the martyr-like serenity of his countenance, his emotions are such as rarely stir the heart of man. When Mr. Porter, the prize master, assured him of his safety, he threw his arms around his neck, while gushing tears coursing down his furrowed cheek, bespoke the overflowing transport of his soul. Every now and then he clasped his hands, and with uplifted eyes, gave thanks to "the Holy Virgin" who had led him out of his troubles. Senor Ruiz has given us two letters for his agents, Messrs. Shelton, Brothers & Co. of Boston, and Peter A. Harmony & Co. of New York. It appears that the slaves, the greater portion of whom were his, were very much attached to him, and had determined after reaching the coast of Africa, to allow him to seek his home what way he could, while his poor companion was to be sacrificed.

On board the brig we also saw Cingue, the master spirit of this bloody tragedy, in irons. He is about five feet eight inches in height, 25 or 26 years of age, of erect figure, well built and very active. He is said to be a match for any two men on board the schooner. His countenance, for a native African, is unusually intelligent, evincing uncommon decision and coolness, with a composure characteristic of true courage, and nothing to mark him as a malicious man.

By physiognomy and phrenology, he has considerable claim to benevolence. According to Gall and Spurzheim, his moral sentiments and intellectual faculties predominate considerably over his animal propensities. He is said, however, to have killed the Captain and crew with his own hand, by cutting their throats. He also has several times attempted the life of Senor Montez, and the backs of several poor negroes are scored with scars of blows inflicted by his lash to keep them in subjection. He expects to be executed, but nevertheless manifests a *sang froid* worthy of a stoic under similar circumstances.

With Captain Gedney, the surgeon of the port, and others, we visited the schooner, which is anchored within musket shot of the Washington, and there we saw such a sight as we never saw before and never wish to see again. The bottom and sides of this vessel are covered with barnacles and sea-grass, while her rigging and sails presented an appearance worthy of the Flying Dutchman, after her fabled cruise. She is a Baltimore built vessel, of matchless model for speed, about 120 tons burthen, and about six years old. On her deck were grouped amid various goods and arms, the remnant of her Ethiop crew, some decked in the most fantastic manner, in silks and finery, pilfered from the cargo, while others, in a state of nudity, emaciated to mere skeletons, lay coiled upon the decks. Here could be seen a negro with white pantaloons, and the sable shirt which nature gave him, and a planter's broad brimmed hat upon his head, with a string of gewgaws about his neck ; and another with a linen cambric shirt, whose bosom was worked by the hand of some dark-eyed daughter of Spain, while his nether proportions were enveloped in a shawl of gauze or Canton crape. Around the windlass were gathered the three little girls, from eight to thirteen years of age, the very images of health and gladness.

Over the deck were scattered in the most wanton and disorderly profusion, raisins, vermicelli, bread, rice, silk, and cotton goods. In the cabin and hold were the marks of the same wasteful destruction. Her cargo appears to consist of silks, crapes, calicoes, cotton, and fancy goods of various descriptions, glass and hardware, bridles, saddles, holsters, pictures, looking-glasses, books, fruit, olives and olive oil, and "other things too numerous to mention"—which are now all mixed up in a strange and fantastic medley. On the forward hatch we unconsciously rested our hand on a cold object, which we soon discovered to be a naked corpse, enveloped in a pall of black bombazine. On removing its folds, we beheld the rigid countenance and glazed eye of a poor negro who died last night. His mouth was unclosed and still wore the ghastly expression of his last struggle. Near him, like some watching fiend, sat the most horrible creature we ever saw in human shape, an object of terror to the very blacks, who said that he was a cannibal. His teeth projected at almost right angles from his mouth, while his eyes had a most savage and demoniac expression.

We were glad to leave this vessel, as the exhalations from her hold and deck, were like any thing but "gales wafted over the gardens of Gul." Captain Gedney has dispatched an express to the United States Marshal, at New Haven, while he has made the most humane arrangements for the health and comfort of the prisoners and the purification of the prize. There are now alive 44 negroes, 3 of whom are girls; about 10 have died. They have been at sea 63 days. The vessel and cargo were worth forty thousand dollars when they left Havana, exclusive of the negroes, who cost from 20 to 30 thousand dollars. Vessel and cargo insured in Havana.

There is a question for the laws of Admiralty to decide, whether captain Gedney and his fellow officers are entitled to prize or salvage money. To one or the other they are most surely entitled, and we hope they will get their just dues. Captain Gedney, when he first espied the Amistad, was running a line of sounding towards Montauk Point. He had heard nothing of this vessel being on the coast till after his arrival in this port."

The Amistad, as has been stated, anchored off Culloden Point, on the — of August, and the Africans went on shore to get a supply of water for their voyage. It appears that three of their number went up to some of the houses in the vicinity of their landing place, and bought of the inhabitants one or more dogs, for which they paid at the rate of three doubloons each. Capt. Green and some others who were on this part of the island, having heard of these circumstances, and having seen the account of the "suspicious looking schooner" in the newspapers, concluded that these black men were part of the crew of this vessel. Capt. Green, with four or five others, then proceeded to the shore, where they found eight or ten blacks on the beach. Cingue, the leader of the Africans, being one of the number on shore, gave a whistle, upon which all the blacks sprung around him: the whites then ran to their wagons for their guns. The blacks seeing this, sat down, and soon came to a parley with Capt. Green, giving up to him two guns, a knife, and a hat, and remained with him about four hours.

It appears from the testimony given on the trial of the case, that the blacks having been made to understand that there was a vessel of war in pursuit of them, and that there were no slaves or Spaniards in this part of the country, agreed to give up the schooner to Capt. Green, to be taken around to another part of the island, from whence they wished Capt. Green to carry them to Sierra Leone. At this time, or soon after, Lieut. Gedney having discovered the Amistad, dispatched a boat with an armed force and took possession, as has been related.

Cingue having been put on board of the Washington, displayed much uneasiness, and seemed so very anxious to get on board the schooner, that his keepers allowed him to return. Once more on the deck of the Amistad, the blacks clustered around him, laughing, screaming, and making other extravagant demonstrations of joy. When the noise had subsided, he made an address, which raised their excitement to such a pitch, that the officer in command, had Cingue led away by force. He was returned to the Washington, and was manacled to prevent his leaping overboard. On Wednesday he signified by motions, that if they would take him on board the schooner again, he would show them a handkerchief full of doubloons. He was accordingly sent on board. His fetters were taken off, and he once more went below, where he was received by the Africans in a still more wild and enthusiastic manner than he was the day previous. Instead of finding the doubloons, he again made an address to the blacks, by which they were very much excited. Dangerous consequences were apprehended; Cingue was seized, taken from the hold, and again fettered. While making his speech, his eye was often turned to the sailors in charge; the blacks yelled, leapt about, and seemed to be animated with the same spirit and determination of their leader. Cingue, when taken back to the Washington, evinced little or no emotion, but kept his eye steadily fixed on the schooner.—The following relative to the judicial investigation, &c. is taken from a newspaper published in New York :

" On Wednesday night, Captain Gedney dispatched an express to the U. S. Marshal at New Haven, who gave information to his Honor A. T. Judson, U. S. District Judge. On Thursday morning, both these gentlemen arrived, and after careful deliberation, concluded to hold their Court on board the Washington, then lying off the Fort, within musket shot of the schooner. Lieut. Wolcott kindly offered the services to the U. S. cutter Experiment to take all interested on board the Washington. The U. S. Marshal politely took us under his protection.

JUDICIAL INVESTIGATION.

At anchor, on board the U. S. cutter Washington, commanded by Lieut Gedney.

NEW LONDON, AUG. 29, 1839.

His Honor Andrew T. Judson, U. S. District Judge, on the bench, C. A. Ingersol, Esq. appearing for the U. S. District Attorney. The Court was opened by the U. S. Marshal. The clerk then swore Don Pedro Montez, owner of part of the cargo, and three of the slaves, and Don Jose Ruiz, also owner of part of the cargo, and forty-nine of the slaves. These gentlemen then lodged a complaint against Joseph Cingue, (the leader in the alledged offense,) Antonio, Simon, Lacis, Peter, Martin, Manuel, Andrew, Edward, Caledonis, Bartholomew, Raymond, Augustine, Evaristo, Casimiro, Mercho, Gabriel, Santaria, Escalastio, Paschal, Estanilaus, Desiderio, Nicholas, Stephen, Thomas, Corsino, Lewis, Bartolo, Julian, Frederick, Saturnio, Lardusolado, Celistino, Epifanio, Tevacio, Genancio, Philip, Francis, Hipiloto, Venito, Tidoro, Vicinto, Dionecio, Apolonio, Ezidiquiel, Leon, Julius, Hippoloto, 2d, and Zinon, or such of the above as might be alive at that time. It was ascertained that Joseph Cingue, and 38 others, were alive, and on the complaint an indictment was framed charging them with murder and piracy on board the Spanish schooner Amistad.

Joseph Cingue, the leader, was brought into the cabin manacled. He had a cord round his neck, to which a snuff box was suspended. He wore a red flannel shirt and duck pantaloons.

Lieut. R. W. Meade, who speaks the Spanish language both elegantly and fluently, acted as an interpreter between the Spaniards and the court.

Several bundles of letters were produced, saved from the Amistad, and such as were unsealed, read. The contents being simply commercial can be of no interest to the reader. Among the papers were two licenses from the Governor of Havana, Gen. Ezpeleta, one for three slaves, owned by Pedro Montez, one of the men saved, and 49 owned by Senor Don Jose Ruiz, the other that has escaped, allowing the said slaves to be transported to Principe, and commanding said owners to report their arrival to the territorial Judge of the district, in which Principe is situated. A license was found permitting Pedro Montez, a merchant of Principe, to proceed to Matanzas, and transact business, which was endorsed by the Governor of Havana, and the officer of the port. Regular passports were produced, allowing the passengers to proceed to their destination. A license was found permitting Selestino Ferrers, a mulatto, owned by Captain Ramon Ferrers, and employed as a cook, to proceed on the voyage. Other licenses for each sailor were produced and read, all of which were regularly signed, and endorsed by the proper authorities.

The Custom House clearance, dated the 18th of May, 1839, was produced. Also another dated the 27th of June, 1839, all regular. Several licenses permitting goods to be shipped on board the Amistad, were read, and decided to be regular.

Lieut. R. W. Meade testified that he was in the boat which boarded the Amistad, and demanded the papers, which were unhesitatingly delivered. Previous to this demand Senor Don Jose Ruiz had claimed protection for himself and Don Pedro Montez, the only two white men on board. The protection was immediately granted and the vessel brought to New London.

Many of the events which are detailed in the narrative, were omitted in the evidence as having no bearing on the guilt or innocence of the accused, in the present state of the proceedings.

Senor Don Jose Ruiz was next sworn, and testified as follows. I bought 49 slaves in Havana, and shipped them on board the schooner Amistad. We sailed for Guanaja, the intermediate port for Principe. For the four first days every thing went on well. In the night heard a noise in the forecastle. All of us were asleep except the man at the helm. Do not know how things began ; was awoke by the noise. This man Joseph, I saw. Cannot tell how many were engaged. There was no moon.

It was very dark. I took up an oar and tried to quell the mutiny; I cried no! no! I then heard one of the crew cry murder. I then heard the captain order the cabin boy to go below and get some bread to throw to them, in hopes to pacify the negroes. I went below and called on Montez to follow me, and told them not to kill me: I did not see the captain killed. They called me on deck, and told me I should not be hurt. I asked them as a favor to spare the old man. They did so. After this they went below and ransacked the trunks of the passengers. Before doing this, they tied our hands. We went on our course—don't know who was at the helm. Next day I missed Captain Ramon Ferrer, two sailors, Manuel Pagilla, and Yacinto ———, and Selestina, the cook. We all slept on deck. The slaves told us next day that they had killed all ; but the cabin boy said they had killed only the captain and cook. The other two he said had escaped in the canoe—a small boat. The cabin boy is an African by birth, but has lived a long time in Cuba. His name is Antonio, and belonged to the Captain. From this time we were compelled to steer east in the day : but sometimes the wind would not allow us to steer east, then they would threaten us with death. In the night we steered west, and kept to the northward as much as possible. We were six or seven leagues from land when the outbreak took place. Antonio is yet alive. They would have killed him, but he acted as interpreter between us, as he understood both languages. He is now on board the schooner. Principe is about two days sail from Havana, or 100 leagues, reckoning 3 miles to a league. Sometimes when the winds are adverse, the passage occupies 15 days.

Senor Don Pedro Montez was next sworn. This witness testified altogether in Spanish, Lieut. R. W. Meade, interpreter.

We left Havana on the 28th of June. I owned 4 slaves, 3 females and 1 male. For three days the wind was ahead and all went well. Between 11 and 12 at night, just as the moon was rising, sky dark and cloudy, weather very rainy, on the fourth night I laid down on a matress. Between three and four was awakened by a noise which was caused by blows given to the mulatto cook. I went on deck, and they attacked me. I seized a stick and a knife with a view to defend myself. I did not wish to kill or hurt them. At this time the prisoner wounded me on the head severely with one of the sugar knives, also on the arm. I then ran below and stowed myself between two barrels, wrapped up in a sail. The prisoner rushed after me and attempted to kill me, but was prevented by the interference of another man. I recollect who struck me, but was not sufficiently sensible to distinguish the man who saved me. I was faint from loss of blood. I then was taken on deck and tied to the hand of Ruiz. After this they commanded me to steer for their country. I told them I did not know the way. I was much afraid, and had lost my senses, so I cannot recollect who tied me. On the second day after the mutiny, a heavy gale came on. I still steered, having once been master of a vessel. When recovered, I steered for Havanna, in the night by the stars, but by the sun in the day, taking care to make no more way than possible. After sailing fifty leagues, we saw an American merchant ship, but did not speak her. We were also passed by a schooner but were unnoticed. Every moment my life was threatened. I know nothing of the murder of the Captain. All I know of the murder of the mulatto is that I heard the blows. He was asleep when attacked. Next morning the negroes had washed the decks. During the rain the Captain was at the helm. They were all glad, next day, at what had happened. The prisoners treated me harshly, and but for the interference of others, would have killed me several times every day. We kept no reckoning. I did not know how many days we had been out, nor what day of the week it was when the officers came on board. We anchored at least thirty times, and lost an anchor at New Providence. When at anchor we were treated well, but at sea they acted very cruelly towards me. They once wanted me to drop anchor in the high seas. I had no wish to kill any of them, but prevented them from killing each other.

The prisoner was now sent to his quarters, and the Court adjourned to the schooner, that she might be inspected, and that Antonio when making his deposition might recognize those who murdered the Captain and his mulatto cook.

Adjourned investigation on board the Amistad.

Antonio, the slave of the murdered Captain, was called before the court, and was addressed in Spanish, by Lieut. Meade, on the nature of an oath. He said he was a Christian, and being sworn, he thus testified :

" We had been out four days when the mutiny broke out. That night it had been raining very hard, and all hands been on deck. The rain ceased, but still it was very dark. Clouds covered the moon. After the rain, the Captain and mulatto lay down on some matresses that they had brought on deck. Four of the slaves came aft, armed with those knives which are used to cut sugar cane ; they struck the Captain across the face twice or three times; they struck the mulatto oftener. Neither of them groaned. By this time the rest of the slaves had come on deck, all armed in the same way. The man at the wheel and another let down the small boat and escaped. I was awake and saw it all. The men escaped before Senor Ruiz and Senor Montez awoke. Joseph, the man in irons, was the leader; he attacked Senor Montez. Senor Montez fought with them and wanted them to be still. The Captain ordered me to throw some bread among them. I did so, but they would not touch it. After killing the Captain and the cook, and wounding Senor Montez, they tied Montez and Ruiz by the hands till they had ransacked the cabin. After doing so, they loosed them, and they went below. Senor Montez could scarcely walk. The bodies of the Captain and mulatto were thrown overboard and the decks washed. One of the slaves who attacked the Captain has since died. Joseph was one, two of them are now below. (The boy then went on deck and picked out the two negroes who had conspired to kill the Captain and mulatto.)

The examination of the boy being finished, the court returned by the conveyance which put it on board the Washington, and after being in consultation some time, came to the following decision:

Joseph Cingue, the leader, and 38 others, as named in the indictment, stand committed for trial before the next Circuit Court at Hartford, to be holden on the 17th day of September next.

The three girls and Antonio, the cabin boy, are ordered to give bonds in the sum of $100 each to appear before the said court and give evidence in the aforesaid case, and for want of such bonds to be committed to the county jail in the city of New Haven. These persons were not indicted. Lieut. R. W. Meade, Don Jose Ruiz, and Don Pedro Montez, are ordered to recognize in the sum of $100 each to appear and give evidence in said case, before the aforesaid court. The court now finally adjourned, having given an order to the U. S. Marshal, to transport them to New Haven. As we were about to leave, the following was put into our hands by Senor Ruiz, with a request that it might be published in all the city papers:

A CARD.

NEW LONDON, August 29, 1839.

The subscribers, Don Jose Ruiz, and Don Pedro Montez, in gratitude for their most unhoped for and providential rescue from the hands of a ruthless gang of African bucaniers and an awful death, would take this means of expressing, in some slight degree, their thankfulness and obligation to Lieut. Com. T. R. Gedney, and the officers and crew of the U. S. surveying brig Washington, for their decision in seizing the Amistad, and their unremitting kindness and hospitality in providing for their comfort on board their vessel, as well as the means they have taken for the protection of their property.

We also must express our indebtedness to that nation whose flag they so worthily bear, with an assurance that this act will be duly appreciated by our most gracious sovereign, her Majesty the Queen of Spain.
DON JOSE RUIZ,
DON PEDRO MONTEZ."

The Africans were put on board of a sloop, under the charge of Lieut. Holcomb, of the Washington, and Col. Pendleton, keeper of the New Haven prison. They arrived in New Haven on Sunday morning, Sept. 1st. Cingue, the leader, was separated from the rest, and was brought in by the revenue cutter Wolcott, Capt. Mather, in irons. The whole, 44 in number, were put into the county Jail, of which, they occupied four apartments.

The following account of the Amistad captives, given individually, is partly drawn from that given by Professor Gibbs, and partly from personal conversation had with them by the compiler, by means of the interpreter. The accompanying profiles were mostly taken by a pentagraph from the wax figures now exhibiting through the country by Pendleton & Curtiss, which are striking and accurate likenesses of the Africans, taken from life by Mr. Moulthrop, and are mathematically correct. [The numbers correspond with those on the wax figures.] The French sound of the vowels is the one adopted in the orthography of names.

[The map (page 9) is given to assist the reader in understanding some parts of the outline history of the individual Africans, which is here attempted. It gives the relative situation of the Mendi country, with regard to other portions of Africa. The distance from Freetown, Sierra Leone, to Monrovia, Liberia, is in a direct line, about two hundred miles. It will be seen on the map, that Gallinas river discharges its waters into the ocean between these two places. Lomboko, the place from where the Africans were embarked for Havana, is an island at the mouth of the Gallinas.]

Map of part of Western Africa.

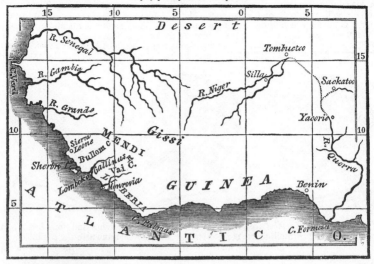

No. 1.

(1.) SING-GBE, [**Cin-gue,**] (generally spelt *Cinquez*) was born in Ma-ni, in Dzho-poa, *i. e. in the open land*, in the Men-di country. The distance from Mani to Lomboko, he says, is ten suns, or days. His mother is dead, and he lived with his father. He has a wife and three children, one son and two daughters. His son's name is *Ge-waw*, (God.) His king, Ka-lum-bo, lived at Kaw-men-di, a large town in the Mendi country. He is a planter of rice, and never owned or sold slaves. He was seized by four men, when traveling in the road, and his right hand tied to his neck. Ma-ya-gi-la-lo sold him to Ba-ma-dzha, son of Shaka, king of Gen-du-ma, in the Vai country. Bamadzha carried him to Lomboko and sold him to a Spaniard. He was with Mayagilalo three nights; with Bamadzha one month, and at Lomboko two months. He had heard of Pedro Blanco, who lived at Te-i-lu, near Lomboko.*

No. 2.

(2.) GI-LA-BA-RU, [**Grab-eau,**] (*have mercy on me*,) was born at Fu-lu, in the Mendi country, two moons' journey into the interior. His name in the public prints is generally spelt GRABEAU. He was the next after Cingue in command of the Amistad. His parents are dead, one brother and one sister living. He is married, but no children; he is a planter of rice. His king Baw-baw, lived at Fu-lu. He saw Cingue at Fulu and Fadzhinna, in Bombali. He was caught on the road when going to Taurang, in the Bandi country, to buy clothes. His uncle had bought two slaves in Bandi, and gave them in payment for a debt; one of them ran away, and he (Grabeau) was taken for him. He was sold to a Vai-man, who sold him to Laigo, a Spaniard, at Lomboko. Slaves in this place are put into a prison, two

* The following is a phrenological description of the head of Cingue as given by Mr. Fletcher: " Cingue appears to be about 26 years of age, of powerful frame, bilious and sanguine temperament, bilious predominating. His head by measurement is 22 3-8 inches in circumference, 15 inches from the root of the nose to the occipital protuberance over the top of the head, 15 inches from the Meatus Auditorious to do. over the head, and 5 3-4 inches through the head at destructiveness.

The development of the faculties is as follows: Firmness; self-esteem; hope—very large. Benevolence; veneration; conscientiousness; approbativeness; wonder; concentrativeness; inhabitiveness; comparison; form—large. Amativeness; philoprogenitiveness; adhesiveness; combativeness; de-

are chained together by the legs, and the Spaniards give them rice and fish to eat.
In his country has seen people write—they wrote from right to left. They have
cows, sheep, and goats, and wear cotton cloth. Smoking tobacco is a common practice. None but the rich eat salt, it costs so much. Has seen leopards and elephants,
the latter of which, are hunted for ivory. Grabeau is four feet eleven inches in
height; very active, especially in turning somersets. Besides Mendi, he speaks Vai,
Kon-no and Gissi. He aided John Ferry by his knowledge of Gissi, in the examination at Hartford.

No. 3.   No. 4.   No. 5.

(3.) **Kimbo** (*cricket*) is 5 ft. 6 in. in height, with mustaches and long beard; in
middle life, and is intelligent. He was born at Maw-ko-ba, a town in the Mendi country; his father was a gentleman, and after his death, his king took him for his slave,
and gave him to his son Ban-ga, residing in the Bullom country. He was sold to a
Bullom man, who sold him to a Spaniard at Lomboko. He counts thus: 1, etá ; 2, filĭ ;
3, kiau-wá ; 4, náeni ; 5, lóelu ; 6, wêta ; 7, wafurá ; 8, wayapá ; 9, tá-u ; 10, pu.—
Never saw any books in his country. When people die in his country, they suppose
the spirit lives, but where, they cannot tell.

(4.) Nazha-u-lu, (*a water stick*,) also called from his country, **Kon-no-ma,** is
5 ft. 4 in. in height, has large lips, and projecting mouth, his incisor teeth pressed outward and filed, giving him rather a savage appearance; he is the one who was supposed
to be a cannibal, (see page 5,) tattooed in the forehead with a diamond shaped figure.
He was born in the Konno country: his language is not readily understood by Covey,
the interpreter. Kon-no-ma recognizes many words in Mungo Park's Mandingo
vocabulary.

(5.) **Bur-na,** the younger, height 5 ft. 2 in. lived in a small town in the Mendi
country. He counts in Tim-ma-ni and Bullom. He was a blacksmith in his native
village, and made hoes, axes, and knives; he also planted rice. He was sold for crim.
con. to a Spaniard at Lomboko. He was taken in the road, and was four days in
traveling to Lomboko. Has a wife and one child, a father, three sisters and brother
living.

No. 6.   No. 7.   No. 8.

(6.) Gba-tu, [**Bar-tu,**] (*a club or sword,*) height 5 ft. 6 in. with a tattooed breast
was born in the country of Tu-ma, near a large body of fresh water, called Ma-wu-a·
His father is a gentleman and does no work. His king, named *Da-be,* resided in the

structiveness; secretiveness; constructiveness; caution; language; individuality; eventuality;
causality; order—average. Alimentiveness; acquisitiveness; ideality; mirthfulness; imitation;
size; weight; color; locality; number; time; tune—moderate and small. The head is well formed
and such as a phrenologist admires. The coronal region being the largest, the frontal and occipital
nearly balanced, and the basilar moderate. In fact, such an African head is seldom to be seen, and
doubtless in other circumstances would have been an honor to his race.''

town of Tu-ma. He was sent by his father to a village to buy clothes; on his return, he was seized by six men, and his hands tied behind; was ten days in going to Lom-boko. There are high mountains in his country, rice is cultivated, people have guns; has seen elephants. *Remark.*—There is a village called Tu-ma, in the Timmani country, 60 miles from Sierra Leone, visited by Major Laing.

(7.) **Gna-kwoi** (in *Ba-lu* dialect, *second born*) was born at *Kong-go-la-hung*, the largest town in the Balu country. This town is situated on a large river called in Balu, *Za-li-ba;* and in Mendi, *Kal-wa-ra:* fish are caught in this river as large as a man's body—they are caught in nets and sometimes shot with guns. When going to the gold country to buy clothes, he was taken and sold to a Vai-man who sold him to a Spaniard named *Péli.* Gna-kwoi has a wife and one child; he calls himself a Balu-man; has learned the Mendi language since he was a slave; 5 ft. 6 in. in height.

(8.) **Kwong** was born at Mam-bui, a town in the Mendi country. When a boy he was called Ka-gnwaw-ni. Kwong is a Bullom name. He was sold by a Tim-mani gentleman in the Du-bu country, for crim. con. with his wife, to Luisi, a Span-iard, at Lomboko. He is in middle life, 5 ft. 6 in. high.

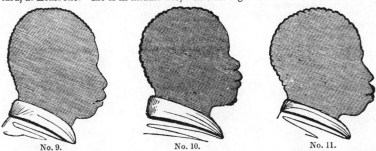

No. 9. No. 10. No. 11.

(9.) **Fu-li-wa,** Fu-li, (*sun*,) called by his fellow prisoners Fuliwa, (*great Fuli,*) to distinguish him from Fu-li-wu-lu, (*little Fuli,*) was born at Ma-no, a town in the Mendi country, where his king, *Ti-kba,* resided. He lived with his parents, and has five brothers. His town was surrounded by soldiers, some were killed, and he with the rest were taken prisoners. He passed through the Vai country, when taken to Lomboko, and was one month on the journey. He is in middle life, 5 ft. 3 in. high, face broad in the middle, with a slight beard. It was this Fuli who instituted the suit against Ruiz and Montez.

(10.) **P-ie,** *Pi-e,* or *Bi-a,* (5 ft. 4½ in. high,) calls himself a Timmani, and the father of Fu-li-wu-lu. He appears to have been distinguished for hunting in his country: says he has killed 5 leopards, 3 on the land, and 2 in the water; has killed three elephants. He has a very pleasant countenance; his hands are whitened by wounds received from the bursting of a gun barrel, which he had overloaded when showing his dexterity. He had a leopard's skin hung up on his hut, to show that he was a hunter. He has a wife and four children. He recognizes with great readi-ness the Timmani words and phrases contained in Winterbottom's account of Sierra Leone. He and his son seemed overjoyed to find an American who could articulate the sound of their native tongue.

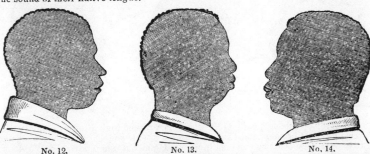

No. 12. No. 13. No. 14.

(11.) Pu-gnwaw-ni, [**Pung-wu-ni,**] (*a duck*,) 5 ft. 1 in. high, body tattooed, teeth filed, was born at Fe-baw, in Sando, between Mendi and Konno. His mother's brother sold him for a coat. He was taken in the night, and was taken a six days' journey, and sold to Garlobá, who had four wives. He staid with this man two years, and was employed in cultivating rice. His master's wives and children were employed in the same manner, and no distinction made in regard to labor.

(12.) **Ses-si,** 5 ft. 7½ in. with a sly and mirthful countenance, was born in Massa-kum, in the Bandi country, where his king, *Pa-ma-sa*, resided. He has three brothers, two sisters, a wife, and three children. He is a blacksmith, having learnt that trade of his brother; he made axes, hoes, and knives from iron obtained in the Mendi country. He was taken captive by soldiers and wounded in the leg. He was sold twice before he arrived at Lomboko, where he was kept about a month. Although a Bandi, he appears to have been able to talk in Mendi.

(13) **Mo-ru,** middle age, 5 ft. 8½ in. with full negro features, was born at Sanka, in the Bandi country. His parents died when he was a child. His master, Margoná, who sold him, had ten wives and many houses; he was twenty days on his journey to Lomboko. He was sold to Be-le-wa, (*great whiskers*,) i. e. to a Spaniard.

(14.) **Ndam-ma,** (*put on, or up,*) 5 ft. 3 in. a stout built youth, born in the Mendi country, on the river Ma-le. His father is dead, and he lived with his mother; has a brother and sister. He was taken in the road by twenty men, and was many days in traveling to Lomboko.

No. 15.   No. 16.   No. 17.

(15.) **Fu-li-wu-lu,** (*Fuli,*) or, as the name has been written, Furie, (*sun,*) called Fuliwulu, to distinguish him from Fuliwa, (*great Fuli,*) lived with his parents in the Timmani, near the Mendi country. He is the son of Pie, (No. 10.) He was taken with his father, by an African, who sold him to a Bullom man, who sold him to Luis, a Spaniard at Lomboko. He has a depression in the skull from a wound in the forehead. 5 ft. 2½ in. in height.

(16.) **Ba-u,** (*broke,*) 5 ft. 5 in. high, sober, intelligent looking, and rather slightly built. Has a wife and three children. He was caught in the bush by 4 men as he was going to plant rice; his left hand was tied to his neck; was ten days in going to Lomboko. He lived near a large river named Wo-wa. In his country all have to pay for their wives; for his, he had to pay 10 clothes, 1 goat, 1 gun, and plenty of mats; his mother made the cloth for him.

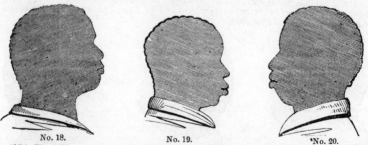

No. 18.   No. 19.   *No. 20.

(17.) **Ba,** (*have none,*) 5 ft. 4½ in. with a narrow and high head; in middle life. Parents living, 4 brothers and 4 sisters; has got a wife and child. He is a planter of rice. He was seized by two men in the road, and was sold to a Gallina Vai-man, who sold him to a Spaniard. High mountains in his country, but small streams; cotton cloth is manufactured, and hens, sheep, goats, cows, and wild hogs, are common.

(18.) **Shu-le,** (*water fall,*) 5 ft. 4 in. the oldest of the Amistad captives, and the fourth in command, when on board the schooner. He was born at Konabu, in the open land, in the Mendi country. He was taken for a slave by Ma-ya, for crim. con. with his wife. Momawru caught both him and his master Ma-ya, and made them slaves, and sold them to a man who sold him to the Spaniards at Lomboko. There is a large river in his country named *Wu-wa,* which runs from Gissi, passes through Mendi, and runs south into the Konno country.

(19.) **Ka-le,** (*bone,*) 5 ft. 4 in. small head and large under lip, young and pleasant. His parents living; has two sisters. He was taken while going to a town to buy rice. He was two months in traveling to Lomboko.

(20.) **Ba-gna,** (*sand* or *gravel,*) 5 ft. 3 in. was born at Du-gau-na, in the Konno country, where his king, *Da-ga,* lived. His parents are dead, and he lived with his brother, a planter of rice.

No. 21.   No. 22.   No. 23.

(21.) **Sa,** 5 ft. 2 in. a youth with a long narrow head. He was the only child of his parents, and was stolen when walking in the road, by two men. He was two months in traveling to Lomboko.

(22.) **Kin-na,** (*man* or *big man,*) 5 ft. 5½ in. has a bright countenance, is young, and, since he has been in New Haven, has been a good scholar. His parents and grandparents were living; has four brothers and one sister. He was born at Sima-bu, in the Mendi country; his king, Sa-mang, resided at the same place. He was seized when going to Kon-gol-li, by a Bullom man, who sold him to Luiz, at Lomboko.

(23.) NDZHA-GNWAW-NI, [**Nga-ho-ni,**] (*water bird,*) 5 ft. 9 in. with a large head, high cheek bones, in middle life. He has a wife and one child; he gave twenty clothes and one shawl for his wife. He lived in a mountainous country; his town was formerly fenced around, but now broken down. He was seized by four men when in a rice field, and was two weeks in traveling to Lomboko.

No. 24.   No. 25.   No. 26.

(24.) FANG, [**Fa-kin-na,**] 5 ft. 4 in. head elevated in the middle, stout built, and middle aged. He was born at Dzho-po-a-hu, in the Mendi country, at which place his father, *Baw-nge,* is chief or king. He has a wife and two children; was caught in the bushes by a Mendi man, belonging to a party with guns, and says he was ten days in traveling to Lomboko after being a slave to the man that took him, less than a month.

(25.) FAHI-DZHIN-NA, [**Fa-gin-na,**] (*twin,*) 5 ft. 4 in. marked on the face with the small pox; was born at Tom-bo-lu, a town of Bombali, in the Mendi country. He was made a slave by Tamu for crim. con. with his wife. Tamu sold him to a

Mendi man, who sold him to Laigo, a Spaniard, the same who purchased Grabeau. He says many people in his country have the small pox, to cure which, they oil their bodies.

(26.) **Ya-boi,** 5 ft. 7 in. large head, stout built, and in middle life; was born at Kon-do-wa-lu, where his king, Ka-kbe-ni, (*lazy,*) resided. His village was surrounded by soldiers, and he was taken by Gillewa, a Mendi man, to whom he was a slave ten years. Had a wife and one child. Gillewa sold him to Luiz, the Spaniard.

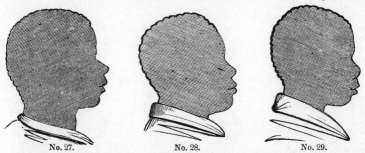

No. 27.   No. 28.   No. 29.

(27.) **Fa-ban-na,** (*remember,*) 5 ft. 5 in. large round head, tattooed on the breast; in middle life; he and Grabeau were from the same country, both having the same king. He has two wives and one child; all lived in one house. His village was surrounded by soldiers: he was taken prisoner, sold twice, the last time to a Spaniard at Lomboko.

(28.) **Tsu-ka-ma,** (*a learner,*) 5 ft. 5½ in. young, with a pleasant countenance; was born at Sun-ga-ru, in the Mendi country, where his king, Gnam-be, resided: has parents living, 3 sisters, and 4 brothers. He was taken and sold into the Bullom country, where he lived for a time with his master, who sold him to Luiz, at Lomboko.

(29.) Be-ri, [**Ber-ri,**] (*stick,*) 5 ft. 3 in. with mustaches and beard, broad nose; in middle life. He was born at *Fang-te,* in Gula, a large fenced town, where his king, Ge-le-wa, resided. He was taken by soldiers, and was sold to Shaka, king of Genduma, in the Vai or Gallina country, who sold him to a Spaniard. Genduma is on a fresh water river, called *Boba.* It is three or four miles from the river, and nine from the sea.

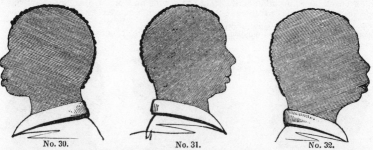

No. 30.   No. 31.   No. 32.

(30.) Faw-ni, [**Fo-ni,**] 5 ft. 2 in. stout built; in middle life. He was born at Bum-be, a large town in the Mendi country: the name of his king was Ka-ban-du. He is married, and has parents, brothers, and sisters living. He was seized by two men as he was going to plant rice. He was carried to Bem-be-law, in the Vai country, and sold to Luiz, who kept him there two months, before he took him to Lomboko. From Bem-be-law to Lomboko is one day's walk.

(31.) **Bur-na,** (*twin,*) the elder, has a cast in the eye; was taken when going to the next town, by three men. His father is dead, and he lived with his mother; has four sisters and two brothers. When his father died his brother married; all lived in the same house. In his country are high mountains, but no rivers; has seen elephants and leopards. He was six weeks in traveling to Lomboko, where he was kept three and a half moons.

(32.) **Shuma,** (*falling water,*) 5 ft. 6 in. with mustaches and beard; in middle life. He can count in the Mendi, Timmani, and Bullom. His parents have been dead a long time; has a wife and one child, was taken prisoner in war, and it was four moons after he was taken, before he arrived at Lomboko. Shuma spoke over the corpse of Tua, after the Rev. Mr. Bacon's prayer. The substance of what he said, as translated by Covey, was, " Now Tua dead, God takes Tua,—we are left behind—No one can die but once," &c.

No. 33.   No. 34.   No. 35.

(33.) **Ka-li,** (*bone*,) 4 ft. 3 in. a small boy, with a large head, flat and broad nose, stout built. He says his parents are living; has a sister and brother; was stolen when in the street, and was about a month in traveling to Lomboko.

(34.) **Te-me,** (*frog*,) 4 ft. 3 in. a young girl, says she lived with her mother, with an elder brother, and sister; her father was dead. A party of men in the night broke into her mother's house, and made them prisoners; she never saw her mother or brother afterwards, and was a long time in traveling to Lomboko.

(35.) **Ka-gne,** (*country*,) 4 ft. 3 in. a young girl. She counts in Mendi like Kwong, she also counts in Fai or Gallina, imperfectly. She says her parents are living, and has four brothers and four sisters; she was put in pawn for a debt by her father which not being paid, she was sold into slavery, and was many days in going to Lomboko.

(36.) **Mar-gru,** (*black snake*,) 4 ft. 3 in. a young girl, with a large, high forehead; her parents were living; she had four sisters and two brothers; she was pawned by her father for a debt, which being unpaid, she was sold into slavery. The foregoing list comprises all the Africans captured with the Amistad, now [May, 1840] living. Six have died while they have been in New Haven; viz. 1, *Fa*, Sept. 3d, 1839 ; 2, *Tua* (a Bullom name) died Sept. 11th ; 3, *We-lu-*

No. 36.   *Antonio.*

wa (a Bandi name) died Sept. 14th ; 4, *Ka-ba*, a Mendi man, died Dec. 31st ; 5, *Ka-pe-li*, a Mendi youth, died Oct. 30 ; 6, *Yam-mo-ni*, in middle life, died Nov. 4th.

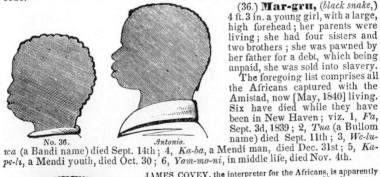

JAMES COVEY, the interpreter for the Africans, is apparently about 20 years of age ; was born at Benderi, in the Mendi country. His father was of Kon-no descent, and his mother Gissi. Covey was taken by three men, in the evening, from his parents' house, at Go-la-hung, whither they had removed when he was quite young. He was carried to the Bullom country, and sold as a slave to Ba-yi-mi, the king of the Bul-loms, who resided at Mani. He lived there for three years, and was employed to plant rice for the wife of Ba-yi-mi, who treated him with great kindness. He was sold to a Portuguese, living near Mani, who carried him, with 200 or 300 others to Lomboko, for the purpose of being transported to America. After staying in this place about one month, Covey was put on board a Portuguese slave-ship, which, after being out about four days from Lomboko, was captured by a British armed vessel, and carried into Sierra Leone. Covey thus obtained his freedom, and remained in this place five or six years, and was taught to read and write the English language, in the schools of the Church Missionary Society. Covey's original name was *Kaw-we-li*, which signifies, in Mendi, *war road*, i. e., a road dangerous to pass, for fear of being taken captive. His Christian name, James, was given him by Rev. J. W. Weeks, a Church Missionary, at Sierra Leone. In Nov., 1838, he enlisted as a sailor on board the British brig of war Buzzard, commanded by Captain Fitzgerald. It was on board this vessel, when at New York, in Oct., 1839, that James was found, amid some twenty native Africans, and by the kindness of captain Fitzgerald, his services as an interpreter were procured.

James Covey.

On the 14th of September, 1839, all the captured Africans, with the exception of Burna, who was left sick at New Haven, were removed to Hartford to await their trial. On Wednesday, the 18th, Judge Thompson took his seat. In the afternoon the council for the blacks, Messrs. S. P. Staples and T. Sedgwick, Jr. of New York, and R. S. Baldwin of New Haven, moved for a habeas corpus to the Marshal, directing him to bring up the three African girls, they not being implicated in the criminal charge. The writ was granted and made returnable the next morning.

On Thursday, the matter of the habeas corpus was postponed till the afternoon, and the District Court was opened by Judge Judson, he quitting the bench of the Circuit Court. The libels and claims in relation to the Amistad were then read and filed as follows ; 1st. Lieut. Gedney and Meade, filed their libel praying for salvage. 2d. Captain Green, of Long Island, by Governor Ellsworth, his Attorney, put in his libel for salvage also. 3d. Pedro Montez filed his libel against part of the cargo, and four of the slaves, three girls and one boy, as his property. 4th. Jose Ruiz filed his libel against the remainder of the slaves and the balance of the property; and lastly, the District Attorney, Mr. Hollabird, filed a claim under Lieut. Gedney's libel, on two distinct grounds: one that these Africans had been claimed by the Government of Spain, and ought to be retained till the pleasure of the Executive might be known as to that demand, and the other, that they should be held subject to the disposition of the President, to be re-transported to Africa, under the act of 1819.

The Spanish Consul also asked leave to file a libel in behalf of the owners abroad. The counsel who appeared for the Spanish owners, were Messrs. R. I. Ingersoll, W. Hungerford, and Mr. Purroy of New York.

The only matter of consequence which occurred at this time, was that the District Judge said he had come to the decision that there could be no claim for salvage as to the Africans.

Thursday, P. M.—The three African girls were brought into Court weeping, and evidently much terrified at the separation from their companions :—the eldest being about eleven years of age. The Marshal then made his return, and justified the detention of these negroes under the libel of Lieut. Gedney—the claim of the United States, the libel of Pedro Montez, and also under an order of the District Judge, committing them as witnesses to appear at this Court. The counsel for the Africans asked leave to consider this return, and it was granted till the next morning.

On Friday, the matter of the habeas corpus was called up, and Mr. Sedgewick read the answer to the Return, setting out at length the Spanish decrees suppressing the slave trade, and alleging these Africans to have been born and still of right to be free. Mr. Baldwin followed in a very elaborate argument, denying the jurisdiction of the Court, as the property was found at Long Island, and in the District of New York— the right of Gedney as salvor—the claim of Montez as a purchaser of slaves illegally imported into Cuba, and the authority of the District Attorney to make any claim in behalf of the Spanish Government, or that of the United States. In regard to their being recognized as witnesses, an offer was made to give security for them, and in relation to the claim of Lieut. Gedney, the Court remarked that, under the decision of the District Judge, they could not be held by any process under that libel.—Thus two of the obstacles to their discharge were removed : there remained the libel of the alleged owner, and the claim of the United States.

Mr. R. I. Ingersoll replied to Mr. Baldwin, insisting that the rights of the owners were the proper subjects of the cognizance of the District Court, and that this Court should not interfere by this summary process to deprive them of the opportunity of establishing those rights. He further insisted that by the treaty of 1795 with Spain, the rights of these owners were guaranteed, and that the President was bound to surrender them.

The argument was now interrupted by the Grand Jury coming in, and requesting the Court to give them instructions respecting the murder alledged to have been committed on board the Amistad. Upon an intimation of the judge, they presented a statement of the facts of the case, and this the Court took time to consider.

On the re-opening of the Court at 2 P. M., the Court delivered its charge to the Grand Jury, instructing them that the offense of Cingue and his associates, (if offense it was,) being committed on board a Spanish vessel, was not cognizable in our courts. This gave a final disposition of the question whether these Africans could be capitally punished in this country, and the Grand Jury having no other business before them were discharged.

On the opening of the Circuit Court on Saturday morning, Judge Thompson said the Court were not prepared as yet, to dispose of the case under consideration, *finally;* and that any intimations he might then throw out, ought not to be taken as the ultimate views of the Court. On the conclusion of his remarks, he proposed that the case should be kept open until afternoon, and then have it argued. A writ of *habeas corpus* was taken out in the course of the forenoon on the petition of Erastus Smith, Esq. of Hartford, for all the other African prisoners returnable before this Court. The Court then took a recess until 2 o'clock. The arguments on the question were closed on Saturday evening. Messrs. Baldwin and Staples addressed the Court in an able manner, about one hour each, on the question of jurisdiction, and were opposed by Messrs. Hungerford and Ingersoll. Mr. Staples, in his plea, argued that if there was jurisdiction any where, it was in the Southern District of New York.

On the opening of the Circuit Court, on Monday the 23d, Judge Thompson delivered the opinion of the Court. He stated that the question now to be decided, was not as to the ultimate rights of either party, but simply as to the right of the District Court to take cognizance of the case. Had the seizure been made within the limits of the District of New York, the District Court of Connecticut could not have jurisdiction; if the seizure was made on the high seas, as it appeared to be in this case, the District Court of any District to which the property was brought, has jurisdiction. Judge Thompson, in denying the discharge of the Africans, under the writ of the *habeas corpus*, wished to be distinctly understood, that, in denying their discharge, he did not decide that they were not entitled to their freedom, but only left the case in a regular way for decision in another tribunal, from whose decision an appeal might be taken to that Court, and if desired, to the Supreme Court of the United States.

After the adjournment of the Circuit Court, the District Court was opened. Judge Judson said that he should direct an examination of the place where the Amistad was taken, should be made, to determine where the seizure was actually made. The Court was then adjourned to meet in Hartford, on the third Tuesday in November, after the Judge had directed the U. S. Marshal, to see that the prisoners should be comfortably provided for, with regard to food, clothing, &c. In pursuance of this direction, the Africans were remanded back to the prison in New Haven.

On the 17th of October, Messrs. Ruiz and Montez were arrested in New York, on two processes, at the suites of Cingue and Fuli, for assault and battery, and false imprisonment. Being unable, or unwilling to give bail for $1000, which was required, the Spaniards were lodged in prison. On a hearing of the case before Judge Inglis, he decided that Montez should be discharged on finding common or nominal bail, and that the amount of bail for Ruiz, should be reduced to two hundred and fifty dollars.

On Tuesday, the 19th of October, the District Court at Hartford, met agreeable to the adjournment, and the examination of witnesses occupied the whole day. On Wednesday, seven of the Africans were brought in Court, and after some further examination respecting the place of seizure, the Court was adjourned to sit in New Haven, on January 7th, 1840.

On the day of the adjournment, Judge Judson held a session at his chamber in the City Hotel, for the purpose of receiving the testimony of Dr. R. R. Madden, who had recently arrived in this country from Havana, on his return to England. He stated that he was a British subject, and had been a resident at Havana for more than three years, and had held official stations there for three years ; that the office he now held was that of Commissioner of liberated Africans, and for one year held that of British Commissioner in the Mixed Court of Justice : that the duties of his office made him well acquainted with the details of slavery and slave trade in Cuba. He stated that for the last three years, from *twenty*, to *twenty-five thousand* slaves from Africa, were yearly introduced into the island of Cuba, although it has been in violation of the Spanish law ever since 1820. The Spanish authorities never interfere to stop this illegal trade, but connive at it, receiving ten dollars a head for every negro thus introduced, which is called a voluntary contribution, but is in reality a tax, which has no legal sanction for its imposition. Dr. M. also stated that he had seen the Africans, who were captured in the Amistad, and that they were of that class called in Cuba, *Bozal*, a term given to negroes recently from Africa : that the document then produced before him, dated June 26th, 1839, and signed by Espelata, the Captain General of Cuba, was a permit for the transportation of 49 slaves on board of the Amistad from Havana : that they are called in the permit, *Ladinos*, a term given to negroes long settled and acclimated in Cuba.

That the custom, on landing the negroes illegally introduced by the slave traders of the Havana, is to take them immediately to the Barracoons, or slave marts, which are fitted up exclusively for the reception and sale of Bozal negroes lately introduced, where they are kept by the slave traders till sold, generally for a period of two or three weeks ; that among the slave traders of the Havana, one of the houses, the most openly engaged and notoriously implicated in slave trade transactions, is that of Martinez & Co., and that the custom of this house is, like all other slave traders of the Havana, to send the negroes they import into the island, immediately after landing, to the Barracoons.

Dr. Madden also stated in his testimony, the trespasses or permits, for all such negroes are commonly and usually obtained at the Havana, simply on application to the authorities. The " Bozal" negroes are called " Ladinos," and no examination is made by the Governor, or any officer of his, into the truth of the statement, but the permit is granted for the removal of the negroes falsely called Ladinos, on the simple application of the buyers, on the payment of the fees, and no oath required of them.

That to apply for these permits, and obtain them, representing Bozal negroes as Ladinos, as in the present case, is a fraud on the part of the purchaser, which cannot take place without connivance at the trade, and collusion with the slave traders on the part of the authorities. That the vast numbers of Bozals thus illegally introduced are by these means carried into the interior, and fall into hopeless slavery.

The efforts of the committee on behalf of the Africans, were, after the adjournment of the September court, crowned with success. Two native Africans belonging to the crew of the British brig of war Buzzard, which came into New York in July, from a cruise on the coast of Africa, were found to speak the same language of the prisoners. With the consent of Capt. Fitzgerald, they were allowed to come on to New Haven. When taken to the prison, the African captives were at breakfast, and the Marshal objected to their entrance till they had finished. One of the captives, however, coming to the door and finding one who could talk in his own language, took hold of him and literally dragged him in. Breakfast was forgotten, all seemed overwhelmed with joy, all talking as fast possible.

The following communication from Mr. Day, of New Haven, gives a summary account of the African captives, as stated by themselves, from the time they left Africa, till the time they obtained possession of the Amistad :

NEW HAVEN, Oct. 8, 1839.

[To the Editors of the Journal of Commerce.]

Gentlemen—The following short and plain narrative of one or two of the African captives, in whose history and prospects such anxious interest is felt, has been taken at the earliest opportunity possible, consistently with more important examinations. It may be stated in general terms, as the result of the investigations thus far made, that the Africans all testify that they left Africa about six months since; were landed under cover of the night at a small village or hamlet near Havana, and after 10 or 12 days were taken through Havana by night by the man who had bought them, named *Pipi*, who has since been satisfactorily proved to be Ruiz; were cruelly treated on the passage, being beaten and flogged, and in some instances having vinegar and gunpowder rubbed into their wounds; and that they suffered intensely from hunger and thirst. The perfect coincidence in the testimony of the prisoners, examined as they have been separately, is felt by all who are acquainted with the minutes of the examination, to carry with it overwhelming evidence of the truth of their story.

Yours respectfully,
GEORGE E. DAY.

MONDAY, Oct. 7.

This afternoon, almost the first time in which the two interpreters Covey and Pratt have not been engaged with special reference to the trial to take place in November, one of the captives named Grabeau, was requested to give a narrative of himself since leaving Africa, for publication in the papers. The interpreters, who are considerably exhausted by the examinations which have already taken place, only gave the substance of what he said, without going into details, and it was not thought advisable to press the matter. Grabeau first gave an account of the passage from Africa to Havana. On board the vessel there was a large number of men, but the women and children were far the most numerous. They were fastened together in couples by the wrists and legs, and kept in that situation day and night. Here Grabeau and another of the Africans named Kimbo, lay down upon the floor, to show the painful position in which they were obliged to sleep. By day it was no better. The space between decks was so small,—according to their account not exceeding four feet,— that they were obliged, if they attempted to stand, to keep a crouching posture. The decks, fore and aft, were crowded to overflowing. They suffered (Grabeau said) terribly. They had rice enough to eat, but had very little to drink. If they left any of the rice that was given to them uneaten, either from sickness or any other cause, they were whipped. It was a common thing for them to be forced to eat so much as to vomit. Many of the men, women, and children died on the passage.

They were landed by night at a small village near Havana. Soon several white men came to buy them, and among them was the one claiming to be their master, whom they call *Pipi*, said to be a Spanish nick-name for *Jose*. Pipi, or Ruiz, selected such as he liked, and made them stand in a row. He then felt of each of them in every part of the body; made them open their mouths to see if their teeth were sound, and carried the examination to a degree of minuteness of which only a slave dealer would be guilty.

When they were separated from their companions who had come with them from Africa, there was weeping among the women and children, but Grabeau did not weep, "because he is a man." Kimbo, who sat by, said that he also shed no tears— but he thought of his home in Africa, and of friends left there whom he should never see again.

The men bought by Ruiz were taken on foot through Havana in the night, and put on board a vessel. During the night they were kept in irons, placed about the hands, feet and neck. They were treated during the day in a somewhat milder manner, though all the irons were never taken off at once. Their allowance of food was very scant, and of water still more so. They were very hungry, and suffered much in the hot days and nights from thirst. In addition to this there was much whipping, and the cook told them that when they reached land they would all be eaten. This " made their hearts burn." To avoid being eaten, and to escape the bad treatment they experienced, they rose upon the crew with the design of returning to Africa.

Such is the substance of Grabeau's story, confirmed by Kimbo, who was present most of the time. He says he likes the people of this country, because, to use his own expression, " they are good people—they believe in God, and there is no slavery here."

The story of Grabeau was then read and interpreted to Cingue, while a number of the other Africans were standing about, and confirmed by all of them in every particular. When the part relating to the crowded state of the vessel from Africa to Havana was read, Cingue added that there was scarcely room enough to sit or lie down. Another showed the marks of the irons on his wrists, which must at the time have been terribly lacerated. On their separation at Havana, Cingue remarked that almost all of them were in tears, and himself among the rest, " because they had come from the same country, and were now to be parted forever." To the question, how it was possible for the Africans, when chained in the manner he described, to rise upon the crew, he replied that the chain which connected the iron collars about their necks, was fastened at the end by a padlock, and that this was first broken, and afterwards the other irons. Their object, he said, in the affray, was to make themselves free. He then requested it to be added to the above, that "if he tells a lie, God sees him by day and by night."

3 feet 3 in. high

[The above engraving shows the position as described by Cingue and his companions, in which they were confined on board the slaver, during their passage from Africa. The space between the decks represented in the engraving is three feet three inches, being an actual measurement from a slave vessel. The space in the vessel that brought the Amistad captives to Havana was, according to their statement, somewhat larger, being about four feet between the decks.]

On the 7th of January, 1840, the U. S. District Court commenced its session in New Haven, Judge Judson presiding. The lawyers in the suit were Messrs. Baldwin, Staples and Sedgewick, for the Africans. Messrs. Isham and Brainard of New London, for Lieut. Gedney. Gov. Ellsworth of Connecticut, in behalf of Capt. Green, and Mr. Cleveland of New London, in behalf of the Spanish owners of part of the property on board of the Amistad, and lastly, Mr. Hollabird, District Attorney, in behalf of the United States. The counsel for the prisoners withdrew the plea which denied the jurisdiction of the court, and acknowledged that if any court in the country could have jurisdiction of the case, this court could. The morning was occupied in discussing technical questions, and the first testimony introduced was on behalf of the prisoners. The deposition of Dr. Madden was read. Messrs. Haley and Janes, of New London, James Covey, the interpreter, and Professor Gibbs, of Yale College, then gave in their testimony, all tending to show that the Amistad captives were recently from Africa. The evidence on this point was so clear, that on the second day of the trial, (Wednesday,) Judge Judson remarked that he was fully convinced that the men were recently from Africa, and that it was unnecessary to take up time in establishing that fact.

Cingue, the leader of the Africans, being called as a witness, Covey, the interpreter, was sworn to interpret the oath to him. The clerk read the oath and Covey repeated it to Cingue in their native tongue. His examination was quite minute, and was listened to by a crowded auditory, with the deepest interest. He testified that at the time of their capture by Lieut. Gedney, a large number of them were on shore, on Long Island. He also gave an account of the voyage to and from Havana, till their capture; and his statements so nearly correspond with the account already given, as to render a repetition unnecessary. While Cingue was on his examination, he described by actions, (which spoke louder than words,) the manner in which Pipi [Ruiz] examined the Africans to ascertain if they were healthy and sound. He also put himself in the position in which they were forced to remain, when packed away on board the slaver. Grabeau and Fuliwa were then sworn and examined, who also testified to the same facts.

Mr. Wilcox, the U. S. Marshal, was examined relative to a conversation he had with Cingue, soon after the arrival of Covey, (the interpreter.) Mr. Wilcox stated that he understood from Covey, (which he now denies,) that Cingue had said that he had sold slaves, and that he himself was seized and sold to pay a debt which he had contracted, and could not pay. Professor Gibbs and Mr. Day who were present at the time, stated that there was much confusion in the room, arising from many asking questions, &c., and think that Mr. Wilcox must have misapprehended what Cingue said.

On Thursday afternoon, after the examination of Antonio, the slave of the Spanish Captain, the District Attorney introduced the deposition of James Ray, and G. W. Pierce, mariners on board of the cutter, giving a detailed account of the capture of the Africans on Long Island. He then introduced the papers of the Amistad, and the permits given to Montez and Ruiz, for the transportation of *Ladinos* to Principe. The license of Capt. Ferrer to carry slaves was from Gaston, who signed himself a Knight of the Cross, a commander of a 74—bearing various insignia of honor, merit, and reward.

The counsel for the Africans introduced Mr. D. FRANCIS BACON, of New Haven, as a witness. Mr. Bacon stated that he left the coast of Africa on the 13th of July, 1839. He knew a place called Dumbokoro [Lomboko] by the Spaniards : it was an island in the river or lagoon of Gallinas.* There is a large slave factory or depot at this place, which is said to belong to the house of Martinez in Havana ; there are also different establishments on different islands. Mr. Bacon stated that he had seen American, Russian, Spanish, and Portuguese vessels at Gallinas. The American flag was a complete shelter ; no man-of-war daring to capture an American vessel. The slave trade on that part of the coast is the universal business of the country, and by far the most profitable, and all engaged in it who could raise the means. Extensive wars take place in Africa, for obtaining slaves from the vanquished. Different towns and villages make war upon each other for this purpose. Some are sold on account of their crimes, others for debts. The slaves are all brought on to the coast by other blacks,

* The following notice from Mr. Bacon, appeared in the New Haven papers, addressed to the editors :

GENTLEMEN,—In connection with the report of the evidence yesterday given in the case of the Amistad, allow me to state a few circumstances explanatory of the manner in which I became possessed of the facts to which I testified.

I was three times in Gallinas during my long wanderings on the coast of Western Africa ;—first, in January, 1838, afterwards, in May of the same year, and last in February, 1839. On each of these visits I was the guest of Don Pedro Blanco, long famous for his large share in the slave trade. From him and all of his agents, and also from those of other establishments, Spanish and Portuguese, in the same business, I received the most unbounded hospitalities. While thus an inmate of their houses, I became familiar with all the details of their business, which was carried on before me in the confidence that I would not abuse their hospitality as a spy ; though they had been cautioned that from my connections I might be dangerous in this way.

In the evidence given, I have therefore been careful to make use of no circumstances relating to the traffic of which I was *thus* informed, and which are not facts of common notoriety on the coast among those who have never been at Gallinas. To those Spaniards at Gallinas and New Sesters, I can never forget my numerous and weighty obligations. When the sea threw me, time and again, a houseless and friendless wanderer on their shore, they received and cherished me, and bade me always seek among them a welcome home in distress. They were anxious to supply every want, and their attentive kindness followed me to the last moment of my residence abroad. At the first tidings of my shipwreck they sent a vessel to search for me and my companions, then surrounded by perils on sea and land, and from savages, while British men-of-war, scouring the coast for "*blood-money*," "passed by on the other side," and carried the news to those who had more charity for mariners in distress.

I make this communication, because I consider it unjust both to them and me that my evidence should go forth on any subject connected with them, without accompanying acknowledgment of my *great* indebtedness to those who could liberally tolerate me as a guest and an inmate friend, when they knew my expressed opinions against their occupation.

Yours,   D. FRANCIS BACON.

and sold at the slave factories, as no white man dare penetrate into the interior. Some of the blacks who have been educated at Sierra Leone, have been principal dealers in the slave trade.

On Friday morning, the District Attorney, according to an arrangement made with the opposing counsel, read the substance of what Antonio G. Viga, the Spanish Consul, at Boston, said he should testify in this case, viz: that he (Viga) had resided in Cuba many years; knew the laws of Cuba; knew of no law in *force*, against the introduction of slaves into the island ; that on some plantations, the native language of the Africans was continued for years; that the papers of the Amistad were genuine. Mr. Janes was then called, who testified that he called on Viga at New London, and asked him when the slave trade was prohibited, or made piracy. He replied he thought it was in 1814, but did not know the penalty.—Here the testimony closed. Mr. Brainard opened the argument on behalf of the libelants, Lieuts. Gedney and Meade. He contended that whether the Africans were or were not, the lawful property of Ruiz and Montez, the Court could not set them free ; crime had been committed on board this Spanish vessel, and this government were bound to deliver up these persons to Spain, that she may execute her own laws. Whether they were delivered up to the Spanish authorities, or to the United States government, his clients had performed meritorious services, for which they were justly entitled to salvage.—Governor Ellsworth, the counsel in behalf of Capt. Green, stated that he could not in accordance with the sentiments he entertained, nor in justice to his client, use the slighest efforts either to have these Africans delivered up to the government of Spain, or to the United States. But if they were to be delivered up, he must claim part of the valuation, for salvage for Capt. Green. He contended that his client had rendered a more valuable and hazardous service than any which Lieut. Gedney and others had rendered, and therefore his right to salvage was paramount to all others. Mr. Cleaveland followed Gov. Ellsworth, in behalf of certain houses in Cuba, who had been shippers in the Amistad. His arguments were confined to the denial of any right of salvage to Lieut. Gedney and others. Being in the service and pay of the United States, they were bound to render assistance without compensation. Capt. Green, having not in fact saved the vessel and cargo, was not entitled to salvage, as that should be given for saving, not for the *attempt* to save.

On Friday P. M., Mr. Sedgewick opened the cause in behalf of the Africans, and was followed on that side by Messrs. Staples and Baldwin. Mr. B. contended that the Africans being born free, were entitled to their freedom, and that every person is presumed to be a freeman until the contrary is proved. The libelants and the United States claim they were slaves, because licenses have been produced authorizing the transportation of *Ladinos* from one port in Cuba to another, a term totally inapplicable to the Amistad captives. It was perfectly evident from the licenses or permits, that a fraud had been committed upon, or by, the Spanish authorities. The decree of Spain of 1817, prohibits the slave trade after 1820, with heavy penalties, and declares all slaves imported from Africa, after that period, free. These Africans owed no obedience to the Spanish laws. When taken at Long Island, they were in possession of their just rights, having the Spaniards Montez and Ruiz in subjection. If not slaves when they set foot on the soil of New York, they cannot be pronounced slaves now. Mr. B. contended, that the Africans were not held here for any lawful purpose, that no human being could be demanded as property, unless specifically named as such by treaty, and no such treaty had been made with Spain. There was no authority in any officer of any foreign government to enter our limits, and take a person thence. The government refers all applications for the delivery of criminals to the authorities of the several States. The interference of the Spanish minister in this case before the Court, was an insult to the government, and the courts of justice of this country.

On Saturday P. M., Gen. Isham, on behalf of Lieuts. Gedney and Meade, made the closing argument in the case. In the course of his remarks, he took occasion to say, that his clients authorized him to say that they would never receive salvage on *human* flesh: all they asked for, was, that if the Court decided that the vessel, cargo, and slaves, should be restored to the Spaniards, it should be upon terms that the owners should first pay them a reasonable compensation for services rendered in preserving their property.

On Monday A. M., Jan. 13th, Judge Judson gave a review and decision of this case, which occupied more than an hour in the delivery. The first point his Honor decided upon, was that respecting jurisdiction. It was necessary in order that the Court have jurisdiction of this case, that the seizure must have taken place within the limits of the District of Connecticut, or upon the high seas. The determination of this point, then rested upon the legal signification of the words *high seas*. It appeared in evidence that the Amistad lay in 3½ fathoms of water off Culloden Point, 5 or 6 miles from Montauk Point, not less than half a mile from the shore, and not in any known harbor, bay, river, or port. Excluding these, the high seas extend to low water mark ; consequently, the Amistad must have been on the high seas. The well known position of Montauk, adds conclusiveness to the argument, as we all understand that Montauk is a point of land projecting into the *sea*.

The next points decided by his Honor, were those respecting salvage. He stated that the services rendered by Lieut. Gedney, were such as justly entitled him to salvage on the *vessel* and *goods*. The decree would be, that the schooner and her effects be delivered up to the Spanish Government, upon the payment, at a *reasonable rate* for saving the property. An appraisement will be ordered, and one third of that amount will be deemed just and reasonable. The next question was, can salvage be allowed upon the slaves ? His Honor here stated that he had in the very outset of the case, decided that the alledged slaves could not be sold. There was no law of the United States nor of the State of Connecticut by which a title can be given under any decree of this Court. Their value in the District of Connecticut was not one cent.

The libel of Messrs. Green and Fordham rested on the claim that they had in effect taken possession of the vessel. His Honor remarked that the facts proved would not sustain this claim, and that therefore their libels must be dismissed. The two great questions still remained to be settled : " Shall these Africans, by a decree of this Court, be delivered over to the Government of Spain, upon the demand of her Minister as the property of Don Pedro Montez and Don Jose Ruiz ? But if not, what ultimate disposition shall the Government of the United States make of them ?"

In Cuba, there are three classes of negroes, *Creoles*, those born within the Spanish dominions : *Ladinos*, those long domiciliated on the island owing allegiance to Spain, and *Bozals*, the name given to those recently from Africa. The negroes in question are recently from Africa, imported into Cuba in violation of Spanish laws, and bought as slaves by Montez and Ruiz. The demand of the Spanish Minister is, that these Bozals shall be given up, that Montez and Ruiz may have them as their property. In order to justify this demand, and require our Government to give them up, according to our treaty with Spain, it is necessary that *property* and title should be proved. The whole evidence offered in support of this claim is a permit or license to transport 54 *Ladinos*, to Guanaja. But these negroes are *Bozals*, not Ladinos. Here then, is the point upon which this great controversy *must* turn. His honor then stated, that he found as a matter of fact, that in the month of June 1839, the law of Spain, prohibited under severe penalties, the importation into Cuba of negroes from Africa. *These* negroes were imported in violation of that law, and by the same law of Spain, such negroes are declared free, and of course are not the property of Span-

24

ish subjects. With regard to the boy Antonio he being a Creole, born as he believes in Spain, recognized by the laws of that country as being the property of Ramon Farrer, a Spanish subject, he should decree a restoration of this slave, under the treaty of 1795.

"The question remains, What disposition shall be made of these negroes by the Government of the United States? There is a law of Congress passed the 3d of March, 1819, which renders it essential that all such Africans as these shall be transported under the direction of the President of the United States to Africa.—I shall put in form a decree of this Court, that these Africans, excepting Antonio, be delivered to the President of the United States to be transported to Africa, there to be delivered to the Agent appointed to receive and conduct them home."

The case of the Africans having been appealed by the District Attorney in behalf of the United States, it came before the Circuit Court held at New Haven, April 29th, 1840, Judge Thompson presiding. The counsel for the Africans objected to the appeal, as coming from the Executive of the U. S. who had no interest in the case, and of whom nothing more could be expected than to assist in bringing the case before the proper tribunal. The arguments of both sides on this point occupied the whole of the afternoon. On Thursday morning the Judge gave it as his opinion that the Government have an interest in the case; these Africans are claimed as the property of Spanish subjects, and Spain demands of this Government that they shall be delivered over to her in compliance with our treaty. The Government therefore have a right to conduct the inquiry, and ascertain the facts. He should not therefore refuse the appeal. The point was a perplexing one, and if he should decide against it, an appeal could be carried up to the Supreme Court on this very point, and in case his decision were reversed, the case would come back for a hearing on the main question, and then would again be appealed, and thus the final disposal of the case be needlessly delayed. He therefore chose, as the case would at all events be appealed, to affirm the decision of Judge Judson *pro forma*, and leave the whole case to be decided by the Supreme Court, leaving the case open to the September term of the Court for the parties to agree on the facts as far as they could, and make out a case to be referred to he Supreme Court which sits at Washington in January, 1841.

Village in Mendi, with Palm trees, &c.

[The Africans are now under the daily instruction of a number of young men connected with Yale College, who are learning them to read the English language, and teaching them the plain and important truths of Christianity. In this laudable object, they receive much assistance from James Covey, the Interpreter. By his aid, and that of John Ferry, a native of the Gissi country, a Mendi and Gissi vocabulary has been made by Prof. Gibbs, and is published in the 38th vol. of the American Journal of Science. The above engraving, copied partly from one in Lander's travels, is recognized by the Africans as giving a correct representation of the appearance of villages in their native country.]

[As there has been considerable interest felt by many persons in the moral and religious welfare of the Africans, it is presumed that the following account furnished by Mr. Benjamin Griswold, of the Theological Seminary, will prove interesting. Mr. G. with a number of other young gentlemen connected with Yale College, have deeply interested themselves in the welfare of these captives. Being in the habit of daily intercourse with them as teachers, they possess great facilities in procuring correct information on the subjects here introduced.]

The reader of the preceding pages has observed, that the history of the captives of the Amistad, as given by Mr. Barber, is confined to the circumstances of their capture, the judicial proceedings relative to them, with short biographical sketches. Friends of the Africans have expressed a desire that an article might be added giving an account of the efforts made for their intellectual and moral improvement, and some notice of the manners and customs prevalent in their native country.

Information relative to the Mendi country and people has been obtained from the captives themselves, mostly through an interpreter; of late, however, they have been able to converse in English. I rely with confidence upon their statements, since a long and intimate acquaintance with them and the interpreter justifies me in saying that I regard them generally as men of integrity.

The limits of the Mendi country have not yet been defined with much certainty. Never has it been visited, so far as we know, by a white man. Park's route lay north; Winterbottom's excursions did not extend far enough into the interior; the Messrs. Landers passed to the south and east. These Africans tell us that they never saw a white man in their country. In attempting to tell one of the teachers how he would be treated if he should return with them—at first they showed signs of fear, then cautiously returned, and presently ventured to touch his clothes and hands, and soon proceeded to a minute investigation.

When winter came, they appeared surprised, not so much at the sight of snow, as at its depth. Inquiry was made if they had ever seen it in their native land. "Yes," was the reply, "*little, little, little,*" accompanying the word with a sign of the same import, and adding, "*water, water, water.*" That is, a very little snow falls, but very soon changes its form to water. This leads us to suppose their country mountainous and probably healthy.

Their government appears to be despotic, and the power goes down from father to son by hereditary descent. Each town appears to have a chief of its own. Attempting once to explain to Cingue the nature of our government, when in answer to his inquiries I informed him that our "*great man*" was not great man for life, but was elected once in four years, he seemed not a little astonished; surprise however soon gave way to boisterous laughter at my expense, in which nearly all his companions joined. The ideas of a democracy, and rotation in office, seemed to him new, strange, and ridiculous. The king receives his support from the contributions of his people. At the appearance of each new moon, they bring their offerings, the rich and the poor, according to their ability.

The apparel of both sexes is the same—the difference consists in the manner of wearing it. The man throws one end of his blanket (as it may perhaps be called) *over* the left shoulder *forward,* the other end is brought around under the right arm and thrown backward over the same shoulder, leaving the right shoulder and arm uncovered. The cloth thus used, being three or four feet wide and two or three yards long, reaches nearly to their feet, and, with the exception just mentioned, envelopes the whole person. The female makes this same garment fast around the waist, and so leaves herself partially unprotected. In youth the dress of both sexes consists merely of a small piece of cloth like a handkerchief fastened around the waist. In childhood till eight or ten years of age, no clothing is worn. The dress of their "*great man*" differs only in this, that his consists of "*plenty, plenty*" of cloth.

Ornaments are much esteemed; the natives adorn themselves with strings of beads, shells, and the like. These tied around their wrists, arms, and ankles, produce in their estimation a very pleasant rattling, when they walk or dance. Many submit to the painful process of tattooing. The breasts and arms of some of the captives display in every part the incision of the knife; both sexes practice this custom in Mendi. We inquired the reason, and received for reply, "*to make them proud,*" i. e. to make them beautiful.

Another custom extensively prevalent on the western coast of Africa is common to them. No observing person can have visited these men without noticing the want of one or two front teeth from the upper or under jaw, or from both. A friend inquired how they were extracted; he was informed that a knife was inserted between the teeth; thus the one they wished to extract is loosened and removed. Sometimes two standing adjacent are cut down so as to leave an opening between them in the form of V, and is done with great skill. The papers designated one of the captives by the name of *cannibal*. The only reason for this appellation is, that his teeth, according to our notions, not being very well arranged, and a degree of emaciation leaving him but a skeleton, made him in fact a frightful object. Some of the front teeth of Konomo have been extracted, others have been sharpened, and made to project from his mouth like tushes. The tooth is pointed thus: a knife is placed upon it on the outside; some hard substance, as a stone or billet of wood, being held against it on the inner side, the knife then receives a blow, and a part of the tooth is thus chipped off. This operation continues till the object is accomplished. This being the manner, he asked the reason. To this question was replied, "*to make the ladies love him.*" It is proper to add, that the captives without distinction appear filled with horror at the idea of feasting upon human flesh.

Their food consists of a great variety of vegetables and fruits, as corn, rice, different kinds of nuts, and flesh furnished by their flocks, herds, and poultry. Of milk they never taste, nor is it drawn from the cow; when informed that it was much esteemed and extensively used among us, they appeared greatly amused, and one observed joking, "*white* man, little cow, eat milk." Reptiles, as snakes and frogs, sometimes form a part of their diet. No animals are used as beasts of burden; the traveller journeys on foot, and the trader transports his articles of traffic upon his back.

Polygamy exists among them. The remark was made by them to one of their friends that in case he returned with them, he should have ten wives, expressing thus the honorable station he would probably hold. Matrimonial matters are managed somewhat after this manner. The gentleman calls upon the lady that pleases him, and presents her some small gift; if she does not feel inclined to encourage his attentions, she refuses its acceptance, and the matter is at an end. But if she receives it, thereby expressing satisfaction with the giver, she carries it after his departure to her parents; they hold a consultation, and if they approve, the suitor is made acquainted with the fact at a subsequent call; then or soon after he makes a present to the parents, and takes the daughter. In case the parents are dissatisfied, it is the lady's duty to return the gift, and this closes the negotiation. In Mendi the woman is made to feel herself inferior to her husband. Seldom does she eat at the same time. To use the language of one of the captives, "man come, eat, eat—go; then woman come, eat, eat—go." Cingue says that his wife eats at the same table and time with himself. The wife attends to the concerns of the house, and sometimes aids her husband in cultivating and often in securing his grain, especially his rice.

The form of a Mendi dwelling is exhibited in the engraving on the 24th page. Circular walls, frequently of mud or clay hardened by the sun, roof thatched with leaves or covered with turf, without windows or chimney. The fire is kindled in the center, and the smoke finds its way out through the single door with which each house is provided.

Their funeral customs resemble much those prevalent among other tribes in Africa. Soon after a person dies, the body is wrapped in a mat, an article somewhat like cloth, made from the fibrous bark of a certain tree that grows in their country; in this, without any coffin, the body is carried out at evening, within two or three days after the decease, and deposited in a place set apart for this purpose with the head always lying to the west. The funeral is attended with weeping and mourning, so loud that the stillness attending exercises of this kind among us seems to them surprising, and to be accounted for only on the ground of insensibility.

The body deposited in the ground, it lies undisturbed, if that of a man till the second day; if a woman, till the third. The reason for this difference is that "*man was before the woman.*" Going to the grave often in great numbers, they remove the earth at the head of the corpse and deposit a vessel filled with food, prepared for this purpose. In it is first placed boiled rice, and palm-oil is then poured upon it; again rice and palm-oil, and so on until the vessel is nearly full. At last the flesh of some animal is added; a spoon is placed in it; a mat thrown over it, and thus is it conveyed and deposited at the head of the deceased friend. "Why this?" was asked. "Because the person is hungry," was replied. "But do you suppose the body will again come to life, and so want the food?" "No, but the spirit is hungry." "How do you know?" "It comes and says so if it is not thus provided for." Often the chief issues his commands, and vast multitudes assemble from the distance of miles even to attend this ceremony. This custom, however, does not prevail in *every* village.

This account having been given by some of the captives, others were called and asked if it was true. One replied that such ceremonies were not common where he lived. The observation was then made, *you* say "*yes*," and *you* say "*no*," here is a contradiction; do you both tell the truth? Fuli after a moment's delay replied, "*Merica all, all, all*," extending his right hand and turning round through half a circle, "so *Mendi, all, all, all*," accompanying the words with the same gesture and motion of the body. The idea he wished to convey was this: "America is a great country, so is Mendi; and because a custom is prevalent in *one* part of it, it is not necessary to conclude that it is universal." The explanation was satisfactory. Nothing has occurred of special interest at the funerals which have taken place since their arrival in New Haven. It has been said that Shuma addressed his companions as they were standing around the dead body of Tua. The interpreter informs us that it was merely the remark that "Tua was dead—God had taken him," &c. They naturally feel themselves restrained, being among and in the hands of those whose manners and institutions are so entirely unlike their own.

At the funeral of Kaperi, a number of the clergymen from the city were present. Prayer was offered in the room, and remarks made, the substance of which was, "Ka-pe-ri is dead. His body is still, and will be laid in the ground. The soul of Ka-pe-ri is alive. It will never die. Our souls will never die. They will live after our bodies are dead and cold. The Bible tells us how our souls may go to the good place. You must learn to read the Bible. Pray to God, become good, and then when your bodies die, God will take your souls to the good place, and make you happy forever." To this they listened with serious attention. Accompanied by a large number of citizens, they then walked in procession to the grave, when a hymn was read and sung, and a prayer offered by Mr. Bacon. In all these exercises the captives appeared interested and solemn.

The Mendi language, so far as we have been able to learn, has never been reduced to writing, nor have the natives characters by which they retain and transmit a history of passing events. Since the captives have been in New Haven, efforts have been made to improve their minds and hearts, by some gentlemen connected with the theological seminary. From two to five hours each day have been spent in imparting instruction. At first their progress was slow and attended with some difficulties. They had been accustomed neither to the requisite effort of mind nor fixedness of attention.

In the first attempts to teach them the English language, the picture of some animal, as a dog or horse, was presented to them, its name was mentioned, and they required to repeat it after their teachers; then was added another and another, their names told in the same way, and repeated till they could readily distinguish one from the other. Then we showed the names printed on separate cards in large characters, directing their attention to the picture at the same time. Very soon we found them able to select and join each picture to its name. This process was continued for some time before we attempted to teach them the letters. When they began to read, it became necessary to explain the meaning of every word. They manifested so deep an interest, that though progress was slow, yet it was perceptible, and labor was pleasant. Sometimes they complained because we did not come earlier, and refused consent to our departure when, at noon or night, it became necessary for us to leave. Their interest still continues, and never perhaps was it greater than at the present time. Not unfrequently in their desire to retain their teacher through the day, they attempt even to hold him, grasping his hands and clinging to his person, and individuals offer to give him their own dinner on condition of his remaining. Sometimes they may be found gathered in two or three groups, all reading and aiding each other. While the teacher is hearing one class, the interpreter is engaged in the same duty with another, and one of the most advanced among the captives gives instruction to another, and thus employed will they sit quietly for hours in the most patient, persevering effort to learn "*Merica*." Especially do they seem anxious to learn that they may read the Bible—this is the great desire of their hearts.

Their improvement is as great as could be expected. Some of them can read in the New Testament. Their situation has been peculiarly unfavorable to progress in speaking the English language. They have been confined exclusively by themselves, and intercourse with each has been in their native tongue. Yet they can converse with one upon any subject with which both have some acquaintance.

One of the most serious obstacles with which we have had to contend is the anxiety occasioned by the uncertainty that hangs over them in respect to the future. They appear much distressed at the idea of going to Havana.

Especial attention has been given to their moral improvement since they have been in New Haven. We have sought to make them acquainted with the vital truths of Christianity, and though we cannot say that they are Christians, yet we can say that they have, some of them at least, manifested a deep interest in the subject of religion.

The system of religion prevalent in their native country appears to be the Fetisch. They reverence the cotton tree. The inquiry was made if they paid their devotions to it because they supposed the *tree* could do them good or evil. The reply was in the negative; but they added that there was a "spirit in it," and they worshipped him that "*they might be well.*" They regard him however as a good deity. His favor is secured by suspending some offering, a fowl perhaps, to the limb, or placing the same at its roots.

The mountain too receives their homage. Worship in this instance consists in praying at its foot, and in depositing a dish of boiled rice or flesh—something that serves the purposes of food. The spirit dwells on the mountain. Water too, or the genius of the stream, has a place among their deities. Respecting the ceremonies of their religion we do not feel confident, for neither Cingue nor any of his companions can give us any other than hear-say information. In such services they never took part—they were too *young;* only the *aged* perform the duties of religion.

Their teachers have religious exercises with them daily. In the morning on their arrival they assemble for prayers—if the room is sufficiently capacious they kneel. The teacher offers his petitions in English, the interpreter translates sentence by sentence, and the captives respond in Mendi. A prayer has been composed and translated into their language, which, in case of the interpreter's absence, is sometimes read by the teacher and repeated by them. Of this prayer I give a few of the first sentences. *O ga-wa-wa,* O great God; *bi-a-bi yan-din-go,* thou art good; *bi-a-bi ha-ni gbe-le ba-te-ni,* thou hast made all things; *bi-a-bi fu-li ba-te-ni,* &c., thou hast made the sun, &c. After prayers, sometimes an half hour is spent in attempting to impress religious truth upon the heart. At this exercise the captives are attentive and solemn, the season is frequently of great interest. On the Sabbath we have one, usually two exercises with them. They ever appear interested in listening to the truths of the word of God. One Sabbath, on account of the absence of the interpreter, the teacher was obliged to dispense with the usual exercises; he left, and Cingue assembled his companions and conducted the service himself. Many of them in their troubles and fears are driven to the throne of grace. A lady in the family of the jailer informs me that the little girls even are mindful of their hours for devotion, and that too when the duty is not pressed upon them by the example of others.

When listening to an explanation of the nature of an oath, on being informed that God would visit the man who violated it with his displeasure, they very naturally inquired, "What will be done to the people of the United States if they send us back to Havana?"

For those who have sought to do them good, and have proved themselves friends, they feel an affection that displays itself in a thousand ways.

The scene when information was given to them relative to the decision of the District Court, was publicly noticed at the time. They were assembled and seated in a commodious room—they knew that their case was pending—

some of them had been called to testify in court—they were of course deeply anxious for the event. All being present and quiet, they were informed that the judge had decreed their return, not to Havana, but to their native land. They leaped from their seats, rushed across the room, threw themselves prostrate at the feet of those who brought them the glad tidings, while "*thank you, thank you*," was the expression of every tongue.

The succeeding day Mr. Baldwin, one of their counsel, entered the jail. Cingue was seated behind a table, and members of his class on either side of him. As Mr. B. approached, Cingue was told that he pleaded his cause; said it would be wrong to send him to Havana. He dropped his book, rose from his seat, seemed for a moment deliberating whether he should leap the table. Seeing this to be attended with difficulty, he reached forward, and seizing the extended hand of Mr. B. with a firm grasp, and looking him in the face, his own countenance beaming with the most grateful emotion, exclaimed, "We thank you, we bless you, this is all we can do for you."

During the winter, one of the teachers was called from the city. After an absence of nearly two weeks, on his return he visited the captives, and the reception he received can never be forgotten by him so long as memory records one event of the past. The first who met him threw his arms around his body, and clasped him to his bosom. Freed from his grasp, he was soon met by others. Some were reading, some on their couches—all rose as soon as his name was announced, left books and beds, and rushing into the room gathered around, a dense mass, all striving to reach him; some threw their arms around his body, some around his neck, some seized his arms, some pressed his hands, and all cried out, "*good, good*, Mr. —— come, Mr. —— come, good, good." Their friend laughed and shouted with them, overcome by this effort to express their joy. Such an outburst of grateful affection we never witnessed before. After quiet was restored, one observed, "when we see you, all of us act like children."

One of their friends received a message from Cingue requesting him to call at the jail, for some of their number had been guilty of faults which ought to be corrected. He went; Cingue said that two of the captives took liberties which he regarded as stealing; that the rest of them were innocent and disapproved of their conduct, and that they wished the two put into a room by themselves. One of the culprits was summoned and questioned; he confessed his crime, and gave assurances of better conduct, in accordance with which, so far as I know, he has acted ever since. "O!" exclaimed Fuli, who was standing by, "I cannot tell how much I hate a thief." "But why," said the friend, "would *you* refuse to steal?" "Because it is wrong." "But suppose you were hungry?" "Then I would beg." "Suppose no one would give you?" "*Then I would die*," was his decided answer. We know not that we have reason to question his sincerity.

After the decision of the District Court, previous to the appeal, their immediate return to Africa was confidently expected by themselves and their friends. They expressed a very warm desire that some of their teachers should go with, to instruct them and their people. Said Burna, addressing one of their friends, and speaking the feelings of many, "If we should be compelled to return without you, we shall all cry; but if you will go with us then shall we all laugh." It was asked how they would treat him. They replied that they would "give him a house and abundance of food, take the best care of him, and not let him be sick." But, said the teacher, though we go by water to Sierra Leone, from thence we shall be under the necessity of making our journey on foot, since no horses go into your country. Now in case I become wearied, what shall I do? how will you dispose of me?

For a moment they seemed perplexed. Cingue soon rose from his seat—called for a blanket—tied the corners of each end together—then putting the broom handle through under the knots—placed one end upon his own shoulder, rested the other upon that of one of his companions, then thrusting his hand into the blanket, and crying out, " *Mr.* —— *in there, Mr.* —— *in there,*" commenced his march. This I doubt not is a faithful expression of the feeling of their hearts. A friend might trust his safety in their hands with the most perfect confidence, not doubting that they would sacrifice their own lives before they would abandon one whom they respected and loved. "Should I go with you," said the teacher, "what good could I do you?" "Teach us, our brothers, sisters, and children," was replied. "But," said the teacher to test their affection, "if I go I must teach you truth. The Bible says that a man must have but *one* wife; will you put away *all* but *one?*" All said, yes. "Well," said the teacher, "suppose I accompany you, since you do not reside in the same town what will you do? I cannot go all over your country—with whom shall I live?" This difficulty was very speedily removed, and one replied, "You may go with whom you please. If you should return with Cingue, we would visit our parents a few days, and then remove with our wives and children, brothers and sisters, to your place of residence, that we might avail ourselves of your instruction."

These men deserve sympathy—they ought to have protection. Let me ask in their behalf, means to carry on their defense; let me ask the prayers of those who care for them and the perishing millions of Africa, that God will so order events as to deliver them from the bloody grasp of the executioner, and that they may return missionaries to their native land to proclaim there the truth of the everlasting Gospel.

[The following facts relative to the case of the Africans are derived from Document No. 185, published in accordance with a resolution of Congress, passed March 23d, 1840, calling on the President for information, &c.]

On the 6th of Sept. 1839, Mr. Calderon, the Spanish Minister at New York, addressed a letter to the Secretary of State, (Mr. Forsyth,) asking that the Amistad, her cargo, including the slaves, should be immediately delivered up without salvage, in accordance with the treaty of 1795. He expresses his fears that if the slaves are not delivered up to the Spanish authorities to be punished for their crimes, it " would endanger the internal tranquillity and the safety of the Island of Cuba," &c—that it would interrupt the good feeling now existing between the people of that island and those of the United States. Mr. Holabird, the U. S. District Attorney, in a letter to Mr. Forsyth, dated Sept. 5, says, " the next term of our Circuit Court sits on the 17th instant, at which time I suppose it will be my duty to bring them to trial, unless they are in some other way disposed of." In a letter dated Sept. 9, he thus writes, " I would respectfully inquire, sir, whether there are no treaty stipulations with the government of Spain that would authorize our government to deliver them up to the Spanish authorities; and if so, whether it could be done before our Court sits?" The Chevalier de Argaiz (the successor of Mr. Calderon) addressed a letter to Mr. Forsyth, Nov. 26, 1839, in which he complained that the treaty of 1795 had not been executed; that great injury had been done to the owners, " not the least being the imprisonment which Don Jose Ruiz is now undergoing;" that " no indemnification can fully recompense for the evils, physical and moral, which the persecutions and vexations occasioned by fanaticism may cause to an honorable man." Another letter was addressed by him to the Secretary, Nov. 29, stating that the injuries of which the negroes complain, should be redressed in Cuba, and by " no means" by the Courts of the United States.

Mr. Forsyth, in a letter of Jan. 6, 1840, to the Chevalier de Argaiz, states that the President " will cause the necessary orders to be given for a vessel of the United States to be held in readiness to receive the negroes and convey them to Cuba, with instructions to the commander to deliver them up to the Captain General of the island. The President has the more readily been inclined to accede to your request in this particular, on account of one of the leading motives which prompted you to make it; that the negroes, having asserted before the Court of Connecticut that they are not slaves, may have an opportunity of proving the truth of their allegation before the proper tribunals of the island of Cuba, by whose laws alone, taking in connection with circumstances occurring before the arrival of the negroes in the United States, the question of their condition can be legally decided."

On the 6th of January, 1840, Mr. Forsyth, in a letter to the District Attorney says, " the President has, agreeable to your suggestion, taken in connection with the request of the Spanish Minister, ordered a vessel to be in readiness to receive the negroes from the custody of the Marshal as soon as their delivery shall be ordered by the Court." The following is the warrant of the President for this purpose.

" The Marshal of the United States for the district of Connecticut, will deliver over to Lieut. John S. Paine, of the U.S. Navy, and aid in conveying on board the schooner Grampus, under his command, all the negroes, late of the Spanish schooner Amistad, in his custody, under process now pending before the Circuit Court of the United States for the District of Connecticut. For so doing, this order will be his warrant. Given under my hand, at the city of Washington, this 7th day of January, A. D. 1840.

M. VAN BUREN.

By the President :   John Forsyth, *Secretary of State.*"

It appears by the following extract of a letter from Mr. Holabird to Mr. Forsyth, dated Jan. 11, that there was a mistake in this warrant.

" *Sir*—Lieut. Paine has shown me the Executive warrant to the Marshal of this District for the delivery of the negroes of the Amistad, in which it is stated that they are now holden in custody under a process from the " *Circuit Court ;*" and also, in his instructions, the same term is used. They are not holden under any order of the Circuit Court, but under an order from the *District Court*, and should have been so stated in the warrant and instructions. Should the pretended friends of the negroes obtain a writ of habeas corpus, the Marshal could not justify under that warrant."

The following is the reply of the Secretary to Mr. Holabird.

" [confidential.]   *Department of State,* Jan. 12, 1840.

Sir—Your letter of the 11th instant has just been received. The order for the delivery of the negroes of the Amistad is herewith returned, corrected agreeably to your suggestion. With reference to the inquiry from the Marshal, to which you allude, I have to state, by direction of the President, that if the decision of the Court is such as is anticipated, the order of the President is to be carried into execution, unless an appeal shall actually have been interposed. You are not to take it for granted that it will be interposed. And if, on the contrary, the decision of the Court is different, you are to take out an appeal, and allow things to remain as they are until the appeal shall have been decided. I am, sir, your obedient servant,   John Forsyth."

Memorandum from the Department of State to the Secretary of the Navy.

"Department of State, Jan. 2, 1840.

" The vessel destined to convey the negroes of the Amistad to Cuba, to be ordered to anchor off the port of New Haven, Connecticut, as early as the 10th of January next, and be in readiness to receive said negroes from the Marshal of the United States, and proceed with them to Havana, under instructions to be hereafter transmitted.

" Lieutenants Gedney and Meade to be ordered to hold themselves in readiness to proceed in the same vessel, for the purpose of affording their testimony in any proceedings that may be ordered by the authorities of Cuba in the matter.

" These orders should be given with special instructions that they are not to be communicated to any one."

There is in the document from which the foregoing is taken, a letter from Messrs. Staples and Sedgwick, dated Sept. 13, addressed to the President, stating the facts of the case, and praying that the Africans may not be given up to the Spaniards till their claim is substantiated in a court of justice. In answer, or in consequence of this, there is a letter addressed to Mr. Forsyth, giving the opinion of the Attorney General, who says, that after a due consideration of the case, he has come to the conclusion that the Amistad captives ought to be given up to the Spaniards. This letter has no signature, nor no date but 1839. In the document, the Spanish passport with a translation is given : the word " *Ladinos*" is incorrectly translated " *sound negroes.*" (See p. 18.)

Part Five

The Black in American Literature

A Century of Negro Portraiture
in American Literature

STERLING A. BROWN

I

OVER A CENTURY AGO, in November, 1863, Harriet Beecher Stowe wrote that she was going to Washington to satisfy herself that "the Emancipation Proclamation was a reality and a substance not to fizzle out. . . ." She meant to talk to "Father Abraham himself." When she was ushered into his study, her frailty startled President Lincoln. As his big knotted hand took her small one, he quizzed: "So this is the little lady who made this big war." Pressed by her eagerness, Lincoln assured Harriet Beecher Stowe that he was determined to issue the Emancipation Proclamation on New Year's Day.

In spite of Lincoln's gallant exaggeration, his estimate of the impact of *Uncle Tom's Cabin* showed his old canniness. His secretary of state, not so given to overstatement, said that "without *Uncle Tom's Cabin* there would have been no Abraham Lincoln," and here William Seward also spoke cannily. For the novel had been an instantaneous success here and abroad. Many of Father Abraham's hundred thousand strong had read it a decade earlier in their forming years; many carried it in their knapsacks, and it had dramatized for both North and South the American moral dilemmas and something of the humanity involved in the controversy over slavery.

Herman Melville had expressed antislavery opinions even earlier in *Mardi.* The approach, however, was oblique, and the antislavery sections were only a small part of a murky allegory, which was to be largely unread in contrast to Mrs. Stowe's popular success. Still, *Mardi* is pertinent here for Melville's clear indictment of slavery, his dread and prophecy of the inevitable clash of the irreconcilable viewpoints about slavery and the Negro. Describing the Capitol of Vivenza (his name for the United States) Melville singled out the creed "All Men are born Free and Equal," noting that an addition, in minute hieroglyphics, read: "all except the tribe of Hamo." On the flag being hoisted over the Capitol, red stripes corresponded to marks on the back of the slave who was doing the hoisting. Strangers visiting the South of Vivenza discovered that the slaves were men. For this a haughty spokesman denounced them as "firebrands come to light the flame of revolt." This grim prophet, a fictionalized Calhoun properly named Nullo, swore that the first blow struck for the slaves would "dissolve the Union of Vivenza's vales." Like his allegorical visitors, Melville was troubled over what seemed an irrepressible conflict between North and South and, dreading war, concluded that only Time "must befriend these thralls." In spite of his doubts about the best course, he was nevertheless certain that slavery was "a blot, foul as the crater pool of hell."

These two significant novelists of a century ago indicate how influential the treatment of Negro life and character has been in American history and literature. From the outset of our national life "Negro character," if such a loose term may be used at the beginning of this essay, has intrigued American authors. Their portraits have evinced varying degrees of sympathy and understanding, skill and power. Their motives have been manifold. Their success has not been marked.

Before the Civil War, creative literature dealing with Negro life was abundant, though not distinguished. Minor efforts at real characterizations—some perceptive, some vague, some tentative guesses about half-strangers—occur in Cooper, Poe, William Gilmore Simms, and the Southern humorists. By and large, however, the Negro in the literature of this period was a mere pawn in the growing debate over slavery. With the overwhelming success of *Uncle Tom's Cabin* in 1852, the battle of the books was joined, and torrents of proslavery replies rushed from the presses. These were ungainly books, crude sentimentalizings and melodramatizings of the proslavery argument of Dew and Harper, of Calhoun and Fitzhugh. Slaves chanted paeans to the Arcadian existence of the old South; others walked the woods as embodiments of the various Bible Defenses of Slavery—one of them, for instance, pulling a much thumbed copy of the Sacred Book out of his overalls to confound a Yankee abolitionist who was haunting this Eden. The wisest slaves rejected freedom; the maladjusted and the half-wits ran away to the North where they either died in snow drifts (they needed master to tell them to come in out of the snow) or else they saw the light and stole away, back to the Southland and slavery (a kind of Underground Railroad in reverse). One novel, *Life at the South, or Uncle Tom's Cabin As It Is*[1] closes with another Tom, disillusioned with the North, heading back South. "And if the reader shall chance to travel the high road, as it winds up the valley of the Shenandoah, above Winchester, he will find no slave more contented than Uncle Tom." A tall, tall order. Carry me back to old Virginny.

They would have to carry him back to get him there, was what a Negro like Frederick Douglass thought; and this opinion was shared by such other stout-hearted fugitives as Martin Delany, David Ruggles, Sojourner Truth, Harriet Tubman, and William Wells Brown. These and many other Negroes fought in the anti-slavery crusade; several used stirring autobiographies, pamphlets, journalism and oratory in the battle. Creative literature, however, was the exception with them; an embattled people used literature as a weapon, as propaganda; not as exploration, but as exposé of injustice. There were a few short stories and novels, and hortatory poetry. The truth of Negro life and character, however, is in such an autobiography as Douglass's *My Bondage and My Freedom* more than in the fiction and poetry of the time.

Also engaged in this crusade were white abolitionist poets—

[1] To illustrate some of the absurdities cited and the repetition that really amounted to plagiarism, compare this novel with one that preceded it by twenty years. In *The Yemassee* (1832), by William Gilmore Simms, a heroic slave, the properly named Hector, is offered his freedom: "I d--n to h---, maussa if I gwine to be free!" roared the adhesive black, in a tone of unrestrainable determination . . . "This onpossible, maussa, and dere's no use for to talk about it. Enty I know wha' kind of ting freedom is wid black man? Ha! you make Hector free, he turn wuss than poor buckra, he tief out of de shop—he git drunk and lie in de ditch—den if sick come, he roll, he toss in de wet grass of de stable. You come in de morning, Hector dead. . . ." Twenty years later, in 1852, in *Life at the South, or Uncle Tom's Cabin As It Is,* the author, W. L. G. Smith, has a character also named Hector, who is also offered his freedom. And he also says: "I damn to hell, massa, if I gwine to be free, roared the adhesive black in a tone of unrestrainable determination . . ." etc. *ad literatim et ad nauseum.*

Bryant, Longfellow, Whittier—and novelists like Harriet Beecher
Stowe. Their hearts were better than their circumstantial material;
they, as Lowell said of Mrs. Stowe, "instinctively went right to the
organic elements of human nature, whether under a white skin or
black"; they knew the right thing—that men should be free. But
they lacked realistic knowledge of Negro life and experience, and
for this lack sentimental idealism could not compensate. Before
the Civil War, therefore, the characterization of the Negro was far
from the complexity that we now know was there; it was over-
simplified—the contented slave and his corollary, the wretched
freedman; the comic minstrel on the one hand, and the persecuted
victim, the noble savage, the submissive Christian, the tragic
octoroon on the other.[2]

II

IF, BEFORE APPOMATTOX, *Uncle Tom's Cabin* was undoubtedly
the champion in the battle of the books, for a long time afterwards
the proslavery defense was victorious. The plantation tradition,
glorifying slavery as a benevolent guardianship, crystallized. Negro
and white characters were neatly packaged. Inevitable were old
marse, the essence of chivalry; young missy, one hundred per cent
southern womanhood, the essence of charm; and young marse, chip
off the old block, the essence of dash and courage; all essences.

[2] "I swear their nature is beyond my comprehension. A strange people!
—merry 'mid their misery—laughing through their tears, like the sun
shining through the rain. Yet what simple philosophers they! They
tread life's path as if 'twere strewn with roses devoid of thorns, and make
the most of life with natures of sunshine and song." "Natures of sunshine
and song." Most readers of this passage would take it to refer to the
American Negro. Instead it is about the Irish, spoken by an English officer
in a play dealing with one of the most tragic periods in the history of the
persecution of the Irish. (From Sterling A. Brown, *The Negro in American Fiction* [Washington, D.C., 1931], p. 1.)

Stereotyping is a thrice-told tale. The treatment of the Jewish character
in English, European, and American literature is certainly another instance. Years ago, a perceptive commentator on our popular art, Isaac
Goldberg, pointed to the startling fact that the three most popular butts
of comedy on our vaudeville stage were the Irishman, the Negro, and the
Jew, the three most persecuted minorities at that moment of American
History.

Negro characters were grooved also: the mammy, proud of her quality whitefolks, the wise upbringer of their children (there is little mention of her own); her male counterpart, also worshipful of his whitefolks, devoted to their glory and service; and the clown, the razor-toting, watermelon-eating singer and dancer, with a penchant for big words he could neither understand nor pronounce, whom the thriving black-face minstrel shows made one of America's favorite theatrical personages.

Among the authors who established the plantation tradition, Thomas Nelson Page and Joel Chandler Harris were most persuasive. These and their fellows were children when the Civil War broke out; they had known Negro children as playmates; they remembered their grandfathers and fathers and uncles with ancestral pride; they saw the old South through the haze of retrospect; they invested the Lost Cause with the glamor of the defeated and the departed. They combined the chuckling of humorous, philosophical slaves with the pathos of ill-starred aristocrats. Frequenters of the Negro quarters, rapt listeners to old Negro yarn spinners in their absorptive years, blessed with sharp eyes and ears and retentive memories, these authors were able to convey the plausible, surface realism of local color. The dialect, often meticulously rendered, rang true; if the words were right, the thoughts behind them had to be right. A Negro folkline, "You can read my letters, but you sho' cain't read my mind," should have caused them and their readers some doubt—but for all of their claim that they knew the Negro, *that* was *one* line, and *one* aspect of his character that they did not know.

So Page has his inveterate old uncles reminiscing on the good old days before the war, to a white stranger who asks just the right question and then stands back while the torrent leaps: a stranger who never for a moment suspects guile or irony or forgetfulness or inaccuracy. "Dem was good ole times, Marster, de bes' Sam ever see," is one refrain that is repeated. These old uncles are more ventriloquist's dummies than people, but to the readers of the eighties, they were appealing and persuasive. A vouched-for legend tells us that Thomas Wentworth Higginson, the abolitionist friend of John Brown, the man who was wounded in a fight in Boston to keep a fugitive slave from being returned to the South, the colonel of a Negro regiment in the Civil War, this man, the legend goes, who had fought so strenuously for the Negro, was discovered thirty years after the war in his study, in tears from reading *In Ole Virginia* by Thomas Page.[3]

Joel Chandler Harris was readier to show some harshness in the ante-bellum South, but his picture remains one of mutual affection and kindness. A surly, intractable Blue Dave is rehabilitated when he finds another master as good as his first one, who had died; Free Joe, who had no one to look after him, a misfit among the happier slaves, dies disconsolate, and ineffectual, and free. Harris contributed minor masterpieces in his Br'er Rabbit Tales; these are his garnerings of rich yield, and without his perceptiveness some of the world's best folk literature might have perished. But despite his disclaimer, Harris *did* doctor the tales he picked up in the slave quarters; they are not genuinely folk—of the folk, by the folk, to the folk, for the folk—but they are told by an old uncle to entertain a little white boy. The framework in which they are told is the plantation tradition. When Harris used Uncle Remus as a kind of columnist for the *Atlanta Constitution,* as he often did, Uncle Remus is closer kin to Henry Grady and the New South than to Remus's African forebears. Still in his inimitable speech he deplores education of Negroes as the "ruination of this country . . . a barrel stave [he says] can fling mo' sense into [his] people in one minute than all de schoolhouses betwixt dis and de State er Midgigan." There are two Uncle Remuses. The inferior one was a dialect-talking version of a Georgia politician, and for all of his pithiness he is more cracker-box philosopher than sage of the quarters.

But Page and Harris, and a horde of followers were popular in the leading Northern magazines and converted much of the North, which was ready to forget the late grueling contest. They presented a glowing picture of the kindlier aspects of slavery. Their cardinal principles were mutual affection between the races and the peculiar endowment of each race to occupy its role: one race the born master, one race the born slave. The road to reunion was opening; tension was relaxing; the troubled past could be forgotten, the wrongs could be covered over, perhaps they had not been so bad, perhaps they could go away. So the Plantation Tradition became fixed.

During the Reconstruction, other stereotypes were added to those

[3] Paul H. Buck, *The Road to Reunion* (*1865–1900*) (Boston, 1937), p. 235.

of the contented slave, the comic minstrel, and the wretched freed-man.[4] These were the brute Negro and the tragic mulatto. Page contrasted the old issue Negro, loyal and contented (in Page's version) with the new issue, who were disloyal, ungrateful, and discontented, ruined by emancipation. These new Negroes were shown as insulting swaggerers. They were often in federal uni-forms, or they engaged in politics. The docile mastiffs had become mad dogs; the carriers of the rabies were carpet-baggers, scalawags, Union troops, and Yankee schoolmarms. A sort of Ku Klux Klan fiction emerged; insolent Negroes, often rapists, were shown in atrocity stories, and the knightly Klan rode, white sheeted, to restore Southern civilization and to protect Southern womanhood.[5] As a colleague, E. Franklin Frazier, used to quip: "The closer a Negro got to the ballot box, the more he looked like a rapist."

The tragic mulatto stereotype stemmed from the antislavery crusade, whose authors used it partly to show miscegenation as an evil of slavery, partly as an attempt to win readers' sympathies by presenting central characters who were physically very like the readers. Antislavery authors, Harriet Beecher Stowe included, held to a crude kind of racism. Their near-white characters are the in-transigent, the resentful, the mentally alert—for biological, not social reasons. In the proslavery argument, the mixed blood char-acters are victims of a divided inheritance[6] and proof of the

[4] The effect, of course, was not confined to the last century. In the first doctoral dissertation written on this subject, the critic pontificates that in one twenty-six line sketch by Joel Chandler Harris about Br'er Fox and Br'er Mud Turtle (I quote): "the whole range of the Negro character is revealed thoroughly." John Herbert Nelson, *The Negro Character in American Literature* (Lawrence, Kansas: The Department of Journalism Press, 1926), p. 118.

[5] Two of the most widely known Hollywood motion pictures have made great use of the formulae of the plantation tradition and especially of the brute Negro. These are D. W. Griffith's *The Birth of a Nation* (based upon the melodramatic novels of Thomas Dixon, *The Clansman* and *The Leopard Spots*), and Margaret Mitchell's *Gone With The Wind,* in which the glamor of Scarlett O'Hara and Rhett Butler should not blind us to the trite stereotyping of character and social background.

[6] What might be called the fractional theory of personality gets its *reductio ad absurdum* in Roark Bradford's *This Side of Jordan* (1929). "The blade of a razor flashed . . . Her Negro Blood sent it unerringly be-tween two ribs. Her Indian blood sent it back for an unnecessary second and third slash." It might be hazarded that her Eskimo blood kept her from being chilled with horror.

disastrous results of amalgamation. Most of the villains in recon-struction fiction are mixed bloods, "inheriting the vices of both races and the virtues of neither." The mulatto, or quadroon, or octoroon heroine has been a favorite for a long time; in books by white authors the whole desire of her life is to find a white lover; then balked by the dictates of her society, she sinks to a tragic end. In our century, Negro authors have turned the story around; now after restless searching, she finds peace only after returning to her own people. In both cases, however, the mulatto man or woman is presented as a lost, unhappy, woebegone abstraction.

The fiction of George Washington Cable pays great attention to the free people of color of old Louisiana, whose rigid caste restric-tions brought tragedy to quadroon and octoroon heroines. But Cable did not limit his sympathy for the victims of slavery to this unfortunate caste; his picture of old Louisiana was colorful but crowded with authoritative antiquarian detail. Whether educated free man of color, or illiterate field hand, or captured African Prince Bras-Coupé, who killed rather than serve as slave, Cable gave shrewd, knowing interpretations of Negro character. The first genuine Southern liberal, Cable knew too much about slavery to idealize the old regime, and he was sensitively aware of the dark shadows of the past on the South of his day. The best local colorist of Louisiana, he found his social sympathies too broad for his native section, and he spent his last years in self-imposed exile.

One of Cable's services to American literature lies in his re-enforcing of Mark Twain's growing liberality concerning Negroes. *Huckleberry Finn* is more telling an indictment of slavery than patently antislavery novels are. The callousness of a small God-

---

Fannie Hurst's *Imitation of Life* contains another gem. Of the fair-skinned heroine, Peola, we get this analysis from her mother: "It may be mixed up wid plenty of white blood . . . but thin out chicken gravy wid water an' it remains [sic!] chicken gravy, only not so good. . . ." She prays for her octoroon daughter: "Lord git de white horses drove out of her blood. Kill de curse—shame de curse her light-colored pap lef' for his baby. . . . Chase de wild white horses tramplin' on my chile's happiness. . . . It's de white horses dat's wild, a-swimmin in de blood of mah chile." It is submitted that with all those horses running wild in Peola's aorta, she could hardly be a stable character. From this novel, of which Holly-wood has made two increasingly saccharine versions, oral tradition among Negroes has taken the name of Peola for a fair skinned girl; not in respect, however, but in burlesque.

fearing town toward Negroes; the conditioning of a small boy, so that the word "abolitionist" is the worst insult he can imagine; the topsy-turvyness of Huck's self-condemnation when he decides that he will help Jim escape only because he hasn't been brought up right and is in the devil's grip; the characterization of Jim, superstitious but shrewd, kindly, self-sacrificial, but determined to be free, not contented in slavery—all of these are vividly rendered. A single passage of dialogue and the pretensions of the plantation tradition are shredded away. Consider this scene: Jim is on the raft; Huck sets off in the canoe, ostensibly to learn the name of the town they are passing but really to betray Jim to the slavehunters.

> "Putty soon I'll be a-shout'n for joy, an I'll say its all on account o' Huck I's a free man; en I couldn't ever been free if it hadn't ben for Huck; Huck done it . . . Dah you goes, de on'y white gen'lman dat ever kep' his promise to ole Jim."

This tobacco-chewing, pipe-smoking, barefooted, one-gallused, Missouri kid, this truant from learning, the delinquent son of the town drunk—now on his way to betray his buddy—becomes "the only white gentleman that ever kept his promise to old Jim." Twain's irony does not leave the old tradition of noblesse oblige much to stand on.

Negro writers at the turn of the century also deepened the portraiture. According to William Dean Howells, Paul Laurence Dunbar was the "first American Negro to feel the Negro life aesthetically and express it lyrically." Influenced almost inevitably by the powerful plantation tradition, most of his poems about slavery echo Irwin Russell, Page, and Joel Chandler Harris, but his poems about the Negro life of his own day are affectionate, sympathetic, and winning. Characters that had been treated as clownish were now revealed as more richly human. Dunbar was of the school of James Whitcomb Riley—of the happy hearthside and pastoral contentment. He was a gentle person, and even if publishing conditions had permitted it, he probably would not have chosen the prevalent harshness to write about. In a few short stories and poems in standard English he showed bitterness, but this is typically oblique as in "We Wear the Mask," a poem containing a true metaphor but more plaintive than revealing.

Dunbar's contemporary, Charles Waddell Chesnutt, was concerned with the harsher—and more typical aspects of life in the

South, and with the problems of the color line. His volume of folk tales (*The Conjure Woman,* 1899) seems to resemble the tales of Page and Harris, but on close reading Chesnutt is quite different. His tales are told by a shrewd, self-serving Uncle, whose characterizations of both Negroes and whites is salty—and no nonsense about the good old days. Chesnutt based one of his strongest novels, *The Marrow of Tradition* (1901), on the riot in Wilmington, North Carolina. This novel and *The Colonel's Dream* (1905) show a grasp of social reality, and a powerful ability to dramatize his material.

The novels of Albion Tourgee, who served as an officer in the Union Army and remained in North Carolina as a "carpetbagger," are informed and powerful, and with the fiction of Chesnutt, are necessary correctives to the Ku Klux Klan fiction of the post-war South. *A Fool's Errand* (1879) and *Bricks Without Straw* (1880) are melodramatic—fighting fire with fire—but they come closer to the complex realities of the time and anticipate the fiction of the twentieth century more than those of any other writer save Chesnutt.

III

AT THE TURN of the century W. E. B. Dubois started his distinguished career with *The Souls of Black Folk,* which is still one of the best interpretations of Negro life and aspirations. On the creative side, Dubois continued to write poems, short stories, novels, autobiographies, and essays, but none of these excel this pioneering work which was marked by impassioned polemics against compromise, incisive irony at hypocrisy, sensitive brooding over the dilemmas of democracy, and affirmation of race pride and solidarity.

A key essay by Dubois, called "The Sorrow Songs," was one of the earliest and best interpretations of the spirituals. Dubois's awareness of the dignity and beauty of Negro folk music was broadened and deepened by James Weldon Johnson. In addition to editing two comprehensive volumes of spirituals with his brother, J. Rosamond Johnson, he commented upon Negro musical shows, ragtime, and the beginnings of jazz from the vantage point of a participant in their history. His novel, *Autobiography of an Ex-Colored Man* (1912), was the first to deal with Negro life on several levels, from the folk to the sophisticated. It is rather more a chart of

Negro life than a novel, but it contains informed analysis and valid interpretation. Johnson's Preface to the *Book of American Negro Poetry* (1922) boldly advanced the claims of the Negro's creativeness. Johnson's own earlier poems, collected in *Fifty Years and Other Poems* (1917), looked backward in genre pieces of the school of Dunbar, and looked at the present and towards the future in hortatory and lyrical verse. In the commemorative title poem, Johnson insisted on the Negro's belonging to America, on his services, and on his potential. As with Dubois, creative literature for Johnson was the other arm to propagandistic work for the NAACP.

Johnson's hope for more adequate and accurate presentation of Negro life was not long in coming. The time—the post-war decade, with its revolt against squeamishness, repression, and Babbittry—was favorable. The lost generation seemed to find itself in Harlem or the Caribbean or Africa; youth rekindled the flame in Harlem where a magazine blazed forth for one issue with the name "Fire!" Carl Van Doren felt that the decided need of American literature for "color, music, gusto, the free expression of gay or desperate moods" could best be filled by the exploration of Negro life and character. Exploitation, however, rather than exploration, was as often as not the result. Eugene O'Neill's *The Emperor Jones* (1920) ushered in the decade: the play was theatrically effective, with a Negro of some aggressiveness and truculence, until then a rarity on the stage, at the tragic center instead of in comic relief, but it relied overly on tom-toms and atavism. So did O'Neill's generally unconvincing *All God's Chillun Got Wings,* which caused a tremendous imbroglio on Broadway, for all of its essential conformity to racial myths.

The technical facility of Vachel Lindsay's *The Congo* (1914) made it too popular; its repetend:

> Then I saw the Congo, creeping through the black
> Cutting through the jungle with a golden track

seemed to be the marching song of the white writers on safari to the newly discovered Harlem and other *terras incognitas.* Even as humane an author as Waldo Frank in *Holiday* defined white and Negro "consciousness" too schematically and too expeditiously. Sherwood Anderson's *Dark Laughter* used "the Negro way of life of levee loungers" to beat such whipping boys and girls as American neuroticism and acquisitiveness. John W. Vandercook brought back from Haiti and Surinam inspiring romances of heroism and noble savagery but, not content with these, he lectured the American Negro for having degenerated from his distinguished forebears in the Surinam bush. In *Tom-Tom* (1926), Vandercook related how the spectacle of a quadroon-octoroon chorus and "several wealthy well-educated mulatto families" in the choice seats—upon his one visit to a Harlem theatre—awoke him to "the supreme tragedy of the Negro." The chorus and the audience clarified race differences for him. "We [the whites]," he states, "are optical —intellectual. They are auricular—emotional." W. B. Seabrooks' books on Haiti exploited the orgiastic and voodooistic. The French novelist Paul Morand wrote a group of stories called *Magie Noire* (1928), in which atavism was luridly and absurdly expressed; in one story, for instance, a Negro intellectual attending a Pan-African convention in Brussels visits a Negro museum and immediately runs berserk. Ronald Firbank's Mayfair burlesque, *Prancing Nigger* (1924), was exactly titled. Perhaps the epitome of the trend was Carl Van Vechten's *Nigger Heaven* (1925), in which Harlem, the heaven, was flamboyant and erotic.

The craft and viewpoint of Carl Van Vechten and his fellows influenced Negro writers, and the frequent interracial parties compounded the interest. Only a few of the Harlem indigènes withstood the blandishments of the aesthetes and the hedonists: the best of those who wrote about Harlem were Rudolph Fisher, an insouciant O. Henry of Baghdad-on-the-Hudson, and Claude McKay, an unvarnished realist. But even these accented the instinctual, hedonistic, and peculiar.

The Harlemites that emerged from the pages of novels by both white and Negro authors in this period were exotic primitives, whose dances—the Charleston, the "black bottom," the "snake hips," the "walking the dog"—were tribal rituals; whose music with wa-wa trumpets and trombones and drum batteries doubled for tom-toms; whose chorus girls with bunches of bananas girdling their shapely middles nurtured tourists' delusions of the "Congo creeping through the black." *Joie de vivre* was a racial monopoly: rhythm and gaiety were on one side—the darker—of the racial line. "That's why darkies were born" sang a Negro jazz musician who should have known better. "The whites have only money, privilege, power; Negroes have cornered the joy" was the theme of a Negro novelist, who did know better.

The amorality and irresponsibility of the youthful rebels was reproved by such genteel critics as Benjamin Brawley. The burgeoning jazz met with disfavor among the Negro middle-class, who wished to conform to socially approved standards. The leaders of the NAACP felt that the characterization of Harlem sweet-backs and hot mammas did injustice to their propaganda and purposes. After chiding younger Negro authors, Dubois turned in *Dark Princess* (1928) to what he considered the proper study of writers: the rising tide of color. Though idealized and contrived, this novel handled Pan-Africanism and the emergence of Asia and Africa with prescience. Walter White's *Fire in the Flint* (1925, an anti-lynching novel) and *Flight* (1926, an anti-passing-for-white novel) were also idealized and tractarian, though informed and somewhat new in material. To Jessie Fauset and Nella Larsen, delineators of Negro middle-class life, proving a point meant more than presenting people. Properly resentful of the nonsense about inherent racial traits; irked by the theories of "race differences," such novelists blinked at the realities of differences (social and cultural) between the races. Occasionally, in their novels about passing Negroes, especially Jessie Fauset's *Comedy: American Style* (1933), the intraracial color snobbishness and the latent self-hatred of anti-Negro Negroes could be glimpsed, but these glimpses were rare, and the usual picture was bland, at once self-pitying and self-congratulatory.

Such novelists, according to Wallace Thurman's *Infants of the Spring* (1932), write only to "apprise white humanity of the better classes among Negro humanity." A sharp-eyed, nay-saying young Negro, Thurman also lampooned the phoney primitivism of his confrères. One of the best satires of the pretense and sham rife at this time came from E. Simms Campbell, whose talent for cartooning extended to pen as well as to brush and palette. He remembered:

> intellectual parties where Negroes who were in the theatre were looked upon as social plums and the dumbest and most illiterate were fawned over by Park Avenue . . . [and where] the intellectual stink could have been cut with a knife—a dull knife.[7]

[7] "Blues," in *Jazzmen*, ed. by F. Ramsey, Jr. and C. E. Smith (New York, 1939), pp. 103–104.

The poets of the period spoke more deeply than the novelists. Claude McKay's *Harlem Shadows* (1922) was original and authentic in its controlled craftsmanship and in its revelation of a personality: an independent, angry radical—now excoriating America for its injustices, now rousing race solidarity, now setting nostalgic vignettes of his native Jamaica against the tragic but fascinating Harlem. Less militant, but as deeply engaged by "race," Countee Cullen also brought disciplined technique to the revelation of a subtle, sophisticated consciousness, as in "Heritage," "The Shroud of Color," and various cutting epigrams. Langston Hughes was less conventional in technique than these two poets, and less subjective, taking the Negro folk—particularly the urban masses—for his subject. For over three decades, in more than a dozen books, Hughes has told their story, interpreted their lives, and made use of their language, lore, and song to point up his own commentary on America.

Among others, Waring Cuney, Frank Horne, and three women poets—Georgia Douglass Johnson, Angelina Grimke, and Ann Spencer—wrote truthfully about themselves, and thereby widened and deepened the self-portraiture of Negroes. One of the finest books of poems of the twenties was James Weldon Johnson's *God's Trombones* (1927), in which he recreated the eloquence of the old Negro preacher. This work not only marked a development from apologistic rhetoric and sentimentalized genre poetry, but also in its respect for the intrinsic dignity of folk-stuff showed younger writers the way to go, much as Yeats and Synge had previously shown young Irish writers.

Two striking books of this movement were Jean Toomer's *Cane* (1923) and Eric Walrond's *Tropic Death* (1926). These authors were alike in being masters of their craft and, unfortunately, in falling silent after the publication of one book each. Toomer is a poet in the few lyrics in *Cane,* and even more so in his evocative prose. No imaginative work since *The Souls of Black Folk* had so deeply explored Negro life in the deep South, in border cities, in the North, among the folk, the urban masses, the bourgeoisie, the intellectuals; and none had revealed it so beautifully. Walrond's *Tropic Death* is a brilliantly impressionistic, obliquely, subtly communicated series of portraits of the author's native West Indies.

In 1925, Du Bose Heyward wrote a poetic novel about a crippled beggar named Porgy of Catfish Row, Charleston, South Carolina.

Through the success of the novel, its dramatization by the Theatre Guild, its several versions in moving pictures, and the folk opera (by Du Bose and his wife Dorothy Heyward, and George and Ira Gershwin), Porgy is the most widely known Negro character (nationally and internationally) since Uncle Tom. Heyward, a white South Carolinian, was a sensitive and sympathetic observer of Negroes, especially on the waterfront. His poem "Jazzbo Brown" and his second novel *Mamba's Daughters* (1925) were fresh and honest. Julia Peterkin, another South Carolinian, was also a careful and absorptive observer of life on the plantations in such books as *Green Thursday* (1924) and *Scarlet Sister Mary* (1928). Both Heyward and Mrs. Peterkin veered toward the exotic primitive, however; a fellow South Carolinian, E. C. L. Adams, gave a fuller picture of the workaday life of Negroes, with none of the harshness minimized, in two books of dialogues: *Congaree Sketches* (1927) and *Nigger to Nigger* (1928). These books, with their vividness of folk-speech, the irony, starkness, and knowingness of the talkers, added a new dimension to the treatment of the Negro folk. No white folklorist (not even Harris), no Negro folklorist (not even Chesnutt) knew so much and rendered it so well as this white country doctor in the Congaree River section of South Carolina. Howard Odum and Guy Johnson at the University of North Carolina studied Negro folk songs for clues to understanding Negro life; as by-products, Odum produced three novels about a synthesized roustabout, Left Wing Gordon, who attains a certain convincingness and complexity; and Johnson wrote the first and best study of the steel driver John Henry, who is now in the pantheon of American folk heroes.

John Henry was debunked and belittled in Roark Bradford's *John Henry* (1932), from which a bad musical was made. Bradford was born on a plantation worked by Negroes, had a Negro nurse, and several Negroes as boyhood friends. He had watched them (in his words) "at work in the fields, in the levee camps, and on the river . . . at home, in church, at their picnics and their funerals." A gifted mimic, like Harris, he was able to reproduce the folk vocabulary and syntax, and books like *Ol' Man Adam An' His Chillun* (1928) and *King David and the Philistine Boys* (1930) are burlesque masterpieces. Dividing Negroes into three types, "the nigger, the colored person, and the Negro—upper case N," Bradford takes his stand by the first type, and though delighted to be in his company, sees him solely as primitive and uproariously funny.[8] Bradford could hardly have respected John Henry who was a steel-driving *man*.

Since Bradford also did not respect the folk-Negro's religion, it is strange that his travesties of the Bible in *Ol' Man Adam An' His Chillun* served as a springboard for Marc Connelly's play, *The Green Pastures*. Connelly, however, though not so soaked in local color as Bradford, was wise enough to know that there was more than farce to the folk, was humane enough to see the true values of material that Bradford underestimated, and was a canny stage artificer. He made full use of the understanding and advice of Richard Harrison and his fine troupe of Negro actors, and finally was inspired to set the play in a framework of spirituals sung authentically by the Hall Johnson choir. A miracle in two senses of the word, *The Green Pastures,* according to Kenneth Burke, exploited the "child symbol":

> The Negroes of "The Green Pastures" with their heavenly clambakes, mildly disconsolate "Lawd," the incongruous Africanization of the Biblical legends, can carry one into a region of gentleness that is, in contrast with the harsh demands of our day, caressing.

In contrast to this play, Burke set Hall Johnson's *Run, Little Chillun!,* a play written from within about a Negro religious cult, which "brings out an aspect of the Negro-symbol with which our theatre-going public is not theatrically at home: the power side of the Negro."[9] Burke was not surprised at the sluggishness of the general public's interest, but he deplored it. In the three decades since, *The Green Pastures* has been revived as a play and movie and has been much anthologized, but the text of *Run, Little Chillun!* is unavailable.

IV

EVEN WHILE BURKE was so writing, however, stress was being shifted from quaint philosophers of the quarters in the good old

[8] *Ol' Man Adam An' His Chillun* (New York, 1928), p. x.

[9] "Negro's Pattern of Life," *Saturday Review of Literature,* X (July 29, 1933), pp. 10–14.

days to the oppressed victims or the aroused laborers in the trouble-some, workaday present. Recognition that the Negro was crucial in labor's march to democracy and that the Negro *belongs,* or must belong, here and now, supplanted delusions of his "special en-dowment," special behavior, and special niche in American life. It was important for writers, both Negro and white, to recognize these truths, though today they may seem truisms. The thirties had this healthy influence in thought about *the* Negro: unfortunately, however, enforcement of economic and political creeds interfered (as did antislavery convictions earlier) with complex and convinc-ing characterization. A new type of Negro did emerge in the force-ful plays of Paul Green, whose dramaturgy, combined with Richard Wright's fervor and understanding, produced *Native Son,* one of America's few distinguished tragedies dealing with racial materials.

In the Depression, various brands of radicalism, whether derived from Socialism, Communism, Garveyism, the IWW, or just grass-roots dissidence, found Negro life and character to be unworked mines. The old firehouse, Scott Nearing, after writing the grim *Black America* (1929), piled the woes of that exposé on the head of a Negro family in *Freeborn* (1932), the first revolutionary novel of Negro life. For all of its veracity the momentum of the novel was lessened by the fact that it was "unpublishable by any commercial concern." A journalistic radical, John Spivak exposed the chain gang system in *Georgia Nigger* (1932), but here, as in so many "proletarian" novels, characterization was strangled by radical theory, with the last twist given by melodramatic clichés. The best "proletarian" works on Negro life were Grace Lumpkin's novel, *A Sign for Cain* (1935), and Paul Peters' and George Sklar's drama, *Stevedore* (1934). Both set at the center of the stage a self-respecting, virile, quiet but strong hero, slowly but surely awakened, capable of the greatest trust, willing and ready to die for the causes of race advance and economic brotherhood. From the nobility of an Uncle Tom we now get the nobility of the working-class hero. We also get repetitions of the despicable, hat-in-hand, tattling Negro, the strong matriarch, and the supposed clown, whose mask is irony; and on the white side, the brutal sheriff, the wishy-washy liberal, and (counterpart to the Negro hero) the courageous organizer. One of the stock incidents in these works is the consummation of the triumphant march, hand in hand, and rank by rank, of the white and black workers of the world.

After thirty years such a march still occurs far less in life than it did in the novels and plays of the thirties.

That there were such people and such events in America goes without saying, but that the actuality of Negro experience and its literary representation do not always coincide should also at this point go without saying. The Negro author most influenced by neo-Marxist literary canons was Richard Wright. After, and even during, his brief visitation with the Communist Party, Wright was uncomfortable with the working-class hero, however, and was more at home artistically portraying lower-class victims and arraigning American injustices: mob violence in the South, ghetto deprivations and frustrations in the North. From "Big Boy" to Bigger Thomas, Wright presented in such dynamic books as *Uncle Tom's Children, Native Son,* and *Black Boy* the searing effects of poverty and prejudice on sensitive Negro youths. Wright's indignation was enormous and his power to communicate the violence and shock was great. Carrying a personal anger too deep for him to master through art, he sought Europe for a resting place. There he became increasingly the interpreter of the American Negro to the European intellectuals, and also, increasingly, he lost touch with the realities of the racial situation in the states. The native son died before he could return home; had he returned he would have found himself not so lost, so alienated, so outside. His own insight, dedication, and craft have helped bring about this changed situation.

At a crucial point in his career, Wright was aided by the John Reed Clubs (leftist writing groups) and the Federal Writers' Project. A child of the New Deal (more accurately a stepchild), the Federal Writers' Project gave employment to Negro authors as diverse as Claude McKay and Frank Yerby; Ted Poston and Willard Motley; Arna Bontemps and Roi Ottley; Zora Neale Hurston and Henry Lee Moon. One achievement of the Writers' Project, through its city, county, state, and regional guides, was the sponsorship of local history and lore, both current and historic. Negro writers benefited from these interests. Far more revelatory than the Harlem fad were Zora Neal Hurston's rewarding novels of her native Florida: *Jonah's Gourd Vine* (1934) and *Their Eyes Were Watching God* (1937), and best of all, *Mules and Men* (1935), in which Miss Hurston, a trained anthropologist, becomes the first Negro to join the many authors who have ploughed the fertile fields of Negro folk life. From a horde of narratives by living ex-slaves, the folklorist B. A. Botkin assembled the indispensable *Lay My Burden Down* (1945), a folk history of slavery of surprising worth; and Roscoe E. Lewis collected a mass of material and fashioned it into *The Negro in Virginia,* the pioneer in a series, doomed by the short life of the Project, that would have dealt regionally with Negro life. Sufficient material was salvaged from the excellent notes on Negroes in New York to supply Roi Ottley's bright, informative narratives, *New World A-Coming* (1943) and *Black Odyssey* (1948). Arna Bontemps in his first-rate novel of a Negro insurrection, *Black Thunder* (1936), turned away from the hedonistic fiction that he exploited in *God Sends Sunday* (1931), to a more important interest in the history of the American Negro—a subject that has busied him fruitfully ever since.

The population of William Faulkner's Yoknapatawpha County contains many Negroes, and they are certainly not the least interesting persons to William Faulkner's readers, or to himself. Faulkner's depth in characterizing Negroes increased with the years; whereas in an earlier novel, *Soldier's Pay,* he accepted the myths of *his* own tribal past, soon he steadily began to see Negroes whole, and with *Go Down, Moses* he defied several of his region's set beliefs concerning the Negro. In his last years, Faulkner was rejected by his fellow Oxonians as too liberal, and accepted (gingerly) by Negro intellectuals as not liberal enough. His essential liberalism on race can be questioned (his correspondence to his "new Southern" spokesman Gavin Stevens, a lawyer who grows in good will to the Negro, but also and better in good understanding, needs study). There is no questioning, however, that in ploughing deeply into the soil of his single county, Faulkner was wise, prescient, and rewarding. What seems at first glance the familiar stereotyping becomes, on true reading, complex and revelatory, e.g., Dilsey is far more than the old mammy; Joe Christmas more than the tragic mulatto; Nancy Manigault more than the depraved "wench." But Faulkner also presents new people, unnoticed before but here candidly portrayed: the admirable Lucius Beauchamps, Sam Fathers, and the Centaur in Brass. When spouting the Southern liberal's ambivalent credo (cf. Gavin Stevens's long-windedness in *Intruder in the Dust*) Faulkner is unconvincing or wrong, but when he stands back and lets his Negro character speak out and act out, Faulkner is right and often superb.

Faulkner's éclat has dimmed the achievement of several other

Southern novelists, who, in dealing with the Negro, often did what Faulkner could not or would not do. One example is Erskine Caldwell, a genuine liberal, who in such stories as "The People Vs. Abe Latham, Colored," "Kneel to the Rising Sun," and "Candy Man Beechum," and in a novel, *Trouble in July,* has snapshots and photographs that are fresh and authentic. Other examples are Hamilton Basso, especially in his *Courthouse Square* (1936), and William March in *Come In at the Door.* Both deal with areas of Negro experience untouched by Faulkner, as does, to cite a current example, Harper Lee's *To Kill a Mockingbird.* A historical novelist, T. S. Stribling, has written a trilogy of a Southern family—both branches, Negro and white—in *The Forge* (1931), *The Store* (1933), and *Unfinished Cathedral* (1934). This masterpiece of re-creating the past is most unfairly neglected today.

Another underestimated novel on race relations is *Strange Fruit* (1944), by Lillian Smith. Here, like Faulkner, Miss Smith explores the conventionally stereotyped liaison between Negro woman and white man. Miss Smith's psychological probing results in much that is clarifying and revealing. The ambivalence of the white youth is dramatized in *Strange Fruit*; it is analyzed and substantiated in *Killers of the Dream* (1949). This book also is neglected by the "Southern critical establishment," though were some of its members to read it they might learn about themselves. *Strange Fruit* was made into a play and created a stir. At the same time, *Deep Are the Roots* by Arnaud D'Usseau and James Gow handled an interracial liaison on a higher level than had been usual. Other dramas getting to grips with the reality of Negro experience were *Jeb,* and a Negro adaptation of a play on Polish life, *Anna Lucasta* by Philip Yordan. The griefs of a Polish family were easily transposed to a Negro family.

The Negro intellectual—as intellectual, not merely victim or malcontent—is missing from American fiction. Even college life has been scanted as a subject. An underestimated book, Bucklin Moon's *Without Magnolias* (1949) is a well-done, serious presentation of a Southern Negro college. It includes sharp *aperçus* and insights, surprising at first when one realizes that the author was a white man, but not surprising when one recalls that George Washington Cable, Mark Twain, Albion Tourgee, and Lillian Smith also wore their color lightly.

Moon's book on Negro academics is broader and more firmly

based than J. Saunders Redding's novel on college life, *Stranger and Alone* (1950). More revealing autobiographically than fictionally, *Stranger and Alone* lacks the power and insight that mark *No Day of Triumph,* Redding's distinguished work of reportage, whose gallery of people—Southern, Northern, Negro, white—and whose searching commentary deserve to be better known. Redding's *On Being Negro in America* has the ambitious reach of books so titled; it grasps both truths and truisms. Although Redding terms it his valedictory to "race," it is no such thing, of course, nor could it be. Instead it signaled the beginning of a career as a sort of Negro roving ambassador, depriving us of one of the sharpest and best informed observers of the American scene. Carl Rowan's career is similar: after keen and persuasive reportage on the Negro in America in *South of Freedom* and *Go Down to Sorrow,* he then traveled and reported on India, Pakistan, and Southeast Asia in *The Pitiful and the Proud.*

While as Director of the United States Information Agency Rowan presented America's cause to the world in Washington, D. C., Chester Himes raged at America's ways in Paris. As rebellious as Richard Wright but even more nihilistic and despairing, Himes has most fully presented the misanthropic, frustrated, furious young Negro, insulted and injured, uprooted and lost, in the novels, *If He Hollers* (1945), *Lonely Crusade* (1947), and the largely autobiographical *Third Generation* (1954), a searing attack on the Negro bourgeoisie. No one can stay long near Himes's characters and feel at all easy with such "racialistic" abstractions as humility, forgivingness, cheerfulness, and contentment.

Another expatriate, Julian Mayfield, wrote three significant novels before departing for the greener fields of Ghana. These were *The Hit, The Long Night* (1958), and *The Grand Parade* (1960). The first two, with Ann Petry's *The Street* (1946), are authentic slices of Harlem life, refuting the repeated lie of Harlem the playground. Many young Negro novelists have found that one novel in everyman's life and have written it in sociological and naturalistic terms, generally in urban settings, under the influence of Dreiser, Farrell, and especially Wright and Himes. William Gardner Smith's *The Last of the Conquerors* centers around the life of Negroes in the armed forces occupying Germany, and the outlook is new and sharp. John O. Killens, in what might be considered a "proletarian novel," showed a man's upbringing in *Youngblood,* a powerful but more hopeful book than any by Wright or Himes. Killens's *And Then We Heard the Thunder* (1962) is so far the best treatment of the Negro soldier in fiction. It is an angry book but rich in sardonic humor and a wide gallery of interesting, diversified people. Similarly sardonic and powerful though less successful as a novel is Hari Rhodes's *A Chosen Few* which deals with Negroes in the Marine Corps. The same qualities of rage, violence, and honesty mark the novels of John Williams, whose novels *Sissie* (1963) and *The Angry Ones,* and anthology *The Angry Black* (1962), mark a newcomer of promise and strength.

Of fiction dealing with Negro life during the last two decades, Ralph Ellison's *Invisible Man* has invited most critical attention. This picaresque novel, something of a black *Candide,* stirred so much interest and belief in its variety and authenticity of characters, both Negro and white, that the old stereotypes were shaken. Carrying his naive hero from boyhood in Oklahoma to manhood in Harlem, Ellison gives a wonderful series of vignettes, rich in farce, comedy, irony, satire, melodrama, tragedy, and grotesquerie, all set solidly in Negro experience. Like Voltaire's Candide, Ellison's hero ends up by cultivating his garden in an underground hole in Gotham. Though he is defeated, his creator is triumphant, and one of his triumphs is that it will be hard for cardboard heroes and villains to occupy the fictional stage any longer.

Because of Ellison's silence since *Invisible Man,* broken intermittently, of course, by his perceptive essays, James Baldwin is today the best known Negro writer and, partly because of the paperback revolution, is probably the best known American Negro writer in history. *Go Tell It On The Mountain* is a winning novel, rich in emotion and understanding, leaning heavily upon Baldwin's autobiography, as almost all of his work does, including his latest, the widely discussed *Another Country.* Baldwin's essays, especially *The Fire Next Time,* mark him as the most powerful and prophetic voice of the young militants in SNCC and CORE. There is such a bond between him and the youngsters that one hopes he has at last come home again. Gifted as a novelist and essayist, he has written two startling plays: *Blues for Mr. Charlie,* a play written in the wake of Birmingham, exacerbated and ferocious, but to at least one critic less lasting than *Amen Corner,* which the gifted Frank Silvera has staged on both coasts.

When *Amen Corner* had its premiere several years ago at

Howard University, it seemed to some that here was the finest grasp of Negro life and character yet encountered on a stage. Lorraine Hansberry's *Raisin in the Sun* belongs in its fine company, for presentation of people, people who happen to be Negroes, people of a different category from Porgy and Scarlet Sister Mary and Lulu Belle and Uncle Tom and The Octoroon. And Ossie Davis's hilarious *Purlie Victorious* also has people in it, of a different section, hemisphere, world, universe from Amos an' Andy, Stepin Fetchit, and Uncle Remus. Incidentally, the humor of Dick Gregory, Jackie Mabley, and Godfrey Cambridge belongs with this type of genuine Negro humor, as remote from the usual radio, movie farce as Charlie Chaplin is from the Katzenjammer Kids.

The plays of Leroi Jones have also caused a stir. In spite of the considerable talents of this young poet-playwright, the unadulterated hatred of his plays seems factitious, not real. That white Greenwich Village audiences are titillated by *The Toilet, The Dutchman,* and *The Slave* is certain, but this says more about them than about Negro life in America. A wave of masochism swings in; cries of *peccavi, peccavimus* fill the air; but this does not mean that the cause is art or insight or revelation.

A healthier kind of writing, less desperate, less frenetic, but as concerned with injustice is the developing literature of the freedom movement. Times of gestation, conception, birth, and early nurturing of a revolution are not necessarily times that produce creative literature. The types of writing for these activists are tracts, pamphlets, advertisements, slogans, squibs, lampoons, parodies, burlesques. Closest to fiction and drama are the autobiographical narratives, fragments recollected in whatever tranquillity is permitted by jail sentences or returns to campuses and jobs. There are signs of such autobiographical renderings from such activists as Michael Thelwell, Len Holt, Claude Brown, Bill Mahoney, and Charles Cobb, to name only the few freedom fighters whom the author knows best. A good anthology has just been issued by *Freedomways* which is called *Mississippi: Opening the Closed Society.* This issue is earnest that the novels and poems and plays will come. As long as these young people hold fiercely to their hope, and to their conviction, singingly proclaimed, that "We Shall Overcome," the good writing will someday come. We can wait. These young people are in a worthy tradition: that of David Walker, David Ruggles, Frederick Douglass, Harriet Tubman, Sojourner Truth, William Nell, Martin

Delany, Henry Highland Garnet, Samuel Ringgold Ward, and William Wells Brown, that driving wedge of Negro propagandists who functioned so ably a century ago.

V

BUT THIS, it seems, is where I came in. The images of Negroes in fiction and drama have increased in number, and their manifold identities have been further recognized. More readers and writers seem aware of the humanist's concern "that the discovery and explanation of the individual . . . in space and time shall not be reduced to a point where his particular character is lost": where he becomes

> indistinguishable from any other person who possesses the same race, milieu and moment. . . . Even when we turn . . . to the study of communities and states, cultures and civilizations, we are equally anxious to make every possible distinction, to recognize every qualitative difference. In the humanist's quest, similarities, whether between individual human beings or between cultural patterns, are useful only insofar as they lead to the discovery of differences; these resemblances are never absolute, they are merely means to discourse, and they have a way of disappearing just as soon as one turns from the larger group to examine the individuals in whom a fleeting resemblance has been caught.[10]

Stereotyping is on the way out. Besides the enormous, comprehensive literature on races and cultures, readers, theatergoers, creative writers, and critics have developed a sophistication boding ill for the allegorical, the simplistic, the superficial characterization of the past. The dangers and unreality of schematic, too well-made plots; the weakness of flat and one-sided characters in distinction to round and complex characters; the pronounced effect of setting on character so that setting itself becomes a character; the ineffectuality of thesis-ridden novels; all of these have grown clearer. Readers and writers learn that deductive, expository, and direct

[10] Harcourt Brown, "Science and the Human Comedy: Voltaire," in *Science and the Modern Mind,* ed. by G. Holton (Boston, 1958), p. 20.

delineation is patently inferior to inductive, indirect delineation; that readers welcome discovery instead of indoctrination; that showing, in fiction, is better than telling. So the expounding, grouping, consigning, assuming, relegating phases of stereotyping disappear.

Fiction and drama have led in the destruction or at least the displacement of the stereotypes. The social revolution at home and the emergent nations abroad have had repercussions in the cultural world.[11] A willingness—nay, an eagerness—to learn the truth is coupled with a willingness to grant dignity to others. Even Hollywood has made a belated start toward pictures of genuine Negro life. It is television, however, that has rushed in where movies and even Broadway long feared to tread.

Nevertheless, stereotyping is not altogether out. The hipster generation, Norman Mailer pontificates, was attracted to what *the Negro* had to offer (italics mine, but let Mailer take over):

> In such places as Greenwich Village, a *ménage-à-trois* was completed—the bohemian and the juvenile delinquent came face-to-face with the Negro, and the hipster was a fact in American life—And in this wedding of the white and black it was the Negro who brought the cultural dowry. Any Negro who wishes to live must live with danger from his first day, and no experience can be casual to him, no Negro can saunter down a street with any real certainty that violence

---

[11] As one instance: nearly forty years ago, when a Negro husband was to be seen kissing his white wife's hand in O'Neill's *All God's Chillun Got Wings,* a mob was threatened in New York City. Today both on and off Broadway interracial liaisons are common in plays, e.g.: *The Owl and the Pussy Cat, No Strings, The Slave.* Odet's *Golden Boy* was wrenched from a play about an Italian pugilist violinist to one about a Negro pugilist-song-and-dance-man whose sweetheart is a white woman.

Concerning television: one single Negro viewer, glowing when he sees his people in unfamiliar roles, still wearies of the word "dignity" in its millionth application and wishes (1) that the Negro lawyer might lose at least one case (Perry Mason did); (2) that Negroes might be arrested for some crimes that they did commit; (3) that some Negroes not so unfailingly noble and sacrificial might also be shown; and (4) that Negroes might be allowed to use language not so stilted—that like other characters, they might be permitted one slave expression, one split verb, one modifier that dangles, and God save us one—just one dialectical trope. Nevertheless if one has to choose between the ennoblement and Aunt Jemima, this reviewer will have to endure the ennoblement.

will not visit him on his walk. The cameos of security for the average white: mother and the home, job and the family, are not even a mockery to millions òf Negroes; they are impossible. The Negro has the simplest of alternatives: live a life of constant humility or ever-threatening danger. In such a pass where paranoia is as vital to survival as blood, the Negro had stayed alive and begun to grow by following the need of his body where he could. Knowing in the cells of his existence that life was war, nothing but war, the Negro (all exceptions admitted) could rarely afford the sophisticated inhibitions of civilization, and so he kept for his survival the art of the primitive, he lived in the enormous present, he subsisted for his Saturday night kicks, relinquishing the pleasures of the mind for the more obligatory pleasures of the body, and in his music he gave voice to the character and quality of his existence, to his rage and the infinite variations of joy, lust, languor, growl, cramp, pinch, scream, and despair of his orgasm.[12]

To which, astounded, one Negro at least can only say, slipping into a consonant Freudian argot: "Poppycock." This is a Greenwich Village refurbishing of old stereotypes.[13] The *ménage-à-trois* of which Mailer speaks derives from this earlier trio (1) the Abolitionist insistence on the utter debasement of slavery, (2) the Marxist theory of the class struggle transferred to race, and (3) the glorification of the exotic primitive rife in the miscalled Jazz Age. If Mailer seeks the real *ménage-à-trois* that birthed this monstrosity let him seek out Harriet Beecher Stowe, Earl Browder, and Carl Van Vechten, with James Ford dropping in. What an unholy triangle that turned out to be!

Concerning stereotyping even Robert Penn Warren has his quandaries; uncertain as to who speaks today for the Negro, he admits to a bewildering diversity among the subjects of his long search. This is a promising sign, for Warren once was sure about the Negro,

[12] *Advertisements for Myself* (New York: Signet, 1959), p. 306.

[13] The quadroon, octoroon hedonists who throng the fiction of the Beats are merely the granddaughters of the tragic mulattoes of the old stereotype. Kerouac's *Subterraneans* has a close cousin to the Tawny Messalina of Seventh Avenue in Van Vechten's *Nigger Heaven*. She has been here before.

using a buzzard to speak for him the prognostication: "Nigger, your breed ain't metaphysical." Today while discussing a Negro metaphysical novelist, Warren praises Ralph Ellison for theorizing about "the basic unity of experience . . ." and also about "the rich variety" of Negroes and their experience in American life. He quotes Ellison approvingly:

> For even as his life toughens the Negro, even as it brutalizes him, sensitizes him, dulls him, goads him to anger, moves him to irony, sometimes fracturing and sometimes affirming his hopes . . . it *conditions* him to deal with *his* life, and no mere abstraction in somebody's head.[14]

Warren finds Ellison refreshing for reinspecting the "standard formulations," the "mere stereotypes" of the Revolution. Well, the sun do move.

But the writer feels no need to default to Warren, even though Warren is currently the authority on the Civil War and Segregation and, in some quarters, of the Civil Rights Revolution. For this is where I came in. Over thirty years ago I wrote

> One manifest truth, however, is this: the sincere, sensitive artists, willing to go beneath the clichés of popular belief to get at an underlying reality, will be wary of confining a race's entire character to a half-dozen narrow grooves. He will hardly have the temerity to say that his necessarily limited observation of a few Negroes in a restricted environment can be taken as the last word about some mythical *the* Negro. He will hesitate to do this, even though he had a Negro mammy, or spent a night in Harlem, or has been a Negro all his life. The writer submits that such an artist is the only one worth listening to, although the rest are legion.[15]

In the intervening years there have been many writers worth listening to, though not so many as hoped for, who saw Negro life steadily and whole. Nevertheless, clichés and stereotypes linger, and even burgeon. The conclusion, in these much later years, still holds. It is here that I take my stand.

[14] *Who Speaks for the Negro* (New York, 1965), p. 351.
[15] "Negro Character as Seen by White Authors," *Journal of Negro Education,* II, 2 (April, 1933), p. 203.

The Problems of the Negro Writer*

SAUNDERS REDDING

L ANGSTON HUGHES, WHO, ON THE STRENGTH of his output,
his attainments, and his years of devotion to the literary
profession, rates as the dean of American Negro letters,
began his contribution to a recent symposium on the problems of
Negro writers with this assertion: "The Negro writer in America
has all the problems any other writer has, plus a few more." LeRoi
Jones, the Beat poet-dramatist, and John A. Williams, the novelist,
who were the other contributors, agreed with this, but instead of
exploring and supporting it as a critical proposition, they, like
Hughes, wandered off into matters that on casual notice appear to
have little relevance to it.

Indeed, this impression of irrelevance is encouraged when Hughes
makes no bones of concerning himself with "areas peripheral to
writing"—that is, lecturing, teaching, and other academic activities
in which Negro writers are not or are too seldom invited to participate; and Jones draws a contrast between the "refined Afro-
American Writing" (whatever that is) of "middle-class Negroes"
(whom he excoriates) and the "richness and profundity of the blues.
. . . Even the best of contemporary literature written by Negroes
cannot yet be compared to the fantastic beauty of Charlie Parker's
music" (as if it should be); and John A. Williams, after expressing a peevish interest in the "themes and techniques" of Negro
writing, levels his verbal shafts at those white reviewers who
"label," "group," and "lump together" books by Negro authors.

While these matters seem way beside the point of those "few
more problems" Negro writers have than whites, they are not really.
As a matter of fact, they illustrate one of those problems rather
specifically—that one that many Negro writers have called the
"problem of identity." This is imprecise. It is much less a problem

* This article was written for *The Massachusetts Review* with the
assistance of a grant from the Philip M. Stern foundation of Washington,
D.C.

of identity than of identification, and the difference, which may seem merely subtle, is substantial. What Hughes, Jones, and Williams do, each in his own way, is deplore the fact that their *identity as Negroes* precludes their *identification with American writing.* It is immediately clear that this is something more than a "literary" problem, a problem in writing. It has nothing to do with the classic search-for-the-father theme, nor with the complex notional formulations in the structure of such novels as *The Auto-Biography of an Ex-Coloured Man, Native Son,* and *Invisible Man.* Neither does it have anything to do with what all serious creative writing is at bottom—the quest for self. As a problem of identity, it is delusive. And when it is set forth in James Baldwin's grandiose verbiage as "this prodigious question, at home so little recognized, seems . . . to grow disproportionately . . . producing tensions and bewilderments," it is an unctuous fraud—which, let it be said, Baldwin has perpetrated so successfully as to attain the status of a cultural hero-martyr among the uninformed, the sophisticated misinformed, and the naive.

The Negro, and especially, later, the Negro writer, has always known who he is. He has known it so well and he has been forced to live in such constant tense awareness of it that his reaction to the knowledge has often just skirted the psychotic. Until recently, he has glossed it, he has sometimes ignored it. Certainly he has not had to seek it. Quite the contrary, he has tried to lose it; for what he was made to suffer in America led, ironically enough by a kind of moral necessity, to a distortion of his identity into something not only base, but evil, and he has had to live with this distortion while trying not to live it. The Negro's identity was locked into the white man's fantasy construct of the slave, and Emancipation did not free him. The fantasy construct, "perpetuated as an historical fiction," as Alain Locke pointed out forty years ago, was the image of the Negro that none but the Negro himself wanted to reject. And in order to do this, he had first to suppress the knowledge and deprive himself of the redemptive uses of his true identity.

This is paradox as well as pathetic irony, but it has a simple explanation. Imposed upon the Negro—with all its shame-inducing particulars: shiftlessness, stupidity, bestiality, and so forth—to relieve the conscience of those who had enslaved him, the slave identity did not change with the Negro's conversion to a free status.

The identity was still useful to the conscience, for it justified the social abuses practiced against the freedman, and since the identity of the Negro was locked into this, he could not rid himself of the one without ridding himself of the other. And this, strange and aberrant though it may be, is what he did, or tried to—in fact, in fiction, and in verse. There is no hint of his Negro ancestry, nor the faintest reflection of his racial experience in the works of William Stanley Braithwaite, the poet and anthologist of poets,[1] who declares flatly in his autobiography that he is "descended from a long line of British" ancestors—a declaration that glosses the fact that his mother was a West Indian Negro who was descended from slaves. Jessie Fauset did not write *vers de société* in French and give some of her English language poems French titles merely to exercise her command of the language. One would never know from reading her poetry that Alice Dunbar was the New Orleans-born, mulatto wife of the Negro dialect poet, Paul L. Dunbar, whose own schizoid bent it was to write "white" novels, and who toward the end of his short life complained wistfully of the reception of his verses, among the most popular in America at the century's turn:

> He sang of love when life was young
> And Love itself was in his lays;
> But, Ah, the world, it turned to praise
> A jingle in a broken tongue.

It is the problem of identification then—as distinct from the problem of identity—that plagues Negro writers still. They glory in and sometimes glorify the Negro identity—what the talented novelist John Oliver Killens calls the "black psyche. . . . I work," he continues, "for the day when my people will be free of the racist pressure to be *white like you;* a day when 'good hair' and 'high yaller' and bleaching cream and hair-straighteners will be obsolete." And this sentiment is not new. It is not owing to the recent rise of Black Nationalism. Three-quarters of a century ago, when Dunbar was climbing to heights of popularity never since attained by a Negro poet, the exaltation of the Negro self was

[1] *The Book of Elizabethan Verse* (1906); *The Book of Georgian Verse* (1908); *The Book of Restoration Verse* (1909); and from 1913, a series of annual anthologies of magazine verse.

forced into a self-conscious and mechanical conformity to the folk tradition of "darky entertainment," which whites found so irresistible. Thus a Negro character, like Black Samson of Brandywine, could be ever so heroic and noble so long as he "talked nigger" and was ignorant of what nobility meant. Thus, too, the loftiest precepts could fall from the lips of a black woman, so long as she was in the white folk's kitchen and spoke her maxims in dialect. This was incongruous, like a monkey with table manners, and just as amusing, and therefore, so far as whites were concerned, permissible. Ascribing praiseworthy attributes and pretty and idealistic sentiments to Negro characters in the folk tradition[2] was the Negro's means of preserving at least a modicum of that racial pride and dignity that whites otherwise would have disallowed.

But for the past thirty years whites have been losing the pleasure of condescendence and the power to disallow pride and dignity to black people. The steady erosion of this authority has been signalized in disparate events, circumstances, and people, including Joe Louis, who, as heavyweight boxing champion of the world, was "majestic Modesty's favorite son"; World War Two and the Korean action, when integration of the armed forces got under way; the birth of African freedom; the Negro American's unremitting cutting through the thickets of proscriptive laws; the Supreme Court decision; the sit-ins; Montgomery, Alabama, and Martin Luther King; Patrice Lumumba; Roy Wilkins and Philip Randolph. Each of these focused a dramatic highlight on another feature of the Negro image. Each made it a little more impossible for whites to believe in the fictive image so carefully elaborated by the school of American romantic historians led by Ulrich Phillips.

Although they are losing the power to annul the Negro's simple human dignity, white people retain the authority to disallow the Negro's participation in American civilization. Although whatever, besides his color, is distinctive about him was made so by the pressures of the American environment, he is not permitted his identification with American culture. He is kept outside it. As every-day citizen and as creative artist, he is relegated to a subculture and required to function within it. John A. Williams complains that

---

[2] Langston Hughes follows a modification of this tradition in his "Simple" pieces, but they are written primarily for a Negro audience, and are not intended to reflect the situation of seventy-five years ago.

Negro writers are confined to a "literary ghetto," which LeRoi Jones describes as "a no man's land . . . almost completely invisible to white America." So invisible, in fact, that the compilers of the standard academic anthologies of American writing, and even compilers of less orthodox, modern collections do not see the larger-than-life figures in that dark landscape, which is nevertheless, as Jones goes on to say, "so essentially part [of America] as to stain its whole being (sic) an ominous gray." The standard anthologies do not contain the writings of Charles W. Chesnutt, who was a far better novelist than his much better known contemporary, William Dean Howells. The verses of Paul Dunbar are missing too, although Howells, who is probably more deserving of lustre as a critic and editor than as a novelist, ranked Dunbar's dialect poems equal to James Whitcomb Riley's. W. E. B. DuBois, whose beautiful book, *The Souls of Black Folk,* is a classic by whatever standards of excellence one cares to set, graces no readily accessible anthology. Even Booker T. Washington, in his day the darling of white America and referred to as a spokesman of the "new South," is not represented—not even by a chapter from *Up From Slavery,* his famous autobiography, which certainly has as much social importance and literary value as the orations of Henry W. Grady.

Very few of the Negro writers of the immediate past and of those presently living are included in recent anthologies of American literature either. James Weldon Johnson, Countee Cullen, and Jean Toomer—no. Langston Hughes and Richard Wright—occasionally. Although Margaret Walker won the Yale Younger Poets award in 1942, and Gwendolyn Brooks won the Pulitzer poetry prize in 1950, neither is represented in Malcolm Brinnin's new anthology, nor in Pack, Hall, and Simpson's *New Poets of England and America,* nor in that big overstuffed book, edited by Clifton Fadiman, *The American Treasury.* Donald M. Allen included LeRoi Jones in his Beat anthology, *The New American Poetry,* and Herbert Gold used a James Baldwin story in *Fiction of the Fifties.* And that is about the extent of it, and the extent does not wipe out the boundaries of the "literary ghetto."

Historians and critics of American literature generally have ignored Negro writing also. The one notable exception is Van Wyck Brooks. In *The Confident Years* he included a chapter, "Eugene O'Neill: Harlem," a lengthy (and critically separate) section of which is devoted to a historical summary of Negro writing from Dunbar to the Harlem literary renaissance of the late 1920's and early 1930's.

But all this has to do with more than the lack of identification with the articulated corpus of American writing about which Negro writers complain. It has to do with more than John A. Williams's point about "lumping" Negro writers and "of always comparing [them] to one another, rather than to white writers." It is indicative as well of the minimizing of Negro writing as projections of a significant aspect of American reality and a distinctive American experience. This, too, is a problem that plagues Negro writers. Indeed, it is a double problem, for it joins the question of what to write about with the question of whom to write for. Since one writes truly out of his own experience—and less than the truth does not count—and out of what he is, it would seem that the problem of what to write about has a simple solution. But not so—not for Negro writers. Three of the best of them have remarked on this difficulty. Each has seen it differently, but it is the same problem for each.

"My fight," writes John O. Killens, "is not to be a white man in a black skin, but to inject some black blood, some black *intelligence* into the pallid main stream of American life." Ralph Ellison discovered that "the greatest difficulty for a Negro writer was the problem of revealing what he truly felt . . . and linked to this was the difficulty . . . of depicting what really happened within our areas of American life, and putting down with honesty and without bowing to ideological expediences the attitudes and values which give Negro American life its sense of wholeness and which render it bearable and human. . . ." And, finally, James Baldwin in one of his early essays—which by contrast make his subsequent novels seem contrived, trivial, and false—wrote that "the difficulty then . . . of being a Negro writer was the fact that I was, in effect, prohibited from examining my own experience too closely by the tremendous demands and the very real dangers of my social situation." One wishes, of course, that Baldwin had given "my social situation" more explicit meaning, but the fact remains that Baldwin the novelist has not examined "too closely" his experience of being Negro since he wrote his first novel, *Go Tell It On The Mountain.*

The trouble rests in the other, the second equation in the problem—the audience the Negro writer wishes to attract, and, more, that he is obligated to attract and must attract if he is to be effective. It is the same audience that makes and sustains any writer's reputation. For the sociological reasons that are summed up in the term "cultural deprivation," there are only a few Negroes in it. In short, it is middle-class and white; and this much is beyond dispute—few Americans of the middle class, or any class, want to share, or are capable of sharing, the experience of being black. Yet it is this experience that is the Negro writer's responsibility and—if he is serious—his commitment to depict. John A. Williams tells us that an editor, rejecting a Williams novel, "said, in essence, in a note to my agent, that it would be wiser if I were to set aside the obviously personal experiences of being Negro." The mask the Negro is asked to wear is not of his own fashioning; the life he lives is not a life of his own choosing; and the reality he knows bears little relation to the "reality" envisioned in the American dream. To tear away the mask, to examine closely the experience of Negroness would be to reveal to whites things about themselves that they dare not face. And the danger of doing this is in destroying the "truce" one has made with what Ralph Ellison calls the white man's "anti-tragic approach" to Negro experience—which "truce," Baldwin notes, "is the best one can hope for."

"Tell it like it is," LeRoi Jones says, and gets hooked on the Beats, whose distinction lies in the very fact that they have nothing to tell; and he writes fantasies like "The Dutchman," in which the allegory, whether intentionally or not, veils more than it reveals, and in which the symbolic devices are exactly those that whites have created for their defense against the reality of the Negro; and he turns to jazz, in which he claims everything to be said about being Negro is said, although "whites don't dig it." Tell it like it is! But he doesn't, for the audience will not listen. "I want," declares James Baldwin, "to be an *honest man* and a *good writer*." This is a startling misplacement of modifiers, but not so startling as it would be had he not told us previously of the prohibition against examining his own experiences too closely.

So there you are. The Negro writer is limited by the limitations of the audience he writes for and is obligated to attract. The obligation is two-fold. It is incurred not only by the writer's—*any* writer's—subjective need for recognition from an audience he has to respect, but also, in the case of the Negro writer, by his racial need for identification with the stream of western culture that flows through America. All the social machinery—education, religion, communications—is geared to the notion that without this identification the Negro artist-writer and man is nowhere, and all experience confirms it. Only when he achieves identification can he attain to respectability and the privilege of being judged by the standards that prevail among Americans and Westerners as artists and men. The manifest implications of Western mythology are that only when he achieves it can he hope to attain to the best the world has to offer.

With but one single exception, as we shall see, there is no resistance on the part of serious American Negro writers to the idea of the superiority of Western standards, disputable though the idea may be. American Negro writers have raised no questions such as those raised by Africans at their All-Africa Writers Conference in Uganda in 1962. Among the handful of guests were representatives of a group of British and American publishers who proposed to offer a sizeable monetary prize for the best fiction work submitted by an African in a competition that would close in 1964–65. Who will judge the competition, you Westerners? the African writers wanted to know. Are our literary sanctions derived from some other racial and social traditions than our own? Is our audience in America and Europe? It is all very well for you to establish a prize competition for us, but aren't your expectations non-African? Do you not expect our work to conform to your standards rather than to our own? And who are you to judge us?

The publishers' representatives were first surprised and then obviously embarrassed by these questions, and they had no answers to them. The offer was withdrawn.

Considering all the historical, cultural, and psychological circumstances, it is not strange that American Negro writers, who have also been invited to compete for literary prizes, have not raised similar questions. Only Julian Mayfield has objected to the "stultifying respectability [that] hangs over the land," and to the immersion, voluntary or forced, in the mainstream, which "seems to be running dangerously shallow." Only Mayfield has cried out against the assimilation, the *integration* that desensitizes the American Negro writer to "philosophical and artistic influences that originate beyond our national cultural boundaries." And Mayfield has gone to Africa to live.

But—if we discount relatively brief periods of expatriation in

Europe, which, anyway, is still the West—most of Mayfield's dark-skin contemporaries have stayed in the land where they were born and in the situation prescribed for them. It is not difficult to understand that for the very reason that the situation sets arbitrary and undemocratic bounds to their lives and to their province as writers, they have responded with greater intensity than white writers to the ideals of American democracy. They are all social moralists. They have assumed a moral responsibility for ideals that their special situation has encouraged them all the while to repudiate. It is a truism that they have come to know America, its flawed character and its bankrupt spirit, better than most Americans, but most Americans reject this special knowledge as disloyal and subversive, and Negro writers cannot even use it in recreating the reality of their experiences, their world. The audience that Negro writers feel duty-bound to attract is fixed in its ideas of what Negroes are, and it is engaged, as Ralph Ellison points out, in a "feverish industry dedicated to telling Negroes who and what they are," and it demands that Negro writers function within this structure of ideology and myth. For here the comic, the frightening, the pornographic, the unnatural and grotesque provide the comforting shock of unfavorable contrast to the social "realities" and the cultural values in its own existence; provide, too, the metaphorical evidence that it has been right about Negroes all along; and provide, finally, the consoling proof that the social acts of alienation and discrimination committed against Negroes are justified. "Oh, look at the niggers! Aren't they queer!"

The inflexibility of this notion has a deadly, corrupting potential. It is not to be doubted that Mayfield, in addition to making a symbolic reaffirmation of his Negro identity, looked upon his removal to Africa as an escape from this potential. Perhaps there he will attain that psychological distance and reduce to nothing that emotional ambivalence in regard to America that embitters many another Negro writer. This is what Richard Wright, who was also an honest writer, hoped to do by his removal to France. Unfortunately, Wright failed disastrously, almost totally. He did not manage to make the psychological distance, and the reduction of the ambivalence of his feelings destroyed, paradoxically enough, the emotional center that inspired his artistic endeavors and was the primary source of his literary power. There was no substitute for that center-of-tension, and none of the technical and mechanical resources of Wright's talent could hide the fact. Wright the novelist was at home only in America. France was never his in the artist's sense; Spain was not his; and Africa, where he also went, broke his artist's heart because it was not his either.

"Oh, look at the niggers!" The ideas, images and sensations that gather around this exclamatory phrase have undermined the creative integrity of some Negro writers. This happened to Wallace Thurman three decades ago, and to Claude McKay in his later years, after his first successes as a poet and novelist; those years when the Harlem renaissance, in which he had been a moving spirit, was prostituted and commercialized by gangster impresarios, who literally bled white the black writers, artists, musicians, and performers. And now the undermining of James Baldwin's creative integrity seems to proceed apace.

In *Another Country,* for instance, while Baldwin steps with authorial warrant into the hearts and minds of his white characters, and is at pains to point to this referment and that in the structures of their lives, their values, and their thoughts, he takes no such trouble with his Negro characters. His examination of their inner lives is perfunctory. It is as if the author grants the validity of the common assumption that whites *react* but Negroes only *act.* His Negroes' behavior has nothing behind it or beyond it, no analyzed causative dependence on the past and without subsequence in the future. It is not only capricious, but impulsive. Rufus Scott's abandonment of his career, his desertion of his friends and family, and his suicide are explicable on no other grounds, and consequently Rufus enkindles no spark of sympathetic understanding, arouses no pang of pity. "Look at the niggers!" There's no figuring them out, and in the case of Baldwin's "niggers" there is no need to figure them out, for even in the moment of action they are mere foils for white characters, and are seen as shadows espied against opaque glass—dramatic, but of no social and moral significance in themselves.

As an essayist of perception and glittering articulateness, Baldwin understands how Negroes think and feel, but as a novelist he scorns the duty to lead his audience to understanding. Is it that the "very real dangers" he sees in snatching away the mythic mask and revealing the "mystery" of Negro life threatens only the artist, the creative writer? Does not the same profound and at once personal and social need to be recognized as man, though black, inspire both the novelist and the essayist? At its best, the novel too is a social declaration and performs a social function. Baldwin the "honest man" is the obverse of Baldwin the novelist and "good writer." And certainly *The Fire Next Time* as well as two other books of essays, represents the obverse—the face of the coin stamped with the symbolic image of the Negro and severely engraved with the legend, "Know me, and deny me at your peril." This is the figuration of that dual commitment of the serious Negro writer: to his people and to his art. It is a commitment that is sometimes violated at the expense of honesty and honor, but it is a commitment that is never completely resigned.

James Weldon Johnson saw it as creating a problem in terms of "two audiences." Calling it a dilemma, he suggested that it could be resolved by the author "working at his best in his best known material to fashion something that rises above race, and reaches out to the universal in truth and beauty." Johnson's *God's Trombones*, "seven Negro sermons in verse," is his supreme effort to do this. W. E. B. DuBois, sometimes a brilliant writer, but seldom a conscious artist, saw the problem too, but thought it was overcome by the author who "served the race by turning his art into conscious propaganda which heralded the true and good and beautiful things about the race." And this is what DuBois attempted to do in *Dark Princess* and *The Ordeal of Mansart*, neither of which succeeds as fiction. Harry A. Overstreet who, as a professor at Columbia University, took a sympathetic interest in race problems, implied, in a somewhat different context, what DuBois had made explicit. "The Negro author," Overstreet wrote in 1944, ". . . dare not take the position that all that is human is his novelist's province [and that] he has a perfect right to describe scoundrel Negroes if he so prefers. He does so at peril to his people, for every scoundrel Negro he describes is [metamorphosed by his white audience into] all Negroes."

It was with the intention of thwarting this metamorphosis (for the intention would be inherent in his commitment to his people) that Richard Wright said of the black scoundrel-protagonist of his novel *Native Son* that "Bigger Thomas was not black all the time, he was white, too, and there were literally millions of him, everywhere. . . . I was fascinated by the similarity of the emotional tensions of Bigger in America and Bigger in Nazi Germany and Bigger in old Russia. All Bigger Thomases, white and black, felt tension, were afraid, hysterical, and restless. . . . Certain modern experiences were creating types of personalities whose existence ignored racial and national lines . . . These personalities . . . were mainly consequent upon men and women living in a world whose fundamental assumptions could no longer be taken for granted."

If the problems created by the Negro writer's dual commitment cannot be solved by a resort to logic, they can be transcended. And not only by the vaulting genius of, say, a Ralph Ellison, or the sheer emotional power of a Richard Wright—both of whom, incidentally, embrace the obligation to their people as a source of creative strength and moral sustenance. They can be transcended by the dedicated exercise of an order of talent and skill such as Ann Petry's, or Julian Mayfield's. Transcendence begins where Wright's begins, negatively, with the rejection of those "fundamental assumptions" that have so long dominated writing *about* Negroes that they have come to permeate writing *by* Negroes. Or transcendence begins positively, where Ellison's and Petry's begins, with a recognition of the fact that Negro behavior—character, sensation, thought—is dredged from the same deep mine of potentials that is the source of all human behavior. Or, finally, trancendence begins with the Negro writer's conviction that, as Ellison has said, "it is important to explore the full range of American Negro humanity and to affirm those qualities which are of value beyond any question of segregation, economics or previous condition of servitude. The obligation was always there and there is much to affirm."

Baldwin's Autobiographical Essays

The Problem of Negro Identity

DAVID LEVIN

THE WORLD and James Baldwin's place in it have changed drastically since the publication of *The Fire Next Time* a year ago. Baldwin, it is true, had already published in *The New Yorker* and the *Progressive* the essays that have since won phenomenal sales in book form. But the Birmingham riots had not yet occurred. Baldwin had not made the electrifying speaking tour that hit Western universities and towns with the force of an old-fashioned revival. Nor had he received the full-scale, public analysis that has since been accorded to him by such divergent journals as *Life, Encounter,* and *Dissent.* Medgar Evers had not been shot. The Birmingham children had not been murdered in their Sunday School. President Kennedy was not only alive but subject to criticism of spokesmen like Baldwin who (along with the madness of segregationists) later persuaded him to speak to the entire country on the moral issue of racial discrimination.

Now, of course, Baldwin has come to represent for "white" Americans the eloquent, indignant prophet of an oppressed people, a voice speaking in print, on television, and from the public platform in an all but desperate final effort to bring us out of what he calls our innocence before it is (if it is not already) too late. This voice calls us to our immediate duty for the sake of our own humanity as well as our own safety. It demands that we stop regarding the Negro as an abstraction, an invisible man; that we begin to recognize each Negro in his "full weight and complexity" as a human being; that we face the horrible reality of our past and present treatment of Negroes—a reality we do not know and do not want to know.

[v, 2, Winter 1964]

This message has always formed the core of Baldwin's auto-biographical writings, those essays that have made *Notes of a Native Son, Nobody Knows My Name,* and *The Fire Next Time* more successful than his fiction. It is a message that seems to me undeniable, in spite of logical difficulties and fluctuations of attitude over a discouraging fifteen years of accelerating conflict and creeping progress, and it is a message that seems now almost too urgent to allow the presumption of literary analysis and historical qualification. Yet Mr. Baldwin has made his desire "to be an honest man and a good writer" the central metaphor through which to express, in his autobiographical writings, his spiritual quest and his evangelical plea to our society. Moreover, this patently topical subject requires us to look with Baldwin at several issues in American and other history and to consider him in relation to writers who seem as remote as Cotton Mather.

The word "identity" recurs over and over again in Baldwin's autobiographical essays. The essential question, for himself and for the American audience that he assumes is white, is: *Who am I?* or: *How can I be myself?* In his answers to these questions we see the strength that places several of Baldwin's autobiographical essays among the best in American literature; we must see there also several inconsistencies and errors that may be the inevitable price of his method.

As he has rearranged them, without regard for chronology, in his books, these essays give great importance not only to the question of identity but to Baldwin's recurrent answer: *I am a writer.* His resolution to be an honest man and a good writer concludes the autobiographical preface to *Notes of a Native Son.* This book tells us at what cost in experience and self-analysis Baldwin arrived at so abstract an acceptance of his humanity. Being a writer meant coming to terms with his condition as native son, first as the individual son of his individual father, then in the ironic sense conveyed by Richard Wright's novel, and finally, with the perspective of his European experience, in reluctant but unqualified acceptance of his complex fate as an American Negro, this new man, "just as American as the Americans who despise him, the Americans who fear him, the Americans who love him"—a man with a peculiar status and a peculiar mission to speak in the Western world at a time when it is imperative to know that "The world is white no longer, and it will never be white again."

The obligation to find a voice with which to speak one's message to the Western world is of course familiar to students of American religion and American autobiography. It did not begin with Richard Wright or with naturalism. Baldwin seems aware of the relationship between his religious experience and his new obligation as the Writer when he recounts his last conversation with his father in the superb narrative essay that gives *Notes of a Native Son* its title. Here, as later in *The Fire Next Time,* Baldwin describes his religious conversion as an adolescent and his youthful success as a preacher. Then he recalls that his father, an unsuccessful preacher who hated white people and deeply suspected the son's literary ambitions, had once suddenly asked him: "You'd rather write than preach, wouldn't you?" And he recalls that his answer was "Yes." He does not pursue the relationship so emphatically as I shall follow it, but it seems clear to me that in his work the writer's mission is very much like the young preacher's, except that the nature of the truth has changed. Released from the beliefs that distorted his view of reality, he can now bear faithful witness to the truth that he believes we all need to see. He can use his special powers to convey, as he says, "something of what it felt like to be a Negro," to give us some sense of experiences that, like grace, can be known only at first hand: the discovery of color and of the society's war on anyone who resists its racial categories; the discovery of one's own rage, of hatred for one's persecutors, one's black father's powdered corpse, one's own color; the resolution to transcend one's hatred. Baldwin's function as a writer is to make us see, and he shocks us with abrupt reversals of our usual point of view—as the first black man, a veritable Gulliver, ever to enter a cold, white Swiss village; as a half-frozen worshipper on Christmas Day in a solitary cubicle in a French prison, "peering through a slot placed at the level of the eye at an old Frenchman, hatted, overcoated, muffled, and gloved [who preached] . . . in this language that I did not understand, to this row of wooden boxes, the story of Jesus Christ's love for men." When Baldwin is "chilled by the merriment" with which Frenchmen who have subjected him to great misery endeavor to warm him, he reminds us of Henry Thoreau. In a "deep, black, stony, and liberating way," he tells us, his own life began the day he endured this merriment, for he learned then that "the laughter of those for whom the pain of living is not real . . . is universal and never can be stilled." Here he reminds us of enthusiasts like Thoreau and Melville and Edwards and Hooker, who persisted in seeing the convicting reality that others would not see.

Throughout *Nobody Knows My Name* and *The Fire Next Time,* the role of the writer as the center of identity remains important. The writer, rather than the statesman, is our most important means of reopening communication between the Old World and the New, Baldwin tells us in the opening essay of *Nobody Knows My Name,* and in this volume he moves as a critical observer through Europe and America, reporting on a conference of African writers and artists, on visits to Harlem and the Deep South, and on his personal relationship with Richard Wright and Norman Mailer.

In *The Fire Next Time,* the main essay brings religion back into the center of autobiographical concern. Here Baldwin describes his early life in Harlem, his conversion, and his successful performance as a preacher in "the religion racket." The experience, of course, is the uniquely harrowing experience of the son of a Negro minister in the ghetto, but his discovery of inadequacies in the Christian God and the Christian people who dominated his childhood differs little from the same discovery in other self-taught American writers: Benjamin Franklin, Thomas Paine, Herman Melville, Mark Twain. Having become a writer, having learned to use the warfare between rage and intelligence that he says destroys many American Negroes, Baldwin goes in this autobiographical narrative on a mission to Elijah Muhammad, leader of the Black Muslims, and the second half of the narrative sets off against the first another religious effort to diminish him by capturing his allegiance. Elijah Muhammad sees that Baldwin wants to become himself, but the Muslim meaning for that phrase simply substitutes one kind of racial power for another. When the prophet asks Baldwin, the former Christian, "And what are you now?" Baldwin replies: "I? Now? Nothing." This was not enough. "I'm a writer. I like doing things alone." Then, as in the account of his earlier conversion (and Martin Luther's supposed account of *his* conversion), Baldwin the narrator adds: "I heard myself saying this."

The writer has won by his experience a place that is separate from both groups, Christians and Muslims. To the presumably white audience he shows the "hypocrisies," he calls them, of Christianity, and he forces us to see that there is much in the Muslim movement to tempt him or any Negro. Yet he cannot be himself unless he faces his American past, his African past, and his indis-soluble relationship to his countrymen and the world. He steps forward at the end to apply the lesson for all of us, speaking in the first person plural for "relatively conscious whites and relatively conscious blacks, who must . . . insist on, or create, the consciousness of others." He demands that we recognize our past and our unique opportunity to abandon the fiction that this is a white nation, and thus to "achieve our country." He calls this achieving our identity, our maturity as men and women. Like many a preacher before him, he admits that we are merely a handful. No matter, he concludes. We must "dare everything" or face the prophetic warning: *God gave Noah the rainbow sign, No more water, the fire next time.*

IN THIS BRIEF STUDY of the writer's mission in Baldwin's auto-biographical essays I have understated his awareness of complexity in human personality and history. The perceptive sensibility of the writer stands in these works for his commitment to respect that complexity. He wants, I believe, to represent the lonely individual trying to achieve dignity in the modern world. Becoming himself requires him to accept with pain the hatred that he has felt for his father, for white men, and for himself. The effect of the entire series is a powerful, if gloomy, reassertion of the American idea—the very notion of the union of the human race that such patriots as George Bancroft celebrated long ago. And the idea gains great force from Baldwin's emphasis (often in Christian language that burns deep) on the Negro's awareness that Americans have so con-sistently betrayed the principle. Through these narratives the Negro becomes, in one of the least felicitous of Baldwin's phrases, "*the* key figure in this country." One reason, of course, is that American treatment of the Negro will test the country's worthiness to survive in a world no longer white. But another, more important to the development of an honest man and a good writer, is that the Negro himself must overcome immense pressures and temptations if he is to transcend the fact of color, the hatred of whites, the restricting bitterness that might keep him from achieving what Baldwin calls his identity. The writer uses his experience as an American Negro to tell us crucial truths about ourselves and all men.

It seems to me that Baldwin accomplishes this task most effec-tively in several of the brilliant autobiographical essays in *Notes of a Native Son.* Especially in the title essay, one of the best autobiographical narratives in our literature, he gives us a sharp sense not only of the pain but of the vigorous diversity of Negro life in America. Even when he is describing the signs warning of the Harlem riots of 1943, signs that reveal a growing union of resentment against the mistreatment of Negro soldiers, he communicates this variety. He is not picturesque or sentimental; he never lets us forget his belief that before reaching puberty every Negro native to this country has been irreparably scarred by the conditions of his life; but he paints a memorable picture of the disparate groups gathering in the streets, and his recognition of the differing responses of "race" men and prostitutes and sharpies and churchly women and newspaper editors keeps us in touch with the human beings to whom our innocence does so much damage.

In almost every essay, however, and especially when he writes about our obligation to face the facts of the past, Baldwin's didactic purpose and his predicament as an American Negro force him to ignore his conviction that color does not matter. They force him to ignore the weight and complexity of human beings. Although he shows magnificently that he knows better, his method leads him to write of Negroes as if they were all of one mind and culture, and of whites (or groups of whites) as if they belong uniformly to another. The uncertainty of method appears most openly in the midst of a superb piece called "The Harlem Ghetto," when Baldwin, having explained the hostility that many Harlem Negroes feel toward Jewish shopkeepers, doubts that "any real and systematic cooperation can be achieved between Negroes and Jews." So sweeping is the generalization, so seriously has he taken his labels, that he feels compelled to enter a qualification familiar to racists who are quick to reassure one about some of their best friends: "This is in terms of the over-all social problem," he says, "and is not meant to imply that individual friendships are impossible or that they are valueless when they occur." Here the writer seems to have forgotten that the only possible kind of friendship in a tragic world is individual friendship and that systematic cooperation can hardly occur between groups that have no existence except through the irrational, unsystematic exclusions of others.

The problem is most serious in Baldwin's discussion of the Negro's past, and it is especially serious because he calls us to face the past honestly and to resist the temptation to invent a false one. When criticizing Richard Wright and when reporting on a conference of Negro and African artists, Baldwin sees plainly the vast difference between Africans and American Negroes; nor does he fail to notice that much of the language, psychology, moral attitude in which Richard Wright's eloquent *Black Boy* protests Western injustices comes from forces that "had nothing to do with Africa." The values of the Negro's special experience, Baldwin perceives, is its double-edgedness, the Negro's separateness from both Europe and Africa. He even goes so far as to contend that the only thing all Americans have in common is their having no identity other than the identity being achieved on this continent. Yet the "I" in these essays often proclaims an undefined African heritage "that was taken from him, almost literally, at one blow." He proclaims what seems to me a specious distinction between the experience of African immigrants, uniquely horrible though that has been, and the experience of all other immigrants. He tells us that a man called Baldwin enslaved him and forced him to kneel at the foot of the cross. He tells us that the most illiterate Swiss villager is related, in a way he himself can never attain, to Dante, Shakespeare, and Michelangelo, and that the cathedral at Chartres and the Empire State Building say something to Swiss villagers (or would if the villagers could ever see them) that these buildings cannot say to him. When he enters a Swiss village, he says, he finds himself among a people whose culture "controls" him, has even in a sense "created" him. "Go back a few centuries," he says, "and they are in their full glory—but I am in Africa, watching the conquerors arrive." The same difficulty persists in a more positive way when at last he affirms his American identity and praises the sturdiness of the "peasant" stock from which he descends: "I am one of the first Americans to arrive on these shores."

The fallacy here lies deep in the method and in the historical assumptions. We must be prepared to accept it as an expression of one sensitive Negro's response to his predicament, and perhaps as a polemical answer to condescending views of the Negro past, but we must reject it when, as in the examples I have just cited, Baldwin seems to offer the argument as truth. For our purposes it will suffice to outline the logical and historical difficulties. The method ignores, first of all, a major truth demonstrated by Melville J. Herskovits and others, that the African Negro's culture was not destroyed by the shock of enforced emigration and slavery. Moreover, as Baldwin himself seems to recognize elsewhere, the choice of genealogical identity for an American can lead (by the methods used here) to strange problems. Where do the descendants of mixed races or nations go in this atavistic game? My own children (if I may use an autobiographical example) can choose to be in their glory in Germany or Denmark or among sea-sick Protestants on the May-flower—or else among Jews in Rumania and Russia. Unless he sub-scribes to a more exclusively genetic theory of culture than he has specified, Baldwin must find it hard to believe that Western culture controls him any more than it controls millions of other Americans who have no African ancestors.

Surely the way in which Baldwin is related to Shakespeare and Dante is more important than the way an illiterate European is related to either of them—more important, too, than the way Baldwin is related to the man in Africa watching the conquerors arrive. The Bible he uses so magnificently is not someone else's Bible but his Bible, and he is not the creature but the master of the language he uses. The American Negro's past to which he calls our attention is much more complex than the demands of Baldwin's autobiographical and polemical techniques have sometimes allowed him to admit; and so is the past of American whites. It will not weaken the force of his indictment to recognize that Thomas Jeffer-son issued a warning as ominous as *The Fire Next Time* several decades before Jefferson himself liberated his slaves. Nor can we take any comfort from the knowledge that our national imper-viousness to the Negro's humanity has resisted the wit of a Ben-jamin Franklin and the eloquence of a Henry Thoreau. Baldwin, however, would honor us all without compromising himself in the slightest degree if he would accept his identity as an original Amer-ican writer whose autobiographical work has already established its place in a tradition that begins with Bradford, Woolman, Franklin, Edwards, Emerson, and Thoreau.

"It'll Be Me"

The Voice of Langston Hughes

DORIS E. ABRAMSON

ASK ANYONE TO NAME the contemporary Negro playwrights, and he will probably answer hastily and as if they were all: Lorraine Hansberry and Langston Hughes. In that order. As a playwright she is probably better known than he is, though he has been writing plays for three decades, whereas her first play is only four years old. Mr. Hughes is known first and praised highest for his poems, one of which gave Miss Hansberry the title for her play, *A Raisin in the Sun.* Both writers have been called propaganda or social protest writers. Neither seems seriously bothered by such labels, and both have had the interesting experience of receiving applause from the objects of their protest.

It is scarcely surprising that Langston Hughes is not more widely known as a playwright. Until the recent publication of his *Five Plays*[1] there was no opportunity for the American public to read his plays. Those of us who didn't see the plays when they were produced knew them only by reputation, which has always been a better way to know the critics than the plays.

Mulatto, the first play in this collection, was a Broadway success during the 1935–36 season. It ran for a year at the Vanderbilt and Ambassador, toured for eight months across the United States (though not in the South, not even in Philadelphia), and has been produced all over the world. It has been translated into Italian, Spanish, French, Portuguese, and Japanese and has been published in Milan and Buenos Aires. Now we may read this remarkable play by a too long neglected American playwright.

In his introduction, editor Webster Smalley blames the commercial nature of our theatres and publishing houses for the delay in the printing of these five plays. And he points out very sensibly that "a Negro playwright has all the woes of a white dramatist,

[1] Edited with an introduction by Webster Smalley. Bloomington: Indiana University Press, 1963.

with a number of others thrown in." Commercial theatre in America (one might just as well say Broadway) shows only occasional interest in Negro drama; little is produced and, consequently, little is published. Miss Hansberry and Mr. Hughes are among a handful (about a dozen) of Negro playwrights who have had their plays produced on Broadway since 1925. Only six of these plays have been published, two of them for the first time in this book. We are indeed indebted to the University of Indiana Press.

THAT THERE HAVE BEEN few productions of plays by Negroes in our time is not to say that history records no early plays of Negro authorship. They are few, but they are impressive both by their very existence and their reflection of the period out of which they came. The first play ever written by an American Negro was probably William Wells Brown's *Experience* or *How To Give a Northern Man a Backbone.* It was not staged, but the author read it during the year 1856 to numerous audiences in New York and Canada. In 1858, he wrote *The Escape* or *A Leap for Freedom.* The title indicates the author's concerns. He was an ex-slave, also credited with writing the first novel ever written by an American Negro. Though before and after these early attempts there were plays by white playwrights *about* Negroes—such plays as *Uncle Tom's Cabin* adapted by George Aiken (1853) and *The Octoroon* by Dion Boucicault (1859)—there was not another play of Negro authorship until 1903, when Joseph S. Cotter wrote *Caleb, the Degenerate,* a play in blank verse, taking Booker T. Washington's side in the Washington–DuBois debate.

Not until the second decade of the century was there a real interest in plays about Negro life, and they were written by non-Negro playwrights (Paul Green, Eugene O'Neill, Ridgely Torrence, Marc Connelly, and others). Langston Hughes once said to a group of Negro writers:

> Sometimes I think whites are more appreciative of our unique-
> ness than we are ourselves. The white "black" artists dealing
> in Negro material have certainly been financially more suc-
> cessful than any of us real Negroes have ever been.[2]

[2] "Writers: Black and White," *The American Negro Writer and His Roots.* Selected papers from The First Conference of Negro Writers, March, 1959. New York: The American Society of African Culture, 1960, p. 42.

These white playwrights, by their treatment of Negro themes and their attempts to destroy an earlier minstrel stereotype, did help make it possible for the Negro to come before the public in serious drama. They paved the way, no doubt inadvertently, for the "real Negroes."

Garland Anderson was the first Negro to have a play produced on Broadway; it was called *Appearances* and ran for three weeks in the 1925–26 season and for nearly five months in 1929. Though there were Negro actors in three of the seventeen roles, the Negro hero was played by a white actor. The author, who had been a bellboy in San Francisco, wrote a moralizing play that called for faith and trust in one's fellow man. He preached Washingtonian virtues in a court room melodrama.

It was not until 1929 that a Negro writer wrote a Broadway play that moved in the direction of the realistic play about Negro life. Wallace Thurman, assisted by William Rapp, wrote *Harlem,* a play about Negro New York of the twenties, complete with rent parties and racketeering. This play provided a transition from the twenties to the thirties, the period in which Negro playwrights began to speak for themselves. When they did gain access to something other than musical-comedy theatre, they were determined to write realistically, to write about Negro life as it is lived by Negroes, not as it is interpreted by white writers.

Langston Hughes made his position clear in the poem, "Notes on Commercial Theatre":

> You've done taken my blues and gone—
> Sure have! You sing 'em on Broadway,
> And you sing 'em in Hollywood Bowl.
> You mixed 'em up with symphonies,
> And you fixed 'em so they don't sound like me.
> Yep, you done taken my blues and gone!
>
> You also took my spirituals and gone.
> Now you've rocked-and-rolled 'em to death!
> You put me in *Macbeth,*
> In *Carmen Jones,* and *Anna Lucasta,*
> And all kinds of *Swing Mikados.*
> And in everything but what's about me—
> But someday somebody'll

Stand up and talk about me,
And write about me—
Black and beautiful—
And sing about me,
And put on plays about me!
I reckon it'll be me myself!

Yes, it'll be me.[3]

It has not been easy for Langston Hughes or for other Negro playwrights to get their plays produced. In a country where only a few years ago Negroes were barred even from attendance at many theatres, it has been exceedingly difficult for Negro writers to serve their necessary apprenticeship in the theatre and to get an audience for their plays. Langston Hughes has been braver (more fool-hardy?) than most of his fellow Negro playwrights. He founded two dramatic groups during the thirties: the Suitcase Theatre in Harlem and the Negro Art Theatre in Los Angeles. In 1941, he established the Skyloft Players in Chicago. "Few playwrights have the heart or energy for such undertakings," Mr. Smalley observes.

On a radio symposium in 1961—in the company of Lorraine Hansberry, James Baldwin, Alfred Kazin, and others—Langston Hughes said: "I am, of course, as everyone knows, primarily a—I guess you might even say a propaganda writer; my main material is the race problem. . . ." He also referred to his famous character Jesse B. Semple, or Simple, as a "kind of social protest mouth-piece." These statements contradict Webster Smalley's insistence that "he is an artist, not a propagandist." What a strange, unneces-sary, and impossible separation. Art that has at its center a social problem must be propaganda. Mr. Smalley correctly says Mr. Hughes is not a belligerent writer, but there is propaganda in his subtle use of humor and deflating irony.

In the plays of Negro authorship written since the 1935 produc-tion of *Mulatto*—which ran longer than any other play by a Negro until *A Raisin in the Sun* broke the record in 1959—the same problems within a problem appear repeatedly. It is not surprising. Certain problems persist in the lives of American Negroes: unem-ployment that breeds poverty and crime; racial tensions that ex-plode in riots, mob violence, lynching; poor housing, slums, the

[3] *Selected Poems.* New York: Alfred A. Knopf, 1959, p. 190.

frustrations of too many people living in one place; miscegenation and its real or imagined unhappy results; political and social evils and educational deprivations too numerous to mention—all the problems that grow out of the ghetto existence and general second-class citizenship forced upon most American Negroes. The plays reflect, with varying degrees of realism, life as lived by Negroes. This is true of plays written for the Negro Unit of the Federal Theatre Project as well as for commercial plays on and off Broadway.

Playwright Alice Childress commented at a writers' conference in 1959 on the possibility of Negro writers forsaking problems and just writing about people. She sees a difficulty, because it turns out that human beings are more than just people.

> Many of us would rather be writers than Negro writers, and when I get that urge, I look about for the kind of white writer—which is what we mean when we say 'just a writer'—that I would emulate. I come up with Sean O'Casey. Immediately, I am a problem writer. O'Casey writes about the people he knows best and I must—well, there you have it![4]

Langston Hughes, too, writes about the people he knows best. The five plays in this book are *Mulatto, Soul Gone Home, Little Ham, Simply Heavenly,* and *Tambourines to Glory.* With the exception of *Mulatto,* a tragedy of the Deep South, they are all comic folk plays with Harlem settings. Only in *Mulatto* is a white man more than a peripheral character.

Mulatto is a play about miscegenation, a subject that both titillated and confused nineteenth-century writers and continues to fascinate in our own time. The "germ idea" was contained in an earlier short story of his called "Father and Son" and even earlier and most effectively in a poem called "Cross."

> My old man's a white old man
> And my old mother's black.
> If ever I cursed my white old man
> I take my curses back.
>
> If ever I cursed my black old mother
> And wished she were in hell,

[4] First Conference of Negro Writers, 1959.

I'm sorry for that evil wish
And now I wish her well.

My old man died in a fine big house.
My ma died in a shack.
I wonder where I'm gonna die,
Being neither white nor black.

Critics of the play have called it melodramatic. (*Mulatto,* too black and white?) The stage version must have been rather sensational, with a rape scene not even in the original text (which is what has been published) and very strong performances by the whole cast. The heroine, Cora Lewis, was played by one of the greatest actresses America has produced, Rose McClendon. This was the last role she played before her untimely death in 1936.

To read *Mulatto* with a forgiving eye, as we have to read many plays of the thirties, is a good experience both emotionally and intellectually. The exposition is obvious, and there's repetition galore. But Cora's long speeches are frighteningly beautiful. (They must have made wonderful arias in the opera, "The Barrier," which was first produced in 1950, with music by Jan Meyerowitz.) Here she speaks to the dead Colonel Tom who has been murdered by their mulatto child who asked to be recognized by his own father:

He's *your* boy. His eyes is gray—like your eyes. He's tall like you's tall. He's proud like you's proud. And he's runnin'— runnin' from po' white trash that ain't worth de little finger o' nobody what's got your blood in 'em, Tom. (*Demandingly*) Why don't you get up from there and stop 'em, Colonel Tom? What's that you say? He ain't your chile? He's ma bastard chile? Ma yellow bastard chile? (*Proudly*) Yes, he's mine. . . . He's ma chile. . . . Don't you come to my bed no mo'. I calls you to help me now, and you just lays there. I calls you for to wake up, and you just lays there. Whenever you called me in de night, I woke up. When you called for me to love, I always reached out ma arms fo' you. I borned you five chilluns and now one of 'em is out yonder in de dark runnin' from yo' people. Our youngest boy out yonder in de dark runnin'. (*Accusingly*) He's runnin' from you, too. . . . You are out yonder in de dark, runnin' our child with de hounds and de gun in yo' hand. . . . Damn you, Colonel Norwood! (*Back-*

ing slowly up the stairs, staring at the rigid body below her)
Damn you, Thomas Norwood! God damn you!

This is less than half of the speech just before the curtain at the end of the last scene but one. The dialect sometimes contributes something to a mood, but often it detracts both from meaning and mood. We learn to put up with it, as we do with dialect in plays by Eugene O'Neill.

We should be grateful to be able to read this play at all. It may not be produced in the United States as often as it is abroad, but now we can read it and ponder why. It is an interesting question. Why should people in France and Spain and Japan still care about problems involving the intermingling of the races to the extent that they produce this play? Why do we not produce it? Is it that we don't care as much as they do, or has our sophistication taken us beyond this particular statement of the problem? We couldn't even begin to ask, let alone to answer, these questions before the play was published.

Soul Gone Home is one of the strangest little plays ever published anywhere. On the book jacket it is called "a fantasy of people so repressed that they can no longer afford love." That's probably true. The editor says it "bristles with implications and reverberates with connotations." Mr. Hughes told me recently that it should be played for broad comedy in order to heighten the tragedy. It gets maudlin if it is done seriously. What is this play about? A dead son comes alive long enough to berate his prostitute mother for being "a no-good mama." A strange subject for a comedy! And strangely enough it works—or one has the feeling that it could work on the stage if the director listened to Mr. Hughes and avoided any hint of sentimentality.

IT IS UNFORTUNATE that *Little Ham* and *Simply Heavenly* are placed side by side in this volume, inviting a comparison in which *Little Ham* is surely the loser. Both plays are urban folk plays in Harlem. In each the hero is a little man with big ideas and a capacity for enjoyment: Hamlet Jones and Jesse B. Semple. Hamlet is a lady's man under the spell of a fat lady named Tiny.

HAM: A sweet little woman like you's got no business at a
fight all alone by her little she-self.

TINY: Now you know I ain't little. (*Coyly*) Don't nobody like me 'cause I'm fat.

HAM: Well, don't nobody like me 'cause I'm so young and small.

TINY: You a cute little man. You mean don't *nobody* like you.

HAM: (*Woefully*) Nobody that amounts to nothin!

This kind of dialogue ripples along with what we take for authenticity, and *Little Ham* moves lightly through a Harlem of the "roaring twenties," introducing us to Madame Lucille Bell, Mattie Bea, racketeers, molls, dancers and kids and all kinds of under- and over-ground characters. The play is a pleasant experience, but it has little more depth than an old Amos 'n Andy sketch. Mr. Hughes has written better plays, one of which should have been put here in place of *Little Ham.* (My choice would have been his agitprop play, *Don't You Want To Be Free?*)

On the other hand, *Simply Heavenly* is a remarkable play about Harlem life, a comedy filled with characters who interest, instruct, transport—and please us. Only Saroyan has created a barroom to match Mr. Hughes's Paddy's Bar. It becomes as vivid a place as the Negroes who people it.

Of the hero, Jesse B. Semple, Langston Hughes has written the following:

Simple is a Chaplinesque character, slight of build, awkwardly graceful, given to flights of fancy, and positive statements of opinion—stemming from a not so positive soul. He is dark with a likeable smile, ordinarily dressed, except for rather flamboyant summer sport shirts. Simple tries hard to succeed, but the chips seldom fall just right.

Saunders Redding once spoke of "the poignant, pain-filled, pain-relieving humor of simple Jesse B." Originally a character in a play called *Simple Takes a Wife,* this little man has become a great favorite in Europe as well as in this country. He turns up in Mr. Hughes's newspaper columns ("I sit in that barber chair, thinking how God must love poor folk because he made so many of them in my image.") And in the earlier play without music as well as the current one with music. His opinions are being heard all over the world. *Simple Takes a Wife* has been done only abroad and is in the repertory at Prague, where it was originally produced in 1961. In that year, Mr. Hughes had this to say about the universality of Simple:

> . . . a regional Negro character like Simple, a character intended for the people who belong to his own race, if written about warmly enough, humanly enough, can achieve universality.[5]

The temptation for a reviewer is to quote great chunks of dialogue from *Simply Heavenly,* for this is a delightful play with a message, a play filled with the rich dialogue of Harlemites who make their lives bearable through humor and affection for one another. Kierkegaard has said somewhere that the more one suffers the more one has a sense for the comic. He speaks of people who have suffered deepest having "true authority in the use of the comic, an authority by which one word transforms as by magic the reasonable creature one calls man into a caricature." Langston Hughes has that authority and in this good sense of the word Simple and his friends are caricatures.

Mamie, an unforgettable woman, has to answer the charge of being a stereotype when she feels the need to defend her tastes in the presence of a "passer," a pretender:

> Why, it's getting so colored folks can't do nothing no more without some other Negro calling you a stereotype, hah! If you like a little gin, you're a stereotype. You got to drink Scotch. If you wear a red dress, you're a stereotype. You got to wear beige or chartreuse. Lord have mercy, honey, do-don't like no blackeyed peas and rice! Then you're a down-home Negro for true—which I is—and proud of it! I didn't come here to Harlem to get away from my people. I come here because there's more of 'em. I loves my race: I loves my people. Stereotype!

The play is bursting with comments, sometimes a bit too obviously.

> SIMPLE: This great big old white ocean—and me a colored swimmer.
>
> BOYD: Aw, stop feeling sorry for your self just because you're colored. You can't use race as an excuse forever. All men have problems. And even if you are colored, you've got

[5] "The Negro in American Culture," WBAI-FM, New York City.

to swim beyond color, and get to that island that is you—
the human you, the man you.

This kind of preaching will bother some readers. But even those
who have an aversion to messages will chuckle at Simple's dream
of leading white Mississippi troops into action in World War III.
They will chuckle, they will wonder, and Mr. Hughes will have
made his point.

Tambourines to Glory, the last play in this collection, is characterized by the editor as a "musical melodrama about some aspects
of Harlem religion." As a play, greatly helped by the songs, it is far
more effective than Mr. Hughes's novel of the same name. Perhaps
the best way to sum up the author's viewpoint in the play is to
quote his own description of it quoted in the Introduction to *Five
Plays:*

> *Tambourines to Glory* is a fable, a folk ballad in stage form,
> told in broad and very simple terms—if you will, a comic
> strip, a cartoon—about problems which can only convincingly
> be reduced to a comic strip if presented very cleanly, clearly,
> sharply, precisely, and with humor.

There is something intriguing about a writer who knows that
the form he has chosen for his work will be right if the presentation of the piece is as honest on stage as his writing was originally.
Langston Hughes, like Bertolt Brecht, writes for the theatre as a
knowledgeable man of the theatre. *Tambourines to Glory* comes
alive on the page; you can hear it.

In this play two women, Laura and Essie, start a church. In Harlem it is quite possible to "set up shop" in an old store, a movie
theatre, any little corner where the faithful poor may gather. In
1930 James Weldon Johnson noted that there were one hundred
and sixty Negro churches in Harlem and that one hundred of
them were "ephemeral and nomadic, belonging to no established
domination and within no classification."[6] There must be many
more by now. Mr. Hughes himself has said that it is difficult to
find a suitable location for a theatre in Harlem, because when the
movie houses go out of business they are bought up by "churches."
Laura and Essie, who start on a street corner, convert an old movie
house into Tambourine Temple.

[6] *Black Manhattan* (New York: Alfred A. Knopf, 1930), p. 163.

Essie is sincere. Laura is a charlatan. Good works with evil to the glory of God ultimately. The devil is in the guise, this time, of Big-Eyed Buddy Lomax, a handsome hustler in the employ of white gangsters. The plot is the least effective thing about the play and does not bear telling. What is impressive is the skillful use of songs to heighten emotional scenes, and the characterizations, especially of the two leading ladies and the devil himself. Mr. Hughes shows sympathy, even pity, for all the participants in this story of hokum and holiness.

Buddy says, "This church racket's got show business beat to hell. But some churches don't have sense enough to be crooked. They really try to be holy—and holiness don't make money." It is the good Essie, however, who wins in the end—at least of this play.

Webster Smalley's introduction is as informative as it is lauda-tory. He gives us a good idea of how productive Langston Hughes —poet, playwright, novelist, short story writer—has been and refers to him as "America's outstanding Negro man of letters." It would seem necessary to qualify that praise since James Baldwin has appeared on the scene. Mr. Hughes, however, is an impressive writer, and this collection of plays gives us a chance to know an important side of his work for the first time. He is still, it seems to me, a better poet than playwright, another reason why *Don't You Want To Be Free?* should appear in print soon; for in that play he uses some of his verses effectively within the framework of a play.

Negro playwrights are scarce at the moment, but they are more than promising: Lorraine Hansberry, Alice Childress, Ossie Davis, Loften Mitchell, William Branch, and James Baldwin, to name most of the handful. They will, no doubt, write out of their experi-ences as Negroes; and they will create white characters, because the time has come for them to let us see ourselves through their art.

It is not likely that Langston Hughes will write about white men —unless they wander into Harlem. Harlem is his home, and he records for us the speech and the dreams, the agonies and the compensating joys alive in that city within a city. We are grateful for his plays and for his wise, warm sense of humor. This book should be only a beginning; his other plays and those of younger Negro playwrights should be made available to us soon.

Mr. William Styron and the Reverend Turner

MIKE THELWELL

W E KNOW WITHIN certain general and stable (though they appear to be constantly expanding) boundaries what a novel is. We know also what a historical novel is, and the terms by which such works can be judged. But when a work of fiction is cast in the form of a novel, utilizes those techniques of narrative, situation, and structure that we associate with the novel, and which concerns an important historical event, but is declared to be "less an historical novel in conventional terms than a meditation on history," then what are we to make of it? Is its historicity more or less important than its meditativeness?

William Styron's *The Confessions of Nat Turner* straddles two genres, claims to be not quite either, and manages to combine the problems of both while to an extent reaping dual dividends as a novel which is in some way also "history." If the book were simply a novel, then there are things that could be said about its structure, characterizations, and language. But how is one to judge the proper and appropriate language of meditation? If it were simply history, then we would point to certain violations of the rules for reconstructing history, and point out that, on the face of any objective reconstruction of the evidence, it could not have been how the book says it was.

The fanfare with which the book has been greeted is largely based on the duality of its claims. It is hailed as a major novel with a significant theme. As a work which recreates and significantly illumines a morally traumatic portion of the American past, it is held, *ipso facto,* to contribute to our awareness of ourselves and our subconscious postures toward present realities. In this context the work becomes a page in that sacred journal that marks the peculiarly American quest to master the truth of our past in a quest for historical and spiritual authenticity. This is doubtlessly an honorable and valid undertaking, but one which borders on absurdity on many sides. It is perhaps a function of this absurdity that I find myself writing in defense of a black rebel, dead since 1831, related to me neither by blood nor obligation, and whose shades, I suspect, have little concern with judgments of posterity as expressed through the person of Mr. Styron.

But my concern is less with the Reverend Turner's memory than it is with the future of his grandchildren—to whom he used to be a hero. And it is reasonably clear—if the notices with which the book was greeted mean anything at all—that Mr. Styron's book is being read as a kind of super historical novel by a public seeking what it seeks in all of its reading, the shock of mildly pleasurable outrage and, incidentally, information and insight.

Because the book is both "historical" and a "novel," a section of the public will invest it with qualities it does not necessarily possess. The facts and situations will be assumed to be accurate because by being "historical" it must of necessity be "true." And just as the facts of history are "true," so are, in a somewhat different sense, the insights of the novel. This is the great advantage of the form. By simulating a cosmos, its terms appear sufficient unto itself, its boundaries definitive and discrete, so that no further possibilities, no moral or philosophical dimensions, other than those existing within those boundaries, seem relevant to that cosmos. It is true, as Negroes are increasingly discovering, that what is excluded by historians is frequently as important as what they choose to record. This must be doubly true of the novel because of the cloak of self-containment which it wears, so that what is an extremely selective process takes on the illusory dimensions of being "the experience." So a book which according to its publishers "reveals in unforgettable human terms the agonizing *essence* of Negro slavery" can certainly be held accountable for what it selects and what it chooses to ignore. It is a solemn and rather prosaic truth that one cannot approach the essence by ignoring the *substance,* either in literature or in the laboratory. For an example, if it were true, or even suggested by the evidence—and this is not the case—that Nat Turner's first nineteen years were spent as a privileged and pampered house slave, favored (beyond all belief) by an ineffectually well-intentioned (beyond all belief) old master of vaguely liberal bent, this would be neither the essence nor substance of the experience of slavery. The substance of that experience, as we well know, was the deadening accumulation of event, the experience of the slave ship, the auction block, the torture of body and spirit, undernourishment, overwork, the violation of spirit and body, the deprivation of a culture, of language, and the overwhelming presence of the apparatus of white power, that is to say the power to coerce, to mutilate, and ultimately arbitrarily to kill. That, it seems to me, is the substance of reality out of which any "essence of Negro slavery" must be distilled. Those are the realities that have conditioned our present situation for both whites and blacks.

Despite the necessary secondary tasks which Styron undertakes in this book, i.e., the fleshing out of various contemporary positions on "the question," the evocation of a historical period, the reconstruction of a culture inherently morally schizophrenic, and so on, the theme of the novel, the central mystery that engages us and clamors for insight, is the personality and motivation of Nat Turner and the determined and desperate band of men who fought and died with him.

It is in this context that the questions which so plague our time become relevant. The question of the moral imperatives and consequences of violent rebellion, of its spiritual and political implications, the existential confrontation with the act of murder, and particularly the exquisitely painful responsibility of the instigator, who not only for himself must choose to resist—that is, to take the irrevocable step—but to be responsible for his followers taking it also. This is the ultimate revolutionary responsibility, and requires a certainty that approaches either love turned to desperation or madness. Styron's Nat Turner, in marked contrast to the historical Nat, has neither; lacking ideology or even the fervor of a prophetic fanaticism, he has only a pallid and unconvincing neurosis. It is perhaps, as one critic has proclaimed, that "only a white southerner could have written this book," this particular book. It is equally true that only a writer who is imaginatively familiar with the agonies of oppression and the morally convoluted dimensions of rebellion and who is in some measure liberated from that experience can do justice to this theme. Mr. Styron is not such a writer.

In selecting the subject and the strategy for this novel, Styron took certain calculated risks. In doing so—and one must assume a full awareness of the purely technical and creative problems they represented—he displays a *chutzpah* which borders on arrogance. First, by selecting Turner, Styron chose a personality with a reality in history, caught up in actual events, within a specific historical situation, about which and whom some facts are known. By so doing Styron placed on his creative imagination the responsibility of working within the facts and events as we know them. This he has not done, and his failure is at once significant and revealing.

Then, by deciding to render the novel through the mind, voice, and consciousness of Nat Turner, he undertook the challenge that finally ruined the book. Assume for a moment that a white Southern gentleman could, by some alchemy of the consciousness, tune in on the mind-set, thought-pattern, impulses, feelings and beliefs of a black slave in 1831. Having accomplished this miracle of empathy, since they lack common language or experience, he will still have the problem of creating a *literary* idiom in which to report his insights to his contemporaries. And as the linguists are discovering, and novelists have always known, language is not only a medium of communication, but also helps shape and express consciousness. It not only functions to formulate attitudes but to create them, it not only describes experience but colors the perception of it, so that dialects and idioms are evolved by people to serve the necessities of their experience. This is one reason why people in Harlem do not speak like people in Bucks County.

When black people were brought here they were deprived of their language, and of the underpinnings in cultural experience out of which that language comes. It is clear that they replaced it with two languages, one for themselves and another for the white masters. It is this latter that has been preserved, parodied is a better word, as the "Sambo" dialect in the works of Southern dialect humorists (even Samuel Clemens at times)—to whom it was often simply quaint and humorous. The only vestiges we have of the real language of the slaves is in those spirituals which have survived. Mere vestiges though they are, most spirituals give a clue to the true tenor of that language. It is a language of conspiracy and disguised meaning, of pointed irony and sharp metaphor. It is a language produced by oppression, but whose central impulse is survival and resistance. It is undoubtedly the language in which Turner's rebellion and the countless other plots for insurrection were formulated. Anyone who has been privileged to catch the performance of a good black preacher in the rural South (or Martin Luther King talking to a black audience) understands something of the range and flexibility of this language. Lacking complicated syntactical structure and vast vocabulary, it depends on what linguists call para-language, that is gesture, physical expression, and modulation of cadences and intonation which serve to change the meaning—in incredibly subtle ways—of the same collection of words. It is intensely poetic and expressive since vivid simile and a creative juxtaposition of images and metaphor must serve (instead of a large vocabulary) to cause the audience to see and feel. It is undoubtedly a language of action rather than a language of reflection, and is as such more easily available to the dramatist than the novelist. Nevertheless it is some literary approximation of this language that the characterization of Nat Turner requires. And Mr. Styron's Nat speaks or rather meditates in (as Spenser is said to have written in) no language at all. His creator places in his mouth a sterile and leaden prose that not even sizeable transfusions of Old Testament rhetoric can vitalize. It is a strange fusion of Latinate classicism, a kind of Episcopalian prissiness, and Faulkner at his least inspired. At times it would seem that Mr. Styron was trying, for whatever reason, to imitate the stodgy "official" prose of the nineteenth-century lawyer who recorded the original confessions. At other times Nat sounds like nothing so much as a conscious parody of the prose voice of James Baldwin, the Negro Mr. Styron knows best. This is not to say that the prose is not lucid, even elegant in a baroque Victorian way, especially in the functionally inexplicable passages of nature writing that continuously interrupt the narrative. But finally it is the language of the essay, heavy and declarative. It does not live.

This language combines with the structure of the novel to disastrous effect. Since the story begins after the fact, with Nat already in prison reflecting on his life, much of the book is in the form of long unbroken monologues, insulated in an inert prose. Even the most violent action or intensely felt experience seems distanced and without immediacy, strangely lumpen. Lacking the allusiveness of thought or the vitality of speech, and the quality of dynamic tension necessary to the illusion of the immediacy of the experience, the language reduces us to spectators rather than participants in the action.

Because the problem of language is inextricably caught up in the problem of consciousness, Styron's inability to solve this problem (and it may well be insoluble) is symbolic of, and operative in, his failure to bridge the gap of consciousness.

Nat Turner operates in this novel with a "white" language and a white consciousness. His descriptions of his fellow-slaves, for example, are not in the language of a man talking about his friends and family; they reveal, rather, the detailed racial emphasis best exemplified by slave-auction advertisements, or the pseudo-anthropological reports sent back from Africa by white missionaries in the nineteenth century. Lacking the idiom in which Nat might communicate intimately with his peers, and apparently any meaningful insight into what they might say to each other, Styron simply avoids this problem by having him spend most of his time in that paradoxically Southern situation, close to but isolated from whites. This isolation in proximity becomes his obsession. And as his language is theirs, so are his values and desires. Styron's Nat Turner, the house nigger, is certainly not the emotional or psychological prototype of the rebellious slave; he is the spiritual ancestor of the contemporary middle-class Negro, that is to say the Negro type with whom whites and obviously Mr. Styron feel most comfortable.

Conspicuously intelligent—in their terms—he aspires hopelessly to the culture and stature of his white masters, to break his isolation by being recognized on their terms. Witness his ecstatic joy when he is able to spell a word, thereby demonstrating his intelligence to his master's guests. Naturally, to Mr. Styron, and his white audience, he must despise and hold in contempt the society of his own people whom he considers dumb, mindless, unsalvageable brutes unfitted either for freedom or salvation. Hating the blackness which limits the possibilities which he feels should be his by right of intelligence and accomplishment he becomes a schizoid nigger-baiter. That the speaker is supposed to be black merely obscures the issue. In the historical context it is impossible to imagine Nat Turner, a minister to his people, teacher, and above all, a venerated leader, displaying the kind of total alienation and contempt inherent in the following:

> A mob of Negroes from the cabins were trooping towards
> the house. Muffled against the cold in the coarse and shapeless,
> yet decent, winter garments Marse Samuel provided for them.
> . . . I could hear the babble of their voices filled with Christ-

mas anticipation and loutish nigger cheer. The sight of them suddenly touched me with a loathing so intense that I was filled with disgust, belly sickness, and I turned my eyes away.

What this Nat Turner really wants is to become white, and failing that, to integrate. This is the Negro whom whites, in the smug, near-sighted chauvinism of their cultural and ethnic superiority, can understand. As a type it certainly exists *today;* 1831 is a different question. What is wrong with this characterization as applied to Nat Turner is simply that it has sprung full-blown out of Mr. Styron's fantasies. It does not logically derive from those facts of Turner's life that have come down to us. Indeed, to develop this characterization, not only did Mr. Styron have to ignore portions of this meager record, but he had to distort, in significant ways, many of the portions he did use.

In an author's note at the beginning of the novel, Mr. Styron says that he has "rarely departed from the *known* facts about Nat Turner and the revolt of which he was the leader." "However," he continues, "in those areas where there is little knowledge in regard to Nat . . . I have allowed myself the utmost freedom of imagination in reconstructing events—yet I trust remaining within the bounds of what meager enlightenment history has left us about the institution of slavery."

One can only assume from this note that the author intends us to regard this novel in a certain way. We must assume that it is an unbiased reconstruction of the events and probable motivations for the Nat Turner rebellion, true to the available facts. Where facts and events are missing, they are imaginatively supplied, carefully based on the logical extension of what is known. By virtue of this claim and the book's being titled *The Confessions of Nat Turner,* thereby tying it to the event, we are led to expect the greatest possible dispassionate, unprejudicial objectivity and accuracy. It is with these minimum expectations that we approach the book, and they must affect how we react to it, and ultimately our attitudes to the subject it illumines. While we cannot realistically expect the novel to escape the influence of the author's private vision, his unique and subjective sensibilities and attitudes, we do expect it to be free of any kind of special pleading, fact-juggling, unsupported theorizing, and interpretations which answer not to the facts or logic of the events, but to an intellectual commitment to a version of history which is not only debatable but under serious question. We do not expect these specious qualities, because they are patently not the terms on which this work is presented to us. Yet Mr. Styron falls victim to all. If Mr. Styron presents his terms in good faith, we must conclude that he was betrayed by his own unconscious attitudes towards slavery, black people, and his ancestors whose myths, prejudices, and self-delusions are faithfully preserved in what must be one of the most touching examples of ancestral reverence outside oriental literature.

The primary source of information, of "known facts," is extremely brief, about four thousand words.[1] Why was it necessary, in this objective reconstruction, to depart from this source? In Nat's confession his formative years are deeply rooted in his family and within the slave society. His mother and father placed his first book in his hands and encouraged him in his efforts to read. His grandmother, to whom he claims to have been very attached, gave him religious instruction and predicted that he was too intellectually curious and intelligent to make a tractable slave. He taught himself reading and writing, and successfully deduced ways to make gunpowder and paper, being limited in these enterprises only by "the lack of means." The white lawyer who took his confession interrogated him about these processes and reports that he was "well-informed on the subject." From an early age, says Nat, he enjoyed the confidence of the "Negroes of the neighborhood," who would take him on their stealing expeditions to plan for them. What emerges from this is that Nat's character and attitudes in his formative years were molded by his family and peers. He becomes a leader and a plotter very early, and is involved with his black brothers in the clandestine resistance to slavery symbolized by stealing. Later he becomes a preacher, that is, a leader and a minister among the slaves. When he stops fraternizing with his peers, it is not out of any disdain or contempt, but for the very good political reason that "having soon discovered to be great, I must appear so, and therefore studiously avoided mixing in *society,* and wrapped myself in mystery."

It is Mr. Styron's inability or unwillingness to deal with the notion of a slave "society"—the presence of a black culture, that is, a system of social organization and modes of collective response—

[1] Gray's "Confessions of Nat Turner," reprinted in Herbert Aptheker, *Nat Turner's Rebellion* (New York, 1966).

with its own values, leaders, and rules, that more than anything else robs the novel of credibility. Because he cannot deal in convincing terms with the "culture" of slavery which produced and shaped Nat Turner, Styron, in contempt for the "known facts," simply isolates Turner from the blacks, places him among the whites, and attempts to create from that situation convincing motives and stimuli for his actions. If the case, historically, had been as Styron reconstructs it, it is difficult to imagine that a single slave would have followed Turner.

In Mr. Styron's "free ranging imagination," Nat's formative years are somewhat different. He has no knowledge of his father. His grandmother, a mute, catatonic, culturally shocked Corromantee wench, barely survives to give birth to his mother after disembarking from the slave ship. Nat's master, who is only mentioned once in his original confession, and then to say only that he was "religious," is elevated by Styron to be the major influence on Nat's life. Discovering Nat with a book stolen from his library (an occasion of great surprise since no nigger ever expressed interest in literacy), he has Nat tutored by his own daughter. Nat becomes a favorite, does light work around the great house, and observes the elegance, enlightenment, and moral superiority of his owners and strives to emulate and impress them. He feels superior to all other "niggers." Of his kindly and benevolent Master Nat reports,

> . . . I hold him in such awe, that I am forced to regard him physically as well as spiritually, in terms of such patriarchal and spiritual grandeur that glows forth from Moses on the mount. . . .

Such awe, indeed, that in his version rather than Styron's he is leading his fellow slaves in raiding his property.

This venerable patriarch is, as Styron is careful to report, educating Nat as an experiment to prove that Negroes are educable. After which presumably he will personally build schools and free them all since he feels that "it is evil to keep these people in slavery, yet they cannot be freed. They must be educated. To free these people without education with the prejudice that exists would be a ghastly crime."

Indeed, Marse Samuel does in due course reveal to Nat that, having educated him, he intends to free him. This contingency terrifies Nat, literate paragon among slaves though he is, since he simply is unable to conceive of assuming responsibility for himself. The wise and kindly master had however, anticipated this insecurity and reassures Nat that he has devised a method to give him his freedom gradually, under his kind and paternalistic guidance. Nat is satisfied. (No explanation—except that time passes—is given in the novel of the process by which Nat moves from this abject dependence to the self-confidence that will allow him to accept responsibility for a colony of free rebels that it was his intention to start in the Dismal Swamps.)

This response (Please good Massa, dis yer Darkie ain't studyin' no freedom) is, of course, one of the favorite clichés coming to us from a certain school of plantation melodrama. Its inclusion here violates the evidence of history. This is not to say that it had no basis in reality, but there were other realities which are not shown. In order to make this response credible in Nat (remember he is the most intelligent and enlightened of any slave shown), Styron includes an image of "The Freed Slave" who is starving, confused, and totally incapable of surviving, and presumably this wretch, who is clearly worse off than the slaves, represents Nat's only experience or knowledge of freedom. This is misleading, since the fact is that every Southern community and many Northern ones had free Negroes, and at times whole colonies of them. These freemen worked as skilled artisans in many instances; some, to their discredit, even owned slaves. What is important here is that both masters and slaves knew this, and for the slaves these free Negroes represented a constant inspiration. What then is the purpose of this fanciful episode concerning Marse Samuel's plantation, Nat's fear of freedom, and the desperate straits of "The Freed Slave"?

The first figure is familiar: the gracious, courtly, humane, landed Virginia gentleman, wracked by conscience, solicitous of his chattel, and obligated by conscience to take care of his slaves who could not survive on their own. For him slavery is not a financial operation, it is the exercise of a moral obligation. (The example of the freed slave proves this.) His home, in which the First Families of Virginia "with names like Byrd, and Clarke" gather in elaborate carriages, rivals Tara in its gentility, charm, and benevolence. This is the Golden Age of Southern Chivalry, and what is being reconstructed for us is the enlightened benevolence of the "Old Dominion" version of slavery, surely the least oppressive serfdom in mankind's history. This only applies, as Mr. Styron is careful to indicate, to slaves fortunate enough to be owned by the enlightened gentry; it is the poor white overseers and small landholders who made the lot of slaves unendurable. Surely we have some right to expect serious novelists in 1967 to eschew this kind of fanciful nonsense? Especially if we know that it is precisely on these large Virginia plantations that the most degrading and debasing form of slavery was developed. Even as early as the 1830's, the Virginia land being increasingly exhausted by tobacco, these enlightened aristocrats had begun converting their plantations to breeding farms—that is to say, the business of breeding black men and women like animals for the purpose of supplying the labor markets of the Deep South. That's one reality which is only fleetingly mentioned in this novel.[2]

In Marse Samuel's great house, Nat becomes "a pet, the little black jewel of Turner's Mill. Pampered, fondled, nudged, pinched, I was the household's spoiled child." Enjoying great leisure, he is enabled to lurk around for "a rare glimpse, face to face, of the pure, proud, astonishing, smooth-skinned beauty," of Miss Emmaline, one of the daughters of the household. It is clear that we are to be rewarded with some psychological insight into the emotional development of the young slave, and we are not disappointed. Nat, in his words, grows to "worship" Miss Emmaline, she who "moves with the proud serenity . . . which was good and pure in itself, like the disembodied, transparent beauty of an imagined angel," with a "virginal passion." For angels, what else?

Imagine then, the trauma of the poor youth who is raised in "surroundings where white ladies seemed to float like bubbles in an immaculate effulgence of purity and perfection" when he finds Miss Emmaline rutting with her cousin on the lawn and in her passion blaspheming God's name. When, having apparently enjoyed the act, she rushes with the inevitable "rustle of taffeta" into the house, she carries with her Nat's innocence and faith.

But for Nat, the experience, shattering as we are asked to believe it is, constitutes a form of emancipation. He had long rejected as too common the idea of sex with black wenches and substituted for

[2] In 1837, the Old Dominion exported to the death camps of the Deep South 40,000 black bodies for a net income of twenty-four million dollars.

it onanistic fantasies with faceless white women.[3] After his "Angel's" fall from grace, he says ". . . in my fantasies she began to replace the innocent imaginary girl with the golden curls as the object of my craving, and on those Saturdays when I stole into my private place in the carpenter shop to relieve my pent-up desires, it was Miss Emmaline whose bare, white full round hips and belly responded wildly to my lust and who . . . allowed me to partake of all the wicked and Godless yet unutterable joys of defilement." Well, after all, that is what comes of all that "fondling, petting, and pinching." Nat becomes an inverted, frustrated, onanistic, emotionally short-circuited lecher after white women. Presumably, if he had given way to this secret lust and raped the white girl he is later to murder, the rebellion would never have occurred. The horror of this experience would probably have driven the young girl insane (almost a moral obligation for her in this tradition of southern literature) but some fifty-five white and two hundred black lives would have been saved. This moonlight, magnolia, and Freud view of history is presented as the basic motivation for the rebellion, a sexual desire (or love if you will) turned malignant in frustration.[4] Even if it did not come dangerously close

[3] There is some indication that the historical Nat, rather than being contemptuous of black women, was either married to one, or at least was the father of several children. Mr. Styron, chose to discount this for several reasons. In the magazine *Per Se* (Summer, 1966) he explains one of these reasons. "He was enormously unusual. He was an educated slave, and a man even of some refinement in a curious way. A man of that sort, I think, in a deep part of his heart would scorn the average, pathetic, illiterate colored woman, slave woman." It is unfortunate for the black woman of this country that Mr. Styron's ancestors, who were beating paths to the slave quarters after dark, were not of Turner's "refinement." This insult to black womanhood (wittingly or unwittingly) is an example of the kind of assumptions which underlie the novel.

[4] To have this thesis seriously put forward is astonishing, and would be laughable if it were not for the easy acceptance that white reviewers have accorded it. It was, Mr. Styron tells us, suggested to him by the fact that the only murder that Turner admits to in his confession is that of a white girl. This is Styron's sole "evidence" for such a view. Along with millions of other Americans, we get another insight into Nat's character, here from the supremely authoritative and anonymous critic of *Time* magazine: "Nat must have been what the book makes of him . . . spoiled by the sweet taste of humanity some of his masters allowed. 'I will say this, without which you cannot understand the central madness of nigger existence,' he

to reiterating the infuriating sexual slander of the Negro male that is the stock-in-trade of the American racist, it would still be unacceptable as a theory of Turner's motives, because this kind of frustration-neurosis expresses itself in solitary, suicidal acts of violence, not in planned, public, political acts of rebellion.

THE SPARE FACTS of Turner's life constitute grounds for a truly fascinating and illuminating mediation. Certainly more useful insight into Nat Turner's character and motives are to be achieved in the effort to reconstruct what it must have been like for the youth growing up in the influence of his family—two parents and a grandmother, his reacting to them and their attitudes towards slavery, his response to his father's running off, his early leadership in the stealing expeditions, his call to the ministry (while ploughing, not serving mint juleps) and his position among his fellows. Surely it is from these experiences that his personality and mission evolved.

Turner tells us, through Gray's, not Styron's, "Confessions," that as he grew to young manhood, the memory of what had been said about him as a child by "white and black"—that he would never be of use to anyone as a slave—began to obsess him, "finding I had arrived to man's estate and was a slave." But he says he is consoled by the spirit of prophecy which indicates to him that there is a preordained role for him in that position. He begins his ministry and continually exhorts his people who "believed and said my wisdom came from God." He obviously occupies a place of some importance among them on his own merit, not from being the favorite of a paternalistic master. That he is a man of charisma and magnetism is evident. He seems totally preoccupied with his God and his people and the only mention of any white person at this time is of an overseer from whom he runs away and is at large for thirty days. He returns voluntarily because the Spirit orders him

[Turner] explains, 'beat a nigger, starve him, leave him wallowing and he will be yours for life. Leave him with some unforeseen hint of philanthropy, tickle him with the idea of hope and he will want to slice your throat.'"
This hodge-podge of cliché, stereotype, and *True Confessions* psychology would be disappointing from a novelist of Mr. Styron's accomplishment, whatever the context. To have it accepted and disseminated as wisdom and insight is simply too much.

to return to his "mission," the exact nature of which he does not yet know. Upon his return the "negroes were astonished and murmured against me, saying that if they had my sense they would not serve any master in the world." This incident either did not impress Mr. Styron enough to be included, or else was at odds with his "interpretation." For one thing their unequivocal condemnation of Turner for returning establishes his peers' attitudes towards slavery, and it is different from the one generally found in the book. This is, significantly, one of the few cases on record of any slave returning voluntarily to slavery. What did it mean? Did Turner return out of a sense of solidarity with his black brothers, out of a sense of divine mission? Was it simply another case of nostalgia for the irresponsible security of slavery, did he get hungry? Subsequent events, and his own explanation, suggest some glimmering of a deliberate motive.

His given reason (at the time) for returning must stand as a masterpiece of irony. He simply quotes one of the Biblical texts best loved by slave owners: "he that knoweth his master's will and does not do it, shall be beaten with many stripes and flogged with a rod." To the slave master this must have been gratifying indeed, evidence further of the faithful darky well steeped in the acceptable slave morality. To Nat, knowing that his master is God, a terrible, vengeful God, who has selected him for a "mission," it meant quite something else. He may even have undertaken the episode simply to establish his trustworthiness, thereby getting the necessary mobility to organize.

Let us examine how this omission serves the "interpretation" presented in the novel. While the historical Turner is trying to regain the confidence of his fellows, who are angry, incredulous, and suspicious at the idea of a man returning voluntarily to slavery, Styron's Nat Turner is fuming and fulminating endlessly at the spiritless subservience and servility of his fellow slaves who are presented as totally lacking in the will or imagination to change their condition. There can be no question that "Uncle Toms" existed, but it is also equally clear that these types and the attitudes they represented were seized upon by apologists for the institution and publicized and exaggerated, out of all proportion, while militance and rebelliousness were played down. Who can doubt this after hearing any contemporary Southern sheriff mouthing his eternal platitude, "our niggers are happy"? History testifies that the desire for freedom among the slaves was a constant problem to their owners.[5]

The reality of slavery was that the slaves were constantly resisting and rebelling, whether by sabotage, malingering, escape to the north, physical retaliation to attack, plotting insurrection (with a frequency that caused the masters to live in a state of constant apprehension and under conditions of continual vigilance and security), running off to join Indian tribes, or else to form small bands of armed guerrillas operating out of swamps and remote areas. It is difficult to imagine why, if the majority of slaves were inner "sambos," broken in mind and spirit as Styron's Nat suggests, Southern governors filled the official record with so many requests for federal troops to guard against insurrection. Why were meetings of slaves forbidden or so severely proscribed? Why were they required to have passes permitting them to use the roads? Why were curfews so rigidly maintained? Why were armed patrols abroad in every slave community at night? Why were firearms considered a necessary part of the overseer's equipment? Is it perhaps because the "Sambo" type was the product of "enlightened" Virginian slavery that no suggestion of this massive machinery of coercion and control is found in the novel? What does its absence do to the "essence of the experience of slavery" that the publishers boast about? It is rather like trying to capture the experience of the Nazi concentration camps without mentioning the barbed wire or armed guards.

Two examples of incidents reported in the original "Confessions" and transformed by Mr. Styron's imagination are worthy of mention, as they are indicative of the pattern of interpretation that runs through the book. Turner tells of converting and baptizing a white man, an event unprecedented in Tidewater, Virginia, of the time, and which would probably cause an equally great furor were it to happen today. The two men are refused access to the church and repair to the river for the ceremony, where they are mocked and threatened by a white crowd.

In Styron's version, the white convert is a drunken, degenerate, child-molesting pederast who is about to be run out of the county anyway, and is shown as the typical sub-human, white trash "cracker" that one might find in Erskine Caldwell. Again the logic

[5] For the testimony of slaves, see B. A. Botkin, ed., *A Folk History of Slavery* (New York, 1962).

dictating such an interpretation is not clear, but this is what happens in this novel to the only white who is shown associating with slaves on anything that looks like simple human terms, outside of the paternalism and implied superiority of the social categories of the time.

The second instance of arbitrary and derogatory "interpretation" concerns a slave called Will, who invited himself to join the insurrection. He is different from the other conspirators by virtue of this fact: Will was not recruited, he volunteered. In the original confession Turner reports finding Will among his men when he joins them on the day of the insurrection.

> I asked Will how he came to be there, and he answered his
> life was worth no more than others, and his liberty as dear.
> I asked him if he thought to obtain it? He said he would or
> lose his life. This was enough to put him in full confidence.

In the subsequent violence Will is identified specifically as "dispatching" a number of people, while most of the other murders are not attributed to members of the band. The most that can be said of Turner's references to Will is that they show him operating with a single-minded efficiency in carrying out the work at hand, which is, after all, the extermination of whites. In the context of Turner's narrative there is no suggestion of dementia or frenzy in Will's actions; like Joshua, he is simply engaged in the destruction of the Lord's enemies. There is one probable explanation for Turner's specific references to Will other than his being particularly impressed by his murderous efficiency. This is simply that Will, being the last of the original band recruited, may have felt it necessary to stay close to the leader so as to demonstrate his sincerity, thus causing Turner to remember his actions more vividly than others in the group.

In the novel, Nat sees "the demented, hate-ravished, mashed-in face . . ." whose "wooly head was filled with cockleburrs. A scar glistens on his black cheek, shiny as an eel cast up on a mud-bank. I felt that if I could reach out I could almost touch with my fingertips the madness stirring within him, a shaggy brute heaving beneath the carapace of a black skin." Will is "streaked with mud, stinking, fangs bared beneath a nose stepped upon and bent like a flattened spoon." His eyes shine "with a malign fire" and he bears a hatred "to all mankind, all creation." We learn that Will has been reduced to this condition of bestiality by the unendurable cruelties of a sadistic master so that his is not the "natural depravity" that another generation of Southern writers would have evoked. But even so, this characterization, this portrait of an evolutionary marvel, half-nigger, half-beast, is surely familiar to anyone who knows such classics of Southern literature as Dixon's *The Klansman*. His has been a long history. He has been constantly and conveniently evoked for any number of purposes, to frighten children with or to justify lynchings. And as he sidles into the scene, stinking and licking his fangs, we recognize his function: like the others of his type who have preceded him, he will rape a white woman. And thirty pages later, despite Nat's injunctions against rape (no sexual incidents are mentioned in the record of the trial), an injunction all the nobler in light of his own perennial, frustrated cravings, we find this scene:

> There deserted of all save those two acting out their final tableau—the tar black man and the woman, bone-white, bone rigid with fear beyond telling, pressed urgently together against the door in a simulacrum of shattered oneness and heartsick farewell. . . .

and it looks as if Nigger-beast has struck again. One had hoped that this particular stereotype had served his time in the pages of Southern fiction and could now be laid to rest. It is, to say the least, disappointing to see him resurrected by a writer of Mr. Styron's unquestioned sophistication—and to what purpose?[6]

[6] William Wells Brown, a Negro whose book on the Negro in the American Revolution appeared in 1867, mentions the Nat Turner rebellion. His version does not in any way contradict the meager record that is the original "Confessions," but it adds information not included. One may speculate as to the source of this information—possibly newspaper accounts of the time, or the testimony of black survivors of the incident—but the account is of interest, representing as it does an early account of the insurrection by a black man. About Will, Brown has this to say: "Among those who joined the conspirators was Will, a slave who scorned the idea of taking his master's name. Though his soul longed to be free, he evidently became one of the party as much to satisfy revenge as for the liberty he saw in the dim future . . . His own back was covered with scars from his shoulders to his feet. A large scar running from his right eye down to his chin showed that he had lived with a cruel master. Nearly six feet in height and one of the strongest and most athletic of his race, he proved to be one of the most unfeeling of the insurrection-

In addition to these (and other) examples of pejorative "interpretation" there is finally the major invention that gives color to the entire novel. Mr. Styron, on no historical evidence, has Turner's final defeat coming as a result of the actions of loyal slaves who fought in defense of their beloved masters. That these slaves are identfiied as "owned by the gentry" further underlines the book's emphasis on the benignity of "aristocratic slavery" which was able to command the loyalty of these slaves who were in one white character's words "living too well." Asked about this in the *Per Se* interview, Mr. Styron, who really talks too much, said: "The slaves in many of these houses—and not at gun point either, but quite voluntarily—were rallying to their masters' defense . . . I'm sure the cliché liberal of our time would ask for proof that this is true. But there are a lot of motives, quite real ones, that would cause a Negro to defend his white master against other Negroes. One was to preserve his own skin. He was shrewd [at all other times in the novel, with the exception of Nat, he is loutish and stupid] and he figured that if he played his cards right he'd get off better. And also I think that there was quite frankly often a very profound loyalty in those days. The fashionable historians can't convince me otherwise, because there's too much evidence."

He never, however, cites any of this evidence. Mr. Styron simply *knows,* like a Mississippi planter of my acquaintance, that "them old time darkies were loyal and true." This is an item of faith. Apart from the fact that there is no evidence of this having happened, is it logical? Can one really believe that a group of outnumbered and frightened slave-holders discovering themselves in the midst of a slave revolt would have armed other slaves, who might themselves have been part of the conspiracy?

---

ists. His only weapon was a broad axe, sharp and heavy." Brown then quotes from the "Confessions" of Will's path of carnage and describes his death in the final skirmish. "In this battle there were many slain on both sides. Will, the blood-thirsty and revengeful slave, fell with his broad axe uplifted, after having laid three of the whites dead at his feet with his own strong arm and terrible weapon. His last words were, 'Bury my axe with me.' For he religiously believed, that, in the next world, the blacks would have a contest with the whites, and he would need his axe." No sociological comment is necessary. But from a purely literary standpoint, it should be clear that Will, lifelong rebel and archetypal destroyer, presents possibilities which Mr. Styron simply ignored in favor of the "ravening, incoherent black beast" stereotype.

This thing which did not happen is made into one of the central motifs of the book. Turner broods on the memory of "Negroes in great numbers . . . firing back at us with as much passion and fury and even skill as their white masters." When his lieutenant, Hark, falls, Turner recalls "three bare-chested Negroes in the pantaloons of *coachmen* . . . kick him back to earth with booted feet. Hark flopped around in desperation, but they kicked him again, kicked him with an exuberance not caused by any white man's urgings or threat or exhortation but with rackety glee. . . ."

This invention makes it possible for a white lawyer at the trial to "revise certain traditional notions about Negro cowardice," because "whatever the deficiencies of the Negro character—and they are many, varied and grave—this uprising has proved . . . that the average Negro slave faced with the choice of joining up with a fanatical insurgent leader such as Nat Turner, or defending his fond and devoted master, will leap to his master's defense and fight as devotedly as any man and by so doing give proud evidence of the benevolence of a system so ignorantly decried by Quakers and other such morally dishonest detractors." The "bravery of those black men who fought bravely and well" at their master's side is to be rceorded "to the everlasting honor of this genial institution."

It is true that those lines are meant to be read as special pleading and polemical defense of the institution *by a single character*. But it was not that character who invented those black loyalists, it was Mr. Styron, and much in the novel—the picture of life at Turner's Mill and Turner's own reflections on the event—support this general position. It is built into the architecture of the novel.

When Gray, the lawyer who is taking Turner's confession, says to Nat,

> . . . you not only had a fantastic amount of Niggers who did not *join* up with you but there was a whole countless number more who were your active *enemies* . . . they were as determined to protect and save their masters as you were to murder them. . . . All the time that you were carrying around in that fanatical head of your'n the notion that the niggers were going to latch onto your great mission . . . the actual reality was that nine out of ten of your fellow burrheads just wasn't buying any such ideas. Reverend, I have no doubt it was your own race that contributed more to your fiasco than anything else.

It just ain't a race made for revolution, thats all. Thats another reason why nigger slavery is going to last for a thousand years.

we are clearly meant to read it as one taunting rationale of an apologist for slavery. Because of the emphasis in the whole book, it is none too clear that this *is* a qualifiable position. Quite literally *nothing* that we are shown in the novel denies the fictional Gray's conclusions. Quite to the contrary, as I have indicated, characters and events which in fact support them are invented in a systematic way.

Turner himself acquiesces in this interpretation. Dispirited and broken, he sits in his cell feeling himself betrayed by his people and his God. He thinks "it seemed . . . that my black shit-eating people were surely like flies, God's mindless outcasts, lacking even that will to destroy by their own hand their unending anguish. . . ."[7]

A pathetic and almost obscene figure, Nat broods and sulks in jail awaiting his death. The night before his execution he is comforted by fantasies of a sexual encounter with the white girl he murdered. In the original "Confessions" Turner shows no such

[7] Brown's version makes it clear, as does the court record, that Turner's defeat came at the hands of whites. No black loyalist mercenaries are mentioned, but he does give an instance of a master's life being saved by a slave. That, too, is instructive. "On the fatal night, when Nat and his companions were dealing death to all they found, Capt. Harris, a wealthy planter, had his life saved by the devotion and timely warning of his slave Jim, said to have been half brother to his master. After the revolt had been put down, and parties of whites were out hunting the suspected blacks, Capt. Harris with his faithful slave went into the woods in search of the negroes. In saving his master's life Jim felt he had done his duty, and could not consent to become a betrayer of his race; and, on reaching the woods, he handed his pistol to his master, and said, 'I cannot help you hunt down these men: they, like myself, want to be free. Sir, I am tired of the life of a slave: please give me my freedom or shoot me on the spot.' Capt. Harris took the weapon, and pointed at the slave . . . The Capt. fired and the slave fell dead at his feet." I do not claim that this incident necessarily took place in exactly the way that Brown relates it. But it also seems too specific to be pure invention by Brown, who was, after all, writing history and not fiction. It seems most probable that this was one of those minor incidents which become part of the "folk-lore" surrounding any major event; it is discussed, passed on, almost certainly distorted in the telling, but for some reason not included in "official" records. In this case, moreover, the nature of the incident suggests a reason for its exclusion.

uncertainty or ambiguity. When asked if he could not see that the entire undertaking was a mistake, he answers simply, "was not Christ crucified?" Gray's final description of him is significant: ". . . clothed with rags and covered with chains: yet daring to raise his manacled hands to heaven, with a spirit soaring above the attributes of man: I looked on him and my blood curdled in my veins." This is the Nat Turner of historical record: the rebel whose "calm deliberate composure" and unshakeable defiance in defeat so troubled and puzzled his white captors. Unfortunately Mr. Styron has not escaped their fate; that is why his Nat Turner is such a grotesque reduction. If this novel is important, it is so not because it contributes anything to our awareness of the Negro's experience and response to slavery, but because of the demonstration it presents of the truly astonishing persistence of white Southern myths, racial stereotypes, and derogatory literary clichés even in the best intentioned and most enlightened minds. Its largely uncritical acceptance in literary circles shows us how far we still have to go, and what a painfully little way we have come.

Its almost wholly favorable reception, up to now, is in some respects more significant and revealing than the book itself. Why, for example, in a book that alleges to deal with important themes and events in Negro history, was no black writer asked to comment on it in any major journal? Is it not a form of cultural condescension and indirect racism that only one white critic bothered to check its historical accuracy? Would a book similarly interpreting the history of any other cultural minority be so uncritically accepted? Would the fate of this novel have been the same had it appeared in 1964, before the liberal literary intelligentsia had begun to feel estranged from the movement for black independence? These are, admittedly, sociological rather than literary questions. But forcing these questions upon us may ultimately prove to be this novel's real contribution to our awareness of contemporary realities.

Part Six

The New
African Humanism

Black Orpheus

JEAN-PAUL SARTRE

W HEN YOU REMOVED THE GAG that was keeping these black mouths shut, what were you hoping for? That they would sing your praises? Did you think that when they raised themselves up again, you would read adoration in the eyes of these heads that our fathers had forced to bend down to the very ground? Here are black men standing, looking at us, and I hope that you—like me—will feel the shock of being seen. For three thousand years, the white man has enjoyed the privilege of seeing without being seen; he was only a look—the light from his eyes drew each thing out of the shadow of its birth; the white-ness of his skin was another look, condensed light. The white man —white because he was man, white like daylight, white like truth, white like virtue—lighted up the creation like a torch and unveiled the secret white essence of beings. Today, these black men are looking at us, and our gaze comes back to our own eyes; in their turn, black torches light up the world and our white heads are no more than Chinese lanterns swinging in the wind. A black poet— unconcerned with us—whispers to the woman he loves:

> Naked woman, black woman
> Dressed in your color which is life . . .
> Naked woman, dark woman,
> Firm fleshed ripe fruit, somber ecstasies of black wine.

and our whiteness seems to us to be a strange, livid varnish that keeps our skin from breathing—white tights, worn out at the

[VI, 1, Autumn-Winter 1964–65]

"Orphée Noir" appeared originally as the preface to an anthology of African and West Indian poets, edited by Leopold Sédar-Senghor (*Antho-logie de la nouvelle poésie nègre et malgache de langue française,* Paris, 1948). A key document in the history of the concept of "Negritude," it has been available in English only in a difficult to come by and out-of-print issue of *Présence Africaine* (Paris, 1951). It appears here with the permission of M. Sartre, in a new translation by John MacCombie.

elbows and knees, under which we would find real human flesh the color of black wine if we could remove them. We think we are essential to the world—suns of its harvests, moons of its tides; we are no more than its fauna, beasts. Not even beasts:

These gentlemen from the city
These proper gentlemen
Who no longer know how to dance in the evening by moonlight
Who no longer know how to walk on the flesh of their feet
Who no longer know how to tell tales by the fireside . . .

Formerly Europeans with divine right, we were already feeling our dignity beginning to crumble under American or Soviet looks; Europe was already no more than a geographical accident, the peninsula that Asia shoves into the Atlantic. We were hoping at least to find a bit of our greatness reflected in the domesticated eyes of the Africans. But there are no more domesticated eyes: there are wild and free looks that judge our world.
Here is a black man wandering:

> to the end of
> the eternity of their endless boulevards
> with cops . . .

Here is another one shouting to his brothers:

> Alas! Alas! Spidery Europe is moving its
> fingers and its phalanxes of ships . . .

Here is:

> the cunning silence of Europe's night . . .

in which

> . . . there is nothing that time does not dishonor.

A Negro writes:

> At times, we will haunt Montparnasse and Paris,
> Europe and its endless torments, like memories
> or like malaises . . .

and suddenly France seems exotic in our own eyes. She is no more than a memory, a malaise, a white mist at the bottom of sunlit souls, a back-country unfit to live in; she has drifted towards the

North, she is anchored near Kamchatka: the essential thing is the sun, the sun of the tropics and the sea "lousy with islands" and the roses of Imangue and the lilies of Iarive and the volcanos of Martinique. Being [l'Être] is black, Being is made of fire, we are accidental and far away, we have to justify our mores, our technics, our undercooked paleness and our verdigris vegetation. We are eaten away to the bones by these quiet and corrosive looks:

> Listen to the white world
> horribly weary of its immense effort
> its rebel articulations crackling under hard stars,
> its steel-blue stiffnesses piercing mystical flesh
> listen to its exhibitionist victories trumpeting its defeats
> listen to its wretched staggering with grandiose alibis
> Have pity on our naïve omniscient conquerors.

There we are, *finished;* our victories—their bellies sticking up in the air—show their guts, our secret defeat. If we want to crack open this finitude which imprisons us, we can no longer rely on the privileges of our race, of our color, of our technics: we will not be able to become a part of the totality from which those black eyes exile us, unless we tear off our white tights in order to try simply to be men.

If these poems shame us however, they were not intended to: they were not written for us; and they will not shame any colonists or their accomplices who open this book, for these latter will think they are reading letters over someone's shoulder, letters not meant for them. These black men are addressing themselves to black men about black men; their poetry is neither satiric nor imprecatory: it is an awakening to consciousness. "So," you will say, "in what way does it interest us, if it is only a document? We cannot enter into it." I should like to show in what way we *can* gain access to this world of jet; I should like to show that this poetry—which seems racial at first—is actually a hymn by everyone for everyone. In a word, I am talking now to white men, and I should like to explain to them what black men already know: why it is necessarily through a poetic experience that the black man, in his present condition, must first become conscious of himself; and, inversely, why black poetry in the French language is, in our time, the only great revolutionary poetry.

IT IS NOT just by accident that the white proletariat rarely uses poetic language to speak about its suffering, its anger or its pride in itself; neither do I think that workers are less gifted than our bourgeois sons: "talent"—that efficacious grace—loses all meaning when one claims that it is more widespread in one class than in another. Nor is it hard work that takes away their capacity for song: slaves used to drudge even harder and yet we know of slave hymns. It must therefore be recognized that it is the present circumstances of the class struggle that keep the worker from expressing himself poetically. Oppressed by technics, he wants to be a technician because he knows that technics will be the instrument of his liberation; he knows that it is only by gaining professional, economic, and scientific know-how that he will be able someday to control business management. He now has a profound practical knowledge of what poets have called *Nature,* but it is a knowledge he has gained more through his hands than through his eyes: Nature is Matter for him—that crafty, inert adversity that he works on with his tools; Matter has no song. At the same time, the present phase of his struggle requires of him continual, positive action: political calculation, precise forecasting, discipline, organization of the masses; to dream, at this point, would be to betray. Rationalism, materialism, positivism—the great themes of his daily battle—are least propitious for the spontaneous creation of poetic myths. The last of these myths—the famous "Upheaval"—has withdrawn under the circumstances of the struggle: one must take up the matter that is most urgent, gain this and that position, raise this salary, decide on that sympathy strike or on some protest against the war in Indo-China: efficiency alone matters. And, without a doubt, the oppressed class must first find itself. This self-discovery, however, is the exact opposite of a subjective examination of oneself: rather, it is a question of recognizing—in and by action—the objective situation of the proletariat, which can be determined by the circumstances of production or of redistribution of property. Unified by an oppression which is exerted on each and every one, and reduced to a common struggle, workers are hardly acquainted with the inner contradictions that fecundate the work of art and that are harmful to the *praxis.* As far as they are concerned, to know themselves is to situate themselves within the context of the great forces that surround them; it requires them to determine both their exact position in their class and their function in the

Party. The very language they use is free from the slight loosening of the screws, the constant frivolous impropriety, the game of transmissions which create the poetic Word. In their business, they use well-defined technical terms; and as for the language of revolutionary parties, Parain has shown that it is *pragmatic:* it is used to transmit orders, watch-words, information; if it loses its exactness, the Party falls apart. All of this tends more and more rigorously to eliminate the subject; poetry, however, must in some way remain subjective. The proletariat has not found a poetry that is sociological and yet finds its source in subjectivity, that is just as subjective as it is sociological, that is based on ambiguous or uncertain language and that is nevertheless as exalting and as generally understood as the most precise watch-words or as the phrase "Workers of all countries, unite" that one reads on doors in Soviet Russia. Lacking this, the poetry of the future revolution has remained in the hands of well-intentioned young bourgeois who found their inspiration in their personal psychological contradictions, in the dichotomy between their ideal and their class, in the uncertainty of the old bourgeois language.

Like the white worker, the Negro is a victim of the capitalist structure of our society. This situation reveals to him his close ties—quite apart from the color of his skin—with certain classes of Europeans who, like him, are oppressed; it incites him to imagine a privilege-less society in which skin pigmentation will be considered a mere fluke. But even though oppression itself may be a mere fluke, the circumstances under which it exists vary according to history and geographic conditions: the black man is a victim of it *because he is a black man* and insofar as he is a colonized native or a deported African. And since he is oppressed within the confines of his race and because of it, he must first of all become conscious of his race. He must oblige those who have vainly tried throughout the centuries to reduce him to the status of a beast, to recognize that he is a man. On this point, there is no means of evasion, or of trickery, no "crossing line" that he can consider: a Jew—a white man among white men—can deny that he is a Jew, can declare himself a man among men. The Negro cannot deny that he is Negro, nor can he claim that he is part of some abstract, colorless humanity: he is black. Thus he has his back up against the wall of authenticity: having been insulted and formerly enslaved, he picks up the word "nigger" which was thrown at him like a stone, he draws himself erect and proudly proclaims himself a black man, face to face with white men. The unity which will come eventually, bringing all oppressed peoples together in the same struggle, must be preceded in the colonies by what I shall call the moment of separation or negativity: this antiracist racism is the only road that will lead to the abolition of racial differences. How could it be otherwise? Can black men count on a distant white proletariat—involved in its own struggles— before they are united and organized on their own soil? And furthermore, isn't there some need for a thorough work of analysis in order to realize the identity of the interests that underlie the obvious difference of conditions? The white worker benefits somewhat from colonization, in spite of himself: low as his standard of living may be, it would be even lower if there were no colonization. In any case, he is less cynically exploited than the day laborer in Dakar or Saint-Louis. The technical equipment and industrialization of the European countries make it possible for measures of socialization to be immediately applicable there; but as seen from Sénégal or the Congo, socialism seems more than anything else like a beautiful dream: before black peasants can discover that socialism is the necessary answer to their present local claims, they must learn to formulate these claims jointly; therefore, they must think of themselves as black men.

But this new self-discovery is different from that which Marxism tries to awaken in the white worker. In the European worker, class consciousness is based on the nature of profit and unearned increment, on the present conditions of the ownership of the instruments for work; in brief, it is based on the objective characteristics of the *position* of the proletariat. But since the selfish scorn that white men display for black men—and that has no equivalent in the attitude of the bourgeois towards the working class—is aimed at the deepest recesses of the heart, black men must oppose it with a more exact view of black *subjectivity;* consequently race consciousness is based first of all on the black soul, or, rather,—since the term is often used in this anthology—on a certain quality common to the thoughts and conduct of Negroes which is called *Negritude* [sic]. There are only two ways to go about forming racial concepts: either one causes certain subjective characteristics to become objective, or else one tries to interiorize objectively revealed manners of conduct; thus the black man who asserts his Negritude by means of a revolutionary movement immediately places himself in the position of having to meditate, either because he wishes to recognize in himself certain objectively established traits of the African civilizations, or because he hopes to discover the Essence of blackness in the well of his heart. Thus subjectivity reappears: the relation of the self with the self; the source of all poetry, the very poetry from which the worker had to disengage himself. The black man who asks his colored brothers to "find themselves" is going to try to present to them an exemplary image of their Negritude and will look into his own soul to grasp it. He wants to be both a beacon and a mirror; the first revolutionary will be the harbinger of the black soul, the herald—half prophet and half follower—who will tear Blackness out of himself in order to offer it to the world; in brief, he will be a poet in the literal sense of "vates." Furthermore, black poetry has nothing in common with heartfelt effusions: it is functional, it answers a need which is defined in precise terms. Leaf through an anthology of contemporary white poetry: you will find a hundred different subjects, depending upon the mood and interests of the poet, depending upon his position and his country. In the anthology which I am introducing to you here, there is only one subject that all the poets attempt to treat, more or less successfully. From Haiti to Cayenne, there is a single idea: *reveal* the black soul. Black poetry is evangelic, it announces good news: Blackness has been rediscovered.

However, this Negritude, which they wish to fish for in their abyssal depths, does not fall under the soul's gaze all by itself: in the soul, nothing is gratuitous. The herald of the black soul has gone through white schools, in accordance with a brazen law which forbids the oppressed man to possess any arms except those he himself has stolen from the oppressor; it is through having had some contact with white culture that his blackness has passed from the immediacy of existence to the meditative state. But at the same time, he has more or less ceased to live his Negritude. In choosing to see what he is, he has become split, he no longer coincides with himself. And on the other hand, it is because he was already exiled from himself that he discovered this need to reveal himself. He therefore begins by exile. It is a double exile: the exile of his body offers a magnificent image of the exile of his heart; he is in Europe most of the time, in the cold, in the middle of gray crowds; he dreams of Port-au-Prince, of Haiti. But in Port-au-Prince, he was *already* in exile; the slavers had torn his fathers out of Africa and dispersed them. And all of the poems in this book—except those which were written in Africa—show us the same mystical geography. A hemisphere: in the foreground—forming the first of three concentric circles—extends the land of exile, colorless Europe; then comes the dazzling circle of the Islands and of childhood, which dance the roundelay around Africa; the last circle is Africa, the world's navel, pole of all black poetry—dazzling Africa, burnt, oily like a snake's skin, Africa of fire and rain, torrid and tufted; Africa—phantom flickering like a flame, between being and nothingness, more *real* than the "eternal boulevards with cops" but absent, beyond attainment, disintegrating Europe with its black but invisible rays; Africa, an *imaginary* continent. The extraordinary good luck of black poetry lies in the fact that the anxieties of the colonized native have their own grandiose and obvious symbols which need only to be gone into deeply and to be meditated upon: exile, slavery, the Africa-Europe couple and the great Manichaeistic division of the world into black and white. This ancestral bodily exile represents the other exile: the black soul is an Africa from which the Negro, in the midst of the cold buildings of white culture and technics, is exiled. An ever-present but concealed Negritude haunts him, rubs against him; he himself rubs up against its silky wing; it palpitates and is spread throughout him like his searching memory and his loftiest demands, like his shrouded, betrayed childhood, and like the childhood of his race and the call of the earth, like the swarming of insects and the indivisible simplicity of Nature, like the pure legacy of his ancestors, and like the Ethics that ought to unify his truncated life. But if he turns around to look squarely at his Negritude, it vanishes in smoke; the walls of white culture—its silence, its words, its mores—rise up between it and him:

Give me back my black dolls, so that I may play with them
My instinct's simple games
that I may remain in the shadow of its laws
cover up my courage
my audacity
feel me as me
me renewed through what I was yesterday

yesterday
   without complexity
    yesterday
when the uprooting hour came . . .
they have ransacked the space that was mine

However, the walls of this culture prison must be broken down; it will be necessary to return to Africa some day: thus the themes of return to the native country and of re-descent into the glaring hell of the black soul are indissolubly mixed up in the *vates* of Negritude. A quest is involved here, a systematic stripping and an "*ascèse*"[1] accompanied by a continual effort of investigation. And I shall call this poetry "Orphic" because the Negro's tireless descent into himself makes me think of Orpheus going to claim Eurydice from Pluto. Thus, through an exceptional stroke of poetic good luck, it is by letting himself fall into trances, by rolling on the ground like a possessed man tormented by himself, by singing of his angers, his regrets or his hates, by exhibiting his wounds, his life torn between "civilization" and his old black substratum; in short, by becoming most lyrical, that the black poet is most certain of creating a great collective poetry: by speaking only of himself, he speaks for all Negroes; it is when he seems smothered by the serpents of our culture that he is the most revolutionary, for he then undertakes to ruin systematically the European knowledge he has acquired, and this spiritual destruction symbolizes the great future taking-up of arms by which black men will destroy their chains. A single example will suffice to clarify this last remark.

In the twentieth century, most ethnic minorities have passionately endeavored to resuscitate their national languages while struggling for their independence. To be able to say that one is Irish or Hungarian, one must belong to a collectivity which has the benefit of a broad economic and political autonomy; but to *be* Irish, one must also *think Irish,* which means above all: think *in* Irish. The specific traits of a society correspond exactly to the untranslatable locutions of its language. The fact that the prophets of Negritude are forced to write their gospel *in French* means that there is a certain risk of dangerously slowing down the efforts of black men to reject our tutelage. Having been dispersed to the

---

[1] *ascèse:* the ascetic's movement of *interiorization.* (translator's note).

four corners of the earth by the slave trade, black men have no common language; in order to incite the oppressed to unite, they must necessarily rely on the words of the oppressor's language. And French is the language that will furnish the black poet with the largest audience, at least within the limits of French colonization. It is in this goose-pimply language—pale and cold like our skies, and which Mallarmé said was "the neutral language *par excellence* since our spirit demands an attenuation of variegation and of all excessively brilliant color"—in this language which is half dead for them, that Damas, Diop, Laleau, Rabéarivelo are going to pour the fire of their skies and of their hearts: it is through this language alone that they can communicate; like the sixteenth-century scholars who understood each other only in Latin, black men can meet only on that trap-covered ground that the white man has prepared for them: the colonist has arranged to be the eternal mediator between the colonized; he is there—always there—even when he is absent, even in the most secret meetings. And since words are ideas, when the Negro declares in French that he rejects French culture, he accepts with one hand what he rejects with the other; he sets up the enemy's thinking-apparatus in himself, like a crusher. This would not matter: except that this syntax and vocabulary—forged thousands of miles away in another epoch to answer other needs and to designate other objects—are unsuitable to furnish him with the means of speaking about himself, his own anxieties, his own hopes. The French language and French thought are analytical. What would happen if the black spirit were above all synthetical? The rather ugly term "Negritude" is one of the few black contributions to our dictionary. But after all, if this "Negritude" is a definable or at least a describable concept, it must subsume other more elementary concepts which correspond to the immediate fundamental ideas directly involved with Negro consciousness: but where are the words to describe them? How well one understands the Haitian poet's complaint:

> This obsessing heart which does not correspond
> To my language, nor to my customs,
> And on which encroach, like a clinging-root,
> Borrowed feelings and the customs
> Of Europe, feel this suffering
> And this despair—equal to no other—

Of ever taming with words from France
This heart which came to me from Sénégal.

It is not true, however, that the black man expresses himself in a "foreign"language, since he is taught French from childhood and since he is perfectly at ease when he thinks in the terms of a technician, of a scholar, or of a politician. Rather, one must speak about the slight but patent difference that separates what he says from what he would like to say, whenever he speaks about himself. It seems to him that a Northern Spirit steals his ideas from him, bends them slightly to mean more or less what he wanted; that white words drink his thoughts like sand drinks blood. If he suddenly gorges himself, if he pulls himself together and takes a step backward, there are the sounds lying prostrate *in front of him*—strange: half signs and half things. He will not speak his Negritude with precise, efficacious words which hit the target every time. He will not speak his Negritude *in prose*. As everyone knows, every poetic experience has its origin in this feeling of frustration that one has when confronted with a language that is supposed to be a means of direct communication.

The reaction of the *speaker* frustrated by prose is in effect what Bataille calls the holocaust of words. As long as we can believe that a pre-established harmony governs the relationship between a word and Being, we use words without seeing them, with blind trust; they are sensory organs, mouths, hands, windows open on the world. As soon as we experience a first frustration, this chattering falls beyond us; we see the whole system, it is no more than an upset, out-of-order mechanism whose arms are still flailing to INDICATE EXISTENCE in emptiness; in one fell swoop we pass judgment on the foolish business of naming things; we understand that language is in essence prose, and that prose is in essence failure; Being stands erect in front of us like a tower of silence, and if we still want to catch it, we can do so only through silence: "evoke, in an intentional shadow, the object "*tu*" by allusive words, never direct, reducing themselves to the same silence."[2] No one has better stated that poetry is an incantatory attempt to suggest Being in and by the vibratory disappearance of the word: by insisting on his verbal impotence, by making words mad, the poet makes

2 Mallarmé, *Magie* (Edition de la Pléiade, p. 400).

us suspect that beyond this chaos which cancels itself out, there are silent densities; since we cannot keep quiet, we must *make silence with language.* From Mallarmé to the Surrealists, the final goal of French poetry seems to me to have been this auto-destruction of language. A poem is a dark room where words are knocking themselves about, quite mad. Collisions in the air: they ignite each other with their fire and fall down in flames.

It is in this perspective that we must situate the efforts of the "black evangelists." They answer the colonist's ruse with a similar but inverse ruse: since the oppressor is present in the very language that they speak, they will speak this language in order to destroy it. The contemporary European poet tries to dehumanize words in order to give them back to nature; the black herald is going to *de-Frenchify* them; he will crush them, break their usual associations, he will violently couple them

> with little steps of caterpillar rain
> with little steps like mouthfuls of milk
> with little steps like ball-bearings
> with little steps like seismic shocks
> Yams in the soil stride like gaps of stars[3]

Only when they have regurgitated their whiteness does he adopt them, making of this ruined language a solemn, sacred superlanguage, Poetry. Only through Poetry can the black men of Tananarive and of Cayenne; the black men of Port-au-Prince and of Saint-Louis, communicate with each other in private. And since French lacks terms and concepts to define Negritude, since Negritude is silence, these poets will use "allusive words, never direct, reducing themselves to the same silence" in order to evoke it. Short-circuits of language: behind the flaming fall of words, we glimpse a great black mute idol. It is not only the black man's self-portrayal that seems poetic to me; it is also his personal way of utilizing the means of expression at his disposal. His position incites him to do it: even before he thinks of writing poetry, in him, the light of white words is refracted, polarized, and altered. This is nowhere more manifest than in his use of two connected terms—"white-black"—that cover both the great cosmic division—"day

[3] Césaire, *Les armes miraculeuses: tam tam II.*

and night"—and the human conflict between the native and the colonist. But it is a connection based on a hierarchical system: by giving the Negro this term, the teacher also gives him a hundred language habits which consecrate the white man's rights over the black man. The Negro will learn to say "white like snow" to indicate innocence, to speak of the blackness of a look, of a soul, of a deed. As soon as he opens his mouth, he accuses himself, unless he persists in upsetting the hierarchy. And if he upsets it *in French,* he is already poetizing: can you imagine the strange savor that an expression like "the blackness of innocence" or "the darkness of virtue" would have for us? That is the savor which we taste on every page of this book, when, for example, we read:

> Your round, shining, black satin breasts . . .
> this white smile
> of eyes
> in the face's shadow
> awaken in me this evening
> deaf rhythms . . .
> which intoxicate, there in Guinée,
> our sisters
> black and naked
> and inspire in me
> this evening
> black twilights heavy with sensual anxiety
> for
> the soul of the black country where the ancients
> are sleeping
> lives and speaks
> this evening
> in uneasy strength, along the small of
> your back . . .

Throughout this poem, black is color; better still, light; its soft diffuse radiance dissolves our habits; the *black* country where the ancients are sleeping is not a dark hell: it is a land of sun and fire. Then again, in another connection, the superiority of white over black does not express only the superiority that the colonist claims to have over the native: more profoundly, it expresses a universal adoration of *day* as well as our night terrors, which also are universal. In this sense, these black men are re-establishing the hierarchy they have just upset. They don't want to be poets *of night,* poets of vain revolt and despair: they give the promise of dawn; they greet

> the transparent dawn of a new day.

At last, the black man discovers, through the pen, his baleful sense of foreboding:

> Nigger black like misery

one of them, and then another, cries out:

> Deliver me from my blood's night

Thus the word *black* is found to contain *all Evil* and *all Good,* it covers up an almost unbearable tension between two contradictory classifications: solar hierarchy and racial hierarchy. It gains thereby an extraordinary poetry, like self-destructive objects from the hands of Duchamp and the Surrealists; there is a secret blackness in white, a secret whiteness in black, a fixed flickering of Being and of Nonbeing which is perhaps nowhere expressed as well as in this poem by Césaire:

> My tall wounded statue, a stone in its fore-
> head; my great inattentive day flesh with
> pitiless spots, my great night flesh with
> day spots.

The poet will go even further; he writes:

> Our beautiful faces like the true operative
> power of negation.

Behind this abstract eloquence evoking Lautréamont is seen an extremely bold and subtle attempt to give some sense to black skin and to realize the poetic synthesis of the two faces of night. When

David Diop says that the Negro is "black like misery," he makes black represent deprivation of light. But Césaire develops and goes into this image more deeply: night is no longer absence, it is refusal. Black is not color, it is the destruction of this borrowed clarity which falls from the white sun. The revolutionary Negro is negation because he wishes to be complete nudity: in order to build his Truth, he must first destroy others' Truth. Black faces—these night memories which haunt our days—embody the dark work of Negativity which patiently gnaws at concepts. Thus, by a reversal which curiously recalls that of the humiliated Negro—insulted and called "dirty nigger" when he asserts his rights—it is the privative aspect of darkness that establishes its value. Liberty is the color of night.

Destructions, autos-da-fé of language, magic symbolism, ambivalence of concepts: all the negative aspects of modern poetry are here. But it is not a matter of some gratuitous game. The black man's position, his original "rending," the alienation that a foreign way of thinking imposes on him, all oblige him to reconquer his existential unity as a Negro,—or, if you prefer, the original purity of his plan—through a gradual "ascèse," beyond the language stage. Negritude—like liberty—is a point of departure and an ultimate goal: it is a matter of making Negritude pass from the immediate to the mediate, a matter of *thematicising* it. The black man must therefore find death in white culture in order to be reborn with a black soul, like the Platonic philosopher whose body embraces death in order to be reborn in truth. This dialectical and mystical return to origins necessarily implies a method. But this method is not presented as a set of rules to be used in directing the spirit. Rather, it becomes *one* with whoever applies it; it is the dialectical law of successive transformations which lead the Negro to coincidence with himself in Negritude. It is not a matter of his *knowing,* nor of his ecstatically tearing himself away from himself, but rather of both discovering and becoming what he is.

There are two convergent means of arriving at this primordial simplicity of existence; one is objective, the other subjective. The poets in our anthology sometimes use one, sometimes the other, and sometimes both of them together. In effect, there exists an objective Negritude that is expressed by the mores, arts, chants, and dances of the African populaces. As a *spiritual exercise,* the poet will prescribe allowing himself to be fascinated by primitive rhythms, letting his thoughts run in traditional forms of black poetry. Many of the poems included here are called *tam-tams,* because they borrow from the night-time tambourine players a percussive rhythm which is sometimes sharp and regular, sometimes torrential and bounding. The poetic act, then, is a dance of the soul; the poet turns round and round like a dervish until he faints; he has established his ancestors' time in himself, he feels it flowing with its peculiar violent pulls; he hopes to "find" himself in this rhythmic pulsation; I shall say that he tries to make himself "possessed" by his people's Negritude; he hopes that the echoes of his *tam-tam* will come to awaken timeless instincts sleeping within him. Upon leafing through this collection, one will get the impression that the *tam-tam* tends to become a genre of black poetry, just as the sonnet or the ode was a genre of our poetry. Others, like Rabemananjara, will be inspired by royal proclamations; still others will draw from the popular well of the Hain-tenys. The calm center of this maelstrom of rhythms, chants, shouts, is the poetry of Birago Diop, in all its majestic simplicity: it alone is at *rest* because it comes directly from Griot narratives and oral tradition. Almost all the other attempts have something contorted, taut, and desperate about them because they aim at *becoming a part of* folkloric poetry rather than emanating from it. But however far he may be from "the black country where ancestors sleep," the black man is closer than we to the great period when, as Mallarmé says, "the word creates Gods." It is practically impossible for *our* poets to resume some closeness with popular traditions: ten centuries of scholarly poetry separate them from such traditions; furthermore, folkloric inspiration is drying up: at the very best, we could only imitate its simplicity from a distance. The black men of Africa, on the contrary, are still in the great period of mythical fecundity and French-language black poets are not using their myths as a form of diversion as we use our epic poems:[4] they allow themselves to be spellbound by them so that at the end of the incantation, Negritude—magnificently evoked—may surge forth. This is why I call this method of "objective poetry" *magic,* or charm.

Césaire, on the contrary, chose to backtrack into himself. Since this Eurydice will disappear in smoke if Black Orpheus turns around

[4] Sartre uses *"chansons"* for what we have translated as "epic poems"; he is referring, of course, to the Medieval French epic poems, the *Chansons de Geste* (translator's note).

to look back on her, he will descend the royal road of his soul with his back turned on the bottom of the grotto; he will descend below words and meanings—"in order to think of you, I have placed all words on the mountain-of-pity"—below daily activities and the plan of "repetition," even below the first barrier reefs of revolt, with his back turned and his eyes closed, in order finally to touch with his feet the black water of dreams and desire and to let himself drown in it.[5] Desire and dream will rise up snarling like a tidal wave; they will make words dance like flotsam and throw them pell-mell, shattered, on the shore.

> "Words go beyond themselves; and just as the old geog-raphy is done for, the high and the low (words) do not allow diversion either towards heaven or towards earth. . . . On the contrary, they operate on a strangely flexible range at one level: on the gaseous Level of an organism both solid and liquid, black and white day and night."[6]

One recognizes the old surrealistic *method* (automatic writing, like mysticism, is a method: it presupposes an apprenticeship, ex-ercises, a start along the way). One must dive under the superficial crust of reality, of common sense, of reasoning reason, in order to touch the very bottom of the soul and awaken the timeless forces of desire: desire which makes of man a refusal of everything and a love of everything; desire, the radical negation of natural laws and of the possible, a call to miracles; desire which, by its mad cosmic energy, plunges man back into the seething breast of Nature and, at the same time, lifts him above Nature through the affirmation of his Right to be unsatisfied. Furthermore, Césaire is not the first Negro to take this road. Before him, Etienne Léro had founded *Légitime Défense*. "*Légitime Défense*," says Senghor, "was more a

---

[5] Sartre seems to have confused his images here, since Orpheus was in-structed not to look back as he was *ascending* from Hades, *after* he had re-trieved Eurydice from Pluto (translator's note).

[6] The French "automatic writing" was so completely untranslatable that we have tried simply to give an English *approximation* of its sense. For those who care to consult the original French text, it runs as follows: "*Les mots se dépassent, c'est bien vers un ciel et une terre que le haut et le bas ne permettent pas de distraire, c'en est fait aussi de la vieille géographie. . . . Au contraire, un étagement curieusement respirable s'opère réel mais au niveau. Au Niveau gazeux de l'organisme solide et liquide, blanc et noir jour et nuit.*"

cultural movement than a review. Starting from the Marxist analysis of the society of the 'Islands,' it discovered, in the Antilles, descendants of African Negro slaves, who had been kept in the dulling condition of the proletarian for three centuries. It affirmed that only surrealism could deliver him from his taboos and express him in his entireness."

However, if one compares Léro with Césaire, one cannot help but be struck by their dissimilarities, and this comparison may allow us to measure the abyss that prevents a black revolutionary from utilizing white surrealism. Léro was the precursor; he invented the exploitation of surrealism as a "miraculous weapon" and an instrument for reconnaissance, a sort of radar with which one probes the depths of the abyss. But his poems are student exercises, they are mere imitations: they do not go beyond themselves; rather, they close in on each other:

> The ancient heads of hair
> Glue to the branches floors of empty seas
> Where your body is only a memory
> Where Spring trims its nails
> Helix of your smile thrown far away
> On the houses we will have nothing to do with . . .

"The helix of your smile," "the spring which trims its nails": we rceognize in these the preciousness and gratuitousness of surrealistic imagery, the eternal process that consists of throwing a bridge between two extremely unrelated or separated terms and hoping—without really believing—that this "throw of the dice" will uncover some hidden aspect of Being. It does not seem to me that, either in this poem or in the others, Léro demands the liberation of the black man: at the very most he lays claim to a categorical liberation of the imagination; in this completely abstract game, no combination of words evokes Africa even remotely. If these poems were taken out of the anthology and the name of their author hidden, I would defy anyone at all, white or black, not to attribute them to a European contributor to *La Révolution Surréaliste* or *Le Minotaure*. The purpose of surrealism is to rediscover—beyond race and condition, beyond class, behind the fire of language—dazzling silent darknesses which are no longer opposed to anything, not even to day, because day and night and all opposites are blended in them and suppressed; consequently, one might speak of the impassiveness and the impersonality of the surrealist poem, just as there is a Parnassian impassiveness and impersonality.

A poem by Césaire, on the contrary, bursts and wheels around like a rocket; suns turning and exploding into new suns come out of it; it is a perpetual going-beyond. It is not a question of the poem becoming part of the calm unity of opposites; but rather of making *one* of the opposites in the "black-white" couple expand like a phallus in its opposition to the other. The density of these words thrown into the air, like stones from a volcano, is found in Negritude, which is defined as being *against* Europe and colonization. What Césaire destroys is not *all* culture but rather *white* culture; what he brings to light is not desire for *everything* but rather the revolutionary aspirations of the oppressed Negro; what he touches in his very depths is not the spirit but a certain specific, concrete form of humanity. With this in mind, one can speak here about *engaged* and even *directed* automatic writing, not because there is any meditative intervention but because the words and images perpetually translate the same torrid obsession. The white surrealist finds within himself the trigger; Césaire finds within himself the fixed inflexibility of demands and feeling. Léro's words are feebly organized around vague, general themes through expansion and a relaxing of logical ties; Césaire's words are pressed against each other and cemented by his furious passion. Between the most daring comparisons and between the most widely separated terms, runs a secret thread of hate and hope. For example, compare "the helix of your smile thrown far away"—which is the product of a free play of the imagination as well as an invitation to revery—with

and the radium mines buried in the abyss of my innocence
will jump by grains
into the feeding-trough of birds
and the stars' stere
will be the common name of fire-wood
gathered from the alluvium of the singing veins of night

in which the "disjecta membra" of the vocabulary are so organized as to allow the supposition that there is a black "*Art Poétique.*" Or read:

Our beautiful faces like the true operative power of negation.

Also read:

> Seas lousy with islands cracking the roses' fingers
> flame-thrower and my lightning-struck body intact.

Here we find the apotheosis of the fleas of black misery jumping in the water's hair, islands in a stream of light, cracking under the fingers of the celestial delouser: dawn with rose-colored fingers, the dawn of Greek and Mediterranean culture—snatched from the sacrosanct Homeric poems by a black thief—whose enslaved princess's fingernails are suddenly controlled by a Toussaint L'Ouverture in order to crack the triumphant parasites of the black sea; the dawn, which suddenly rebels and is metamorphosed, which opens fire like that savage weapon of white men, the flame-thrower, the weapon of scientists, the weapon of executioners, strikes the tall black Titan with its white fire, and he arises intact and eternal in order to begin the assault on Europe and heaven. In Césaire, the great surrealist tradition is realized, it takes on its definitive meaning and is destroyed: surrealism—that European movement—is taken from the Europeans by a black man who turns it against them and gives it a rigorously defined function. I have pointed out elsewhere how the whole of the proletariat completely shut itself off from the destructive poetry of Reason: in Europe, surrealism languishes and pales, rejected by those who could have given it a transfusion of their own blood. But at the very moment when it is losing contact with the Revolution, it is, in the Antilles, grafted onto another branch of the universal Revolution; it develops into an enormous somber flower. Césaire's originality lies in his having directed his powerful, concentrated anxiety as a Negro, as one oppressed, as a militant individual, into this world of the most destructive, free, and metaphysical poetry at the moment when Eluard and Aragon were failing to give political content to their verse. And finally, *Negritude-object* is snatched from Césaire like a cry of pain, of love, and of hate. Here again he follows the surrealist tradition of *objective* poetry. Césaire's words do not describe Negritude, they do not designate it, they do not copy it from the outside like a painter with a model: they *create* it; they compose it under our very eyes: henceforth it is a thing which can be observed and learned; the subjective method which he has chosen joins the objective method we spoke about earlier: he ejects the black soul from himself at the very moment when others are trying to interiorize it; the final result is the same in both cases. Negritude is the far-away *tam-tam* in the streets of Dakar at night; voo-doo shouts from some Haitian cellar window, sliding along level with the roadway; the Congolese mask; but it is also this poem by Césaire, this slobbery, bloody poem full of phlegm, twisting in the dust like a cut-up worm. This double spasm of absorption and excretion beats out the rhythm of the black heart on every page of this collection.

What then, at present, is this Negritude, sole anxiety of these poets, sole subject of this book? It must first be stated that a white man could hardly speak about it suitably, since he has no inner experience of it and since European languages lack words to describe it. I ought then to let the reader encounter it in the pages of this collection and draw his own conclusions about it. But this introduction would be incomplete if, after having indicated that the quest for the Black Grail represented—both in its original intention and in its methods—the most authentic synthesis of revolutionary aspirations and poetic anxiety, I did not show that this complex notion is essentially pure Poetry. I shall therefore limit myself to examining these poems objectively as a cluster of testimonies and to pointing out some of their principal themes. Senghor says: "What makes the *Negritude* of a poem is less its theme than its style, the emotional warmth which gives life to words, which transmutes the word into the Word." It could not be more explicitly stated that Negritude is neither a state nor a definite ensemble of vices and virtues or of intellectual and moral qualities, but rather a certain affective attitude towards the world. Since the beginning of this century, psychology has renounced its great scholastic distinctions. We no longer believe that the "facts" of the soul are divided into volitions or actions, knowledge or perceptions, sentiments or blind passiveness. We know that a feeling is a definite way of establishing our rapport with the world around us, that it involves a certain comprehension of this universe. It is a tension of the soul, a choice of oneself and of another, a way of going beyond the raw facts of experience; in short, a *plan* quite like the voluntary act. To use Heidegger's language, Negritude is the Negro's being-in-the-world.

Furthermore, here is what Césaire tells us about it:

My negritude is not a stone with its deafness flung
    out against the clamor of the day

My negritude is not a dead speck of water on the
    dead eye of the earth
my negritude is neither a tower nor a cathedral
it plunges into the red flesh of the ground
it plunges into the ardent flesh of the sky
it perforates the opaque pressure of its righteous patience.

Negritude is portrayed in these beautiful lines of verse more as
an act than as a frame of mind. But this act is an *inner* determination: it is not a question of *taking* the goods of this world in one's
hands and transforming them; it is a question of *existing* in the
middle of the world. The relation with the universe remains an
adaptation. But this adaptation is not technical. For the white man,
to possess is to transform. To be sure, the white worker uses instruments which he does not possess. But at least his techniques are
his own: if it is true that the personnel responsible for the major
inventions of European industry comes mainly from the middle
classes, at least the trades of carpenter, cabinet-maker, potter, seem
to the white workers to be a true heritage, despite the fact that the
orientation of great capitalist production tends to remove their "joy
in work" from them. But it is not enough to say that the black
worker uses instruments which are lent to him; techniques are also
lent him.

Césaire refers to his black brothers as:

Those who have invented neither powder nor compass
those who have never tamed either steam or electricity
those who have not explored the seas and the sky . . .

But this haughty claim of non-technicalness reverses the situation: what could pass as a deficiency becomes a *positive* source
of wealth. A technical rapport with Nature reveals Nature as
simple quantity, inertia, exteriority: nature dies. By his haughty refusal to be *homo faber,* the Negro gives it life again. As if the
passiveness of one of the members of the "man-nature" couple
necessarily produced the other's activity. Actually, Negritude is not
passiveness, since it "perforates the flesh of the sky and of the
earth": it is "patience," and patience appears like an active imitation
of passiveness. The Negro's act is first of all an act on oneself. The
black man stands erect and immobilizes himself like a bird-charmer,
and things come to perch on the branches of this fake tree. A

magic inveigling of the world—through silence and rest—is involved here: the white man, by acting first of all on Nature, loses himself when he loses Nature; the Negro, by acting first of all on himself, claims to win Nature while winning himself.

> Seized, they abandon themselves to the essence of
>   every thing
> ignorant of the surfaces but seized by the movement of
>   every thing
> heedless of counting, but playing the world's game
> truly the elder sons of the world
> porous to all the breaths of the world . . .
> flesh of the world's flesh palpitating from the very
>   movement of the world.

Upon reading this, one can hardly help thinking of the famous distinction between intelligence and intuition established by Bergson. Césaire rightly calls us

> Omniscient and naïve conquerors. . . .

Because of his tools, the white man knows all. But he only scratches the surface of things; he is unaware of the duration of things, unaware of life. Negritude, on the contrary, is comprehension through instinctive congeniality. The black man's secret is that the sources of his existence and the roots of Being are identical.

If one wanted to give a sociological interpretation of this metaphysic, one would say that an agriculturist poetry is here opposed to an engineer prose. Actually, it is not true that the black man has no techniques: the rapport between any human group and the exterior world is always technical in one way or another. And inversely, I shall say that Césaire is imprecise: Saint Exupéry's airplane folding the earth below like a carpet is a means of disclosure. However, the black man is first of all a peasant; agricultural technique is "righteous patience"; it trusts in life; it waits. To plant is to impregnate the earth; after that, you must remain motionless and watch: "each atom of silence is a chance for ripe fruit," each instant brings forth a hundred times more than man gave, whereas the worker finds in the manufactured product only as much as he put into it; man grows along with his wheat: from minute to minute he goes beyond himself and becomes more golden; he intervenes in this watchful wait before the fragile swelling belly, only to protect. Ripe wheat is a microcosm because the cooperation of sun, wind, and rains was needed for it to grow; a blade of wheat is both the most natural thing and the most improbable chance. Techniques have contaminated the white peasant, but the black peasant remains the great male of the earth, the world's sperm. His existence is great vegetal patience; his work is the yearly repetition of holy coitus. Creating and nourished because he creates. To till, to plant, to eat, is to make love with nature. The sexual pantheism of these poets is undoubtedly what will impress us first of all: it is in this that they join the dances and the phallic rites of the Negro-Africans.

> Oho! Congo lying in your bed of forests, queen of tamed Africa
> May the phalli of the mountains carry your banner high
> For, through my head, through my tongue, through my
>   belly, you are a woman,

writes Senghor. And:

> and so I shall mount again the soft belly of the dunes
> and the gleaming thighs of the day. . . .

and Rabéarivelo:

> the earth's blood, the stone's sweat and the sperm of
> the world

and Laleau:

> The conical drum laments under the sky
> And it is the very soul of the black man
> Sultry spasms of men in rut, lover's sticky sobs
> Outraging the calm of the evening.

Here, we are far from Bergson's chaste asexual intuition. It is no longer a matter of being congenial with life, but rather of being in love with all its forms. For the white technician, God is first of all an engineer. Jupiter orders chaos and prescribes its laws; the Christian God conceives the world through his understanding and brings it into being through his will: the relation between the created and the creator is never carnal, except for a few mystics whom the Church looks upon with a great deal of suspicion. Even so, erotic mysticism has nothing in common with fecundity: it is the completely passive wait for a sterile penetration. We are *steeped* in alluvium: statuettes come from the *hands* of the divine sculptor. If the manufactured objects surrounding us could worship their ancestors, they would undoubtedly adore us as we adore the All-powerful. For our black poets, on the contrary, Being comes out of Nothingness like a penis becoming erect; Creation is an enormous perpetual delivery; the world is flesh and the son of flesh; on the sea and in the sky, on the dunes, on the rocks, in the wind, the Negro finds the softness of human skin; he rubs himself against the sand's belly, against the sky's loins: he is "flesh of the flesh of this world"; he is "porous to all its breaths," to all its pollens; he is both Nature's female and its male; and when he makes love with a woman of his race, the sexual act seems to him to be the celebration of the Mystery of Being. This spermatic religion is like the tension of a soul balancing between two complementary tendencies: the dynamic feeling of being an erect phallus, and that more deaf, more patient, more feminine one of being a growing plant. Thus Negritude is basically a sort of androgyny.

> There you are
> Upright and naked
> alluvium you are and remember yourself as having been
> but in reality you are the child of this parturient shadow
> feeding on lunar lactogen[7]
>
> then you slowly take the form of a bole
> on this low wall jumped over by the dreams of flowers
> and the perfume of summer at rest.
> To feel, to believe that roots are pushing your feet
> and running and twisting like thirsty serpents
> toward some subterranean spring . . .

(Rabéarivelo)

And Césaire:

> Wornout mother, leafless mother, you are a flamboyant[8]
> and now wear only husks. You are a calabash tree
> and you are only a stand of *couis*. . . .[9]

[7] "lactogen": This is a neologism in the French text as well.

[8] *flamboyant:* a plant found in semi-tropical countries, especially in the Antilles: a *poinciana* or *peacock flower* (translator's note).

[9] *couis:* apparently some kind of tree found in the Antilles. (translator's note).

This profound unity of vegetal and sexual symbols is certainly the greatest originality of black poetry, especially in a period when, as Michel Carrouges has shown, most of the images used by white poets tend to mineralize the human being. Césaire, on the contrary, "vegetalizes," "animalizes" sea, sky, and stones. More precisely, his poetry is a perpetual coupling of men and women who have been metamorphosed into animals, vegetables, stones, with stones, plants, and beasts metamorphosed into men. Thus the black man attests to a natural Eros; he reveals and incarnates it; to find a point of comparison in European poetry, one must go back to Lucretius, the peasant poet who celebrated Venus, the mother goddess, when Rome was not yet much more than a large agricultural market. In our time, only Lawrence seems to me to have had a cosmic feeling for sexuality. Even so, this feeling remains very literary in his works.

However, although Negritude seems basically to be this immobile springing-forth, a unity of phallic erection and plant growth, one could scarcely exhaust it with this single poetic theme. There is another motif running through this collection, like a large artery:

Those who have invented neither powder nor compass . . .
They know the most remote corners of the country of
    suffering. . . .

To the absurd utilitarian agitation of the white man, the black man opposes the authenticity gained from his suffering; the black race is a chosen race because it has had the horrible privilege of touching the depths of unhappiness. And even though these poems are anti-Christian from beginning to end, one might call Negritude a kind of Passion: the black man who is conscious of himself as the man who has taken the whole of human suffering upon himself and who suffers for all, even for the white man.

On the judgment day, Armstrong's trumpet will be the interpreter of man's sufferings.

(Paul Niger)

Let us note immediately that this in no way implies a resigned suffering. A while ago I was speaking about Bergson and Lucretius; I would be tempted now to quote that great adversary of Christianity: Nietzsche and his "Dionysianism." Like the Dionysian poet, the Negro attempts to penetrate the brilliant phantasm of the day, and encounters, a thousand feet under the Apollonian surface, the inexpiable suffering which is the universal essence of man. If one wished to systematize, one would say that the black man blends with the whole of nature in as much as he represents sexual congeniality with Life and in as much as he claims he is Man in his Passion of rebellious suffering. One will feel the fundamental unity of this double movement if one considers the constantly tighter relationship which psychiatrists establish between anguish and sexual desire. There is only one proud upheaval which can be equally well described as a desire plunging its roots into suffering or as suffering fixed like a sword across a vast cosmic desire. This "righteous patience" that Césaire evokes is both vegetal growth and patience against suffering; it resides in the very muscles of the Negro; it sustains the black porter going a thousand miles up the Niger under a blinding sun with a fifty-pound load balanced on his head. But if in a certain sense, one can compare the fecundity of Nature to a proliferation of suffering, in another sense—and this one is also Dionysian—this fecundity, by its exuberance, goes beyond suffering, drowns it in its creative abundance which is poetry, love, and dance. Perhaps, in order to understand this indissoluble unity of suffering, eros, and joy, one must have seen the black men of Harlem dance frenetically to the rhythm of "blues," which are the saddest sounds in the world. In effect, rhythm cements the multiple aspects of the black soul, communicates its Nietzschian lightness with heavy Dionysian intuitions; rhythm—*tam-tam,* jazz, the "bounding" of these poems—represents the temporality of Negro *existence.* And when a black poet prophesies to his brothers a better future, he portrays their deliverance to them in the form of rhythm:

What?
rhythm
sound wave in the night across the forests, nothing—or
    a new soul
timbre
intonation
vigor
dilation
vibration which flows out by degrees into the marrow

revulses[10] in its progression an old sleeping body, takes
it by the waist
and spins it
and turns
and once more vibrates in its hands, in its loins, its
sexual member, its thighs, its vagina . . .

But one must go still further: this basic experience of suffering is ambiguous; through it, black conscience is going to become historic. In effect, whatever may be the intolerable inequity of his present condition, it is not to that condition that the black man first refers when he proclaims that he has touched the heart of human suffering. He has the horrible benefit of having known bondage. For these poets, most of whom were born between 1900 and 1918, slavery—abolished half a century earlier—lingers on as a very real memory:

Each of my todays looks on my yesterday
with large eyes rolling with rancor with
shame
Still real is my stunned condition of the past
of
blows from knotted cords of bodies calcinated
from toe to calcinated back
of dead flesh of red iron firebrands of arms
broken under the whip which is breaking loose . . .

writes Damas, a poet from Guiana. And the Haitian, Brierre:

. . . Often like me you feel stiffnesses
Awaken after murderous centuries
And old wounds bleed in your flesh . . .

During the centuries of slavery, the black man drank the cup of bitterness to the last drop; and slavery is a past fact which neither our authors nor their fathers have actually experienced. But it is also a hideous nightmare from which even the youngest of them are not yet sure of having awakened. From one end of the earth to the other, black men—separated by languages, politics, and the history of their colonizers—have a *collective* memory in common.

[10] *revulses:* referring to the medical term *revulsion:* a counter-irritant. (translator's note)

This will not be surprising if one recalls the French peasants who, in 1789, were still aware of the panicky terrors that went back to the Hundred Years' War. Thus when the black man goes back to his principal experience, it is suddenly revealed to him in two dimensions: it is both the intuitive seizure of the human condition and the still-fresh memory of a historic past. Here, I am thinking of Pascal who relentlessly repeated that man was an irrational composite of metaphysics and history, his greatness unexplainable if he comes from the alluvium, his misery unexplainable if he is still as God made him; that in order to understand man, one had to go back to the simple basic fact of man's downfall. It is in this sense that Césaire calls his race "the fallen race." And in a certain sense I can see the *rapprochement* that can be made between black conscience and Christian conscience: the brazen law of slavery evokes that law of the Old Testament, which states the consequences of the *Fault*. The abolition of slavery recalls this *other historic fact:* Redemption. The white man's insipid paternalism after 1848 resembles that of the white God after the Passion. The difference being, however, that the expiable fault that the black man discovers in the back of his memory is not his own, it belongs to the white man; the first fact of Negro history is certainly a kind of original sin: but the black man is the innocent victim of it. This is why his concept of suffering is radically opposed to white "dolorism." If these poems are for the most part so violently anti-Christian, it is because the white man's religion is more clearly a hoax in the eyes of the Negro than in the eyes of the European proletariat: this religion wants to make him share the responsibility for a crime of which he is the victim; it wants to persuade him to see the kidnappings, the massacres, the rapes, and the tortures which have covered Africa with blood, as a legitimate punishment, deserved tests. Will you say that it also proclaims equality for all men before God? *Before God,* yes. Only yesterday I was reading in *Esprit* these lines from a correspondent in Madagascar:

> I am as certain as you that the soul of a Malagasy is worth the soul of a white man. . . . Just as, before God, the soul of a child is worth the soul of his father. However, if you have an automobile, you don't let your children drive it.

One can hardly reconcile Christianity and colonialism more elegantly. In opposition to these sophisms, the black man—by a simple investigation of his memory as a former slave—affirms that suffering is man's lot and that it is no less deserved for all that. He rejects with horror Christian stagnation, melancholy sensual pleasure, masochistic humility, and all the tendentious inducements to his submission; he lives the absurdity of suffering in its pure form, in its injustice and in its gratuitousness; and he discovers thereby this truth which is misunderstood or masked by Christianity: suffering carries within itself its own refusal; it is by nature *a refusal to suffer,* it is the dark side of negativity, it opens onto revolt and liberty. The black man promptly *transforms himself into history* in as much as the intuition of suffering confers on him a collective past and assigns to him a goal in the future. Only a short while ago he was a sheer *present* surging of timeless instincts, a simple manifestation of universal and eternal fecundity. Now he calls to his colored brothers in quite another language:

> Negro pedlar of revolt
> you have known the paths of the world
> ever since you were sold in Guinée . . .

And:

> Five centuries have seen you with weapons
> in your hands
> and you have taught the exploiting races
> passion for liberty.

There is already a black Epic:[11] first the golden age of Africa, then the era of dispersion and captivity, then the awakening of conscience, the heroic and somber times of great revolts, of Toussaint L'Ouverture and black heroes, then the *fact* of the abolition of slavery—"unforgettable metamorphosis," says Césaire—then the struggle for definitive liberation:

> You are waiting for the next call
> the inevitable mobilization
> for that war which is yours has known only truces
> for there is no land where your blood has not flowed
> no language in which your color has not been insulted

[11] Epic: the French here reads *"Geste,"* as in *Chanson de Geste;* Sartre is comparing the Negro Epic with the themes of Medieval French epic poetry (translator's note).

You smile, Black Boy,
you sing
you dance
you cradle generations
which go out at all hours to the
fronts of work and pain
which tomorrow will assault bastilles
onward toward the bastions of the future
in order to write in all languages
on the clear pages of all skies
the declaration of your rights unrecognized
for more than five centuries . . .

Strange and decisive turn: *race* is transmuted into *historicity*, the black Present explodes and is temporalized, Negritude—with its Past and its Future—is inserted into Universal History, it is no longer a *state*, nor even an existential attitude, it is a *"Becoming"*; the black contribution to the evolution of humanity is no longer savor, taste, rhythm, authenticity, a bouquet of primitive instincts: it is a dated enterprise, a long-suffering construction, and also a future. Previously, the black man claimed his place in the sun in the name of *ethnic* qualities; now, he establishes his right to life on his mission; and this mission, like the proletariat's, comes to him from his historic position: because he has suffered from capitalistic exploitation more than all the others, he has acquired a sense of revolt and a love of liberty more than all the others. And because he is the most oppressed he necessarily pursues the liberation of all, when he works for his own deliverance:

Black messenger of hope
you know all the hymns of the world
even those of the timeless building-works of the Nile.

But, after that, can we still believe in the interior homogeneousness of Negritude? And how can one say that it exists? Sometimes it is lost innocence which had its existence in some faraway past, and sometimes hope which can be realized only within the walls of the future City. Sometimes it contracts with Nature in a moment of pantheistic fusion and sometimes it spreads itself out to coincide with the whole history of Humanity; sometimes it is an existential attitude and sometimes the objective ensemble of Negro-African traditions. Is it being discovered? Is it being created? After all, there are black men who "collaborate"; after all, in the prefaces he writes for the works of each poet, Senghor seems to distinguish between degrees of Negritude. Does the poet who would be the Prophet for his colored brothers invite them to *become* more Negro, or does he disclose to them what they *are,* by a sort of poetic psychoanalysis? Is Negritude necessity or liberty? For the authentic Negro, is it a matter of conduct deriving from essences, as consequences derive from a principle, or is one a Negro in the way that the religious faithful are believers, that is to say in fear and trembling, in anguish, in perpetual remorse for never being enough what one would like to be? Is it a given fact or a value? The object of empiric intuition or of a moral concept? Is it a conquest of meditation? Or does meditation poison it? Is it never authentic except when unmeditated and in the immediate? Is it a systematic *explanation* of the black soul, or a Platonic archetype which one can approach indefinitely without ever attaining? Is it, for black men, like our engineer's common sense, the most widely shared thing in the world? Or do some have it, like grace; and if so, does it have its chosen ones? One will undoubtedly answer this question by saying that it is all of these at once and still other things. And I agree: like all anthropological notions Negritude is a shimmer of being and of needing-to-be; it makes you and you make it: both oath and passion. But there is something even more important in it: the Negro himself, we have said, creates a kind of antiracist racism. He wishes in no way to dominate the world: he desires the abolition of *all* kinds of ethnic privileges; he asserts his solidarity with the oppressed of every color. After that, the subjective, existential, ethnic notion of *Negritude* "passes," as Hegel says, into that which one has of the proletariat: objective, positive and precise. Senghor says: "For Césaire, 'white' symbolizes capital, just as Negro symbolizes work. . . . When writing about the black men of his race, he is writing about the worldwide proletarian struggle." It is easy to say, not so easy to think. And it is certainly not just by accident that the most ardent cantors of Negritude are also militant Marxists. Nevertheless, the notion of race does not mix with the notion of class: the former is concrete and particular; the latter, universal and abstract; one belongs to what Jaspers calls comprehension, and the other to intellection; the first is the product of a psycho-biological syncretism, and the other is a methodic construction starting with experience. In fact, Negritude appears like the up-beat of a dialectical progression: the theoretical and practical affirmation of white supremacy is the thesis; the position of Negritude as an antithetical value is the moment of negativity. But this negative moment is not sufficient in itself, and these black men who use it know this perfectly well; they know that it aims at preparing the synthesis or realization of the human being in a raceless society. Thus Negritude is *for* destroying itself, it is a "crossing to" and not an "arrival at," a means and not an end. A poem by Jacques Roumain, a black communist, furnishes the most moving evidence of this new ambiguity:

> Africa I have held on to your memory Africa
> you are in me
> Like a thorn in a wound
> like a guardian mascot in the center of the village
> make of me the stone of your sling
> of my mouth the lips of your wound
> of my knees the broken columns of your humbling
> however
> I want to be only of your race
> peasant workers of all countries.

With what sadness he still retains for a moment what he has decided to abandon! With what pride as a *man* he will strip his pride as a Negro for other men! He who says both that Africa is in him like "a thorn in a wound" and that he *wants* to be only of the universal race of the oppressed, has not left the empire of afflicted conscience. One more step and Negritude will disappear completely: the Negro himself makes of what was the mysterious bubbling of black blood, a geographical accident, the inconsistent product of universal determinism:

> Is it all that climate extended space
> which creates clan tribe nation
> skin race gods
> our inexorable dissimilarity.[12]

[12] Although the poem itself and Sartre's interpretation of it suggest that there should be a question mark here, there is none in the text from which this was translated (translator's note).

But the poet does not completely have the courage to accept the responsibility for this *rationalization* of the racial concept; one sees that he limits himself to questioning; a bitter regret is visible beneath his will to unite. Strange road: humiliated and offended, black men search deep within themselves to find their most secret pride; and when they have found it at last, it challenges its own right to exist: through supreme generosity they abandon it, just as Philoctetes abandoned his bow and arrows at Neoptolemus. Thus the rebel Césaire finds the secret of his revolts in the bottom of his heart: he is of royal blood:

> —it is true that there is in you something which has
> never been able to yield, an anger, a desire, a sadness,
> an impatience, in short a scorn, a violence . . . and now
> your veins carry gold, not mud; pride, not servitude.
> King you have been King in the past.

But he immediately thrusts aside his temptation:

> There is a law that I cover up with a chain unbroken
> as far as the confluence of fire which violates me
> which purifies me and burns me with my prism of amal-
> gamated gold. . . . I shall perish. But one. Whole.

It is perhaps this ultimate nudity of man that he has snatched from him the white rags that were concealing his black armor, and that now destroys and rejects that very armor; it is perhaps this colorless nudity that best symbolizes Negritude: for Negritude is not a state, it is a simple going-beyond-itself, it is love. It is when Negritude renounces itself that it finds itself; it is when it accepts losing that it has won: the colored man—and he alone—can be asked to renounce the pride of his color. He is the one who is walking on this ridge between past particularism—which he has just climbed—and future universalism, which will be the twilight of his Negritude; he is the one who looks to the end of particularism in order to find the dawn of the universal. Undoubtedly, the white worker also becomes conscious of his class in order to deny it, since he wants the advent of a classless society: but once again, the definition of class is objective; it sums up only the conditions of the white worker's alienation; whereas it is in the bottom of his heart that the Negro finds race, and he must tear out his heart. Thus Negritude is dialectical; it is not only nor above all the blossoming of atavistic instincts; it represents "going beyond" a situation defined by free consciences. Negritude is a sad myth full of hope, born of Evil and pregnant with future Good, living like a woman who is born to die and who feels her own death even in the richest moments of her life; it is an unstable rest, an explosive fixity, a pride which renounces itself, an absolute that knows it is transitory: for whereas it is the announcer of its birth and of its death agony, it also remains the existential attitude chosen by free men and lived *absolutely,* to the fullest. Because it is tension between a nostalgic Past into which the black man can no longer enter completely and a future in which it will be replaced by new values, Negritude adorns itself with a tragic beauty that finds expression only in poetry. Because it is the living and dialectical unity of so many opposites, because it is a complex defying analysis, Negritude is only the multiple unity of a hymn that can reveal both it and the flashing beauty of the Poem which Breton calls *"explosante-fixe."* Because any attempt to conceptualize its various aspects would necessarily end up showing its relativity—even though it is lived in the absolute through royal consciences—and because the poem is an absolute, it is poetry alone that will show the unconditional aspect of this attitude to be fixed. Because it is subjectivity written in the objective, Negritude must take form in a poem, that is to say in a subjectivity-object; because it is an archetype and a value, it will find its most transparent symbol in aesthetic values; because it is a call and a gift, it will make itself heard and offer itself only by means of a work of art which is both a call to the spectator's liberty and absolute generosity. Negritude is the content of the poem, it is the poem like a thing of the world, mysterious and open, obscure and suggestive; it is the poet himself. One must go still further; triumph of Narcissism and Narcissus' sucide, tension of the soul beyond culture, beyond words and beyond all psychic facts, luminous night of unknowing, deliberate choice of the *impossible* and of what Bataille calls "torture" [*supplice*], intuitive acceptance of the world and refusal of the world in the name of "the law of the heart," double contradictory postulation, demanding retraction, expansion of generosity—Negritude is, in essence, Poetry. For once at least, the most authentic revolutionary plan and the most pure poetry come from the same source.

And if the sacrifice is achieved one day what will happen then? What will happen if, casting off his Negritude for the sake of the

Revolution the black man no longer wishes to consider himself only a part of the proletariat? What will happen if he then allows himself to be defined only by his objective condition? if, in order to struggle against white capitalism, he undertakes to assimilate white technics? Will the source of poetry run dry? or in spite of everything, will the great black river color the sea into which it flows? That does not matter: each era has its poetry; in each era, circumstances of history elect a nation, a race, a class to take up the torch, by creating situations that can be expressed or that can go beyond themselves only through Poetry; sometimes the poetic *élan* coincides with the revolutionary *élan* and sometimes they diverge. Let us greet today the historic chance that will permit black men to

> shout out the great negro cry so hard that the world's foundations will be shaken.[13]

[13] Césaire, *Les armes miraculeuses,* p. 156.

Sartre's Theory of "Antiracist Racism" in his Study of Negritude

W. A. JEANPIERRE

U SING HEGELIAN CONCEPTS to analyze Negritude in his famous essay, *Orphée noir* Sartre concluded that Negritude is the antithesis, the weak beat of a dialectical progression, a moment of negativity in counter responses to the thesis of white supremacy, and exists only to destroy itself, finally, once the goal of a society without races is achieved. The reaction provoked by this position gave rise to much controversy and confusion, because a rapport was established between Negritude and racism instead of a direct relationship between Negritude and Humanism.

Many opposed to this view pointed out that Sartre, in effect, really wanted to contribute to this "antiracist racism" because he felt it to be the only effective, necessarily revolutionary, instrument at the disposal of the Negritude poets capable of bringing about the demise of white racism. Negritude, to them, could not be relegated to being simply an operational weapon adopted for purposes of strategy. It was symbolic of values peculiar to the African by virtue of geography, temperament, and unique historical experiences. It existed prior to, and independent of, the African's confrontation with European colonialism, although enslavement and racism added new and far-reaching dimension to it.

Frantz Fanon, author of *Les Damnés de la Terre* (*The Wretched of the Earth*), accused Sartre of having dealt a fatal blow to Negritude and of having destroyed the enthusiasm felt by black people at having rediscovered the real self which lay buried beneath the alien personality imposed upon them by cultural domination.

As Lilyan Kesteloot (*Les Ecrivains noirs de langue française*, Brussels, 1963) has pointed out, however, Sartre was speaking in philosophical terms when using the expression "negativity," which is not, therefore, in this context, at all pejorative (pp. 120–121). In Hegelian dialectics the thesis inevitably calls forth its antithesis, and as a result of the struggle which takes place between the two, the synthesis which emerges contains the best features of both elements rid of their imperfections.

According to this logic, white racism is the thesis, while Negritude is assigned an antithesis value. In Hegelian dialectics, this value is negativity. The third phase, or the synthesis which finally emerges, is superior to both and is called *Aufhebung* by Hegel— which means to go beyond, to suppress, and to conserve. Negritude, then, as the "negative phase," cannot be equated with sterile opposition content only with denying the thesis of white supremacy, and bringing nothing positive in its wake, destined, after the struggle has taken place, to disappear. To the contrary, it embraces qualities which will make for a richer synthesis. In Hegelian dialectics then, to negate the negative is not synonymous with rejecting it, but rather with bringing the issue to a successful conclusion by recognizing and conciliating the respective rights of all parties involved.

Sartre's oversight was in not keeping in mind that his analysis of Negritude in Hegelian, philosophical terms was destined for the public-at-large who could easily misread the equation: Negritude = negativity.

Sartre even went as far as to posit a world in which neither black nor white would exist but only men enriched by mutually profitable contact with each other. While the chances of such a possibility ever occurring are highly remote, even its desirability is debatable.

The founders of the Negritude movement did not finally come to rejoin that part of themselves which had been systematically insulted, scoffed at, and distorted, in order to surrender it after a Hegelian synthesis had been operated. They were not seeking a world without races, but one without racism. Their principal concern was to force a recognition of their humanity as black men in a world that would be that much richer because it is culturally pluralistic. The problem that faced Césaire, Damas, and Senghor was that of having to affirm themselves fully as black men without becoming racists in the process. They had to reconcile the very definite feeling of belonging more particularly to the black community of the human family (by virtue of a common community of suffering and background), with a goal that opened on the universal. They knew that for them the only way to attain the universal was by affirming the particular, by exalting their specific humanity in their relationship with men racially different from themselves. By affirming their Negritude they affirmed their humanity. And although Senghor (in *Cahier No. 3 Pierre Teilhard de Chardin,* Paris, 1962) agrees that Sartre was correct in applying the label "antiracist racism" to Negritude, he points out that: "Si nous refusions la condamnation de la Négritude, ce n'est pas seulement que ses valeurs étaient les nôtres, c'est surtout qu'étant de l'Homme, elles étaient nécessaires au monde: à la 'Civilisation planétaire' qui s'édifie sous nos yeux . . ." (p. 27). (If we refuse to accept the condemnation of Negritude, it is not only because its values were ours, but especially because its values being that of Man, were necessary to the world: to the planetary Civilization that was being erected under our very eyes. . . .")

Negritude is racial, therefore, but it is not racist. It is racial because it is consciousness of being black, a consciousness brought about more particularly by experiences peculiar only to those of African descent. When it first made its appearance in the nineteen-thirties, the rich psychic dividends it yielded, the positive feelings it generated among a people whose dignity had been sorely trampled underfoot, gave birth to a system of reference that reflected, especially, an extra-African Negritude that was mainly social in content. Sartre's brilliant study of it emphasized, almost exclusively, its socio-political, extra-African manifestations, in terms of racially persecuted people of color reacting to this persecution. This position is valid as far as it goes. But does it go far enough? It would seem not, since the founders of Negritude—for the most part colored French West Indians—sought an identification with the *spirit* of African civilization, with *that Africa* prior to its confrontation with Europe.

Sartre erred, it would seem, in concluding that Negritude exists, finally, in order to destroy itself. Césaire pointed out in a recent interview that Negritude is the *sine qua non* of creation in whatever area black artists choose to exercise self-expression, since it is based on a community of culture, history, and temperament. As such, then, it would seem more permanent than transitory in character.

Today, more than twenty-five years after the appearance of the concept of Negritude, it is obvious that the conditions which once operated to make it inevitable have been considerably modified.

The African writers of the sixties seem to be drawing more and more from the traditional and actual sources of their own societies. Their works, in the main, are devoid of that tenseness which characterizes the work of Afro-American and Caribbean writers, who are subjected to a more subtly discriminatory way of life. Nevertheless, it should be kept in mind that in its extra-African manifestations, at least, Negritude is the literary embodiment of vigorous protest against the experiences endured by the expatriated African and his descendants. It nourished a universal revolt out of a universal servitude, and it was only when black writers and poets began to make meaningful the facts of *their* reality, of *their* existential condition, that their works were stamped with an originality that commanded universal attention. But to do this, they had to indulge in an "orphic" quest, as Sartre put it, to discover how they really thought and felt. It was necessary to go beyond the three or four hundred years which marked the pilgrimage to the sources of their origin—as Senghor put it. This "négritude des sources" was to be found only in Africa, and pre-dates the confrontation between Europe and Africa. It refers to basic African values which are uniquely cultural. It does not seem that these values are destined to disappear.

Africa's Olympiad of the Arts

Some Observations on the Dakar Festival

THOMAS CASSIRER

ON A PROMONTORY jutting out into the Atlantic at the extreme western point of Africa, the government of Senegal built a new museum in preparation for the First World Festival of Negro Arts, held in Dakar from March 30 to April 24, 1966. As the visitor approached the museum along the shoreline highway, he was both delighted and surprised to discover in this African setting a beautiful modern re-creation of a Greek temple. Framed by the expanse of the Atlantic and the dry, brown earth, the flat-roofed building with its surrounding peristyle stood out gleaming white in the brilliant sun. For a moment the architecture, the light, the climate, and the blue sea evoked a vision of ancient Greece itself.

Inside the museum the illusion was quickly dispelled. Here the art of Africa was brought together from museums and private collections in Africa, Europe, and America through a joint effort of the Senegalese and French governments, with the technical help of UNESCO. The arrangement of the exhibition stressed various perspectives of African art. Prehistoric rock paintings in the Sahara, two-thousand-year-old terra-cotta sculptures from the Nigerian village of Nok, and the striking statue of King Misha Pelenge Che seated before his drum (created by an anonymous Congolese sculptor in the early nineteenth century) stood out among many reminders of the "Historical Dimension" of African art. In this as well as in the arrangement along geographic regions ("The Geographical Dimension") no one could fail to be impressed by the astonishing diversity of African art.

Most of the exhibits came from West Africa and the Congo region. South Africa did not participate for political reasons. A few well-chosen pieces, among them a small, powerful bull sculpture of wrought iron from Tanzania, illustrated the Negro art of East

Africa. Ethiopian art, with its ornate tryptics, crosses, and illuminated manuscripts, was well represented. Geographical representation, however, soon became a question of minor importance in the face of the large array of wooden and bronze masks, of sculptures in wood, ivory, and metal, some of them covered with cowrie shells or brightly colored pearls. In style, these ranged from the bird-masks of the Dogon and the stylized antelopes of the Bambara in Mali to the Benin bronzes of Nigeria, and included as well the colorful art of Cameroon with its thrones out of which rise the stylized sculptures of the royal couple, covered entirely with brightly colored glass beads.

Until recently it was customary to relegate the artifacts of Africa to ethnographic, rather than art, museums. A narrow conception of art as pure self-expression prevented an unprejudiced appreciation of the artistic value of the artifacts brought from Africa by archeologists. The section "Aspects of Life" acknowledged the utilitarian and ritualistic purpose of traditional art. At the same time the similarity of some of the pieces with those in other sections of the exhibition emphasized that the separation between utilitarian art and "pure art" is too limited as an approach to African art objects. Next to a large exhibit of spears and ceremonial batons used by the chief's messengers as symbols of authority, one could find intricately carved ceremonial seats that resembled those in the other groupings of the exhibition. The stylized animal figures which served as weights for gold dust with the Baoule and Ashanti tribes were very similar to the animal sculptures in the geographic and historical groupings.

Africa's "Dialogue with the World," its long contact with other countries and continents, was illustrated by several pieces of ancient Nubian art, some sculptures from Madagascar, as well as several objects from the Congo and Angola in which African and European motifs intermingle. A replica of the famous Fang mask, given by Vlaminck to Derain in 1905, that gave the initial impetus to the interest in African art by the Paris school, as well as a Baoule mask and a Benin bronze, pointed to the impact of the discovery of African art on twentieth-century European painting and sculpture. They were juxtaposed to Picasso's *Les Demoiselles d'Avignon* and works by Modigliani, Braque, Zadkine, and Juan Gris. The exhibition ended on this fusion, this "symbiosis," as Senghor would call it, between African and European art that brought the traditional art of Africa out of its isolation into the mainstream of modern art.

Once the visitor left the calm and air-conditioned comfort of the museum and explored the center of the city, he found himself engulfed in the confusion of the Festival itself. His pocketbook and his ingenuity in procuring tickets often enough narrowed down the choice from an overwhelming variety of ongoing activities and programs. Ideally he should have been possessed of superhuman stamina as well as the magic gift of simultaneity to enable him to be present at several performances every evening. Anyone so equiped could attend plays in French and English by Negro troupes from such diverse points of the globe as Leopoldville, Ibadan, Bathurst (the capital of Gambia), Paris, and London; he could sit in bewilderment through a five-act tragedy on Hannibal performed by Ethiopian actors in Amharic, take in folkdances from more than twenty African countries, listen to Duke Ellington's band (if he was lucky enough to get a ticket), as well as to steel drummers from Trinidad, the De Paur Choir and other singers from the United States. There were opportunities to enjoy music and dancing fom Brazil and Haiti, to attend an Easter mass where the music was performed on African instruments, or to witness the Passion according to Saint Luke sung in jazz rhythm and danced by actors from the London Negro Workshop. Every night of the week also brought another performance of a pageant on the island of Gorée, staged by the French in the best *son et lumière* tradition, during which a group of actors, assisted by many of the islanders, re-enacted scenes from the history of that former center of the slave trade. As if all this were not enough, one also had the choice of poetry recitals in French and English, as well as a series of films on Africa—some of them produced by Africans—that were the special responsibility of an Italian film crew sent by the Italian government as its contribution to the Festival. Even the penniless spectator could share in the festival atmosphere: every weekend the city resounded to the beat of the *tam-tam* until the early morning hours as groups of Senegalese folk dancers engaged in what the local paper referred to as the "animation" of the city, and several times a week the main thoroughfares were blocked off to give passage to such distinguished visitors as André Malraux, the brother of the Sultan of Morocco, the President of the German Bundestag, and his Imperial Majesty the King of Kings of Ethiopia, Haile

Selassie. It was an exhilarating experience in all its confusion, for there was a spontaneity about it that is unusual for an art festival.

The theatre mirrored the extraordinary fluidity and the rapid change of the African cultural scene. The performances ran the gamut from the most primitive to the sophisticated, and from the amateurish to the work of polished professionals. Much of the theatre, as one might expect in Africa, took the form of dance, and it was possible to sit spellbound one night as villagers from the Congo enacted an initiation ceremony that had heretofore been a secret, open only to the men of that particular village—what a perplexing experience to watch it in air-conditioned comfort in a theatre with the most up-to-date lighting and scenery! A few nights later one could see an expertly trained troupe from Sierra Leone present such comic scenes as a satire on British colonialism and the courtship of two rivals for the hand of the chief's daughter, by means of dances that combined in perfectly polished form slapstick humor and exuberant acrobatic dancing.

Since the development of an African spoken theatre is even more recent than other literary forms, this part of the Festival was of special interest. The plays were in the realist tradition and commented on the contemporary African scene. The comedies presented aspects of African society while the tragedies touched on political problems. Psychological drama was almost entirely absent.

As one of their official offerings, the Nigerians staged a comedy, *Danda,* by Nkem Nwankwo, a picaresque farce concerning a young ne'er-do-well in a Nigerian village. The hero gets into scrapes both with the harbingers of Westernization, and the stalwart representatives of the village traditions, but always carries the day with his high spirits. The Senegalese audience, most of whom knew no English, much appreciated the slapstick humor in such familiar village situations as a palaver of the elders and the efforts of the local catechists to convert the remaining pagan villagers. Indeed, its folk character made this the only play that transcended the language barrier and enabled English and French speaking Africans to laugh together at Western mannerisms and old-fashioned traditions. Another Nigerian comedy, *Wind Against Polygamy,* by Obi Egbuna, was performed by a Negro troupe from London. Its plot was built around one of the oldest comic situations: the heroine is forced to marry for money rather than love but after many complications escapes her predicament and marries the young man of her dreams. The heroine of this play ultimately finds conjugal happiness in a monogamous marriage but the author knows how to exploit his theme to show polygamy in an advantageous light as well.

The three plays with serious themes all dealt with the problem of dictatorship, but differed in their point of view. The one play in English, *Kongi's Harvest,* by the Nigerian Wole Soyinka, voiced outright criticism of the trend toward dictatorship in Africa and seemed to many to allude very directly to Kwame Nkrumah. The absolute ruler appeared in a more favorable light in the two plays in French. This would seem to be less a reflection of the current political situation than a consequence of the French political and literary tradition. *La Tragédie du Roi Christophe,* by the West Indian Aimé Césaire, transposes the problems of newly won independence into the historical setting of early nineteenth-century Haiti. Christophe, a former coachman, makes himself absolute monarch of one part of the island, and tries to teach his people that freedom brings with it hard work and self-discipline. The natural desire of the Haitians to enjoy their freedom drives Christophe to take increasingly severe measures to impose his vision of grandeur, and he finally dies a broken man, abandoned by his former subjects. Within the framework of this tragic plot Césaire successfully introduces a broad satire of the relations between "developed" and "underdeveloped" countries, and in the polished performance by a group of professional Negro actors from Paris, *La Tragédie du Roi Christophe* proved the hit of the Festival.

The other tragedy in French, *La Mort de Chaka,* by Seydou Badian, Minister for Economic Development in Mali, is a thesis play in which the absolute ruler is presented as the embodiment of political mystique. The famous Zulu warrior, Chaka, spurs his people to feats of heroism to fulfill his vision of their destiny. Ultimately he is killed by his generals who do not share his visionary goals and fight only for material gain. In his death, however, Chaka leaves to later generations of Africans an example of the heroism and self-discipline they will need to free themselves from the effects of European colonial rule.

Many of the writers incorporated elements of African music and dance into their plays, none more successfully than Aimé Césaire. In order to poke fun at the doubtful value of some aid projects, he created the figure of a French dancing master sent as "technical aid" from France to teach the court of Christophe the ceremonies and dances of the Old Regime which were out of date by then in France itself. The incongruous combination of these stilted ceremonies with native Haitian dancing not only makes for good theatre but also expresses visually Césaire's criticism of the Negro's desire to imitate European culture.

What contribution can the Negro tradition bring to the fine and applied arts today? This question confronted the writers, artists, critics, and professors from three continents who met during the first ten days in a conference on "The Negro Arts in the Life of the People." Under the direction of the African Society of Culture (publishers of *Présence Africaine*), they discussed the traditional function of art in Africa and examined the possibilities of assigning art a similarly significant role in the new Africa. Their deliberations dealt primarily with the dance and the visual arts, and they concerned themselves with such topics as the teaching of African art in the schools, the development of an African architectural style, and the character of modern Negro-African music. The conference had certain practical results: it established permanent commissions that will concern themselves with the preservation of African art, the protection of wooden art objects against termites, the development of modern African music, and other problems affecting the arts in Africa. It also voted a series of resolutions appealing to African governments to give more active support to the arts. The government of Senegal showed the way on this point by appointing Katherine Dunham, an active participant in the conference, as a technical advisor charged with setting up a school of the dance in Senegal. It was announced at the end of the Festival that Senegal would begin work on one project proposed at the conference by building a center for African art, a *Cité des Arts,* in Dakar to which young artists from all parts of Africa would be invited to come for work and study.

The conference also gave rise to a re-examination of the concept of Negritude. As President Senghor pointed out in his welcoming speech, Negritude had provided the impetus for the entire Festival. "If we have assumed the terrible responsibility of organizing this Festival," he said, "it is for the Defense and Illustration of Negritude." Just as Joachim Du Bellay's sixteenth-century manifesto *Défense et Illustration de la Langue française* had proclaimed the emancipation of French from the cultural prestige of Latin, the

Festival should proclaim the cultural emancipation of the Negro people from their colonial dependency on Western civilization. In Senghor's words, the Festival was to demonstrate that the Negroes of today, like their ancestors, were once again "producers of civilization."

As president of the host country, prime mover behind the Festival, and the most prestigious African poet in French, President Senghor set the theme of the conference with his speech, and yet a nagging question remained in the minds of many participants on the validity of Negritude. Was this ideology not out of date in an independent Africa, whatever it might have contributed to the battle against colonialism? and did the stress on Negritude, on *Negro* art and architecture and music, on the necessity of identifying oneself with the precolonial traditions of Africa, not act as a limiting, restraining influence just when Negro Africa needed to change and develop? These doubts remained unspoken for the first few days. It was difficult to criticize the ideology of Negritude without at the same time unintentionally criticizing the Festival and the Conference. Indeed such well-known critics as the Nigerian writers Wole Soyinka and John Pepper Clark preferred to keep silent in the ideological discussion. Thus when the controversy came out into the open it turned largely into a debate within the Negritude movement, with some of the French-speaking writers and artists voicing their apprehensions that this concept of "antiracist racism"—as Sartre had called it in *Black Orpheus*—was becoming a barrier that isolated Africans from the mainstream of modern culture.

Their apprehensions were largely laid to rest by the remarks of Aimé Césaire, Senghor's old comrade-in-arms in the Negritude movement. Before a large and wildly cheering audience he stressed the historical elements of the concept. In the thirties and forties, Negritude served as a rallying point to counter the white man's assumption of cultural superiority. In the Africa of the sixties this psychocultural assertion against colonialism had served its usefulness. Africa was now "irrevocably committed to the atmosphere and dynamism of Western civilization." In other respects, however, the original view of the situation and the potential of the black man held continuing challenge. Césaire was still convinced that the African genius tended toward expression through the arts rather than technology and science. Its strength in this respect should be further developed so that it could contribute a counterweight to the "desiccating" and "depersonalizing" effect of modern civilization.

The emphasis given to the development of the arts inevitably raises the question of African economic and political stability. Can Africa assume the function of a "mother country of the arts" on the shaky political and economic base as it now exists? Aimé Césaire, while mindful of this problem, alluded to it only in the most general terms when he appealed to his audience—some of whom had come as the official representatives of other African nations: "We ask you to create a good Africa for us, an Africa that gives us reason to hope and cause to be proud."

The economic question becomes even more puzzling in regard to Senegal itself. Senegal, a country of three million inhabitants with a one-crop economy, relies heavily on French subsidies. At first glance it seems astonishing that President Senghor should envision it as a "land of dialogue," a center of cultural interchange between Africa, Europe, and America. Both Athens and Paris, Senghor's two models, benefited, as is well known, from a very different economic environment. Yet Dakar does have the advantage of an unusual geographical location because of its proximity to both the Americas and Europe. The friendly social climate of the city encourages cultural exchange, a fact which was much commented on by the visitors to the Festival. The ingenuity and persistence of President Senghor could certainly be called an additional asset. Having inherited a modern city and administrative center from the French, Senghor was able to enlist the cooperation of countries in three continents to make it into the most modern African cultural center as well, and in the course of this realized a dream of forty years. The meeting in Dakar marked the triumph of an idea.

The Festival set a high beginning for future events of this type. Plans call for a repetition of such an African Olympiad of the arts every five years in a different host country. It was a most successful Pan-African event, yet at the same time its ideological theme, the active participation by Americans and Europeans, the fusion of cultures in its artistic offerings, even its architectural setting confirmed that the Atlantic Community is both black and white.

Notes on Contributors and Index

Notes on Contributors

DORIS E. ABRAMSON directs plays and teaches acting at the University of Massachusetts and is the senior drama editor of *The Massachusetts Review;* she is the author of *Negro Playwrights in the American Theatre* (1925–1959) (Columbia, 1969).

JOHN W. BARBER (1798–1885) was an American historian.

LEONARD BASKIN, well-known sculptor and graphic artist, is Professor of Art at Smith College. He recently received the medal of the American Institute of Graphic Art.

GENE BLUESTEIN is a collector and performer of folksongs who teaches American literature and folklore at Fresno State College.

ROSELLEN BROWN taught at Tougaloo College; she has published poems in *The Nation, Arts in Society, North American Review,* and the *Denver Quarterly.*

STERLING A. BROWN, poet, critic, editor of *The Negro Caravan,* has long been a Professor of English at Howard University; a pioneer in the study of Negro literature and folklore, he has been an important teacher to several generations of black intellectuals.

TREVOR N. W. BUSH left his Anglican ministry in South Africa after the Sharpville massacre, becoming a political refugee because of his opposition to apartheid and the Verwoerd government; at present he is teaching English in Nigeria and contributes a regular letter from Africa to *The Massachusetts Review.*

TONI CADE is a teacher at the CCNY Experimental College, an essayist, and a fiction writer whose work has appeared in *Prairie Schooner, Liberator, Negro Digest;* she has compiled a forthcoming anthology of literary, political, and critical pieces on and by contemporary black women called *New Breed* (Doubleday).

STOKELY CARMICHAEL is a former national chairman of the Student Nonviolent Coordinating Committee (SNCC) and author (with Charles V. Hamilton) of *Black Power: The Politics of Liberation in America* (Random House, 1967).

466 · NOTES ON CONTRIBUTORS

THOMAS CASSIRER teaches in the Romance Languages Department of the University of Massachusetts, specializing in French and African literature; his attendance at the Dakar Festival and the Conference on the African Arts was made possible by a travel grant from the Five-College Asian and African Studies Committee.

JULES CHAMETZKY, Professor of English at the University of Massachusetts and a founder of *MR*, has been co-editor of the journal for five years.

LUCILLE CLIFTON lives in Baltimore and is the mother of six children; her first book of poetry will be published by Random House in 1969.

ROBERT COLES, a child psychiatrist on the staff of the Harvard University Health Services, is a contributing editor to *The New Republic* and serves on the editorial board of *The American Scholar*; he is the author of *Children in Crisis, Dead End School*, and *Still Hungry in America*.

WILLIAM CORRINGTON is the author of *Lonesome Traveler and Other Stories* and editor-at-large for the *New Orleans Review*; he is Professor of Literature at Loyola of the South.

W. E. B. DUBOIS, 1868–1963.

BOB FLETCHER was a staff photographer for SNCC for several years.

ANDREW GOODMAN wrote his poem in a class at Queens College, New York, in the spring of 1964 before going to work for civil rights in the SNCC Summer Program; he was murdered, at the age of twenty, in Philadelphia, Mississippi, along with James Cheney and Michael Schwerner.

NAT HENTOFF has been a staff writer for the *New Yorker* and a regular contributor to *Commonweal, The Village Voice, Liberator*, and other periodicals; he is the author of several books on jazz, a biography of A. J. Muste, an educational study (*Our Children are Dying*, Viking, 1966), and two novels.

W. A. JEANPIERRE teaches French at New York University; he was formerly Educational Consultant and Writer of Programs for Haryou Act, Inc., and Lecturer in French at the University of Ghana.

SIDNEY KAPLAN, Professor of English at the University of Massachusetts, has written on Melville and Poe and on the Negro in American history, literature, and art. He was managing editor of *MR* at its inception and then co-editor for several years.

MARTIN LUTHER KING, JR., 1929–1968.

JOSEPH LANGLAND, Professor of English at the University of Massachusetts, has had his poems widely anthologized and has recorded them in the Folkways-Scholastic series and for the Library of Congress; his volumes include *Adlai Stevenson* (1969), *The Wheel of Summer* (1963), and *The Green Town* (1956).

DAVID LEVIN, at present working on a biography of Cotton Mather, is the author of *In Defense of Historical Literature: Essays on American History, Drama, and Fiction* (1967); he is Professor of English at Stanford.

JAMES O. LONG was on the Public Information Staff of the U. S. Navy when he wrote the description of a lynching.

JOHN MACKAY was a student at Bowdoin College when he heard Ellington in concert; he is now an assistant editor for the American Geophysical Union in Washington.

MAX MARGULIS, a professional musician for many years, was co-founder of Blue Note Records and guided its first decade's recording program, assembling jazz players of the epic and classical periods; he is the author of a forthcoming evaluation of the European singing tradition called *The Belcanto Singer.*

MILTON MAYER, author of *They Thought They Were Free* (1955) and *What Can a Man Do* (1964), has written magazine articles which have won for him the Polk Memorial Award and the Benjamin Franklin Citation for Journalism; he has been a guest professor at universities here and abroad and has lectured for the American Friends Service Committee, the Fellowship of Reconciliation, and the Jewish Peace Fellowship; he is a Visiting Fellow to the Center for the Study of Democratic Institutions.

HOWARD N. MEYER, a lawyer by profession, has contributed essays on the history of race relations to various periodicals; he is the author of lives of U. S. Grant and T. W. Higginson, whose *Army Life in a Black Regiment* he edited in a paperback edition (1962).

WILLIAM STUART NELSON, Professor Emeritus of Christian Theology at Howard University, also served as Dean of the University and Vice-President for Special Projects; among his publications are *La race noire dans la démocratie américaine* (1921) and *Bases of World Understanding* (1949); he is Editor Emeritus of *The Journal of Religious Thought.*

G. C. ODEN, a lecturer on Negro poetry at the New School for

Social Research, has read her poetry in and around New York City under the sponsorship of the Academy of American Poets; she has written a study of James Baldwin for the University of Minnesota Press.

CHARLOTTE PAINTER, a former Fellow at the Radcliffe Institute, is a lecturer in Creative Writing at Stanford; she has published stories in the *New Yorker* and the *Western Review* and is the author of a journal, *Who Made the Lamb* (1965), and two novels, *The Fortunes of Laurie Breaux* (1962) and *The God Book* (forthcoming).

SAUNDERS REDDING is the author of many books, including *Stranger and Alone, On Being a Negro in America,* and *The Lonesome Road;* he has been Director of the Division of Research and Publication in the National Endowment for the Humanities, a member of the U. S. Committee for the first World Festival of Negro Art, and has taught at Hampton Institute, Duke, Brown, and George Washington.

LOUIS RUCHAMES, Professor and Chairman of the Department of History at the University of Massachusetts-Boston, is the author of *Race, Jobs, and Politics: The Story of the F.E.P.C.* and editor of *A John Brown Reader, The Abolitionists: A Collection of Their Writings,* and *Racial Thought in America: From the Puritans to Abraham Lincoln;* he is co-editor of *The Letters of William Lloyd Garrison,* to be published in six volumes by Harvard University Press.

JEAN-PAUL SARTRE was awarded and refused the Nobel Prize for Literature in 1964.

STERLING STUCKEY has taught in Chicago public schools, the University of Illinois, Northwestern, and freedom schools in the south; he has lectured widely and published articles, texts, position papers on a variety of subjects in the field of Afro-American history and culture; he is co-author of *From Negro History to Black Studies* (Doubleday, 1969).

MIKE THELWELL, a former staff member for SNCC and the Mississippi Freedom Democratic Party, has been a Writing Fellow at the University of Massachusetts and a Fellow in Humanities at Cornell; his article on Styron and Turner has been widely reprinted; he won first prize in *Story 1968* and is at work on a biography of Nat Turner and a novel.

W. W. [WILLIAM WOOD] is a recent graduate of Tougaloo College who has had summer study at Columbia and Yale; he will do graduate work in Southern history, particularly on the Civil War and the Reconstruction Period.

S. A. WILLIAMS sets many of her stories in the Central Valley of California, her birthplace; she earned her B.A. at Fresno State College in 1966 and is working towards a graduate degree at Howard; she has been active as a teacher and administrator in Black Studies programs in California, Washington, and Georgia.

HOWARD ZINN is Professor of Government at Boston University and the author of numerous articles and half a dozen books, including *The Southern Mystique* (1964), *SNCC: The New Abolitionists* (1964), *Vietnam: The Logic of Withdrawal* (1967), and *Disobedience and Democracy* (1968); he was Chairman of the Department of History at Spelman College, Atlanta, 1956–1963.

Index